6.25 MN
1

THE ANGAMI NAGAS

Kāsākrē of Kigwema—An Angami Warrior
From a Sketch by Col. Woodthorpe

THE
ANGAMI NAGAS

With Some Notes on Neighbouring Tribes

J. H. HUTTON *1885 - 1968.*

C.I.E., D.SC., M.A.

Published by direction of the Government of Nagaland

OXFORD UNIVERSITY PRESS
1969

Oxford University Press, Ely House, London W.1

GLASGOW NEW YORK TORONTO MELBOURNE WELLINGTON
CAPE TOWN SALISBURY IBADAN NAIROBI LUSAKA ADDIS ABABA
BOMBAY CALCUTTA MADRAS KARACHI LAHORE DACCA
KUALA LUMPUR SINGAPORE HONG KONG TOKYO

Oxford House, Apollo Bunder, Bombay 1 BR

J. H. Hutton 1885-1968

First published by Macmillan and Co. Limited, London 1921
Second edition by Oxford University Press 1969

Printed in India by
S. M. Balsaver at Usha Printers, National House, Tulloch Road,
Bombay 1 BR, and published by John Brown, Oxford University Press,
Bombay 1 BR

TENGIMA KEHUPORI KERIAKI KWE-NIE U
MU U ZHO-U KHAWAMODI SEKETO MIA U NGU
KEMIATHODI, MU U KRÜ U PHIPFÜMIA VA KEZEVIDI,
UKO ZA NU LESÜ HAU RULETE

PREFACE TO THE FIRST EDITION

The late Mr. S. E. Peal, in his "Fading Histories," lamented the delay in the study of the Naga tribes, and the consequent loss of much material out of which their past histories might have been recovered. He points out the remarkable rapidity with which they are changing and indeed have already changed. He urges the "unearthing of some local history from these people ere it has faded for ever," and the careful study of the Naga tribes before they are "reformed and hopelessly sophisticated." But if the Eastern Nagas of whom Mr. Peal was thinking have changed much in recent years the Western Nagas have changed far more. It is barely forty years since Captain Butler wrote, but many customs of the Angamis at war which he records are almost or entirely forgotten by the sons of those from whom he learnt them. With the Aos and Lhotas matters have gone even further. Old beliefs and customs are dying, the old traditions are being forgotten, the number of Christians or quasi-Christians is steadily increasing, and the spirit of change is invading and pervading every aspect of village life. All this must be the excuse for a mere amateur's venturing to undertake a monograph on the Angamis. It is work which should be done by a trained anthropologist, but though occasional German and American scientists have paid hurried visits to the Naga Hills, the anthropologists of Great Britain have consistently passed them by on the other side.

Their opportunity, however, is not entirely gone, for there are still across the frontier happy tribes, which have not yet touched pitch and become civilised like their administered brothers; which pay no house-tax, and do no reluctant coolie work ; which know not the seed of conversion and the sword of dissension which missionaries bring, nor have yet been made to eat of that forbidden fruit which drove our first parents into fig-leaves and banishment. The diseases which follow like the jackals in the wake of invasion have not yet touched them, and they go clothed on with modesty rather than with " dhutis." No paternal Government forbids them the taking of heads or their fittest to survive, and no profane hand is raised against their customs of primæval antiquity. " *O fortunatos—sua si bona norint,*" which some of them by this time undoubtedly do.

I should like to take this opportunity of expressing my obligation to all those who have helped me ; to Colonel Gurdon for valuable advice ; to Mr. Balfour of the Pitt-Rivers Museum, Mr. Barnes, Colonel Woods, Mr. Reid, and Dr. Rivenburg for some valuable hints ; to Colonel Shakespear, formerly Political Agent in Manipur, for his very ample notes on the Memi which I have reproduced as an appendix ; to Professor Dixon of Harvard for letting me have the use of anthropometrical data and photographs taken by him in the Naga Hills ; to Miss Poynter, of the Oxford Natural History Society, for very kindly arranging for the preparation of my manuscripts for the press. I should also like to acknowledge my indebtedness to some manuscript notes of Colonel Kennedy's on the Memi ; to the fourth edition of *Notes and Queries on Anthropology,* edited by Miss Freire-Marreco and Professor Myres ; and to Dr. Rivers' pamphlet on the Genealogical Method. The arrangement of this monograph follows in general the syllabus laid down by the Assam Administration, and is not my own.

In particular my thanks are due to those Angamis and other Nagas who have given me very much help in the collection of my information, among whom I would mention Hrichale Pienyunuo, and the interpreters Zelucha, Srisalhu, Vidilhu, Kruzeto, Thepfuvitse, Vise, Tahemo, and Nihu, all of the Deputy-Commissioner's staff, and for other tribes Ongli-Ngaku, Vikhepu, Inato, Chamümo, Etsizao, and Innamiran, interpreters of the Mokokchung Subdivision. For the original typing of a somewhat obscure and involved manuscript my thanks are partly due to Rai Sahib Sitanath Barbara and Babu Hemakanta Barthakur, but the first five parts were almost entirely typed by an Angami, Visanyü Lizechu of Kohima, to whom I am obliged for the correction of a number of inaccuracies, and whose necessary perusal of my work is in some sort a safeguard against mistakes, if not of omission, at any rate of commission.

Many of the stories in Part V have already appeared in a slightly altered form in " Folklore," and I am indebted to the courtesy of the Folklore Society for their republication here, though I have given them here in the original form in which I recorded them, as the alterations were not mine. I have also taken advantage of the valuable notes which appeared appended to the stories in the same journal. Part VI consists principally of verbatim extracts from Sir George Grierson (*Linguistic Survey of India*, Vol. III., Pt. 2) and McCabe (*Outline Grammar of Angami Naga*), as it would be an impertinence on my part to attempt any original treatment of the language. In this connection Sir George Grierson, while kindly giving permission to use his material, writes that he would be sorry if he " got all the credit for others' work," and asks that it should be made clear that his account of Angami is mainly based on McCabe's Grammar and that he was indebted to Mr. Davis for additions and corrections.

Of the illustrations, those from coloured originals are from sketches by the late Colonel Woodthorpe, which were kindly lent me by the Curator of the Pitt-Rivers Museum, Oxford, while of the photographs a few are by Captain Hensley, Professor Dixon, Mr. Barnes, and Mr. Shuttleworth, and some of the best are by Mr. Butler of the P.W.D., to whom I owe many thanks. I also acknowledge my indebtedness to the Royal Anthropological Institute for permission to reproduce an illustration from Colonel Woodthorpe's article in 1881. The remainder of the illustrations are from photographs of my own.

Specimens of a considerable number of the objects described in this monograph will be found in the Pitt-Rivers Museum at Oxford, and a glossary of common native terms

(other than Naga) used in the monograph will be found in
the Appendix. For the Index I am again indebted to
Colonel J. Shakespear.

I would add that the monograph was originally intended
for publication in 1915, but was postponed owing to the war.
Hence some items of additional information in footnotes
which might be expected in the text proper.

J. H. H.

PREFACE TO THE SECOND EDITION

This account of the Angami Nagas was completed by the year 1915, though on account of the war it could not be published for seven years. It is therefore out of date now by more than 50 years, and that a period of rapid change such as humanity has probably never before experienced. The account here given of the Angami Naga tribe must therefore be regarded rather in the light of an historical document than a contemporary survey. Since, however, no people can be understood nor any estimate of their character made without at least some knowledge of their past, the account here given cannot have been rendered valueless by the mere passage of time; indeed its value may perhaps in some respects have thereby even been enhanced. Of its faults and shortcomings, I am only too conscious. I started it when, transferred to the Naga Hills from Eastern Bengal in 1912, I was rather shocked to find that of a tribe I had to work and live with there was no systematic or informed account to which I could refer for customs and ways of life entirely different from those I had known in Dacca or Bakarganj. I had little knowledge of anthropology at that time and having been always a poor linguist and with a bad ear for music, I found the highly tonal languages of the Naga Hills difficult to acquire. The defects of this volume will be manifest therefore to those trained in a discipline of social anthropology and no less so to the linguist, for in the chapter on language I have attempted to give an account of an agglutinative tongue in the entirely unsuitable terms of the inflected grammar of Greek or Latin. I know better now, but I am too old and too far off to rewrite the volume, and can only hope that this jejune effort may still contribute to the knowledge of a people in whose delightful company I passed what were probably the happiest years I had known since I left childhood for a boarding-school.

New Radnor   J. H. H.
   1967

CONTENTS

PART I

GENERAL

PART II

DOMESTIC LIFE

PART III

LAWS AND CUSTOMS

PART IV

RELIGION

xiii

PART V

FOLKLORE

PART VI

LANGUAGE

APPENDICES

LIST OF ILLUSTRATIONS

xv

MAPS

NOTE

The word " genna " is used in the Assamese " lingua franca " of the Naga Hills District to convey the meanings of the following Angami words :—

(1) *Kenna* = " forbidden," *e.g.*, " *a ki vor kennawe*" = it is genna to come to my house—my house is tabued. *Kenna* is applied to the individual while *penna* is applied to the community.

(2) *Penna* = a non-working day (as opposed to *Lichu* = field going, a working day) on which it is genna, or forbidden, for the village to go to work, and also, as a rule, to hold intercourse with strangers.

(3) *Nanü* = a tabu and the whole ceremony connected with it. It differs from *penna* in that it includes the whole period during which any prohibition continues, whereas *penna* merely covers the period during which work in the fields is prohibited.

Naga words, other than proper names, have, generally speaking, been printed in italics, while words of Assamese or similar origin have been printed between inverted commas and will be found translated in the glossary (Appendix XII).

The words *kenna* and *penna* are linguistically linked both etymologically and in meaning and association with the more familiar "tabu", an Austric word to be traced from the SE. Asia mainland to the southern confines of Oceania through the Malayan *kĕna*, *kĕmpunan*, Jakun *punan*, Sea Dyak *puni*, Maori and Samoan *puni-puni*, Hawaian *puni*, Tongan *buni*, *tapbuni*, *tabu*, all with the meaning of seclusion in a literal or metaphorical sense; cp. Malay *buni* = hide, and Marquesan *pana-le* and *penant*. The same word is apparent in the Sema Naga *pini*, and much further south in Assam in the Lakher *pana* all with the same significance as *penna*. See J. H. N. Evans in *Man*, 1920, art. 38; Delmas, *La Réligion . . . des Marquises* (Paris, 1927); and N. E. Parry, *The Lakhers* (1932).

PART I

INTRODUCTORY —THE NAGA HILLS —THE ANGAMIS : HABITAT,
AFFINITIES, APPEARANCE, DRESS AND ORNAMENTS,
WEAPONS, CHARACTER

MAP TO SHOW TH

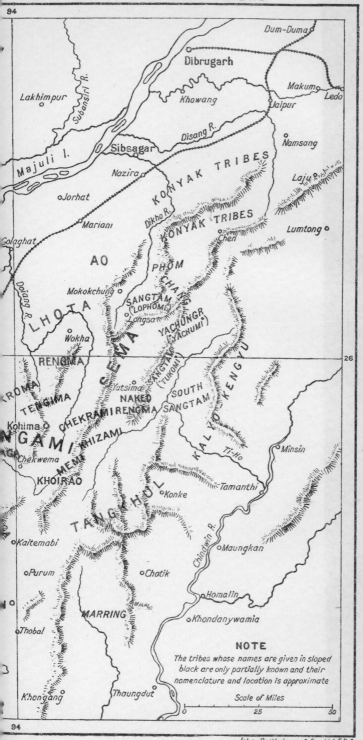

Dum-Duma

Lakhimpur

Subansiri R.

Dibrugarh

Khowang

Makum
Ledo

Jaipur

Disang R.

Namsang

Majuli I.

Sibsagar

Nazira

Laju R.

Jorhat

KONYAK TRIBES

Mariani

Dikho R.

KONYAK TRIBES

Lumtong

Golaghat

AO

Chen

PHOM

Doiang R.

Mokokchung

CHANG

SANGTAM
(LOPHOMI)

LHOTA

ohgsa

YACHUNGR
(YACHUMI')

Wokha

SEMA

RENGMA

26

KROMA)

Yatsima

SANGTAM
(TUKOMI')

TENGIMA

NAKED
RENGMA

SOUTH
SANGTAM

KALYO KENGYU

Kohima

CHEKRAMIRENGMA

NGAMI
RHIZAMI

MEMI

Ti-ho

Minsin

Chekwema

KHOIRAO

Tamanthi

Konke

TANGKHUL

Kaitemabi

Chindwin R.

Maungkan

Purum

Chatik

Homalin

MARRING

Khondanywamia

Thobal

NOTE

The tribes whose names are given in sloped
black are only partially known and their
nomenclature and location is approximate

Khongang

Thaungdut

Scale of Miles

25   30

94

THE ANGAMI NAGAS

PART I

INTRODUCTORY—THE NAGA HILLS—THE ANGAMIS : HABITAT,
AFFINITIES, APPEARANCE, DRESS AND ORNAMENTS,
WEAPONS, CHARACTER

RUNNING southwards from the eastern ends of the Himalayas until it reaches the Bay of Bengal is a strip of irregular
hills dividing Assam and Bengal from Burma. At the
northern end of these broken ranges the valley of the
Brahmaputra makes, as it were, a deep inroad into the hills.
It is in the hills immediately to the south of this encroaching
valley that the Nāga[1] tribes have their present home.
Westward is the valley of the Dhānsīrī, southward the
state of Mănĭpūr, the Raja of which has Naga subjects in
the northern hills of his territory. To the east is Burma.
Of the intervening territory the western half forms the
administered district of the Naga Hills, east of which is a
gradually diminishing tract of unadministered territory
populated by Naga tribes more or less closely related to
those within the district itself. Of these latter there are
roughly seven. The Kăcha Nagas at the south-west end
of the district ; the Àngāmis, occupying the section to the

[1] The word "Nāga" has been given all sorts of derivations; the
most probable explanation of it is that it is merely a European lengthen-
ing of the Assamese "năga" (pronounced "nöga")? = naked—Sanskrit
năgna. All along the foot of the hills an Assamese may be still heard
daily addressing himself to the scantily attired hill man with " Oh, Năga."
Lieut.-Colonel Waddell explains "Nāga" as meaning "hill man," deriving
it from the Hindustani năg = a mountain. Mr. Peal derives it from nok
a word used by some Eastern Naga tribe for " people "(" Fading Histories,"
Journal of the Asiatic Society of Bengal, No. 1, 1894, p. 14), but I suspect
that the alleged word nok is merely the familiar log = "people" of
Hindustani.

north of Manipur ; the Rengmas in a little triangle north of the western Angami country ; north of the Rengmas the Lhōtas, and east and north-east of them the Sĕmas. North of the Semas and Lhotas are the Aos, and to the north-east of them in the north-east corner of the district are the Kŏnyăk tribes. Immediately south of them are Chăngs, but there are only two Chang villages inside administered territory, while the Săngtăms, between the Changs and the trans-Tizu Semas, have only one village inside the district. East of these tribes from north to south are Konyăks, Yàchūmi,[1] Tūkomi, Sangtams, naked Rengmas, and the Tangkhuls of Somra, and in the unexplored area north of the Tangkhuls and east of the Yachumi and Sangtams are the Kālyo-kengyu—" slated-house-men."

The history of how the Naga tribes came precisely to occupy their present position has, of course, passed into the dim obscurity of vague traditions. But enough of them remain to give some indication of the course which the migrations took. The legends of the Aos and of the Semas give those tribes a more or less autochthonous origin, though these legends are probably the old legends of the race which have been given a local value. The Angamis, too, spring from ancestors who emerged from the bowels of the earth, but that not in Angami country, but in some other land to the south. And all the weight of tradition points to migration from the south, except in the case of the Kacha Naga, who believes that his ancestors came from the direction of Japvo mountain, whence they spread towards the south, which indeed would be the natural course if they came through the Mao gap and spread south where the other Naga tribes spread northwards. The Lhota traditions say that they once occupied the country which is now Angami : that the Aos broke off from Lhota stock and went north, and as the Angamis pressed in their rear the Lhotas followed

---

[1] " Yachumi " is the Sema name for this tribe, the members of which call themselves " Yimchurr." The tribe is commonly spoken of as " Yachumi " by the local officers, and is mentioned under that name in Sir G. Grierson's *Linguistic Survey of India*. The " Lophomi " and " Tukomi " Sangtams are really the same tribe. See Appendix.

MIGRATIONS
OF
NAGA TRIBES
according to their own tradi

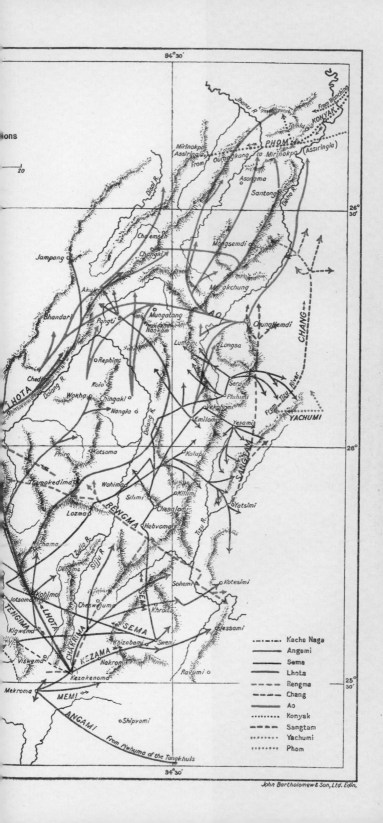

suit, going first west, then crossing the Dăyang at Baghti-
mukh and spreading up the Dăyang to the Ao country or
avoiding the Dăyang and going north-east towards Sema
country. Even now they point to Lhota genna stones
erected on long-deserted and tree-grown hills to the south
of the Dăyang as marking the sites of their former homes,
and remember stories of the great Lhota chief Pemevo, who
led them against the Angamis. And it is possible that the
migration of part of the Rengmas to the Rengma hills in
Golaghat was partly the result of the north-eastward pressure
of Lhota migration. Traditions are extant of a mighty
struggle between the combined Rengma villages and the
Lhota village of Phiro, the southernmost village of the
eastern Lhotas. The Semas again, or at least the Semas
of the Dayang Valley, have a clear tradition that they once
occupied the country now Angami, and point to Swemi[1]
village near Kezobama as the home of their race, and with
this Angami traditions agree. From Swemi, after being
severely defeated by the Angamis, they went to Sedzuma
near the Zubza river, whence they turned north-east again
to Cheswezuma and thence again north-west to Lazemi.

Again, while the Semas point southwards to the village
of Swemi or to the hill of Tŭkahū (Japvo) in the Angami
country as the place from which they sprung, and the
Rengmas to Sŏpvŏma (Mao), the Angamis point to Mao and
the country south of that as the home of their race, and to
this day the priests of the Angami villages wait for the
priests of Mao and Maikel to give the word before appointing
the day for the celebration of any of the regular village
festivals, and point to the ceremonial of the Mao village of
Mekroma ("Maikel") as the type of Angami ceremony *par
excellence*. The Sĕzemi, Sŏpvŏma or Mĕmi Nagas of Mao
again have legends connecting them with the plain lands of
Manipur, and it is conceivable that the magnificent system of
irrigation by which the Memi and other Angami Nagas, who

---

[1] This village is a Sema village in the middle of the Angami country.
Though conforming outwardly to Angami customs, it retains Sema as its
own language for internal use, the women speaking Sema as well as the
men, which shows that the Sema language is not a trading acquisition.
Swemi = Semi = Sema or Simi.

differ in little but language, turn a steep hillside into rice fields is a legacy bequeathed to these tribes by a sojourn in the lowlands of Imphal as they migrated north, but traces of terraced cultivation in the Angami manner have been noticed as far south as Champhai in the Lushai Hills, and the system generally is so like that followed by the Bongtoc or Igorot tribes in Luzon in the Philippines that it would appear to have something other than a purely local origin, while the stone terracing is totally unlike the easy cultivation of the Manipur plain.

Where the Nagas came from before they reached the country near Manipur is a much more difficult problem and one quite beyond the scope of this book.[1] All sorts of origins have been ascribed to the race. They have been connected with the head-hunters of Malay and the races of the Southern Seas on the one hand, and traced back to China on the other. Probably some ingenious person has by this time rediscovered in them the lost ten tribes of Israel, though why anyone, once having lost them, should want to rediscover the ten tribes so successfully put out of the way passes ordinary comprehension. On the basis of language their origin is assigned by Sir G. Grierson to the second wave of emigration, that of the Tibeto-Burmans, from the traditional cradle of the Indo-Chinese race in North-Western China between the upper waters of the Yang-tse-kiang and the Ho-ang-ho rivers. The Naga languages have been differently classified by different philologists, but the classification of Sir George Grierson is now generally accepted (vide Census of India, 1911). According to this classification Angami Naga is of the Tibeto-Chinese family, Tibeto-Burman sub-family, Assam-Burmese branch, group Naga, sub-group Western Naga. The Angami Kezama,

[1] It is undeniable that for some time migration in this part of the world has been from south to north, but it cannot be said how long this has been going on. Colonel L. W. Shakespear suggests that the Naga fancy for marine shells may point to a bygone home on the sea (History of Upper Assam, p. 197). In any case, the Nagas have very strong cultural affinities with the natives of the Asiatic Islands, notably Borneo, and the Philippine Islands, and perhaps physical affinities with some of them (Journal of the Royal Anthropological Institute, vol. xliv, p. 57).

Sema, and Rengma Naga languages are classified in this sub-group, while the Memi language falls under the Naga-Kuki sub-group, and the Lhota language under the Central-Naga sub-group, the position of the negative before or after the verb being taken as the test of distinction between the Western and Central sub-groups. It should be noted, however, that the linguistic distinction between sub-groups can hardly be said to correspond to any sort of racial distinction, and monosyllabic languages like those of the Naga groups grow apart from one another very rapidly, particularly under conditions of isolation such as obtained till recently in the Naga Hills.

It is worth while on this point to quote from McCabe a sentence which bears not only upon Naga languages and dialects but on their customs, habits, and even personal appearance :—

" It is only necessary," says McCabe, " to glance at the peculiar conditions of a Naga's life to grasp the fact that they strongly favour the growth of dialects. Grouped in small communities of from 100 to 3,000 persons, the Nagas have remained isolated on their hill tops, only deigning to visit their immediate neighbours when a longing for the possession of their heads has become too strong to be resisted. Even in a single village this isolating influence is at work. . . . As an example of how rapidly isolation produces dialectical change, I would mention the fact that the Rengma Naga families, who migrated some seventy[1] years ago from Themokedima to the hills along the Koliǎni, are now almost unintelligible to members of the parent stock."

And this is not only the case with dialect. So pronounced is this isolating tendency that there are a number of villages the inhabitants of which may be recognised as such by their facial characteristics after a comparatively short stay in Kohima. Indeed, types of mind as well as features are readily established in such a degree as to distinguish a village from its neighbours ; thus while Khŏnoma and Jàkhǎma are remarkable for the stature of their men, and Kezabama for the " beauty " of its women, Kĭdǐma and

---

[1] It is now about one hundred years.

Nerhăma are noted even among Angamis for litigiousness, and Tŏfĭma for falsehood. On the other hand, while features differ greatly, from the round face and protruding ears of the men of Phūlāma to the very long faces of men of Khonoma, anthropometrical measurements show little or no difference between one type of Angami's head and another, or even between an Angami and a Sema.

It is interesting to note that while the traditions of the Rengmas, Lhotas, Semas, and Angamis all ascribe a common origin to these tribes, they take no account of the tribes across the rivers Lànier, Tizu, and Dikhu. It seems not improbable that while a Naga migration was proceeding northward through the Mao gap and spreading up west of the rivers mentioned, a similar migration was going on to the east of these rivers. It is true that .there are now Semas east of the Tizu, but they have recently migrated from its west bank. Indeed, the north-easterly migration of Semas at the expense of the Sangtam and Yimchurr (Yachumi) tribes is still going on, and Yĕpŏthōmi Sema villages, which all derive their ultimate origin from Yezami on the west bank, have pushed two days' march across the river and are still throwing off colonies further east. Moreover, the Konyak villages round Tamlu and the Changs of Yangiemdi have undoubtedly come west in comparatively recent years from across the Dikhu. The Aos also claim for themselves a trans-Dikhu origin and in every way have far more in common with the trans-Dikhu tribes than they have with the tribes immediately to the south of them (vide Appendix). It cannot, I think, be doubted that the Lhota, Rengma, Sema, and Angami tribes are more nearly connected with one another than any one of them now is with the Aos and the tribes across the Dikhu and Tizu.

In dress, custom, and traditions isolation has led to divergence no less surely than in dialect, and it must not be assumed that a custom set down here as an Angami custom, or a story given as an Angami tradition, will be found in precisely the same form in all Angami villages. As far as possible the villages of the Tengima group have been drawn on first, and Angami customs given in the form in which they are observed there, the divergences of other groups being in some cases noted. At the same time, no interesting material wherever picked up has been discarded, and statements will doubtless be found here given as relating to the Angamis unlocalised which really do not hold good of the whole tribe. Nor is it possible even to attempt to give in detail the manifold divergences of any given custom from village to village. Such an undertaking would necessitate a separate monograph for each Angami village.

It is not without reason that Khonoma, in particular, has been chosen as a typical Angami village. Before the coming of the " Sarkar " no Angamis enjoyed such prestige or levied such widespread tribute as Khonoma. In spite of serious clan dissensions within the village, they were known and feared from Henima to Themokedima, and from Razama to the Mikir Hills in Golaghat. Kōhǐma,[1] it is true, were too numerous for Khonoma to attack with any hope of success, and perhaps had the greater influence over the East Angami country and did all the trade on that side. It is only of recent years that Khonoma have taken to trading far afield in that direction.

But this hegemony, if it may be called such, of Khonoma merely meant that Khonoma was stronger than most other villages, and consequently bullied, and levied a sort of " Danegelt " wherever it could. The general polity of the country may probably be accurately gauged from the reports of the doings of trans-frontier villages which now reach Kohima from time to time. Thus : " In May a man of Thàchūmi and a man of Lazimi hid near the salt hole of Phōza-Nàgwemi and fell upon two men and three women who came to make salt. They killed one man outright and wounded two others, who escaped back to their village, where one of them died later. The two raiders ran off with the head of the man they had killed and evaded pursuit." Clumsily managed but very typical. Again : " In June the Lūkrāmi clan of Thachumi planned a raid upon the village of Phōza-Nàsami, and sent fifty men to cut it up. Another

---

[1] Really Kĕwhīma with the accent on the first syllable but the second syllable long.

clan of Thachumi, however, being on bad terms with the
Lukrami clan, sent round warning to Phōzami and the
neighbouring villages. When the fifty raiders found that
their enemies had been warned (a man of the other Thachumi
clan told them of this shouting across a valley), they returned
home sticking ' panjis ' in the path by which they had
come. When they got back to Thachumi they paid a visit
to the unfriendly clan and killed and carried off four or five
pigs as a punishment for their interference."

These two instances, taken from South Sangtam villages just
across the Angami frontier, are probably typical of the state
of village relations among the Angamis before the British
occupation, and the defeat of the intentions of one clan by
the unfriendly interference of another clan must have
happened over and over again in Khonoma, as well as in
most Angami villages at one time or another. Of course,
the Angami traditions of their village feuds point to pitched
battles of a most sanguinary description, as when Kohima
had a battle with Pūchāma and a Kohima detachment cut
off Puchama from their village. Kohima were aided by the
Vīhotsūma clan of Mezoma, and Puchama by Kigwĕma.
On this occasion so much blood flowed in the gateway of
Puchama and the narrow approach to it that men's hands
clave to their spears owing to the clotted blood, and men
were suffocated in the blood that ran in the pathway.
Again, when the Lhota village of Moilang attempted to storm
the village of Phekĕkrīma, the Lhotas were prevailing and a
local Samson had killed thirty Angamis with his own spear ;
a detachment, however, slipped out the other side of the
village and engaged the Lhotas in the rear, killing many
Lhotas and taking Chàkerōmo prisoner, whom they carried
off to Phekekrima. There he was tortured to death by the
boys of the village, who cut small pieces off him with their
knives, a rare case of the deliberate torture of a prisoner by
Nagas. It is certainly probable that on occasions the
Angamis, like other Nagas, fought pitched battles. When
Captain Reid visited Kĕkrīma in 1851 the village braves
turned out armed with spear and shield and fought a pitched
battle with his sepoys and Naga allies. But while the

Angamis doubtless indulged in pitched battles on occasion, the normal method of carrying on war was undoubtedly characterised by stealth and ambuscade rather than by open fighting, and the stories of the heroic combats of the men of old time have probably been very much magnified by tradition. At the same time, tribal migrations may have led to fighting on a larger scale than was customary after the tribes had settled down into their present areas.

What the precise relations the Naga tribes had with the various nations of the plains before the coming of the British Raj, we have no means of knowing. They must have come into contact with the Kacharis, whose capital was at Dīmāpūr on the edge of the Angami country, and legends of the Kachari King Bhim are still current among the Kacha Nagas and the Angamis of Khonoma. They believe that he yet sleeps in a cave among the hills immediately to the south of Japvo, whence he will come at some time in the distant future to struggle with the British Raj and eventually to rule over all who eat from the wooden platter. There is also a legend current among the Kacharis of Diger Mauza below Hĕn ma that when Bhim Raja built his great keddah at Sōnapūr, in that mauza, he fell in love with a Nagini whom he found in the jungle and who became by him the ancestress of the Diger Kacharis, who pride themselves on their descent. The Ahom kings, again, enlisted Angamis and other Nagas together with Singphos and Kakhos in the hill regions of their armies, and furthermore had relations with Manipur and must have come into contact with whatever hill tribes separated them from their allies ; while a nation spoken of locally as the Chinese, but presumably the Burmese, had an iron foundry and a salt well just below the village of Khŏrō in the Lhota country, where Nagas still search for bits of iron to turn into hoes or " daos." Some Lhota and Ao villagers also held grants of plains lands from the Assam Rajas.

With the Manipuris the relations of the Angamis, at any rate, were anything but friendly, as somewhere about 1833 a Manipuri raid was made into Angami country as far as Kohima, which the Manipuris attacked and burnt, slaughtering a large number of the inhabitants. There are still living in Kohima an old man and an old woman who were alive at the time and escaped the slaughter by hiding in the jungle, and the stone which the Manipuris set up in Kohima over the body of a Kohima boy buried alive is now to be seen in the public garden at Kohima, whither it has been moved from its original site. On the flat stone are carved the footprints of the Manipuri Raja, while the upright slab bears the carvings of a dragon and a cow underneath an inscription in Manipuri.[1]

The Kukis were migrating north when the Sarkar came into contact with the Angamis, and the Kacha Naga villages had begun to call in Kukis to defend them against raiders from Khonoma, which maintained a fluctuating suzerainty over the Kacha Naga villages. It is only the establishment of British rule in the Naga Hills which has prevented the Kukis from occupying the Lanier Valley in south-east corner of the Angami country and advancing up to the Tizu valley.

It would be out of place here to go into the history of the British occupation which has been already written. It is enough to say that after the occupation of the plains of Assam as far as the foothills, Government has been compelled to move gradually further east towards Burma generally for the protection of its frontier villages.

The Angamis. Of all the tribes inhabiting the Naga Hills District the Angamis, or, to give them the name which some of them, at any rate, give themselves (for " Angami " is apparently a corruption of the name " Gnamei " given to them by the Manipuris), " Tengïma," occupy the largest area and are far the most numerous. They are situated roughly in the area bounded on the north by a line running from a point slightly south of where the Däyang river issues into the plains through the peaks Thĕvükĕpü (above Themoketsa, the most southerly Rengma village) and Mutuhu (on the edge of the Sema country) to the junction of the Loï and Tizu rivers between Kivekhu and Chipokitema. Thence on Habitat. the east the boundary of the Angami country coincides approximately with the eastern boundary of the Naga

[1] See the illustration in Mr. Hodson's monograph on the Meitheis.

View from Losama — looking eastwards

The Kezakanoma Stone (to the right)

[See p. 19

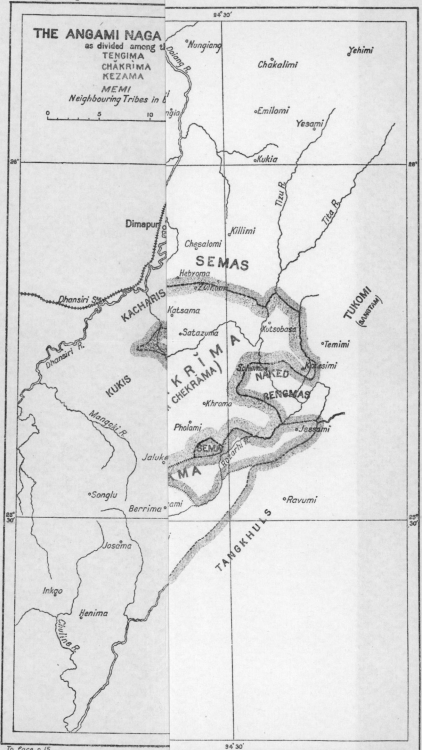

THE ANGAMI NAGA
as divided among th
TENGIMA
CHAKRIMA
KEZAMA
MEMI
Neighbouring Tribes in b

0   5   10

Nungiang   Chakalimi   Yehimi

Emilomi
Yesami

Kukia

Dimapur   Killimi
Chesalomi
SEMAS
Hebyoma
Zulhami
Dhansiri Sta.   KACHARIS   Katsama
Kutsobasa   TUKOMI (SANGTAM)
Satazuma
Temimi
K R I M A   Schemi   Kolasimi
CHEKRAMA)   NAKED
KUKIS   RENGMAS
Khroma
Pholami
Jessami
Jaluke   SEMA   Rozarhi
M A
Songlu   Berrima   Ravumi
Dhansiri R.
Mangchi R.
TANGKHULS
Josama
Inkgo   Henima
Chulile R.

John Bartholomew & Son Ltd. Edin.

Hills District, though the sub-tribe of Memi is south-east of
it, until the Barail range is reached. On the south the
Angamis are bounded by the Barail range and the Diphu
river and on the west by the Nambar forest. With the
exception of one or two villages just outside it, the whole of
the Angami tribe is located in the above area. It is, however, divided into several distinct groups. That group
which is generally regarded as being Angami *par excellence*
is the Khonoma group, consisting of the six large villages
of Kwünoma (Khonoma), Sachema, Mezoma, Kīrūfēma
Jŏtsoma, Kigwema, and their offshoots, Thekrojenoma
and Sàchĕnōbama. The villages nearer the plains, generally
known as the " Chākrōma " villages, Rŏzĕphīma, Chĭmŏkĕ-
dīma (Samaguting), Kàbvŏma, Pĭphīma, Phĕrīma, Mĕzĭ-
phīma, Chōwŭma (Choloma) and Sĕtĭkīma, seem to be
derived principally from the Khonoma and Kohima groups.
The Kohima group, consisting of Kohima and the neighbouring villages, and the Viswema, or " Dzünokehena,"
group to the south of it, differ slightly, but not very much,
in dialect from the Khonoma group, and from one another,
and may be regarded as a link between the genuine Angamis
or Tengima, and the Chakrima (or Chĕkrāma) Angamis who
inhabit the villages north-east and east of the Kohima
group. East of the Viswema group and wedged in between
the Chakrima, Tengima, and Mĕmi are several villages
known as " Kezāmi " or " Kezāma," of which Kezakenoma
and Kezabama are the principal villages. These Kezama
villages, although in external respects like other Angami
villages, have a language and to some extent customs of
their own, though the men, at any rate, speak the Angami
as well as Kezami tongue. The term " Eastern Angami "
has been used in this monograph to signify generally the
Chakrima and Kezama, and those of the Memi who live on
the Kezama borders, in distinction from the Tengima
proper, or Western Angamis, of the Viswema, Kohima,
Khonoma and Chākrōma groups of villages. (Chā-krō-ma =
" Road-below men," the name being perhaps caused by the
situation of the villages with regard to the old Samaguting-
Kohima bridle path.)

Affinities. Of the neighbouring tribes the Khoirao Nagas on the east, though speaking a different language again, approximate closely to the Angamis in culture and appearance, being naturally closer to the Memi than to the Angami proper. On the south the Kacha Naga tribe is apparently derived from much the same stock as the Angamis and resembles them in dress, but speak a very different language ; owing, however, to the domination of Khonoma in the Kacha Naga country, it is very difficult to say at this time what customs are originally Kacha Naga and what have been imposed by Angamis. In many Kacha Naga villages exogamous clans are found bearing the names of the Khonoma clans and probably adopted as a result of their subjection to Khonoma. The Kăbuis of Manipur are probably their closest relatives. (See also Appendix.)

To the north-east of the Angami country is a group of three or four Naked Rengma villages which are an offshoot of the Rengmas proper. The largest of them is Mĕlŏmi, which, like Làpvŏmi, is a colony from Sōhĕmi. The men of Sohemi say that their village was founded by some Rengmas who were benighted in the jungle when hunting, having followed a wounded sambhar all day. When darkness found them on the far bank of the Tizu river, they started to cut bamboos to build shelters. One of them, cutting a bamboo, found it to contain cooked rice,[1] and taking this as an omen, the party decided to build a village in that place. These three villages undoubtedly speak a language closely resembling that of the Rengmas, and much nearer to the Rengma language than it is to that spoken by the neighbouring Angamis or Semas. They differ, however, from the Rengmas in being naked, whereas the Rengmas wear a small " lengta." Another village which may be grouped with these is Temimi, but its language differs from the Rengma, and indeed from any known Naga language, and a small " lengta " is worn. The population seems to be

---

[1] Compare the legend of the Dusun tribe of Tempessuk in British North Borneo, in which the children of Nohok Kurgung get rice by cutting down bamboo stems, the rice coming out from inside the stem. (*Journal of the Royal Anthropological Institute*, vol. xliii, p. 431.)

a cross between Naked Rengma and Tukomi Sangtam and claims kinship with both these tribes. The Rengma tribe proper has already been alluded to, and it would appear to be of the same stock as the Angami, Lhota, and Sema tribes, to the last of which it most nearly approximates. It has the same story of origin as the Angamis have, and the Rengmas in the Mikir Hills of Golaghat are said to wear round the leg, below the knee, the black cane rings worn by the Angamis, but these are not worn by the Rengmas in the Naga Hills. The Rengmas wear the "lengta" and not the Angami kilt.

Apropos of the kilt, Colonel Woodthorpe, in his paper on the Naga tribes, draws a sharp distinction between the kilted and the non-kilted tribes, the Sema, Rengma, and Lhota, that is, and Butler also speaks of the dark, " squat," and " sulky Lhota " as belonging to a different race. It is difficult, however, to believe that the Angami differs from his northern neighbours so radically as has been suggested. It is true that the Lhota is darker than the Angami and of poorer physique, but then he lives in a much hotter and less healthy climate, and throughout the Naga Hills it will be found that the men of the higher and colder villages are, on the whole, taller and fairer than those in lower and hotter situations. This distinction is as noticeable between Semas and Angamis of different villages as between the Angamis and the Lhotas generally. To brand the Lhota in general as " sulky " would be a most unjustifiable stricture upon a friendly and cheerful race.[1] Differences of dress again

[1] Colonel Woods agrees with Colonel Woodthorpe, saying that even the Lhotas who live in the villages at an elevation as high as many of the Angamis are far inferior in physique and darker in colour, although there are many very fair Lhotas even in the villages lying low. He adds that his experience of the Lhota is that "he is not near so cheerful as the Angami or Sema. He has usually a grievance."

It may seem presumptuous to disagree with an officer of Colonel Woods experience. At the same time, I cannot agree at all. The Lhota, it is true, is less ready to grin than the Angami, but I have found him anything but sulky. Nor can I agree that Lhotas are on the whole inferior in phy-sique to Angamis occupying similar altitudes, while my experience is that the Angami villagers at lower altitudes have a vastly inferior physique to Lhotas living at the same height. It must also be remembered that the traditions of the few Lhotas who live at a high altitude point to their

between different tribes are not confined to a broad line
between kilts and " lengtas." Some tribes are naked, like
the Naked Rengmas, some wear a mere flap about eight
inches by two depending from a string round the waist like
the Zŭmŏmi Semas, some wear the small " lengta " of the
southern Lhota villages (the " lengta " consists of a narrow
girdle, one end of which, coming down at the back between
the legs and widening out to conceal the private parts,
comes up in front, passes under the girdle, and ends in a
hanging flap), and some wear the large " lengta " of the
northern Lhotas. The date is probably not really very
far distant when the majority of Nagas were naked, and no
doubt those living nearer to the more fully dressed peoples
adopted a fuller form of loin-cloth than the more remote
tribes. Again, a close connection between the Angamis,
the Lhotas, the Semas, and the Rengmas is indicated by
their legends of origin and by their folk tales, which though
sometimes differing in detail are obviously the same in
substance throughout the three tribes, and it has to be remembered that until quite recent years these tribes have been
kept asunder by impassable barriers of language and of
hostilities. As for external difference of dress, the Semas
themselves have a story which is perhaps worth quoting
here. The Angamis, the Aos, the Lhotas, and the Semas,
they say, are descended from four brothers. The eldest of
the four was very virtuous, and so his parents dressed him
like themselves and were very kind to him. From him are
descended the Angamis. The second, who was the ancestor
of the Aos, was a little troublesome and was punished by a
more scanty allowance of clothing. The father of the
Lhotas was much the same as the Ao, his conduct possibly
a shade less satisfactory, and he was dressed accordingly.
As for the youngest, he was thoroughly wicked. He never
obeyed his parents and was always getting into mischief.
At last, when being sent to scare birds, he neglected his task

previously having sojourned in a lower locality. Some of the Semas who
have recently gone from Nikoto to a site on the Phekekrima-Changsung
range near the plains, where there was once a Lhota village, have visibly
darkened in colour in less than a year at the time of writing.

to eat all the pumpkins in the field, and, tired of his naughtiness, his parents tied a flap round his waist and turned him out of the house. That is why the Sema only wears a flap while the other tribes are more decently clothed.[1] It may be noted, however, that the Lhotas assert that the Ao adopted his " lengta " from them, and that when they first came into contact with him the Ao had a garment of the most scanty description, while he actually calls his full-dress garment " *Moiya längtăm*," *i.e.*, " Sema loin-cloth." In the same way the Sema is now rapidly adopting the " lengta " in place of the narrow flap.

The Angami story of the origin of the Naga tribes centres in the Kezami village of Kezakenoma. There was, the story goes, once upon a time an old couple with three sons living in that village. Every day they used to spread paddy to dry upon a great flat stone, and at dusk a single load spread to dry had become two loads, for the stone was inhabited by a spirit. The three sons used to take it in turns to spread their paddy on this stone, but one day they quarrelled bitterly as to whose turn it was, and their parents, fearing bloodshed, broke eggs on the stone, covered it with brushwood, laid faggots about it, and set the whole on fire. The stone burst with a crack like thunder, the spirit went up to heaven in a cloud of smoke, and the virtue of the stone departed. The three sons then separated and became the ancestors of the Angami, Lhota, and Sema tribes, while from the parents who remained are descended the seven Kezami villages. Variant details of this story are sometimes given ; the name of the village is only known to the Angamis, who still point out the great cracked stone, a flat raised slab opposite the house of the " kĕmŏvō," who is supposed to occupy as a general rule the site believed to have been occupied by the original founder of the village. With this exception substantially the same story is told by the Memi,

[1] The Angami story is that Naga tribes were all descended from one father, but that the Angami ancestor was the son of a second wife. The children of the first wife received proper cloths, which they wore in the ordinary way, continuing naked underneath, but the child of the second wife got only half a cloth, which was too small to wear as a cloak, so he wrapped it round his waist, and hence his descendants still wear the kilt.

Lhotas, Semas, and Rengmas.[1] As regards the Angamis, it does
not quite fit in with the story of the origin of the exogamous
clan, but that is a logical position which it is perhaps too
much to expect of any race. Butler mentions a story of the
foundation of the Angami race by an exile from the Court of
Jaintiapur who went first to Dīmāpūr and thence into the hills.
This history, he says, originated in "an old and intelligent hill
Kachari," but he could himself find no confirmation of it. The
village of Kohima contains one clan which claims an origin
from the west in contradistinction to prevailing accounts.

Appear-
ance.

In appearance the Angami Naga is by no means unpre-
possessing. His stature, tall for a hillsman, is ordinarily
about five feet nine and not infrequently goes up to six feet.
The young bucks are usually very fine, light, beautifully
built, and powerful, though the men of the Khonoma group
are generally made on rather heavier lines and are on the
whole taller than the Eastern Angamis.

The physical powers of the Angami are considerable, for
though he is not athletic in a gymnastic way, he has great
powers of endurance, being able to do forced marches of
thirty to forty miles on successive days over exceedingly
steep country. In fact he prefers marching over hilly
country to marching on the level. He can stand exposure
well, both to the cold, wet, and sun, ordinarily wearing no
covering on his head, but is unable to tolerate the heat of
the plains in the hot and rainy season, or the deep snow of
the Himalayas. He is also able to carry very considerable
burdens, the standard load being 60 lb., which is carried
easily for sixteen miles or so on a sling passing over the
forehead. The women can also carry loads, but with less
endurance. The Angamis are naturally expert hill climbers
and climb trees well, but cliffs indifferently and unwillingly.
Those in the high hills can seldom swim, but near rivers
some of them become expert swimmers and divers, usually
diving with a stone. The Angami's body is lithe and
frequently very finely developed, particularly as to the calf
and chest and shoulders, for which the climbing of hills
and the hoeing of terraced fields are doubtless responsible.

[1] See Appendix—Rengmas.

The toes are often widely separate, the big toe branching away from the others. The features of the Angami are mobile, pleasant and often decidedly handsome, while his voice is on the whole musical. But it would be impossible to give any general description of the type of Angami features, as it varies from village to village and even from house to house in a remarkable degree. The flattened nose and slightly oblique eyes of a decidedly Mongolian type may be seen side by side with a straightness of eye and nose that might be purely Aryan. The colour of the eye is always brown ; the lips are sometimes fine, sometimes very thick, and the hair, which in childhood is often of a reddish colour, though it turns black later, is generally straight and sometimes wavy, very rarely curly, and never woolly like a negro's. Hair does not grow freely on the face, and beards and moustaches are seldom seen. The women, except in one or two villages, are seldom really pretty, and very quickly lose whatever looks they have, but their rather plain features and stumpy figures are more than redeemed by a very taking geniality of expression and an undoubtedly attractive manner, while the tones of their voices offer a very pleasing and melodious contrast to the grating falsetto of the average plains-woman. In the higher and colder villages the skins of both men and women are sometimes exceptionally fair, and a ruddy, almost pink, tinge may be noticed in their cheeks, on which freckles, too, occasionally appear. As far as their persons go they are cleanly and wash frequently, even in cold weather—a quality only too rare amongst hill folk. Near an Angami village washing places are always to be found. A jet of water carried out in a bamboo from some stream, a basin made of hollowed stone or wood, a soap-dish, similarly hollowed and containing Naga soap. This last is made of the fibrous stalk of a creeper, which, when pounded with a stick provided for the purpose, gives a lather not unlike that obtained from European soaps. Here men and women stop to wash on their way to and from the field, while in the villages infants may sometimes be seen being washed in hot water. The teeth are washed by filling the mouth with water and rubbing round the closed teeth with the forefinger, which is followed by rinsing.

There are many different kinds of hair-dressing in vogue among the Naga tribes. The Tangkhuls cut their hair back at the sides, leaving a point in front, giving a sort of cockscomb effect. The Konyaks grow a long tail at the back, sometimes reaching to the ground, which, instead of being plaited, is tied round with cloth and done up into an elaborate knot at the back of the head. The Aos, Changs, Yachumi, Sangtams, Rengmas, Semas, and Lhotas shave the lower hair, and let the hair at the top of their head grow long, cutting it off to the same length all round the head, while the Kacha Naga does not seem to do his hair at all. The real Angami method is to let the hair grow naturally in front while tying up a small knot at the back. The hair which goes to form this knot is separated from the rest by a narrow circle of shaved skin, but this is omitted by the Eastern Angamis, and the Kezami Angamis in certain cases let the back hair fall untied to the neck. In the front a fringe is worn without a parting by the unmarried men, while the married men brush their hair back from the forehead, often parting it in the middle. Cosmetics are not used for the hair, except by those Nagas who have adopted their use from the people of the plains, but by old men whose hair has turned white wigs are frequently worn. These are made of bears' hair worked on to a hard wicker framework for which the head is measured, the tail at the back of the wig being made of human hair, as bears' hair is not long enough to tie up in the way the natural hair is usually tied. Hair does not grow freely on the face, and depilation is resorted to to remove the few hairs that do grow long on the chin or upper lip, the instrument used being a small forceps. Shaving is sometimes practised, but appears to be an innovation. The primitive method of cutting the hair is with a dao and sort of wooden hammer (*sīvü*), the dao being held under the hair and tapped along the edge with the piece of wood.

Dress and Ornaments. Ceremonial dress excepted, a variety of ornaments are worn in the ears. Little plugs of black wool, bits of red

paper or cloth, brass rings, cogwheels from the inside of
watches, anything, in fact, that the individual fancy may
dictate.[1] Round the neck beads of some sort are invariably
worn, the kind made of an opaque red stone flecked with
black and known to the Assamese as " deo-mani " being
perhaps the most highly prized, a small string of which is
sometimes worth as much as Rs.100/-. The white beads
made from the insides of conch shells, cornelian, and a black
bead made by the Kacha Nagas from the seeds of a plaintain
are also very popular, while triangular pieces of conch shells
are worn as well. With the exception of the varieties
above mentioned, however, the wearing of beads is largely
dictated by fashion, which is no less arbitrary in the Naga
Hills than in Bond Street ; the value of bead or similar
ornament is often decided by qualities apparently quite
immaterial to its intrinsic beauty and in every way as
unreasonable as the whims and fancies of civilised people ;
as the whim, for instance, of dog fanciers which rules a
" dudley " out of the show ring. The beads worn by the
Angami proper are numerous in the case of young men, but
the Eastern Angami wears a huge necklace of from six to
ten strings of conch-shell beads, black beads, and cornelian
in rows threaded on the same pattern with the cornelians in
front, the string passing through transverse pieces of horn or
bone at intervals. These pieces of horn serve to keep the
lines of beads apart, and are themselves decorated with
geometrical patterns in black. As well as beads the Angamis
wear necklets of plaited cane, yellow and red or yellow and
black, and at the back of the neck a polished conch shell of
which part has been cut away for the comfort of the wearer.
This shell, which is worn in front in the case of renowned
veterans, and is frequently so represented on the effigies set
up on the graves of the dead, is fastened on by a strip of
black cloth in the case of the Tengima, and by a collar of
blue and white beads with horn spreaders in that of the

---

[1] Children, girls, and young men often wear orchids or other bright
flowers in their ears, particularly on genna days, and the young men often
stick bits of fern or other green stuff into the cotton bindings of their
hair knots.

Eastern Angamis. Boars' tusks, worn by the Semas, Lhotas, Aos, Changs, and Sangtams, are very rarely worn by the Angamis. A piece of twisted cotton the thickness of a rope may often be seen worn round the neck of young un-married men. It is given to them by their sweethearts and worn as a love token.

On the arms the principal ornament worn is the ivory armlet, a complete section of elephant's tusk from $2\frac{1}{2}$ inches to $3\frac{1}{2}$ inches deep, but in addition to this brass armlets are often worn, particularly by the Eastern Angamis. These usually consist of a long ring of narrow brass encircling the upper arms perhaps a dozen times, and of a heavy brass bracelet with solid bugle-shaped ends which cross one another. The latter is worn both above the elbow and on the wrist or fore-arm, and in the latter case is sometimes slipped down into the hand to serve as a weapon, and becomes a very formidable sort of knuckle-duster.

On the legs, just below the knee, rings of cane dyed black (with indigo[1]) are worn. These are not particularly orna-mental, and the object of them is disputed ; for while some affirm that the object is purely ornamental, others say that these " *pissoh*," as they are called, are worn as an aid to hill climbing. They are, however, sometimes said to cause varicose veins, and are less invariably worn by the Eastern Angamis than by the Angami proper. It is interesting to notice that although none of the intervening tribes wear " *pissoh* " or anything resembling them, the Konyaks of Tamlu and the trans-Dikhu villages and the Sibsagar border wear a very similar ornament, differing only in being made of red cane instead of black. The Rengmas of Rengma-pahar in Golaghat also wear black " *pissoh* " like the Angamis, but the Rengmas of the Naga Hills district never wear them. In addition to these ornaments, the dress of the Angami male consists, under ordinary conditions, of a black kilt and one or more cloths. The kilt is generally embroidered with cowries in three or four lines,[2] the real significance of which

[1] Obtained from the plant *Strobilanthes flaccidifolius*, which is cultivated in most Angami villages.

[2] Some old kilts in the Indian Museum, Calcutta, have little cowrie trefoils sewn on between the lines.

is rapidly changing. In Butler's time three lines of cowries signified that the wearer was a warrior, and four lines were only assumed by veterans of renown. Nowadays any grown man may wear three lines of cowries, and the fourth line is supposed to signify that the wearer has taken a head, but as a matter of fact is generally worn by anyone who has thrust a spear into a dead body of an enemy shot by the sepoys, and by many even who have merely accompanied some trans-frontier expedition when any fighting has taken place. In course of time the fourth line will probably cease to signify anything more than social standing. The cowries, it should be mentioned, are rubbed down on stones, so as to fit closely together. Over the kilt a belt is tied round the waist, usually of tubular construction, to contain money. The cowries a man wears may not be sewn on to the kilt by a woman, but are sewn on by the owner himself.

In the case of the Chakrima and Kezama Angamis, the fourth line denotes prowess not in war but in love, and may be worn for any one of the four following achievements :—

1. An intrigue with a married woman living with her husband ;
2. A simultaneous intrigue with two girls of the same name ;
3. or with two daughters of one father ;
4. or with a mother and her daughter.

A man who achieves any one of these is called *jàsejā*. One of the headmen of Takhubama village wears a fourth line of cowries on the third count.

Of the cloths worn there are many varieties, the predominant pattern being black with red and yellow stripes down the two sides. These stripes, which are few and broad in the Angamis of the Khonoma group, are narrow and more numerous in Kohima and the Eastern Angami country. In a few villages, notably Kirufema, these cloths are still made of home-grown and home-dyed cotton, but generally speaking the indigenous plaid has given way to cloths introduced from Manipur or woven with Burmese thread bought from that place. Green stripes may nowadays be often seen in these cloths, though no green dye is known to the Angami, and fancy cloths generally are beginning to supplant the traditional patterns. In the case of Khonoma and of most Eastern Angami villages the unmarried man wears a different cloth. That in Khonoma is black with a broad border of terra-cotta red along each side, while that of the Chakrima is blue with scarlet borders. The Kezami villages also have distinctive cloths, one of which is black with three or four very narrow stripes worked of red and white cotton, each stripe being red one side and white the other, the colours being interchanged halfway down the line. The other is white with blue stripes. A white cotton cloth with black and brownish striped borders and a white cloth of nettle fibre with black stripes are universal. There is one cloth—it is white with a black and red border—which may only be worn by men who have reached a high social standing owing to the number of " gennas " of a semi-public nature performed by him (see Part IV). The Angamis, however, are not in this respect so precise as the Lhotas, who have a regular scale of cloths, from which it can be told at a glance precisely to what status in the performance of such ceremonies the wearer has reached. Besides the " *zhāvā-kwe* " mentioned which is worn by the performer of the " *zhāthō* " genna, the Angamis have only one cloth distinctive of social status—this is the " *pitsü-kwe* " worn by the priest. The Lhotas have also a separate series of cloths relating to exploits in war as distinct from those in society (see Appendix).

In wet weather a large hat of leaves and basket work is worn, as well as a rain-coat of plaited strips of *pandanus* leaf, the ends of which hang out loose, to keep off the water.[1]

The cloths principally in vogue among Angami women are a plain blue cloth and a white cloth with black marginal stripes of varying width, but they may be often seen wearing the bright striped cloth of men. The Eastern Angamis have a cloth with a red edge and a petticoat with a broad white band. The dress of the ordinary Angami woman

---

[1] A similar rain-coat is made by the Konyaks north of the Dikhu, though not by the intervening tribes.

consists of a sort of sleeveless bodice formed by a cloth crossed under one arm and fastened on the opposite shoulder, and of a petticoat made by wrapping a cloth round the waist and tying it or tucking it in so as to keep it from falling, and covering a smaller petticoat called *nikro* (= "loin-cloth-under "). The hair of unmarried girls is shaved,[1] or cropped quite close, universally, as is also the case among the Semas and Lhotas and some of the Aos, while the hair of the married women is dressed differently by different groups. The women of the Khonoma and Kohima Angamis tie their hair up in a knot behind as soon as it is long enough, nor do they hesitate to supplement it, if scanty, with purchased tresses. They wear no hair ornaments, but the Viswema and the Eastern Angami women wear their hair down their backs, and also wear a long brass ring through the top of each ear, the pair being joined by a string across the top of the head, and a second round the back of the head, thus keeping the hair on the top of the head smooth and tidy. The general effect of this is very becoming. The Kacha Naga and Ao women wear somewhat similar brass head-rings.

Cowries are never worn by Angami women, though Sema women wear them strung horizontally as a belt, while the Rengma and some of the Dayang valley Sema women whose husbands have performed certain ceremonies in feasting the village are allowed to wear cloths embroidered with cowries. The Angamis, however, speak of cowrie cloths as essentially " the males' dress," and this idea is the pre-vailing one among Naga tribes, cowries usually being worn as a sign of martial achievements. It is said that before

[1] No explanation of this practice is given by the Angamis, but the Changs, who shave the heads of their young girls until they are old enough to go and work in the fields, give the reason that as long as their heads are shaved it does not matter what they say to men of their own kindred, but that when once they are grown up, they must not utter words which would shame them or men of their kindred to whom they were spoken. The idea seems to be that when the girls are old enough to know what may be fitly said and what may not, then it is safe to let their hair grow. Possibly this originates in a notion that the shaven head is a bar to sexual attraction and can be forgone when girls are old enough to know with whom they may not so associate. If this is so, the reason has been quite lost sight of by the Angamis.

cowries were known their place was taken by the white seeds ("*sĭkre*") of the wild Job's tears, still frequently used as a substitute.

Angami women wear no ornaments on their legs or feet, but wear the bugle-shaped bracelet already mentioned on the upper arm above the elbow, and curious brass wristlets, the ends of which are palmated and turn outwards away from one another. They also wear plain brass bracelets, sometimes in large numbers. The Eastern Angami women wear the same necklaces as their menfolk, while the women of the Angamis proper wear a somewhat similar necklace strung from two half conch shells worn at the back and hanging down squarely to the breast on each side. Here the centres of the square ends are joined at the bottom by one or two strings of cornelian beads. Earrings are not worn by women except the brass rings mentioned above and the white shell worn by all girls and women who have not yet borne a child. When their first child is born, they take out these shells and present them to their husbands, who carefully preserve them. Finger rings are not as a rule worn by either sex. Wives of men who have performed the requisite number of gennas are allowed to carry an iron staff with an ornamental wooden top.[1]

The clothes worn by women on the occasion of ceremonies in which women take part differ from their everyday clothes only in the addition of two long scarlet tassels of dyed goats' hair worn hanging down from the ears in front, a thread fastening them together running round the back of the head over the hair, which is worn hanging down the back. It is, however, usual for a girl on such occasions to squeeze her arms into as many brass bracelets as she can beg or borrow, regardless of fit, and, like her more civilised sisters, she will allow her vanity to put her to unlimited inconvenience. At the Thekrangi genna girls may be seen with their wrists all swollen and lacerated by extra bracelets two or three sizes too small.

The ceremonial dress of the men, on the other hand, is

---

[1] Women rarely if ever wear flowers, as if they do people laugh at them and say, "Someone or other has been giving her flowers."

strikingly picturesque. In the case of younger warriors, a
bearskin fringe adorns the front of the head, while the back
is bound in ropes of white cotton, the whole being surmounted
with a wheel of hornbill feathers, varying in make in different
groups, which is sometimes extended on each side right
down the back. The feathers are loosely set so as to revolve
in a breeze. Among all Nagas the right to wear the tail
feathers of the great hornbill is regarded as peculiarly
belonging to warriors who have taken a head, and those who
have not done so are allowed to wear merely some substitute,
or else imitation feathers made of paper. When a substitute
is used it is customary to wear either the silky feathers of a
Burmese domestic fowl or else to fasten small white feathers
on to a little piece of hollow stick running upon a thin piece
of bamboo and twirling in the slightest breeze like the paper
windmills used by English children. Hornbill feathers are
worn one for each head taken up to five, after which only
may they be worn for every corpse touched in war, but this
rule is a dead letter. The veteran warriors, if they wear any
head-dress at all, wear a pair of horns, sometimes quite
small and sometimes very large, made of buffalo horn and
sometimes ornamented with dyed cane and hair. These
horns should properly be worn only by warriors who have
led an attack upon the enemy and fought him hand to hand.

The ears of warriors in ceremonial dress are ornamented
with a sort of rosette of about $1\frac{1}{2}$ inches in diameter, of which
the centre is formed of the emerald beetle's wing in a ring of
the hard shiny white seeds of the wild Job's tears, the
whole being enclosed in a circle of red hair cut short and
stiff, except in the front, where it falls in a long streamer to
the shoulder. This rosette is made on a sort of wooden cup,
the stem of which is inserted into the lobe of the ear, and,
passing through it, is fitted with a boar's tusk bound at the
broad end with dyed cane. The younger men wear little
fanlike feather ornaments in their ears, usually made from
the feathers of the blue jay. To these some villages add
two white balls of down worn at the top of each ear.

No special necklace is worn with ceremonial dress, but
an ornament is worn on the breast suspended from the neck

for which it is difficult to find an English name. It is more
like a *sabretache* than anything else, and consists of an
oblong piece of wood of from eight to ten by four to six
inches, covered with alternate rows of black and red, or
black, red, and yellow hair, and adorned with lines of
cowries or of the above-mentioned white seeds. The edges
are fringed all round with goats' hair dyed scarlet. In the
case of warriors who have taken a head this ornament is
worn in a vertical position and suspended from the neck by
cloth bands ornamented with human hair and cowries, the
human hair being understood to be that taken from the
scalps of slain enemies, though nowadays this is rarely, if
ever, the case. In the case of young men the ornament in
question is worn horizontally and frequently adorned with
horns tufted with red hair or adorned at the tip with rosettes
like those worn in the ears. These horns are usually made
of the upper or lower part of a hornbill's beak split in two.
This ornament is suspended from the neck by a cord in the
case of the young men and worn singly. Warriors sometimes wear two or even three of these " sabretaches," one
on the chest and one under each arm. Among the Viswema
Angamis, that worn by the young men is circular. A
broad white sash embroidered in lozenge patterns in red
hair and cotton of various colours used to be worn over each
shoulder, the pair being tied together at the back, while
similar bands were worn on the wrists. But there is only
one man now alive in the Angami country at present entitled
to wear these ornaments, though sashes embroidered with
red wool instead of hair are worn regularly by young
men. On the upper arm armlets of cane covered with human
hair and lines of white seeds or cowries are worn, a long
fringe of hair falling down to the elbow, but this ornament is
only worn by warriors, its real significance being that
the wearer has succeeded in bringing back to his village the
whole arms of his vanquished foe. The young men only
wear armlets of plaited red and yellow cane on the upper
arm. Above the elbow the ivory armlets already described
are worn, those who do not possess them putting on, for
ceremonial occasions, imitation armlets carved from a close-

VISITING CLAN IN KOHIMA VILLAGE

[Photo by Mr J. P. Mills

CHAKRIMA ANGAMI

[Photo by Mr J. P. Mills

[See p. 25

grained white wood which at a distance are not distinguishable from the genuine article. Similar imitations are used by some of the other tribes, while the Konyăk tribes of Tamlu and the hill area north of the Dikhu between Sibsagar and the Patkoi range use both ivory armlets and wooden imitations cut to a different pattern. On the forearm gauntlets of red plaited cane fringed towards the elbow with human hair were formerly worn by warriors, but for some reason have fallen into disuse and are very rarely seen at the present day. On the legs in addition to the "*pissŏh*," which are surmounted by a single narrow ring of white cane, leggings of plaited red and yellow cane are worn. These leggings are, in the case of the Viswema and Eastern Angamis, woven on the leg, where they remain until they rot off, being covered for everyday purposes with old rags or cloth, while a special raised bar is put on the bed to lift the knees at the back and keep the leggings from being crushed during sleep. The wearer must of course sleep on his back. The Tengima Angami slits his leggings at the bottom and laces them up, thus removing them at pleasure. The Kālyo-Kengyu tribe far to the north, and east of the Dikhu, makes similar cane leggings, but open all down the sides. The intervening tribes do not make them.

The waist is belted with a strip of white cloth ornamented with lozenge patterns in coloured hair or wool, and a tail of about a foot long is worn by veterans sticking straight out behind. This tail, ornamented with white seeds and long human hair as well as red goats' hair, contains a small receptacle at the root in which "pānjīs" are carried. These "panjis" are spikes of sharpened bamboo hardened in the fire, and are used when retreating to encumber the path of the pursuing enemy, and the tail is regarded as the decoration of the warrior who has been the last to retreat before superior numbers. It is sometimes worn double in the case of warriors of peculiar distinction who have speared two of the enemy on one spear. A sort of sporran formed of long ropes of cotton encircling the waist and hanging down in front, bound at the end with coloured thread, is worn by the younger men and celebrates their prowess in love as the other ornaments denote prowess in war. By the Eastern Angamis each rope is said to signify a flirtation pushed to its logical conclusion, but this is denied by the Kohima and Khonoma Nagas, who say that no meaning is attached to this article of dress.

Colonel Woodthorpe has remarked that all Nagas' personal decorations have a defensive purpose in view, like our old military stocks and epaulettes, and are planned to ward off the spear or axe, while the long hair which is so profusely used, waving about with every movement of the wearer, distracts the eye of the foe levelling his spear at him, and disturbs the aim. This is an ingenious theory, but does not agree with the explanation given by the Angamis themselves, who, like the North American Indians, explain their ornaments as significant of exploits performed in war. Thus the breast ornament signifies a man killed, the hornbill feathers worn on the head denote each an enemy's head taken, the hair armlets inform the spectator of the fact that the enemy's arms have been taken by the wearer ; the gauntlets have a similar significance as regards his hands, and the leggings as regards the feet. The explanation is that when a man kills an enemy he should, if possible, bring home the whole body and perform ceremonies over it. This, of course, is rarely possible, and the head and perhaps a limb are brought, but in case of an enemy killed by more than one man the first spear is entitled to the head and the others bring back what they can. Even now the Naga coolies on any transfrontier expedition usually manage to return with a finger, ear, or other trophy secreted somewhere about their persons. A Naga coolie returning from the Abor expedition, when asked what he had brought back, lifted his arm and showed a little finger hanging in the armpit by a string round his neck. The significance of the horns and the tail have already been mentioned. In the same way the little figures worn on the back by some Eastern Angamis denote a prisoner taken in war and enslaved. On the shield the full figure of a man has a similar significance. Mere heads have their obvious meaning, while it is inferred from the figure of a man represented upside down either that he has been killed by treachery, or that the wearer has taken the enemy's children and dashed their heads against the stones. It is true, of course, that in the case of pitched battles the Angami warrior would go into the field wearing the elaborate costume described above, perhaps with the object of terrifying the enemy by indicating the valour and prowess that have brought him successfully through previous engagements. On the other hand, for a raid into the enemy's country, an ambuscade by one's neighbour's well, or for a looting expedition against plains villages, both clothes and weapons seem to have been chosen with a view to utility purely. Plain spears would be taken instead of ceremonial spears, and ordinary clothes would be worn without any head-dress or hairy paraphernalia. It should be added that, owing to the annexation of the whole Angami country by the British Government and the consequent cessation of head-hunting and fighting generally, the ceremonial ornaments are nowadays assumed on very slight pretences, particularly among the longer annexed villages. Some marks of distinction, however, which have always been very difficult to attain, like the horns worn on the head, are very rarely seen in Angami villages, and then only worn by old men who have a real claim to wear them.

In spite, however, of the local explanation of the origin of ceremonial dress, it must be granted that one part of it at any rate—the tail—has a purely utilitarian origin. The Konyak tribes across the Dikhu regularly use a plain buffalo horn slung at the back from the girdle for carrying "panjis" on the war path. For ceremonial purposes this horn tail is decorated with hair and colours. Now the Semas wear a tail for ceremonial purposes designed exactly like the wooden Angami tail. This they call "*avĭkĕsăphū*," *i.e.*, "bison-horn tail" (in distinction from "*àsàphū*," the straight tail), although it is invariably made of basket work, thus obviously indicating the real origin of the ornament.

Mention has just been made of ceremonial weapons. Weapons. The spears carried with full dress are always ornamented. In the case of young men the shaft is covered with an elaborate and tightly fitting cover of fine plaited cane, the groundwork being red and the patterns yellow.[1] The ordinary warrior bears a spear covered with red hair for halfway down the shaft, after which a pattern of black, white, and red hair succeeds for another foot or so. The veteran carries a spear entirely covered with long human hair or having an unusually long head and an iron spike which comes almost up to the base of the head, leaving only a foot or so of hair-covered wood to form the shaft. There are, however, other patterns of spears. The Eastern Angamis generally use that very common Naga type which has a space in the middle for the hand, while their young men merely swathe the plain spear with cloth and wool. For ceremonial spears, too, a spear-head with a shank adorned by a series of purely ornamental barbs cut from the solid metal is used by Eastern Angami warriors of renown, the number of barbs, which are regular and bilateral, varying according to the martial achievements of the owner, but very rarely exceeding five. For ordinary purposes a spear of plain light wood is used, the heart of a tree that is particularly light and tough or the bark of the sago palm being preferred. The shaft is about 4 to 5½ feet in length and the shape of the head varies somewhat, but in all Naga spears the head is so devised as to afford a projecting check before the sharpened edge of the blade, to prevent its slipping through and cutting the hand when the spear is being used as an alpenstock.[2] The prevailing type of the Angami spear-head narrows above this check and swells out gradually into a broad leaf-shaped blade longer than that affected by other tribes. It has no mid-rib. All spears are tipped at the butt with an iron spike for sticking into the ground, as the spear is never left leaning against a wall. Even inside the house it is usually kept stuck in the ground, although sometimes hung up. Both the head and the butt contain sockets, into which the shaft is fitted without the

[1] In speaking of red and yellow canework, *passim*, it should be understood that while for the red cane real cane split fine and dyed scarlet is used, for the yellow part the stem of an orchid, brilliant yellow when dried, is usually employed.

[2] Mr. Balfour, however, regards this projection as merely a survival of the side points of a lozenge-shaped blade.

aid of glue, binding, or rivets. Angami spears have no
sheath and no counterpoise, though the latter is used by the
Konyak tribes. Two spears are carried on the warpath—
one to be thrown, the other retained. The usual method of
carrying a spear is " at the slope " on the right shoulder,
when it is not being used to assist progress.

The shield used in war by the Angamis is a long strip of
rhinoceros, elephant, or buffalo hide from 5 to 7 feet high,
but generally about 5 or $5\frac{1}{2}$ feet. At the top it is about
$2\frac{1}{2}$ feet broad, and narrows to 18 inches at the bottom. It
is suspended by a rope going over the right shoulder and
manipulated by the left hand with the aid of a small horizontal cane handle set low on the inside of the shield. For
ceremonial purposes a lighter shield is used. This is made
of bamboo matting, and in the case of young men is painted
in black with devices representing mithan horns and earrings, and patterns of concentric circles said to represent
the sun, while the older men cover the matting with bear.
leopard, or tiger skin fastened on with bamboo ties. Veteran
warriors are allowed to wear a shield ornamented with heads
cut out of bearskin and with figures of men. The open
spaces of bamboo matting are covered with red goats' hair
wedged into the interstices, and the whole has sometimes a
border of bear skin all round. These particular shields
have a strip of hide down the centre of the back so that
they can be used for warfare, as the veterans who are
entitled to them are supposed to be getting too old to use
the plain but rather heavy war shield. From the upper
corners of the ceremonial shields spring two long cane horns
from 2 to 3 feet in length, ornamented with tresses of human
hair,[1] while from the centre rises a tall, thick plume of about
the same length made of thick goats' hair dyed scarlet for
two-thirds of the way up but left white at the top. Along
the upper edge of the shield, which in the case of ceremonial
shields may be cut into two concave curves, runs a fringe

[1] It is said that the hair for these horns used to be presented to the
warrior by his sisters, who were expected to give him some locks of hair
every time he took a head. (See Grange's " Expedition into the Naga
Hills," *Jour. Asiat. Soc.* 1840, p. 959.)

of white down, and the rear edge is adorned with a string of tassels made of the feather of the peacock-pheasant (polyplectron), cock, blue jay, green parrot, etc., wrapped at the base in a bunch of white down. In the case of the shields of young men already mentioned, the horns are made of plain white wood without the use of hair.

The only other Angami weapon is the " dao," a sort of hand-bill carried in a wooden sling worn at the back of the waist, the blade hanging bare against the rump. The shape of the dao varies considerably among different tribes. The proper Angami dao is a single-handed weapon with a blade about 12 or 14 inches long. This blade gradually increases in breadth from about an inch in the base to four at the tip, the back of the dao being almost in a straight line with the handle, and the blunt top of the blade curved convexly. The blade is fitted to the handle by a tang, the handle being bound with cane-work. The Eastern Angami dao is a two-handled implement with a somewhat shorter blade, which is more nearly the same breadth throughout, and the end of which is indented. Colonel Woodthorpe mentioned a double-bladed dao, used by the Eastern Angamis, but this variety, if it still exists, is most uncommon. It appears to have been imported from the Tangkhuls. The writer has once seen a Sema dao with two blades, but only one was sharpened. Unlike the Sema, Ao, and Chang daos, the Angami daos are never decorated with red hair, nor is the wooden sling ornamented to any appreciable extent by genuine Angamis, though the Memi group bore patterns and holes in theirs, and Lhota, Sema, and Ao slings almost always have a pattern cut into them[1]. The use of the bow and arrow[2] is unknown to the Angami, though the

[1] The Angami like the Lhota carries his dao with the edge down and outwards when in the sling. The Semas and Aos carry the dao with the edge inwards and upwards. The dao is usually slung at the back over the right buttock. The Chang dao has a very long blade and long handle and is drawn over the right shoulder.

[2] With regard to this statement that the Angamis do not use the bow or crossbow (except possibly in the case of villages bordering on the non-Angami tribes to the north-east), it is stated by Major Casserly in his *Manual of Training for Jungle and River Warfare*, p. 109, that the Angamis in their attack on Kohima fort used " arrows tipped with burning

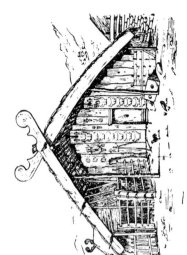

Fig 4 EASTERN ANGAMIS of THEMIJUMA.

Fig. 7 WHITE SHELL FOR NAPE OF NECK.

Fig. 8 ANGAMI EAR ORNAMENT

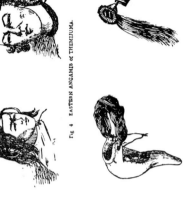

Fig 6 EASTERN ANGAMI DAO

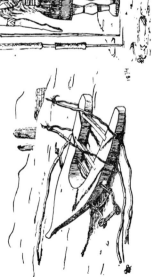

Fig. 3 ANGAMI HOUSE in REZAMI

Fig 5 EFFIGY ON NAGA GRAVE

From Sketches by Colonel Woodthorpe, R.E.

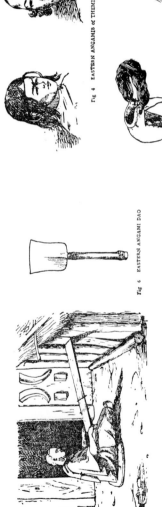

Fig 1 UNMARRIED GIRL of JOTSAMA, WEAVING

Fig 2 SLEDGE FOR DRAGGING STONES UPHILL

Changs, Kalyo-Kengyu, Sangtams, and Naked Rengmas use powerful crossbows and poisoned arrows. The Angamis never poison their weapons. A pellet bow, similar to that used by the Kukis, is used for killing birds and small animals. It is made of bamboo with a double string, and clay balls are fired from a pouch between the strings.

All who know the Angami Naga will readily admit his Char-
acter. high degree of intelligence, and it has been estimated that his cranial capacity is little less than that of the average European. At the same time, he is less receptive than the somewhat less intelligent tribes to the north of him. It must be acknowledged, however, that his reluctance to adopt new manners is rather the result of his superior intelligence than of any flaw in it. New ideas he very readily assimilates, and immediately perceives and takes advantage of the value of such novelties as, for instance, vaccination. His methods of thought, too, allowing for the differences of outlook and mental grouping caused by environment, are but little different from our own, but where it is different, he holds to his own views with great tenacity, convinced that he is really right, and that the foreigners' views of the causes of things are mere foolishness, in spite of the fact that a spurious value seems to attach to them by reason of their (the foreigners') superiority in mechanical inventions. Indeed the Angami's attitude to the European civilisation is probably to be summed up in the distich quoted by Noorna bin Noorka of Kadrab when the old beggar-man whom he had kicked into the air disappeared in the sky :—

> " Oh, world diseased! oh, race empirical !
> Where fools are the fathers of every miracle."

It is probably, however, a great mistake to think that a primitive form of civilisation, as we understand it, entails

---

oil-steeped rags " and that they made entrenchments within 400 or 500 yards of the British stockade, and, " under a heavy covering fire, advanced to the assault behind logs and rocks pushed before them." He adds that the Angamis " are fond of night attacks and have proved themselves excellent guerrilla warriors". The arrows referred to were not shot from bows, but from muskets, a method used by the Angami in my time for elephant hunting.

mental processes necessarily at variance with ours. The least that can be said of the Naga is that in general he has mental outlooks and mental processes far more consonant with those of the European than has the ordinary native of India, whose thought has for generations been stunted by the cumbrous wrappings of caste and Hinduism. Much the same may be said of the Angami character. Independence is its keynote, and wherever independence is found, frankness and honesty usually go with it. Generally speaking, the Angami, while by no means free from that other concomitant of independence, swashbuckling, does possess the attribute of honesty. At the same time the Angami, and more particularly the Eastern Angami, undoubtedly looks on a lie as a very present help in certain circumstances. If he badly wishes to acquire a piece of land he will not hesitate to asseverate audaciously that he bought it, or that he, his father, and his grandfather have successively sown and reaped its harvest without a murmur of dissent from any quarter, the real fact being that the land is, and has been for many generations, in the possession of another family. A village head-man when house-tax is being assessed will not infrequently solemnly affirm that the sole occupant of such and such a house is a decrepit old woman quite unable to pay revenue. He will point to an ancient dame huddling in the doorway under a mass of horrid rags. On searching the house, however, a spear, an extra bed, or some men's beads may be found, indicating unerringly the habitation of a male, while the old woman, possibly imported for the occasion from another family, proves to be wearing new clothes under her filthy coverings. Another favourite trick is to extinguish the second fire, remove the cooking stones and rake over the hearth with dust, when two families inhabit one house. This trick, however, is quickly apparent to the bare soles of an inquiring interpreter. On such occasions as those mentioned an Angami's oath is usually reliable, and it is almost always accepted among Angamis themselves—not that the Angami respects an oath as such, but that he greatly fears the wrath of heaven, that visits the forsworn and all that is his.

Exaggeration too, is common—excessive exaggeration, that is. A man will tell you that an elephant has tusks four feet long when they measure in reality a foot and a half. It is also necessary to beware of being given an answer that is politely intended to please the questioner, or to save the trouble of thinking or the shame of admitting ignorance on the part of the questioned. But on the whole, truth is the rule and falsehood the exception, and Angami servants and Angami subordinates can be trusted to treat those they serve with a remarkable degree of candour and honesty. And they are capable of very great loyalty and fidelity.

One of the first characteristics that strikes a visitor to the Angami's country is his hospitality, a hospitality which is always ready to entertain a visitor and which forms a curious contrast to the very canny frugality of his domestic economy. Nothing whatever is wasted in an Angami household, not even the bad eggs, which if positively too high to be relished by the ordinary palate are given to the old men whose taste is dulled by age, and it is perhaps not unjust to say that rarely is anything given away without the expectation of a solid *quid pro quo*. Nevertheless, great kindness and consideration are shown to the mentally or physically deficient, and the Angami is a model of devotion to his family.

Another very striking trait of the Angami is his geniality. Both men and women are exceedingly good-humoured and always ready for a joke. They will, moreover, break into merriment under the most adverse circumstances and on the slightest provocation. And yet behind their spontaneous geniality lies a vein of deep melancholy. The thought of death is never far from them, and the fear of it is a potent factor in their lives. This is particularly noticeable in their songs ; their music, invariably solemn and dirge-like, being reminiscent of the fifty-first Psalm, even though the subject is love, as it almost invariably is. But this is not all. There is a tendency in the vast majority of their songs to animadvert on the brevity of life and the dread finality of death. As an example at random it may not be out of place to give a rough rendering of a part-song sung at the Thekrangi genna by the young men and girls of Khonoma, and being in point of fact of an almost flirtatious tendency.

Men : Seeds are in the earth, and seeds keep falling
to the earth.
Men take them away, but still they spring up,
But if man die, he riseth not again.

Women : Girls delay not too long to marry !
When your hair groweth long, you grow old ;
When you grow old you die.

Both : The moon waneth, yet it waxeth again,
But when I lose my belovèd, there is no more
meeting.

PART II

PART II

DOMESTIC LIFE

THE Angami village is invariably built either on the summit of a hill, on a high saddle, or perhaps more frequently on the ridge of some spur running down from a high range. This site, though generally in a position highly defensible if not impregnable from the point of view of Naga warfare, has not been chosen with a knowledge of the weapons of civilisation, and could usually be easily commanded by firearms from some adjoining peak or ridge. The name given to the village is not infrequently ascribed to some local feature. Thus Kwünoma (Khonoma) are the men of the " Kwüno " trees, a large number of which are said to have been cleared from the site selected when the village was first built ; Setikima is named after an ancient pipal tree, now dead, which crowned the peak of the hill on which the village stands, and great reverence is still paid to the successor of the original tree. Some villages owe their names to some incident in their history ; Kigwema, for instance, " The Old House-men," owes its name to the return of part of the former members of that village from the site of Jotsoma, whither they had migrated, to their ancient site. Sachenobama, again, are the inhabitants of the place of the men from Sache, the village having been first thrown out from Sachema, then deserted, and again reoccupied by others. Some names have been inspired by the sort of whim that has designated as the " Chicken roost " (Thevokepü) the lofty peak above Themoketsa, while to the other names a legendary origin is assigned. The ancestor of the Angamis and kindred tribes is said to have cut up a mithan. The ancestors of the Kacha Naga

43

village of Kenima are said to have received the head
("*Pomi*"), though the derivation seems somewhat forced.
Sachema are the descendants of those who received the
dewlap ("*Voche*"), while Mima are the men of the tail
("*Mi*"). One is inclined to surmise that the name of
Mima gave rise to the whole legend, but it is possible that
there is some connection between this legendary mithan
and that other which was cut up and divided among the
ancestors of the Naga tribes when the Semas were awarded
the fore-quarters, since when they have never been able to
keep their hands from picking and stealing.

The Angami villages must, before their annexation, have
been elaborately and effectively fortified. They have lost
the less permanent of their original defences, but their
ditches, approaches, and great doors have so far survived
the insidious ravages of the " Pax Britannica." Captain
Butler has thus described an Angami village :—

" Stiff stockades, deep ditches bristling with panjies, and
massive stone walls, often loop-holed for musketry, are
their usual defences. In war-time, the hillsides and
approaches are escarped and thickly studded over with
panjies. The panjies, I may here explain, are sharp-pointed
bamboo skewers or stakes, varying from six inches to three
or four feet in length, some of them as thin as a pencil,
others as thick round as a good-sized cane, and although
very insignificant things to look at, they give a nasty and
most painful wound, often causing complete lameness in a
few hours. Deep pitfalls and small holes covered over with
a light layer of earth and leaves, concealing the panjies
within, are also skilfully placed along the paths by which
an enemy is expected to approach, and a tumble into one
of the former is not a thing to be despised, as I have had good
reason to know. The approaches of the villages are often
up through tortuous, narrow, covered ways, or lanes, with
high banks on either side, lined with an overhanging tangled
mass of prickly creepers and brushwood, sometimes through
a steep ravine and along the bed of an old torrent, in either
case admitting of the passage of only one man at a time.
These paths lead up to gates or rather doorways, closed by
the strong, thick and heavy wooden doors, hewn out of one
piece of solid wood. The doors are fastened from the inside

and admit of being easily barricaded, and thus rendered impregnable against all attack. These doors again are often overlooked and protected by raised look-outs, on which, whenever the clan is at feud, a careful watch is kept up night and day ; not infrequently the only approach to one of these outer gates is up a notched pole from fifteen to twenty feet high. The several clans, of which there are from two to eight in every village, are frequently divided off by deep lanes and stone walls, and whenever an attack is imminent, the several roads leading up to the village are studded over with stout pegs, driven deep into the ground, which very effectually prevents anything like a rush. On the higher ranges, the roads connecting the several villages, as well as the paths leading down to their cultivation, are made with considerable skill, the precipitous hills being turned with easy gradients, instead of the road being taken up one side of the hill and down the other as is usually the case among hillmen."

Nowadays the panjies and the stockades, the pitfalls and the pegs of Captain Butler's description have disappeared, but the ditches and the walls remain in part, and the former are still sometimes crossed over by a single log as they were when the bottom was studded with panjies. The narrow lanes by which the villages are approached are no less narrow, no less overhung with thorny creepers, and, it should be added, no less evil-smelling than in Captain Butler's day. In fact, added years have perhaps brought added filth to them.

The stone walls that divide the different clans or encircle the village are sometimes very massive, and in the case of that defending the Thekronoma clan of Jotsoma the wall, some twelve feet or more in thickness, is pierced by a narrow passage with a right-angled turn in it so arranged that no spear could be thrown through the openings, while one man standing in the angle with a spear could hold any number at bay.

As for the Naga paths, Captain Butler's description applies really to the paths leading down to permanent cultivation, which are often wide and well made, and sometimes to paths joining adjacent villages. But the Naga paths that

link up one village to another some miles away are usually
the tracks of men going in single file over hill and through
jungle in the most direct route possible. As these paths
are normally, if cleared at all, only cleared once a year at
the Chadangi (Tsüngi) genna, they are not usually by any
means easy going. The Naga, however, prefers them to the
metalled road, as owing to their angles they are less tiring
to the foot. The steepness of acclivities and declines is
more or less immaterial to him. Bridges, where necessary,
are well and securely constructed. When the stream is
narrow a single tree suffices, either simply felled across the
stream or cut level and perhaps embossed on the flat surface
with mithan heads. Sometimes two trees from opposite
sides meet in the middle, forming a jamb, but where a long
span is necessary, a suspension bridge made of a long cane
cradle, carrying at the bottom of its V a couple of bamboos
to walk on, is slung from high trees on either bank by
strong ropes of single canes. The paths between villages,
and the bridges as well, are sometimes determined by the
location of the year's " jhum " lands, but not so much as in
the case of the tribes whose cultivation is entirely " jhum."
The permanent roads from the villages to the terraced fields
are usually provided with a rest-house at some distance
from the villages where parties returning from their fields
can halt to drink rice beer.

The arrangement of the houses in an Angami village is
irregular. Often, as in the Sema, and differing from the Lhota
village, the houses are built here and there, facing this way
and that at every angle and at all levels to suit the lie of the
ground or the taste of the builders. There is, it is true, a
theory that the Angami house faces, or should face, east,
and on the assumption that it does so, the west is called
" Kisatsa," " the side behind the house." [1] But although, if
convenient, the Angami does prefer, perhaps for the sake of
some tradition as well as for the sake of his own personal comfort, that the front of his house should catch the morning
sun, he quite as often as not builds it to face some other way.

[1] An eastward orientation of the dead appears in some Naga tribes.

2. Married (*Tengima*)

Angami Girls

[See p. 27

1. Unmarried (*Khizami*)
acting as nursemaids

[See p. 29

TENGIMA ANGAMIS SHOWING GENNA DRESS OF YOUNG MEN

Each house has a small open space in front of it, and irregular paths and steps connect it with other houses. Small enclosures by way of gardens containing little patches of " kachu," maize, or mustard are frequently made near the house when there is room. Nasturtiums may be seen growing in some villages, but it is very rarely that flowers are grown at all.

A noticeable feature of Angami villages is sitting-out places. These were originally, it may be supposed, look-outs from which a watcher might descry the approach of possible enemies, but they are, nowadays at any rate, frequently so constructed as to be useless for such a purpose. Some of them are built of stone and are arranged with tiers of seats one behind the other in a straight line, an arc, or in the form of an E without the central projection. They vary in height from three or four feet to twenty feet or more, and are often carefully and solidly built of heavy masonry, though without the use of mortar, which is unknown. Sometimes they surmount the walls, and sometimes occupy a central position among the houses in one of the open spaces which are to be found in almost all villages and which serve as meeting-places for general purposes and parade grounds for ceremonial occasions. In the Eastern Angami villages these look-out places are usually to be found at all the higher points of the village, and are built of undressed logs arranged horizontally one behind the other at a steep incline, and sometimes rise to a height of as much as thirty feet. Sometimes, on the other hand, they are merely low platforms of roughly-hewn planks.

Another feature of the Angami village is its graves. These are normally built of stones and are either circular or rectangular and are to be found in the village itself, or by the side of one of the village paths in the immediate vicinity of the village, while all round the outskirts of the village are similarly constructed memorials built to commemorate deceased warriors.[1] These memorials are frequently surmounted, particularly in Eastern Angami villages, by life-size wooden effigies of the dead, dressed, when first erected, in the ornaments and garments of the

---

[1] Sir J. Frazer (" Golden Bough", viii, p. 100) referring to Dr. Burton Brown says that such memorials are intended to deceive the spirits as to the place where the real grave is, but I think myself that they represent a change in funeral customs from exposure of the corpse, as, e.g. by Konyaks, to interment.

deceased, and decorated with symbols in wood or stone recording his prowess and achievements in love and war. It also very often happens that a number of graves of men long dead, including among them the heroes of almost legendary times, are found surrounded by one great wall banked up inside to a level top and furnished with a ring of large stones as a sitting-place opposite the *Kemovo's*[1] house. Such a sitting-place, comprising a considerable area and of perhaps a dozen feet in height, may also be used as a coign of vantage in clan disputes, and, to mention one instance out of many, the erection of such platforms by the hostile Semoma and Tevoma clans of Khonoma gave rise to very serious riots and still more embittered a dispute previously quite troublesome enough to the local officials. The sitting-place in front of the *Kemovo's* house is called "*tehuba*," and is used as a dancing place at festivals (see Thekrangi genna in Part IV).

Near the gate to the part of a village occupied by a particular clan is often to be found a large stone called " *Kipuche*," which is the subject of veneration. If earth falls on to it a day's *penna* is observed, and it plays an important part in the head-taking genna. Dotted all over the village and its outskirts may also be seen numbers of monoliths, some of them of inconsiderable size, others occasionally so massive as to make the observer wonder at the labour which must have been necessary to haul the huge stones up to the village and erect them where they stand. These monoliths are erected to commemorate the personal " gennas " performed by individuals at which they have feasted the village, and are set up either in front of the house of the giver of the feast or in some conspicuous place near one of the paths to the terraced fields. In the Lhota villages the same practice prevails, but the stones are always erected in a line down the centre of the broad street that divides the two opposite rows of houses. No carving or ornamentation of any kind decorates the Angami monoliths, though the Lhotas sometimes ornament theirs with rough designs traced in oil of pigs' fat. Though the monoliths are generally put up to

[1] *Kemovo*—see Part IV.

commemorate a feast, they are sometimes erected to commemorate a person merely, as in the case of the stone erected
at Sakhabama in honour of Captain Butler, and of the stones
pulled in some Angami villages to commemorate the dead.

The " Morung " or young men's house (*Kichüki*), which is
such an important feature of most Naga tribes, is insignificant in the Angami village. Sometimes one finds a house
definitely set apart for the young men. More often one
finds a house that is only nominally set apart for them,
but is in reality built and occupied by a family in the ordinary
way, though it is recognised as being also the Morung house,
and is furnished with a large wooden sleeping platform in
the outer compartment which is absent from the ordinary
house, or in some cases with a high machan on the verandah.
In many Angami villages there is not even a nominal
Morung, though among the Memi they are used by the
young girls as well as the young men, both in some cases
using the same house, the young men sleeping on an upper
shelf and the girls below them. The publicity probably
entails great propriety of behaviour. In any case among
the Angamis proper the " Morung " is not habitually used
by the young men, as it is in the Ao and trans-Dikhu tribes,
but it is used on the occasions of ceremonies and gennas
which by traditional usage call for a house definitely allotted
to the young men of the clan ; such an occasion, for instance,
as that of the Thezükepu genna. At other times it is used
merely as a casual resort for the village bucks, and perhaps
as an occasional sleeping-place for a young man finding it
temporarily inconvenient to sleep in the outer chamber of
his father's or elder brother's house, although in some
villages the young men regularly sleep there.

The village obtains its supply of water usually from a
spring outside the village and at a short distance down the
hill. This spring may be really a hole in the ground which
keeps more or less full of rather dirty water, or it may be
an elaborate stone well, a sort of great trough with a stone
platform running all round it and water pouring out into a
lower stone basin. A big village will frequently have several
water-holes, but in some villages the supply is scarce, and in

any case the labour of bringing water up to the house causes a certain economy in its use.

A word must be added on the general condition of the Angami village. It is not a subject on which it is pleasant to dwell. Sanitary arrangements are nil. The offices performed by the sewer farm of an English town are carried out for the Naga by his fowls, pigs,[1] and dogs, destined themselves to be eventually eaten. Meanwhile these same fowls, dogs, and pigs, mightily assisted by the cattle, do their utmost to further befoul every inch of space that is not built over and which is already made noisome by the refuse which the human inhabitants cast out of their houses. In wet weather the filth is indescribable, and one must be prepared to wade ankle deep in middens if one wishes to perambulate the village. In dry weather the dust and dirt through which one walks are crawling with fleas. The only time when an Angami village is in anything approaching a sanitary condition is when it has just been burnt, an accident which occurs periodically to most villages and is probably as salutary as it is distressing for the time being.

The House.

The typical Angami house, built in one storey on the ground, the bare earth roughly levelled forming the flooring, varies in length from 30 to as much as 60 feet, and in width from 20 to 40 feet. The front gable, which is often furnished in the case of men of wealth with heavy beams carved with the heads of mithan or men, and other symbols of riches or valour, rises from 15 to 30 feet in height, while the back gable is usually lower, being only about 10 or 15 feet high. On each side the eaves almost touch the ground, doubtless to secure the roof from the March winds. The house is constructed by setting up eight posts, four on each side, with four higher corresponding posts, to bear the roof tree, down the centre of the house. These posts are notched at the top, the arms of the notch being of equal length, and a hole bored below the notch to take the cane lashings which secure the roof tree, and the beams for the two sides, which are laid over the top of them and securely tied with cane

---

[1] Pigs have been described as the "peripatetic sanitary installations" of Naga villages.

thongs passing through the hole. The posts, both upright
and horizontal, are merely trees roughly trimmed. On
this framework an open trellis is made of split bamboos
crossing one another at right angles and similarly tied with
cane thongs. On this trellis the roof is constructed. The
Angami roof is of four degrees. The first degree is of plain
thatching grass, and anyone is at liberty to roof his house
thus. The second degree has the front gable edged by two
barge-boards running up from the eaves to the point of the
gable. For these and for the further marks of social distinction the builder of the house must duly qualify. In the
roof of the third degree these barge-boards are continued into
two great massive horns of wood known as *kika*, " house-
horns," usually bored with a round hole in their palmated
ends. The object of these holes is said to be to reduce the
resistance offered by the horns to the wind and so lessen the
likelihood of their being destroyed or broken. In some
villages, Razama, for instance, which is unusually sheltered,
these holes are dispensed with. The ends of these horns
are usually square, among the Memi rounded, but always
wider than the breadth of the beam immediately beneath
them. They have, that is to say, a neck. In Viswema the
broad ends are sometimes split up into prongs resembling
the palmated antlers of deer. Dummy birds of wood are
often fancifully made to perch on the horns and sometimes
on the beams. Very rarely a third horn is erected bisecting
the angle between the first two, and, like them, ending in a
bored square. The house of Pule in Kezakonoma has such
a horn. The roof of the fourth degree, which may only be
made by those having attained to the uncommon distinction
of " *Kemovo*," is not made of thatch at all, but of rough
wooden shingles. House-horns, of course, accompany this
roof too, but are sometimes pointed instead of palmated,
while sometimes a pair of horns is erected at the back as
well as at the front of the house.

The sides and back walls of the Angami house are generally
of bamboo matting from the ground, though they are
occasionally built up of dry masonry to the height of three
feet or so. The front wall is made of great boards of wood.

to the making of one of which the whole thickness of a tree must go, while the partition is made of smaller planks. Those in front are often carved with the heads of men, mithan, pigs, etc., usually represented by more or less conventional designs. These planks are dug into the ground at the foot and kept in place by cross pieces formed of two smaller beams, one on one side and one on the other, tied at intervals with cane thongs, and resting on the side beams connecting the corner posts.

The building of a new house is attended by certain ceremonies. When a site has been selected, the man who is going to build goes and places two flat stones on the site ; [1] that night he dreams, and if the dreams have been favourable, the next day, which must be a working day (lichu), he goes in the evening with his wife, taking fire, fuel, a fowl and other food, and builds a fireplace with three stones and makes a fire. The couple sit for a few minutes and take their food and return and dream again that night. If they do not dream of copulation, excretion, or any other ill-omened thing, the site is definitely adopted. When the house is finished fire must be brought from the house of a kika kepfüma, i.e., a man who has performed the Lesü genna[2] and has horns on his house. This in many villages is all the ceremonial necessary, and in Khonoma, where there are no kika kepfüma at present, fire is brought from the house of any person none of whose children have died. In the Chakrima, Kezama, and Memi villages the ritual is more elaborate. First of all two pieces of thatching grass and a little leaf of rice beer are put where the hearth is to be, and on the day that this is done the Kemovo and a kika kepfüma must remain on the site. The middle post is erected, and all those present, which includes all who will help in the building, partake of rice beer at the expense of the builder. Then the house is built with the exception of the roof, and the thatch for the roof is placed ready.

---

[1] This may be to receive any evil influences there may be and so avert them from himself and his wife ; a Kuki who wishes to break a genna puts up in the ground a little upright stone which remains at home and. observes the tabu instead of the real man, who goes about his business.

[2] See Part IV.

Then the owner of the new house, dressed in ceremonial dress, enters the house carrying a spear and fire brought from the house of the *kika kepfüma*, who must be a man of his clan. After three more days' genna have expired the thatch is put on. Including the first day, five days are observed as genna, and during those days the man and his wife may take rice beer only—no rice may be eaten, though their children may be given rice by any *kika kepfüma* of their clan.

During the building of houses bamboos armed at the top with panjies pointing four ways are put up at each corner to keep off evil spirits, or to prevent the possible misfortunes consequent on anyone's inauspiciously praising the work. This apparatus is called *kethie thedi*, and is the same as that used for crops, etc.

The interior of the house is divided into three compartments. The front room (*kiloh*), comprising half the length of the house, contains the paddy, which is stored in great baskets of from five to eight feet high, ranged along one or both of the side walls. It also contains the bench, *pikeh*, for rice-pounding, a massive table-like object, five to ten feet long, with a broad wooden keel and round holes at intervals of about one and a half to two feet burnt into the wood, in which the paddy is pounded. This article of furniture is an almost invariable appurtenance of every Angami household, though in the case of the very poor it may consist merely of a round section of a tree trunk with a single hole, *kedu*. Otherwise it must be hewn from the trunk of an exceptionally massive tree (for it is made in a single piece) and has to be pulled into the village by the owner's kinsmen, who go *en masse* to fetch it, which they do to the accompaniment of dancing and singing, and the consumption of much liquor provided by the owner. The second compartment (*mipu-bu*) is separated from the first by a plank wall in which there is an unclosed, or usually unclosed, opening by way of a doorway. It contains the hearth, composed of three stones embedded in the earth so as to form a stand for a cooking pot set over the fire which burns between them. On two of the inner sides of this fireplace are rough planks raised about two feet from the ground and laid level so as to form beds. The Angami does not, like the Sema chief, sleep on a vast bed hewn out of a single tree. Behind this compartment there is usually a third (*kinutse*) of three or four feet only in depth, but extending the whole width of the house. Here is kept the liquor vat, a hollowed section of a tree with three legs hewn in one block. The third room is sometimes furnished with a bamboo door which affords a second entrance and exit to the house. The door in the front of the house is made of solid wood and is fastened on the outside by a couple of large sticks or bamboos crossed through a fibre or hide thong that passes through the middle of the door and is supported against the wall on either side by the weight of the door itself—sometimes a wooden socket of a piece with the door is provided to take a cross bar. When inside, bars are fastened to the wall on each side. In front the broad projecting eaves of the gable form a porch where wood is stored and where in cold weather a fire is sometimes built, round which men sit and talk. Sometimes half of this porch is fenced in to form a cattle shed or a dwelling place for some solitary person, but this can only be done by those who have performed the *zhatho* genna. In many villages each house has the space in front of it surrounded with a low stone wall marking off its compound. Besides the furniture mentioned there are, of course, numerous miscellaneous possessions filling up the house. The whole is covered with the dust and dirt of ages, nor is it ever cleaned save by fire, and that by no choice of its owner. The real condition of an Angami house can only be appreciated by one who has slept there. Mithan (*Bos frontalis*) in the porch ; cows in the front room ; hens sitting on their eggs in baskets hung up for the purpose ; cocks, pullets, pigs, and dogs foraging and rummaging in all directions at their own sweet will, and every interstice of the walls and the open floor of the house alive with vermin of more than one variety—such is the dwelling of the Angami family (see plan on plate facing p. 52).

The human occupants of the Angami house do not seem to be put to any inconvenience by their immediate surroundings. They seldom exceed five in number. A man and his wife with perhaps two or three children, perhaps an aged and widowed parent, perhaps a younger brother still unmarried—such is the usual family. Children are not numerous, and, owing perhaps to a high death rate among infants, it is the exception to see more than three children to a family. Five children are considered an unusually large one. Occasionally a second family occupies part of the house, a separate space being fenced off and a separate hearth provided. This usually happens when a son, newly married, is unable to build his house at the prescribed time and has to remain where he is till the following year.[1] In some villages, however, where house-room is scarce and costly, such an arrangement may be permanent, and sometimes two quite different families will be found sharing one house.

Apart from the carving on the front beams there is little ornamentation about the average Angami house. Rich men, however, sometimes adorn the fronts of their houses with painted representations of men and women, of shields, of mithan, hornbill feathers, and geometrical designs usually in the form of concentric circles. The Eastern Angamis (Chakrima, Kezama, and Mĕmi, that is) frequently adorn the fronts of their houses with little models in clay of men in ceremonial dress, mithans, dogs, and other animals, executed with considerable ingenuity. These are either placed upon one of the cross beams or on a shelf put up on the outside wall on purpose. Brightly coloured insects and the plumage of birds are utilised in the same way. Inside the porch and the front room are the skulls of animals killed by the householder in the chase or slaughtered by him on festal occasions, and in some houses, particularly those used as morungs, huge reproductions in white pith and coloured wood of ordinary Naga bead necklaces are to be seen. These are frequently about ten times the size of the original and are festooned along the walls.

---

[1] In such a case the son lives in the back half of the house. It is genna for a parent to live behind the children, and an aged parent sharing the house of children lives in the front room or the porch.

The fireplace has already been described. Wood only is burnt in it, and if possible it is not allowed to go out. Should this happen, however, it may be relit with matches, not necessarily with the firestick, though the incident is looked on as ominous. It is regarded as genna, or at least as a serious offence, to put out a man's fire, though there seems to be no definite reason for this except that it is contrary to custom and unlucky for both parties. It is seldom, if ever, done. There is no chimney and the smoke is allowed to find its own way out of the house, nor is there any extra covering hung over the fire, as in the case of other tribes, as a precaution against the roof being set on fire by sparks. The only precaution taken against fire is the organisation of a fire-guard by the clan, which arranges for watches to be taken when the population of the village is at work in the fields, and sometimes at night, during the dry weather, when most danger is apprehended from fire. This practice is not, however, universal. The method of lighting fire is by the ordinary firestick (*segomi*) used throughout the Naga tribes. A piece of wood of almost any sort, though certain soft trees like the lime are preferred, is split at one end, which is slightly notched to keep the thong from slipping, and the two parts wedged a little apart, usually with a stone. A piece of split bamboo is peeled down to a pliant thong about two feet long, the shreds whittled from it being used with cotton-wool, thatch, and shreds of old cloth, as tinder. Some of this wool and bamboo shreddings is placed in the fork of the stick and some beneath it. One foot is placed on the unsplit end of the stick and the thong drawn under the fork in the notch and pulled swiftly to and fro until a spark catches in the tinder, when a little blowing soon produces a flame. Except matches, which are freely used, no other means of producing fire is known to the Angami,[1] and the firestick is exclusively used on ceremonial occasions.[2] Torches are made of bundles of split bamboo or ekra. The

[1] The Aos use flint and steel freely. Both Aos and Semas use the firestick frequently to take omens, but the Angamis only take omens from it when its use is otherwise a necessary incident of some ceremony, as at the Sekrengi genna.

[2] See the Sekrengi Genna and the Derochü ceremony in Part IV.

only other artificial light in use is that of cheap tin kerosine lamps which are now frequently to be found in Angami houses.

The utensils found in the house of the Angami usually include an assortment, more or less varied, of tin and enamel mugs, bowls and plates, iron or aluminium cooking-pots, beer bottles and the like, and occasionally brass dishes. These are, of course, the result of a recent contact with European and Assamese civilisation. Such vessels are in no way indigenous and until recently were practically unknown. The principal indigenous household utensils are comprised in the following list :—

1. *Earthen Pot for Cooking.*—This is a large clay vessel used for cooking meat or rice, or for boiling water and making liquor. The clay from which they are made is only obtainable from certain villages, and the villages of Viswema and Khuzama have almost a monopoly of earthen pot-making for the Angami country.

2. *Baskets for Straining and Mixing Liquor.*—These vary in shape from village to village, the normal type of mixing basket being a fairly deep and closely woven basket of bamboo with four legs to raise it from the ground. The baskets for straining are sometimes pointed and are woven with a looser mesh through which the water can percolate freely.

3. *Vats, Troughs, and Jars for Fermenting Liquor.*—The wooden vat has been already described. The trough is merely a hollowed log. Both of these may be covered with flat wooden lids with a projecting handle. For ceremonial purposes rich men sometimes make huge liquor vats of enormous dimensions, hollowing out the trunk of a tree like a dug-out canoe, but these are not kept in the house. An earthenware jar with a narrow neck, made in the same villages as the cooking-pots, is also used as a receptacle for liquor.

4. *Gourds for Storing and Carrying Liquor.*—These are the ordinary " lao " of Assam, grown and used by all Naga tribes. Small laos with curved necks are fitted with a bamboo sling for attachment to the belt when walking.

Laos are also cut to form *ladles*, the broad end being used for ladling, while the neck forms the handle and an aperture at the end of the neck is used for tasting the brew.

5. *Horns of the Domestic Mithan for Drinking Vessels.*— The horns of the wild variety (*Bos gaurus*) are also used when obtainable, but the larger horns of the tame mithan are preferred. Fine specimens of these horns often fetch large sums, costing as much as Rs. 40/- when the colouring and shape are perfect. The colour preferred is black for the lower half, merging into a transparent yellow top. The horn should be the right-hand horn of the animal so curved that, when held as a drinking vessel in the right hand with the point towards the left, the flat side of the horn may face outwards.[1] This makes a considerable difference to the value of the horn. Some, however, prefer left-handed horns. Buffalo horns are also used occasionally, but are not sought after as are mithan horns.

6. *Cups and Drinking Vessels of Bamboo.*—These are drinking vessels in ordinary use and are of several different shapes. Rekroma and some other villages make regular cups, wide at the brim and narrow at the base, for which a white wood is used, but the commonest type is a tall, straight bamboo vessel, shaved thin towards the top and similarly shaved away towards the bottom, the middle of the vessel being the thickest part. These cups are carefully made and well finished, and usually provided with a handle of plaited cane to receive which small holes are drilled in the side of the cup. These vessels, like all Angami wooden vessels, are made with the dao except for the small holes drilled in the side, which are made with the cold point of a spear-head or the iron butt point of the spear heated in the fire, or with a rough drill made of an iron point set vertically at the end of a straight handle which is rolled between the two palms.

Plaintain leaves are always kept in the house to make temporary drinking cups, as well as for wrapping up the

---

[1] The horns of *Bos frontalis* and of *Bos gaurus* are not cylindrical. The side of the horn which is towards the animal's back is very much flatter than the front. This is the case with all members of the buffalo family and distinguishes them from the true bison of Europe and America.

cold rice taken to the fields for the midday meals. They are called, in fact, *tekwe-ni*, " rice-covering leaf."

7. *Wooden Spoons* of various shapes, some having almost flat, others hollow, cone-shaped bowls. The handles vary in length and are usually ornamented with a rough pattern cut into the wood. The rings or notches cut at the end of the handle of the spoon are sometimes, and not inappropriately, a tally of the *liaisons* of the owner.[1] The spoons with cone-shaped or with long, flat, narrow bowls are used when drinking the ordinary rice beer. Spoons with broad, flat bowls are used for eating.

8. *Basket-work Dishes* with little wooden feet, usually four of them, are used for various purposes and are of various sizes. One of the commonest uses to which they are put is to hold salted beans or similar appetisers which are eaten when drinking rice beer, a proceeding which occupies most of the day when there is nothing else to do. The long bamboo cup and the appetiser dish are held together in the left hand, leaving the right hand free.

9. *Wooden Platters.*—These are of all sizes and several patterns. Little wooden saucers are used like the smaller baskets as appetiser dishes, and large ones as plates from which to eat. There is a very popular round four-legged pattern cut from solid wood in all sizes, from six inches to perhaps eighteen inches or more in diameter. Another similar dish of what may be called a chalice pattern is imported from some non-Angami Naga villages. By some the wood is wound round with a fibre rope and the two ends of this are pulled to make it revolve against a dao, and it is thus cut circular with a waist. The top is hollowed by being similarly turned against a stone, and apertures are cut in the foot. More often, however, these dishes are merely shaped with a dao.

10. " *Jappas,*" or large baskets, narrow at the bottom and swelling towards the top, which is covered with a pointed cover, are used for keeping clothes and other possessions.

---

[1] A Memi bridegroom gives his bride a present of wooden spoons. See Part IV, under " Marriage."

These, however, are usually bought from the Kacha Nagas and Kukis.

11. Water is generally carried in the narrow-necked earthenware jars mentioned above, not, like most Naga tribes, in bamboos, though these are used by several of the Eastern Angami villages.

12. Rude *wooden stools* are also used as seats.

Implements and utensils for special purposes will be found mentioned in their own place.

Manufactures.

Angami cloths, though now widely made of the fine thread imported from Burma, were originally made of entirely local materials. Cotton, it is true, is now not much grown in the high hills, but the lower villages grow plenty and still sell it in its raw state to the villages higher up. The cotton is seeded by a little wooden machine (*Meza tsangyusi*) like a mangle, the ends of the rollers being each cut into the shape of two thick strands twisted, thus forming a cog. These machines are, however, seldom made locally, being usually purchased from the Kacha Nagas, as the name implies. The real Angami method of extracting the seeds is by rolling with a stick on a flat stone. After seeding the cotton it is spun on to a spindle, the spindle being spun with the right hand against the thigh and the cotton held in the left. Both hands are used in twisting the cotton. This spindle (*themwü*) is made of a long spike of hard wood (frequently of the sago palm) with a point at the bottom, the greatest thickness being just above this point. Above this again is a round flat stone spindle-whorl cut and trimmed and bored in the middle, through which the wooden stem is passed from its upper end. This stone weights the spindle, which spins readily and for a long time, the point being placed in a potsherd, covered with a rag, to keep it from wandering. The thread is gradually wound round the wooden stem as it is spun. From the spindle the thread is wound on to a sort of double T-shaped stick, called *tsaki*. From this it is unwound and steeped in hot rice-water, hardening as it dries, and when dry it is wound on to a light bamboo frame (*dulo*) made to spin readily round a central upright. From the *dulo* it is wound into a ball, *lodzi*.

The loom itself is a tension-loom of the simplest description. To set up the warp the single thread from the ball is wound off on to the lease-rod (*jippu*) and on to two upright sticks (*jizyeh*), set at a distance apart of 4 or 5 feet. The beam (*dzippa*), a stout bamboo 3 or 4 feet long, is inserted into the warp at one end, a couple of small breast-rods, also called *dzippa*, are inserted at the other end, and the shedstick and heddle (*jinyeh*) in between. The two uprights (*jizyeh*) are then removed and the warp set up in a horizontal position. A quicker, more ingenious, and probably commoner method of setting up the loom is to put out more or less in line all the rods required, sticking them upright in the ground and laying out the warp round them from two balls of thread, one at each end. These threads are held one in each hand and wound round the uprights simultaneously so that the threads fall alternately into the required positions. Great swiftness and dexterity are acquired in this by the women. The positions taken by the alternate threads are as in the diagram shown on plate facing p. 58.

When set up horizontally the beam is fastened to two upright stakes of from 2 to 3 feet in height, or to the wall of a house or anything else that comes in handy. The weaver, sitting at the other end, fastens each end of one of the two small *dzippa* to a plaited cane band (*chepvü*) that passes round her waist. The warp is shed with a single heddle, and the shuttle (*jirr*), a sort of wooden needle of sago palm wood with two or three notches at the top for the attachment of the woof, is shot by hand. The woof is tied round the notches at the end of the shuttle and then rolled up on it, leaving just enough free to shoot it twice or thrice, more yarn being let out as required. The pick is beaten up with a sword (*dzükri*) made of a flat piece of wood of the sago palm pointed at both ends. On this loom, of course, only the plain, or chequer, textile pattern can be woven. Lines of colour are introduced into the warp by laying out threads of different colours on to the *jizyeh*, but the woof is always of a single colour, either white or black, among the Angamis, while the Semas and most of the Lhotas likewise employ a woof of a single colour. The Aos, however, intro duce transverse lines of colour into some of their cloths by changing the woof. The breadth of a piece of cloth made on one of these looms runs from 18 to 30 inches, the length from 4 to 5 feet.[1] An ordinary Angami cloth consists of three breadths of 18 inches sewn together.

The whole operation is performed by women, and among the Angamis by all women, but there is no prohibition against the touching, etc., of the implement by men. The only embroidery (*kweku*) worked on the cloth is done by working little patches of colour design into the cloth as it is woven by hand with a bamboo needle and a fine pick of hard wood (bamboo or sago palm), which is also used to beat up the stitches. The pattern is always one of the triangles and lozenges[2] forming a small rectangular patch. The material used is either the same cotton thread as that used for weaving, or wool brought from the plains. The needle used nowadays is sometimes a steel one, imported.

Besides cotton the fibres of a species of nettle, *wüve*, and of a species of jute, *gakeh*, are used in making cloth. The fibre obtained from the former is spun in fairly fine threads and makes a very durable drab-coloured cloth in which black lines (of dyed cotton) are woven at broad intervals. The jute plant, on the other hand, is only used for a very coarse material. The outer skin is stripped from the green plant, twisted by hand into stout twine, and rolled on to bits of stick. It is then spun into a very coarse and rough cloth, which is, however, very durable. This cloth is seldom worn, but is used for bedding. In dyeing, only five colours are known to the Angamis—black, blue, scarlet, pale terra-cotta, and yellow. They are not mixed to make different shades. The first two are made from the indigo[3] plant (*tsoprü*), which is grown in most villages. Scarlet dye is made from the juice of a creeper called '*nki*, and a pale terra-cotta dye from a creeper called *tsenhü*. In both cases the wood of the creeper is cut up into small

---

[1] I have, however, seen one of about 15 feet.
[2] No doubt originally representing the human figure.
[3] Not the real indigo, but *Strobilanthes flaccidifolius*. *Wüve* is a stinging nettle. A dead nettle—*ganyü*—is also used occasionally. *Gakeh*, jute, is also called *wükwi*.

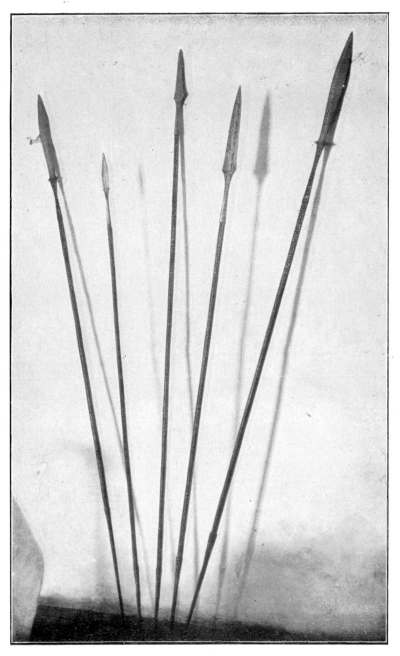

ANGAMI FIGHTING AND HUNTING SPEARS
(N.B. : The one with a small head is of Sema manufacture.)

[See p. 31

DOTSOLE OF CHEDIMA

[See p. 35

pieces and boiled together with the hair, thread, or cloth to be dyed. Yellow dye is similarly made from a tree called 'nthoh.

After weaving, which is practised by all Angami women, the most important industry, other than cultivation, is blacksmithy. This is practised by individuals (there are usually two or three or even more in most large villages) who either live on it alone or combine it with the cultivation of whatever fields they have. Spear-heads and butts, daos, axes, and spade-hoes and knives are their principal productions; sickles and a few awls and drill points are also made. The blacksmith's anvil (*rekri-chi*) is a large flat stone. His hammers (*rekri jivü*) are made of smooth oblong or egg-shaped stones of various sizes picked from the bed of a mountain stream and bound tightly to a short stout stick by means of a sort of cane cradle, which leaves the nose of the stone free for use.[1] A split and flattened bamboo serves for pincers (*jibbeh*), and these, excepting his bellows, are all the instruments he needs. The bellows (*kuru*) are made of two sections of a large bamboo, or more often in the Angami country of hollowed sections of a tree placed upright together on the ground. From a hole in the bottom of each of these a short bamboo tube is led. These two tubes meet at the place where the fire is to be made, being brought through holes in a flat sandstone [2] set upright, against which the charcoal is heaped. The air is pumped to the fire by means of two pistons, the ends of which are usually covered with the skin of the flying squirrel or with chicken feathers. These are worked alternately by a man standing behind the bamboos and holding a piston rod in each hand. The soft fur, or feathers, with which the end of the rod is bound fits closely in the bamboo and acts as an efficient pump. The iron which is used for making the spear-heads, etc., is brought from the plains in the form of cheap spades (in old times it was got from Manipur), and wrought by the smith into weapons of soft steel easily kept sharp by whetting with water on a stone. It is tempered

[1] Similarly hafted hammers are used in the Philippines.
[2] A regular trade in such stones is done by Jotsoma village.

by cooling with water mixed with salt, and particularly
with chillies, with bamboo pickles, or with all three. The
water evaporates, leaving a sediment on the blade, which is
again heated and the process repeated a number of times.
Old weapons are also treated in this way to renew them.
A spear-head is, of course, sharpened on both sides, as well
as both edges, but a dao is only sharpened on one side of its
edge, and, unless made on purpose for a left-handed man,
can only be used effectively on solid substances by a downward blow from the right. The sickle has a serrated edge,
the edge being notched with a dao after the blade is cold.
The only other form of metal work is the making of brass
earrings from brass wire. These are usually in the form of a
plain coil on a stem, or are merely a plain brass ring.

Pots (*rüga*) are only made in certain villages, notably
Viswema and Khuzama, where clay is available.[1] They are
modelled from the lump by hand, without the aid of any
wheel or implements, roughly round, with a somewhat
greater circumference near the base than at the mouth, the
lip of which is turned outwards. They are made of different
sizes, and those for liquor have narrow necks. They are
neither glazed nor varnished. A great number crack in the
firing, which is done in an open fire. They have no ornamentation of any kind, nor are pots with handles made.
For firing they are placed in rows on a platform of green logs
and covered with a layer of leaves, when dry sticks are
placed on the top, and underneath a fire lighted. Except
for shields, no hide or leather work is used, nor is any form
of preparation of hide known beyond stretching and sun-
drying.

Basketry is a very important industry, as baskets are
made for a variety of uses. All baskets are made either to
stand in the house or to carry on the back, some, of course,
serving both purposes. Of the carrying baskets the principal
are baskets for carrying firewood, for carrying miscellaneous

---

[1] Among the Semas and some other tribes pots are made exclusively by
women, but among the Angamis I have seen both sexes making them.
The Sema women, as also the Chang, forbid men to approach when they
are making pots. If men approach the pots break in the firing.

articles, and for carrying husked rice. The first (*thekrakor*) is a loose basket with a broadish bottom, though broader at the top. It is woven of cane in an open lozenge-shaped or hexagonal mesh cross-warped and twined at the top and the bottom. The other two are pointed at the bottom and woven in the chequer, twilled or wicker pattern. In the case of the basket (*kodi*) for carrying husked rice the mesh is so fine as to make the basket virtually water-tight. The latter two baskets are sometimes given a slightly truncated point and four feet, formed by the ends of four of the bamboo stays, which run from the point to the rim. For the coarse basket (*kola*) cane is employed, while the third kind is made of bamboo split and peeled into very fine thongs. The baskets inside the house have already been mentioned. Those for storing rice are woven in the twill, chequer, or wicker pattern, and stand, with their pointed lids, from 5 to 8 feet high, and measure as much as 4 feet in diameter. Another very large basket (*lithi*), woven as a rule in the twill pattern so closely as to be water-tight, is used for mixing rice beer. It runs to 3 or 4 feet in height and about the same in width, and is more or less square, having bamboo stays at the four corners. Other small baskets are made usually with the twilled pattern for mixing and straining rice beer, and numbers of small baskets are used for various purposes. They are never made with handles.

Mats are made of split bamboo, usually in the twilled pattern, and are some of them very finely woven. Head-bands for carrying loads also are plaited, usually in the chequer pattern, from cane or finely shredded bamboo thongs. Necklets, armlets, and leggings are also woven from fine strips of dyed cane.

The carving and woodwork of the Angamis is decidedly superior to that of the Semas and Lhotas. Only three or four tools are used, however, the dao (*zhe*), the axe (*merr*), the hand-drill (*chügeh*), the chisel (*rüzhe*), and the knife (*tsukwe*). The axe is an iron blade, decidedly suggestive of a long stone celt in form, fitted to one of two hafts by the mere insertion of the butt of the blade into a rectangular hole made to receive it. When the axe is required for splitting

wood the blade is fitted in its vertical plane and called
merr or *sidure ;* when it is required as an adze for planing or
chiselling wood it is fitted in its horizontal plane and called
kethi. The drill has been already described and is really
just a smooth round stick, into the lower and cane-bound
end of which an iron point, often of umbrella wire, is fitted.
It is manipulated by rolling the handle between the palms
of the hands. The chisel sometimes has a wooden handle,
otherwise it is of plain iron. With these tools all sorts of
articles are made from husking-tables to platters. With
them the solid doors of villages, planks for the fronts of
houses, house horns, liquor vats, and single-span bridges
are hewn in the solid block from trees of huge girth, and with
them are made the bamboo cups and wooden dishes used at
every meal. Holes are made either with fire or the drill or
the head or butt of a spear. The shape of the article to be
made determines how the tree is to be cut. The grain of
the wood is not taken into account. When planks are made
the tree is split in two with the *sidure* and each half planed
down with the *kethi* from the round side until a plank of the
required thickness is left.

The carvings on wood are usually of conventional designs
which vary in villages and are nowhere of a very strict
uniformity. Figures and symbols in very high relief are
the prevailing form, but carvings almost flush with the wood
are also found. In the latter case they are sometimes
coloured with the colours used for dyeing cloth, and with
lime for white paint. The representation of the human
head is naturally common, and in the Eastern Angami
villages a careful differentiation is made between the ordinary
head taken from a neighbour and the heads taken from
Tangkhul villages. The Tangkhul " cockscomb " is clearly
shown in the representation of the latter. Perhaps the
commonest conventional form of all is that of the mithan
head (see plate facing p. 58). This is symbolic of wealth,
as is the horn-bill feather of valour, and is usually represented with rather exaggerated horns, square projections
for ears, and a purely conventional nose ; a still more
conventionalised form with squared horns is also occasion-

ally seen. The carving of a pig's head is even more conventional still, being little more than a lozenge with the ends squared off. Another conventional carving which is symbolical of prosperity is so vague that while some say it represents the breasts of women, others affirm that it is merely a tale of baskets of dhan. Of course, the form of a breast and that of the top of a dhan basket are not wholly dissimilar. These carvings and others may be seen in large numbers on the great doors of villages, on the front gables of houses, and even on the wooden bridges that span the streams.

The human figure is executed in life size for erection over graves, particularly in Eastern Angami villages, while wooden dolls are also made, some of them with considerable elaboration and dressed up in miniature reproductions of Angami costume. The original manufacture of these dolls seems to have been a case of " Art for Art's sake " merely, but those who know how to make them are usually willing to manufacture them for sale. It is generally considered improper for any but old men to make them, but nevertheless comparatively young men do make them, if they expect to gain anything thereby.

Hard materials like shells, ivory, bone, and horns are bored with the drill and rubbed on stones to make them smooth. Cutting is done with the dao, and if a hammer is needed a stone serves the purpose, but in the preparation of conches and cowries for wear, rubbing on a stone is the important process. Polishing is not resorted to and the finished article is left to acquire polish by wear. Ivory armlets seem to have been cut from the tusk with a dao, notched so as to give it a saw edge, the cut surface being rubbed smooth on stones. They are nowadays cut with a saw. The trade in shells and beads and the making up of shells into forms popular among Nagas is almost entirely in the hands of the village of Khonoma. Numbers of this village go down to Calcutta to trade and come back through Burma and Manipur, one man of a party perhaps being able to speak a little bad Assamese or worse Hindi.

In the treatment of hard substances, as in woodwork and

blacksmithy, there is a growing tendency to add to the very limited stock of tools used by the Nagas in the ordinary way by purchase from shops at Kohima or in the plains.

Musical instruments are made with one exception from wood only, and, like other woodwork, are made by the person who intends to make use of them, for their manufacture is not confined to particular individuals. The Angami trumpet (*ketsü*) is made from the dried and hollow stem of the shrub of that name, the mouthpiece being formed merely by cutting obliquely across the narrow end. At the broad end, the mouth is usually left closed and an opening of the same pattern as that in a common English metal whistle cut just above it. The instrument is 6 or 7 feet long and its sound carries for a considerable distance and a number of notes can be blown upon it. The Angamis of Samaguting make a variety of trumpet which is a deliberate attempt to copy the bugles which they have seen used by the military police, an outpost of which was at one time stationed there. These bugles are made of short sections of bamboo fitted one into another and fastened by gum, made of rubber and cactus juice, so as to give a straight tube of gradually increasing width. The mouth is made of the upper half of a gourd. The mouthpiece, however, is made like that of the genuine Naga trumpet and does not seem to be blown like the English bugle with a loose lip. Military bugle-calls picked up by ear may be heard reproduced on this instrument with very fair accuracy by the bucks of the village. The Angami, however, is not so clever at this as the Lhota, who is somewhat gifted musically. The Lhota villages, after the Abor expedition on which many Naga coolies were taken, fairly rang with bugle-calls picked up by ear on the expedition and not even practised until after the return home. One non-wooden musical instrument was mentioned : this is the buffalo-horn (*reli-ki*) made particularly, but not by any means exclusively, in Khonoma. It is usually made of about a foot and a half of buffalo horn, roughly trimmed and cut square at the wide end. Into the narrow end a wooden mouthpiece is fitted. This mouthpiece is merely a wooden tube about 2 or 3 inches long, cut oblique at the mouth end.[1]

In addition to the instruments mentioned, flutes (*lowü*) and Jews' harps (*theku*) are made. The flute is made of a piece of bamboo about 18 inches to 2 feet in length, solid at one end and open at the other. There are two holes, one at each end, a couple of inches or so from the end in each case. The player, though sometimes standing, usually plays seated, the solid end of the flute being rested on the ground. Just above the aperture at this end the flute is grasped between the thumb and either the first or second finger of the right hand, the second or first finger being used to close or open the aperture. The flute, particularly if a small one, may also be played without resting the solid end on the ground, but in that case a continual pressure has to be exerted to keep the open end against the left hand. The left hand is extended and the thumb and fore finger rested against the cheek, the open end of the flute being stopped by the palm, and the mouth applied to the hole in the side. The holes are burnt with a heated drill. The pitch of the flute varies according to its size, and the few notes produced are particularly musical and liquid.

The Jews' harp is made out of a piece of thin flat bamboo about 1 inch wide and 4 or 5 inches long. The centre is cut away so as to leave a prong attached to the frame at one end. A string is fastened to this end, either to a sort of handle or through a small hole where the prong joins the frame ; by jerking this the prong is made to vibrate, and another string in the form of a loop is attached to the opposite end of the frame, the fore finger of the other hand being passed through this loop. The instrument is made to vibrate between the lips of the open mouth, which acts as a sounding board, and a skilful player can produce a quite unexpected volume of sound.

The Jews' harp is, generally speaking, the only musical instrument played by women. Among the Semas also

---

[1] Some of the Konyak tribes use a similar buffalo horn, but without the wooden mouthpiece, which appears to be used by the Angamis so that the horn may be blown in precisely the same manner as the *ketsü*.

women play the Jews' harp, while it is absolutely tabu for them to play the flute, which is regarded as belonging exclusively to males. The trumpet and horn are not used by Semas. Among the Lhotas women do not, in point of fact, play any instrument except the Jews' harp, though it is not positively said to be tabooed to play on the other instruments, while Angami women occasionally do play the *lowü*, though but rarely.

Some villages of the Dzuno-kehena group, in particular Viswema, use an instrument called *übo* (see plate facing p. 65), probably adopted from the Memi group and possibly originally suggested by some instrument in use in Manipur. It is played both with one and with two hands. With one hand the back of the nail of the fore-finger of the right hand is used, the rod being held in the left hand. The sounder is a half-gourd covered with a pig's bladder or a bit of goatskin fastened to the gourd by pegs of wood. The bridge is of wood, and there is a hole at the bottom of the gourd. The string (there is only one) is made from a strand of sago-palm fibre or, if pro-curable, wire. The key to which the end of the string is fastened is a peg which is twisted in its hole in the rod when necessary.

Salt, though nowadays very seldom, if ever, made in Angami villages, deserves mention in a list of manufactures, as it must have been made by Viswema and other villages possessing brine wells before the pacification of the Angami hills, and it still forms an important article of commerce. Naga salt, as opposed to salt bought in the Kohima bazaar, is nowadays purchased from the Kacha Naga, Sangkam, or Tangkhul country. It is said to have medicinal properties denied to ordinary salt and is used as a thirst-raiser, a cake being nibbled at intervals of draughts of rice beer. The method employed in preparing it by the Kacha Nagas, Tangkhuls, Sangtams, and others probably differs little from that formerly employed by Angamis. Where there is no natural well, a hole is dug and a hollowed tree-trunk sunk, where the salt spring is, in such a manner that the end of the trunk projects. A receptacle on a string is let down to haul up the brine. This receptacle is emptied into other vessels for evaporation. In some cases the latter is a flat earthen or iron dish lined with a leaf which adheres to the block when the moisture has been evaporated. The block with the leaf adhering is taken from the dish, and the edge bound with another leaf tied on by bamboo thongs, when the whole is ready for trade. In other cases the brine is poured straight into a small round earthenware pot in which it hardens, when the whole pot with its contents is sold. Evaporation takes place either over an ordinary fire, the pot being placed on the three hearth-stones, or over a regular oven which has holes in the top to receive the evaporation dishes ; ovens of this sort are built of clay and sticks. Wood ashes from the fire are sometimes sprinkled into the boiling brine, apparently to prevent its boiling over during evaporation and to increase the bulk of the salt product. These ashes, of course, become a part of the final salt block, which, whether ashes are with it or not, is composed of a coarse grey or brown substance, in texture not unlike pumice-stone and in taste suggesting brackish earth and iron. It is generally preferred by the Angami to purified salt for every purpose, but costs much more. Tangkhul Nagas about to make salt must remain chaste on the preceding night and speak to no one the next morning until the salt wells are reached and the fires for evaporation lit.

A word may here be added as to currency. Before the Currency. coming of the British and the rupee, barter was undoubtedly the principal method of trade, but a currency of a sort existed in conch shells and iron. One conch shell, in length equal to the breadth of eight fingers, is said to have been worth a cow, and small iron hoes brought from Manipur were also used as a currency, it being possible to make an Angami hoe from three of these Manipuri hoes, which were about 6 inches long by 3 inches broad. Iron was likewise used as a currency by the Aos in the form called in bastard Assamese " chabili," a piece of thin iron, roughly key-shaped,[1] and about 8 inches long. These " chabili," however, were tokens merely, having no use except as money, and one " chabili " was reckoned the equivalent of a day's labour. Large numbers of these " chabili " are still to be

[1] The likeness to a key is not great and there is no doubt all that these " Chabili " represent spears degraded into the form of a currency

seen in the houses of rich men in the Ao country. Among the Yachumi and other trans-frontier tribes there is a form of currency, which still does duty, consisting of a string composed of quite worthless pieces of broken conch shell beads alternated with bits of bamboo, one string having the token value of about four annas of Indian money. The Chang use flat metal gongs, each being worth now not more than two rupees, though their value was formerly much higher ;[1] also the worn-out blades of daos, which are used for making new daos as well as for money. They used at one time, too, to use small conch shell beads as money.

Salt is said by the Angamis to have been too precious to be in general use as a medium of exchange.

Agriculture.

The most striking difference between the Angamis and their neighbours on the north is their cultivation of wet rice. While the Lhotas, Semas, Aos, and trans-Dikhu and trans-Tizu tribes cultivate only by " jhuming " (that is, by clearing land and growing crops on it for two years and then allowing it to return to jungle), the Angami has an elaborate system of terracing and irrigation by which he turns the steepest hill sides into flooded rice-fields, and in dealing with his cultivation, this terraced cultivation and " jhuming " must be treated separately. All the Angamis, however, do not practise this wet cultivation, as the Chakroma Angamis living nearer to the plains have so much jhum land that they are able to live on this alone, and good jhum land, cleared once in twelve or fifteen years, say, is said to produce a better crop than the " pānikhēts " or terraced fields.

The method of preparing land for wet cultivation is to dig and build the side of the hill into terraces of from 2 to 20 feet broad—200 feet broad if the ground is level enough. The stones taken out of the soil are used to bank up the walls of the terraces. The terraces are irrigated by channels which carry water from some stream or torrent for a distance that may sometimes be measured in miles, many fields

---

[1] Since writing the above, the value of the brass " gong " now current has dropped to eight annas. The bell metal gongs which represented the value of five rupees or more a few years ago have been driven out of circulation by the brass substitute.

being fed on the way. Each terrace, of course, cannot have its own channel, but usually obtains water either from the next terrace above it or from one of the terraces in the same row, the terraces being so carefully graduated that the water may flow from terrace to terrace round a whole spur and back again to a point little below that from which it started. Water is also often carried from one terrace to another terrace in a hollow bamboo passing over other terraces and channels in between.

The rainfall in the Angami country being very heavy, many terraced fields can, if necessary, be flooded at almost any time of the year. These are usually the most valuable lands. On the other hand, of course, many fields cannot be put under water at will, and a spring drought, or dry spring winds lasting later than usual, may cause a delay in flooding terraces which considerably impairs the yield of the crop. Water is, of course, regarded as property, and very valuable property. The first man to dig a channel tapping some new stream acquires a right to the water drawn in the water channel to the exclusion of anyone else wishing to tap the stream higher up, though there are certain large streams like the Siju which are regarded as common property and in the water of which no right can be established. The water that is drawn naturally becomes in the course of time itself the subject of all sorts of rights, rights of purchase, of custom, and of inheritance. The overflow, for instance, from the field of one man may be utilised by another who has no connection with him, and may even be of a different village. This latter, by using the overflow, establishes what might be called a right of easement in the overflow, and although the original owner might perhaps successfully maintain his right to absorb that overflow into new fields made by him, any attempt to turn the overflow to the fields of a third party, even when bought by the owner of the water, or to sell or otherwise divert it from the existing user, would be regarded as illegal.[1] Ownership of terraced fields is not communistic but strictly individual, and sales, divisions between heirs, and similar circumstances have made the water rights in an Angami village a very complicated

[1] See Appendix XIII, p. 453.

affair. Water is divided up, either by tapping the channels or by partitioning them into two or more runnels, and rights of overflow, tapping, etc., may be transferred. It may thus happen that one man's fields will be dry while those immediately adjoining will be flooded, or a field at the end of one line is dry while that immediately above is full, but the water has to go right away round the spur of a hill and back again before the dry field gets its share. The owner of the dry field then not infrequently resorts to the obvious device of running the water off the field above to his field below, to the intense annoyance of the owner of the water and of those entitled to prior use of the overflow. Hence abuse, a rough-and-tumble, and probably a visit to the Kohima " kacheri," for the Angami is nothing if not litigious.

Though no manuring of jhum land is ever attempted, manure in the form of cow-dung collected by the owners of cows outside (and inside) their houses is frequently applied to terraced fields, and cattle are often turned into the terraces to graze in the cold weather with the same end. In addition to manuring, the only other preparation of the fields for the crop consists of digging them over with the Angami spade, of which a description is given below, and, when the fields have been flooded, of puddling them. The flooding of the fields drowns the weeds already overturned in the surface soil, and when they have sufficiently decomposed and the mud is well puddled, the field is ready for transplantation. In the task of digging and puddling a man is usually helped by his friends or his kindred, he in his turn going to work on the fields of those who have helped him. The owner of the field on which work is being done is expected to provide those who come to work on his land with a meal at midday which is cooked in the small field-house which every owner of land erects. Meanwhile the seed paddy has been sown thickly on a patch of dry ground late in March or early in April, and the seedlings are ready for transplantation about the beginning of June.[1] The seasons naturally vary in different villages according to the altitude and climate. At transplantation the seedlings are never planted in bunches, as in the plains, but separately by ones or twos. After transplantation the fields need

[1] See Appendix XIII, p. 453.

cleaning two or three times—the usage varies in different villages, and as the grain begins to ripen scarecrows are put up. The varieties of scarecrows are legion and some of them very ingenious. Perhaps the commonest form is that of the human figure—occasionally a solid stuffed British-looking scarecrow on sticks, but usually made of basket work with a rag or two and a gourd for a head, and swinging on a string at the end of a bamboo. Basket-work hawks are also made, and a woven cane circle open at the centre is used, as well as other patterns of various sorts down to mere strings tied across the field, to which strips of cloth and bark are fastened. Some varieties of scarecrows are ingeniously contrived with bamboo clappers which keep up an incessant rapping when there is any wind, and perhaps the cleverest of all is an automatic scarecrow to be seen at Jessami, worked by water. A piece of bamboo, consisting of two segments with the node at the top of the upper segment cut off to admit water, is set up on a pivot consisting of a horizontal stick running through a hole in the bamboo just below the node in the middle. The whole is erected so that a bamboo pipe from a water channel runs into the upper segment. As this fills with water it tilts forward on the horizontal pivot, overbalances and empties itself, when the lower segment, which is longer and therefore heavier than the emptied top half, swings back to its original position and bangs hard upon a horizontal bamboo set in the ground at its foot. The upper segment then starts to refill and so keeps up a constant clatter by repeating the process every minute.

The harvest is usually ready about the end of October and the first half of November, and is reaped with a saw-edged sickle. Usually the head only of the plant is severed and thrown into a basket on the bearer's back, but sometimes the whole stalk is cut.[1]

---

[1] The Semas, alone of Naga tribes, strip the standing ear straight into the basket by hand. The reason given is that a Sema once slashed open his stomach, thus killing himself, when reaping with a dao, since when reaping has been done by hand.

Among the Angamis it is genna to take fire into the fields at harvest, though the precise opposite is the case among the Rengmas. The Semas and Lhotas consider it genna to take matches to the fields at harvest, though the firestick may be taken.

Before it is brought up to the house the grain is trodden out of the ear by foot, and after being brought home for storage it is dried gradually in small quantities on bamboo mats in the sun, a process to which it is subjected at intervals until consumption. The rice when spread out is turned and shifted with a blunt rake called *lhavahu*. It is stored in the large baskets already described, and husked as required for use by pounding on the paddy husking bench, when the grain is separated from the husk by winnowing on basket-work trays. The stalk of the rice is left standing until the whole crop has been cut. It is genna to cut the straw before all the grain has been harvested.

The rice grown in wet rice-fields is of a number of varieties, some sorts being suitable to low and hot situations and others doing better in cold and high fields. The varieties differ also in the time taken to mature.

The principal kinds of rice used in the Khonoma terraces are the following : " *Teverr* " (white), " *Zugarr* " (white ; only grown in cold situations), " *Mocha* " (white ; grown in hot situations), " *Perrhi* " (red ; hot situations), " *Tsorenungo* " (red), " *Ngoba* " (red ; only sown in temperate situations and unsuited to extreme heat or cold), " *Zivichango* " (white), " *Thekwerr* " (white with black husk ; cold situations), " *Ngoseno* " (red) ; all these varieties are used for consumption in the ordinary way. " *Soppa* " (white ; hot situations), " *Makrirr* " (red ; large grain), and " *Yeponya* " (similar to " *makrirr*," but small grain and very susceptible to wind) are grown particularly for the manufacture of rice beer, to which they are more suited than other grains. Two varieties, " *Nyaseno* " (white) and " *Nyami* " (red), are grown in very small quantities for consumption as parched rice.

For dry rice, terracing is not ordinarily employed, but when the hillside is very steep logs are placed at irregular intervals to keep the earth from slipping down hill. In some villages, notably Mozema, terraces are built for jhum almost as elaborate as those made for wet cultivation. These dry terraces are plentifully supplied with pollarded alders, which were doubtless saved when the fields were first cleared of jungle. A " jhum " field is cultivated for two successive years, when owing to the excessive multiplication of weeds it is allowed to lie fallow for from five to fifteen years, according to the amount of land available for cultivation. It is usual to sow rice in a " jhum " which is newly cleared, following this crop by millet, maize, or Job's tears in the second year, unless rice is sown again.

Among Angamis " jhum " land is cleared by first felling the trees and then burning the low jungle and as much of the trunks of the trees as possible. The land is then cleaned, and before sowing, the fresh weeds which may spring up again are cleaned away at least twice. After sowing, the land is cleaned from three to six times before reaping. The crop is ready in October before the rice in the wet fields is ripe. The principal kinds of rice grown in the dry fields round Khonoma are " *lakarr*," " *kethorr*," " *rihawü*," " *chakrau* " (white varieties grown in hot situations), " *thekeh* " (red ; hot situations), " *ketsorr* " (red ; cold situations), and " *mezharr*," a white grain suited to cold situations and grown in wet terraces as well as in jhum-fields.

In addition to the main crop, whether of rice or of millet, other crops of an incidental nature are generally grown in small quantities and sprinkled here and there among the main crop. Little lines of Job's tears, or occasional stalks of maize (when these do not constitute the principal crop), " menitessa," beans, oil seeds, gourds, cucumbers, chillies, spinaches, mustard, " kachu,"[1] etc., may be found scattered about, particularly near the field-houses or near the machans built on the hillside to scare the birds, and along the edges of the fields. Cotton and a species of jute used for making coarse cloth are grown in patches by some villages.

Of what might be called natural crops, the principal is thatching grass, which is, in some villages with little jhum land, of great importance. It is protected from damage and encroachment, but not otherwise cultivated, and is usually village or clan property. Wood, including bamboo, is also preserved near the villages, and private property is

---

[1] *Kachu*—i.e., *Colocasia antiquorum*

well recognised in it, plantations being highly valued and carefully looked after. Pollarding is practised with a view to reducing to a minimum the destruction of trees, which are used not only as firewood, but for fencing fields. There is also a recognition of property in special trees, though they may grow on the land of another person—so much so that a dispute will arise as to the ownership of a tree which is actually growing on the ground of a third person not a party to the dispute. It is apparently enough for a man to say that he is preserving such and such a tree, and, provided that no one has previously set up a right to that tree, the tree becomes the property of the preserver, and he can claim damages for destruction or injury. This custom, generally speaking, is only applied to trees valuable for their timber for constructive purposes, and is not universal. Paths, streams, trees, and natural features of any sort may serve as landmarks, or there may be no landmark at all, while in the case of terraced fields the embankment of the field itself serves. When land is demarcated large stones are used, unless advantage is taken of water or some other natural boundary.

The implements used in agriculture are (1) the axe (*merre*), described above ; (2) the spade or hoe (*kejü*), an implement made of a flat spoon-shaped blade, the handle of which is bound with thongs of cane or bamboo to a crooked stick, making an implement in the shape of an inverted V, the blade of which is about 6 to 8 inches broad in the broadest part ; (3) the mattock (*sivü*), a T-shaped wooden hammer, the head being about a foot or a foot and a half in length and the handle 3 to 4 feet : it is made both in one piece and in two ; (4) the rake (*paro*), made of a bamboo split at the end into four or five spikes which are bent at a right angle to the handle and bound with bamboo thongs and a cross-piece into this position ; (5) the hoe (*saro*), used as a hoe for jhum-fields by some of the Eastern Angami villages : it is made of a simple piece of bamboo bent into a small hoop, the crossed ends forming the handle, and the blade, if it may be so called, being formed by cutting away half the thickness of the bamboo, so as to make it more pliable and

2. Jotsoma

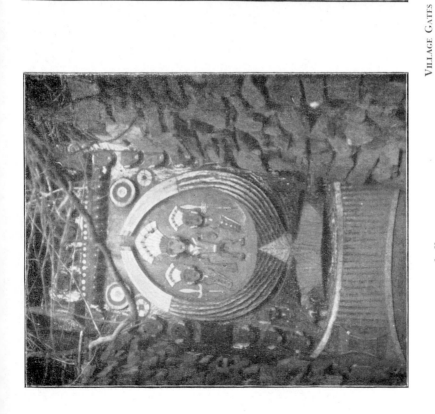

1. Kigwema

Village Gates

[See p. 44

STONE FORTIFICATIONS (*tsa*) AT JOTSOMA

[See p. 45

STONE LOOK-OUT PLACE (*daho*) AT JOTSOMA

[See p. 45

to prevent breaking ; seven or eight of these may be used in a day : the Semas use the same implement, while the Lhotas, Aos, and some of the Konyak tribes use one of exactly similar design but with an iron blade ; [1] (6) the sickle (*zupfino*), consisting of a light curved iron blade about a foot long set by a tang in a wooden handle, and having a rude saw edge. One other accompaniment of agriculture, for it can hardly be called an implement, needs mention. This is the stake and panjis called *kethi-thedi*, which is set up to mark jungle, thatch, etc., chosen by some person or family for cutting, or, in an elaborated form, to preserve crops from the unlucky results of someone's too favourable comments on their condition. [2] In its simple form the *kethi-thedi* is just a cleft stake with two roughly pointed cross-pieces at right angles to one another like the points of the compass on a vane. In its more elaborate form it has a series of such cross-pieces, made of carefully pointed and trimmed bamboo tied one below the other in a bamboo upright, the top of which is split in four.

The domestic animals of the ordinary Angami household are restricted to a few varieties. Though not the most numerous, the principal of these is the "mithan" (*Bos frontalis*). This magnificent animal is a form of wealth in which men invest what are for the Angamis large sums of money, but except for trading purposes and for consumption at feasts the mithan is of no particular value, and the breed-ing of mithan for trade is always a speculative undertaking, as losses from tiger, wild dog, and cattle diseases are con-siderable. The mithan varies in value according to size, length of horn, and colour, the colour preferred being black with four white stockings and a white blaze, which in point of fact is the predominant colour. Colour, however, would seem to tend to vary according to the method of keeping the mithan, for where mithan are allowed to roam at their will in the jungle and grazing lands round the village, black

[1] This iron-bladed hoe is subsequent to the wooden one. A similar wooden hoe is described and illustrated by Mr. S. E. Peal in his " Visit to the Naga Hills," *J.A.S.B.* 1872.

[2] The Nagas ascribed the death of a very big dog of mine to the fact that it was so frequently talked about on account of its size.

predominates. But in some of the Eastern Angami villages, where the mithan are usually kept tied up in front of the owner's house, being supplied with fodder brought in by the owner and grazed in the keeping of a cowherd, black and yellow pied mithan are not uncommon. In the case of the unconfined mithan, the animals live almost in a wild state and are merely visited from time to time by their owner, to whose call they come in order to get salt, and when once accustomed to be given salt in a certain place they rarely stray very far. Females and young males make excellent beef, and mithan milk, though not used by the Angami, is very rich.

Cows are kept in large quantities for their meat and for sale, for the Angami, though by no means refusing milk when offered to him, does not care about it particularly, and never attempts to milk his cattle. The reason he gives is that as he has never done it he does not know how to do it. Occasionally one is told that it is genna to drink milk, but most Angamis take it readily. A separate cowshed is sometimes built for cattle near the owner's house, but more often the cattle live in the porch and front part of the house itself. They are taken daily to grazing ground in the charge of a cow-herd, who is frequently a child, sometimes an idiot. In some villages a proper cow-herd is kept who does no other work, but gets two baskets of paddy per annum per cow kept from the owners of the cattle in his charge. Wooden cow-bells are tied to the necks of mithan and cows. This bell is made of a box cut from a single piece of wood or bamboo, and having one to three wooden tongues.

In addition to mithan and kine, a very fine breed of hybrid cattle is kept, bred from cows by mithan bulls. These hybrids are usually black with a tan line down the back, and are fertile. Being less feral than the mithan and less domestic than the cow, they are particularly apt to haunt cultivated land and damage crops.

Cattle are identified by their natural marks and by different ways of slitting and cropping the ears. If one beast kills another in a fight, both the living and the dead are divided between the two owners. This custom prevails in most Naga tribes.

Pigs are kept by all but the very poorest Angamis. They are allowed to roam at will, and though regularly fed on paddy husks and the waste rice that remains as refuse after making rice beer, pick up the greater part of their substance by scavenging round the village. On pigs alone, of their livestock, do the Angamis practise castration. The extraordinary thing about this is that *all* the males are castrated, and that before they are more than three months old, by which time they are mature enough to have begotten offspring. All Naga tribes seem to treat their pigs in the same way. At the time of castration the Angamis also slit the ears and dock the tails of their young boars.[1]

Dogs are kept under much the same circumstances as pigs, except, perhaps, that they are better fed. They share with the pigs the scavenging of the village, and like them are used for food. Dogs are eaten in great numbers at the Sekrengi genna, probably on account of a belief in the medicinal properties of dogs' flesh. The eating of dogs at the Sekrengi is not compulsory. They are eaten much as turkeys are eaten at Christmas in England, as a matter of custom. Dogs used for hunting are treated much better than the ordinary cur. They are, it is true, sometimes sold for food when past work, but are never killed or eaten by the man who has trained or kept them for hunting purposes, and when they die a natural death are buried with a cloth, in recognition of the services they have rendered their owners. Indeed a man who kills a hunting dog has to leave the village for five days, and on the day of his departure and again on the day of his return the whole village observes *penna*. A genna of this sort was observed in Jotsoma in 1916. Hunting dogs are not of any distinct breeds, but an attempt is sometimes made to ensure that both sire and dam are of a hunting strain, and hunting dogs will in any case usually be found to be out of a hunting bitch, as the usual method of training a puppy is to take it hunting with its dam, from whom it learns what is expected of it. It is

---

[1] No Angami ever attempts to drive a pig. When he wishes to transport it he straps it to a bamboo frame and carries it on his back. Little pigs, like fowls, are carried in small cane cages.

seldom, however, sufficiently disciplined to be of much use until it is three years old, and is usually considered at its best at about five years, and begins to get too old for work at seven. Good hunting dogs are never punished, and are distinguished from the ordinary village dog by their fearlessness of men. All male dogs have their tails docked and their ears cropped close to the head. Bitches do not have their ears cropped, but their tails are sometimes, not always, docked. No clear reason is given for either docking or cropping. Some say that the ears of the dogs are cropped so as to distinguish them from the bitches. Some say that they crop dogs' ears merely because they are males, just as the ears of male children are bored in several places but those of girls only in the lobe, and in the Eastern Angami villages at the top. Others say that if the ears are not cropped they are a hindrance to dogs working in the jungle, but this hardly explains why all dogs have their ears cropped and not bitches, although the latter are equally used for hunting. It is to be noticed in this connection that the ears of pigs, and occasionally of cats, are slit or bored in the case of males. No reason at all is given by Angamis for the docking of tails except custom.[1]

Cats are not kept in anything like large numbers, but there are usually a few in most villages, and their possession is sometimes valued. They are subject to certain superstitions, and it is usually regarded as " genna " to sell cats for gain, though a man transferring a cat to another man is at liberty to receive the actual amount which in his estimation has been spent by him on the keep of the cat.[2] It is not, however, at any rate in most Angami villages, forbidden to kill cats, and they are sometimes, but rarely, eaten as

[1] On these points the forthcoming monograph on the Sema Nagas may be referred to. The distinction between the male and female is probably to prevent the latter being chased and killed (for the pot) by mistake.

[2] The Bantu of East Africa have a saying, "It is forbidden to eat the wages (or 'hire') of a cat," and never buy or sell cats, and the Ama-Xosa of South Africa say that "a cat is never sold, but always given away" (*Folklore*, vol. xxvi., No. 1). It seems possible that the Angami respect for cats is connected with the services rendered in the destruction of rats, whose depredations are much feared (see Part IV, the Thezukepu genna).

food, though this was formerly "genna." · It is not now usual to kill cats for any "magico-religious" purpose. A case of one such killing did once come to the notice of the writer. A man of Nerhema killed a black cat in the village path (the usual place for such ceremonies) with a view to his recovery from illness. The village found the body lying in the path on their way to their fields later in the morning, and were exceedingly disturbed. They observed a "genna" that day, returning to the village instead of going on to their work, and, although the sacrifice of the cat proved to have been made at the suggestion of the village priest (*pitsu*), punished the sacrificer by keeping the non-working day on account of his action, a proceeding which would perhaps cause his death, saying that such a thing had never been heard of and was contrary to all custom and tradition. Cats, however, used to be sacrificed at the making of peace between hostile villages, and are still employed as a sacrifice in a genna for the cursing of an unknown thief.

The fowls kept in all Angami villages are usually smallish and in type resemble the local jungle fowl, which is of the red, not the grey, variety. In some of the Chakroma villages where jungle fowl are plentiful, the domestic fowls are said to inter-breed occasionally with the wild ones. Fowls are fed by their owners, not liberally, but enough to keep them from straying to different houses. They also aid the pigs and dogs in their scavenging operations.

Bees (*mekwi*) are kept by a good many Angamis. They are hived in a broken pot, a cracked gourd, or some similar receptacle placed in the roof, and the honey is taken either by smoking the bees to a stupor, or after smearing the hands and arms with honey, when the bees are said not to sting.[1] The variety of bee which is usually kept (*kevü*) does not, however, give a very severe sting, and may sometimes be taken in a wild state without any aid but a dao to cut the tree down, and with absolute immunity to the robber provided the day is cold and misty. The variety known as *kwidi*, a large dark blue hornet with a red head, is kept for the sake of its grubs, which are eaten with great relish. It is caught alive by fastening a bit of carrion (a dead locust

[1] See Appendix XIII, p. 454.

will do) to the end of a switch which is raised to the hole in some tree which these hornets frequent either for food or for the purpose of getting building material. A hornet at once starts to feed on the meat, which is then lowered and the insect carefully caught by the waist in a bit of grass bent double, which is tied and stuck into the ground until all in the tree have been captured one by one. Bits of white pith are tied to them, by means of which they are followed to their nest after they have been released, one by one as the one before is lost sight of, and allowed to fly home.[1] When found, the nest is taken and placed with the hornets in a hole in the earth somewhere near the village, where they accommodatingly remain, provided the queen is in the nest. The sting of this variety is most severe.

In addition to the livestock mentioned above, Angamis occasionally keep goats, but it is the exception rather than the rule, and very rarely they keep buffaloes obtained from Nepali graziers. In one or two of the villages near the plains ducks may be seen now and then, probably recent purchases merely awaiting the stewpot.

Hunting. The large number of guns, principally Tower muskets, which were dispersed over the neighbouring hills after the Manipur rebellion of 1891 and the consequent dissolution of the Manipuri army, has very considerably altered the hunting practices of the Angamis. So many of these guns found their way into Naga villages, and so many remain in spite of very numerous confiscations, that a Tower musket is always known in the hills as a "Manipuri gun." Some villages possess from thirty to forty of such guns, with the result that game is nowadays hardly obtainable in the Angami country. At the present time, in all villages where guns are fairly numerous, what hunting is done is done by owners (or borrowers) of guns, who go into the jungle and stalk their game, at which they are extremely clever. An Angami can move through jungle as silently as a leopard. It is generally held to be genna for a man to eat game killed (by whatever means) by himself until he has killed 100 or 150 head, excluding little birds and quite small mammals. It need hardly be said that this rule is not too rigidly observed.

[1] See Appendix XIII, p. 454.

In any case it is the huntsman himself who keeps the score.
This rule holds good not only in the Khonoma and Kohima
group, but in the Kezama villages as well. In the more easterly
villages, where guns are still absent or very scarce, the old
method of hunting is still occasionally followed, and the hunt
is on this wise: A valley is chosen to which deer have recently
been marked down. It may be two miles long and a mile
broad. The whole male population turns out to take part.
The men are armed with spears, boys with sharpened bamboos. Stops are put all round the sides of the valley, with
stronger pickets where depressions lead over the hill into the
next valley, and the lower end of the valley is stopped by
more pickets. The owners of hunting dogs enter the valley
at the top, and the dogs start giving tongue as soon as they
light upon a fresh scent. The dogs follow the scent down the
valley at their top speed, yapping vociferously, while their
owners cheer them on from behind with a deep call almost
like a laugh. This cheering is an important item, as if not
continued most dogs are apt to give up as soon as they become
tired. The yapping of the dogs informs the pickets and
stops along the sides of the valley of the whereabouts of the
game and the direction it is taking, for the thick jungle
prevents anything from being seen. As the barking of the
dogs goes down the valley, the stops who are passed by it
move down too, taking fresh positions lower down. The
deer almost invariably tries sooner or later to cross from the
valley it is in to the next valley parallel to it. Then it is
that the spearmen along the ridge get their chance. From
the barking of the dogs they know that the deer is coming
up their side of the valley (the passes which are usually
followed by hunted deer crossing to the next valley are
well known), and by the time the animal breaks cover there
are plenty of spears waiting for it. If it comes within a
range of twenty yards of the spears the hunt for that particular deer is at an end, for a running deer at twenty yards is
a fair target for a Naga spear. If, however, the deer is
missed or only wounded, it breaks back to the valley again
to emerge at the lower end or perhaps up the other end or
lower down the same side. In any case there are probably

several spears waiting for it, and its chance of ultimate escape is a poor one. Serow, wild dog, and bear are hunted in the same way. In the case of tiger and leopard, shields are sometimes carried by those who hunt them, and usually a V-shaped stockade is built into which the animal is driven and in which it is speared. Similar methods of hunting are also followed on a smaller scale by small hunting parties of from five or six to a dozen or more, who go out with dogs and kill their quarry in the same way as when the whole village turns out, by an accurate knowledge of the habits of the game and the line it will take when hunted. Before annexation elephants were legitimate game and, owing to the quantity of flesh they yielded as well as to the value of their tusks for armlets, were prized above all animals of the chase. The use of pitfalls was, of course, common, and though forbidden is still indulged in in out of the way corners of the district. These pitfalls differ only in size from those made for bison, serow, and deer—large holes from six to sixteen feet deep with long and stout panjies stuck all over the bottom and a covering of thin branches, leaves, and earth spread carefully over the top. Not a few fatal accidents have happened to men hunting in the jungle who have come on such pitfalls unawares. But elephant spearing, if the accounts given by Khonoma and Samaguting may be trusted, must have been a sport almost more exhilarating than head-hunting itself. The method followed was to detach an elephant, the big tusker, of course, for preference, from a herd and drive or follow him to some part of the jungle open enough to engage him, but having enough big trees to afford shelter from his charges. Here the elephant, already irritated and perhaps wounded, would suddenly see before him right in his path a Naga dancing up and down, shouting defiance, and spinning his spear. As the enraged animal charged the figure would speedily vanish (probably up a tree), but unlooked for spears would take him in flank and rear. As he turned on his new assailants, spears and shouting would come from another direction. And so in time the huge beast, probably more feared by the Angami than any other wild animal, would be speared to death.

Nowadays, however, elephants are usually killed by means of an ordinary gun with an iron barbed arrow instead of a bullet—a weapon probably borrowed from the Kukis.

But whatever the excitement of hunting—and Nagas are no less sensible than Europeans to the attractions of the chase for its own sake—trapping is probably a more profitable method of filling the Angami larder. Pitfalls have been described already ; simple fall traps are also used, a log being weighted with heavy stones and placed over a run in such a manner that the animal when passing underneath displaces a stick which releases the string by which the log is suspended. The jungle on each side of the run is also fenced so as to induce the animal to take the required path. This sort of trap is usually employed for the smaller animals, otters for instance, though it is also sometimes used for serow and barking-deer (*Cervulus muntjac*), while for wild cats especially such a trap is baited by a live mouse tied by a string to a peg in a hole in the side of a hillock, the fall being set in front of the bait. Snares are used very largely, being set at the edges of the rice-fields and in the jungle for birds and animals of various sorts. In the autumn numbers of woodcock and pheasant are caught in springes and brought into Kohima for sale, while fields may be sometimes seen surrounded with a low hedge in which little runs have been made for rats, snares being set inside each hole. The hornbill is also snared, a bright red fruit, which is a favourite with the bird, being placed over the snare at the top of a tree. Snares made by the Angamis are of two or three sorts, but the commonest (*Kesheh*) is made of a small cane triangle, one side of which is double, and which has for its base a strip of bamboo extending two or three feet beyond the double side of the triangle.[1] From the end of this bamboo slat to the foot of the double side is a cane or fibre thong containing a wooden spike. To set the snare the bamboo is bent like a bow and the near end of the thong gathered in a loop inside the triangle through the double side. The point of the spike rests on the apex, and a string, with a little peg attached, runs from the thick end of the spike to the double side against which the peg is held in place by

[1] See Appendix XIII, p. 454.

a stem of grass or thin twig running across the loop of twine inside the triangle. When the twig is displaced the bow is sprung and the leg of the bird or the neck of the rat is held between the thong and the double side of the triangle. A trap almost identical with this one is found in Borneo (see figures I. and II. on plate opposite).

Another snare, also used for small game, consists of a notched wooden peg (a) which is driven into the ground, and of a slip-noose of shaved and tapered cane (b) left fairly stout at the butt end, though pliant enough at the noose end. To this butt a string (c) is fastened which is tied to a bough bent down as a spring. The cane is then caught back in the notched peg, from which it is freed at once by the struggles of the victim, which is whipped up off the ground and suspended by its neck beyond possibility of escape (see figure III. on plate opposite).

Running nooses (kipreh) are sometimes set for deer and other animals, and their feeding grounds are " panjied," as barking-deer may frequently be taken in this way at the edges of rice-fields. Bird-lime (ketsa) for catching small birds is made from the gum of trees called pri and naku, and spread along the boughs of any tree to which birds may be expected to resort in any numbers for feeding purposes.

While on the question of hunting, the taking of omens should be mentioned. The ordinary method used by the Angamis when any sort of hunt is to be undertaken is that of slicing a twig on to the ground or a flat stone and watching the fall of the slices, the method of interpretation apparently frequently varying with different persons. These omens are always taken, and occasionally an unfavourable result will deter a hunting party from further proceedings, but as a rule too much faith is not placed in them, as almost any Angami will admit. Probably they are only believed in when performed by someone who has gained a reputation for producing correct results. Every Angami dreams before going a-hunting and believes most heartily in the truth of such prognostications, and, at any rate with certain dreamers, these hunting dreams have a remarkable way of coming true.

The training and treatment of hunting dogs have been

already described, but it should be added that the owner
of a hunting dog which takes part in a hunt is always entitled
to take the dog's share, usually a hindquarter or part of a
hindquarter of the game, and part of this share is always
given to the dog. The man first wounding the animal gets
the head, though among the Lhotas this goes to the dog's
owner. The names given to hunting dogs usually have
reference to the dog's colour, and one hears dogs called by
such names as "Black and White," "White Collar" ("*voka*"),
"Red'un" ("*kemerriye*"), or "Wolf" ("*soki*" = the wild red
dog). Sometimes, however, names denoting qualities, such
as "Growler" ("*jesho*"), are met with, as well as "*nere*" =
"Ear-cut." Among the Semas hunting dogs are frequently
called after some chief, though the chief whose name is chosen
regards this as a very serious insult if he comes to hear of it; but
the Angamis do not seem to do this at all. Calves are named
by their owners as well as dogs, but no other animals as a rule.

Hunting rights are usually admitted to be conterminous
within the land belonging to the village, subject to the
right to pursue a wounded animal on to the land of another
village, but there is no very strict custom on the question.

The most interesting method of catching fish employed Fishing.
is by the use of " poison." But though very common among
most other Nagas, it is only practised by a very few of the
Angamis. The " poison " consists of the roots, stem, leaves,
or fruit of certain plants, the juice of which when beaten
into the water intoxicates or stupefies or even kills the fish.
The various tribes use several different poisons. The Ao
prefers the fruit of a particular tree, the Chang uses walnut
leaves ; but all tribes use the root and stem of a certain
reddish creeper. This is cut into sections of about 2 feet
long, split up and frayed out, and done up into small bundles,
in which condition it is brought to the river. There long
sort of benches are built across the river of stones and logs.
On these the bundles of fibres are laid, beaten into pulp, and
dipped from time to time in the water. As the juice of the
creeper impregnates the water the fish become excited,
leaping at first as though merely in play, but many of them
coming in to the bank, where they can easily be captured
by a net or by a blow from a dao. Some of them become

quite stupefied, while bottom-feeding fish and the fresh-water shark appear to die. The men and women who are not beating wait lower down the river at shallows or other convenient places, and after the " poison " has once begun to take effect the women and children catch a large number of the smaller fish among the stones. This method is practised by some of the Chakroma villages. Among the Lhotas it is regarded as unlucky for women to come to a fishing of this sort, but the women are not only allowed to come, but take an active part in the fishings of Angamis and Semas. One common method of fishing is to dam the river so as to leave half of it dry, when the fish are taken by hand. The dam in such cases is made of stone, sand, earth, or any handy material. Something approaching a ceremony usually precedes " poisoning " operations, but this cere- mony, in the case of the Angamis, amounts to little more than the flourishing of daos and a great deal of " ho-ho-ing " by the men as they approach the river.[1] Fishing with rod and line is also practised, the hook being home-made, of a piece of bent iron or brass wire (old umbrella wires do excel- lently well), and the line being made of fibre attached to the end of a stick, and worms, grasshoppers, or crickets used as bait. Crabs, fresh-water shrimps, prawns and periwinkles, and several kinds of small fish are taken by hand among the stones of the smaller streams and caught with the aid of a basket-work tray in the wet rice terraces. Basket traps like eel or lobster traps are also regularly used, being placed with their mouths up stream, as a rule, and forming openings in a light dam or fence which make the entrance of the fish into the trap more likely. In and round Kohima the Angamis have taken to cast-nets, but the use of these has been acquired from Kukis or Gurkhalis or other foreigners and is not indigenous. The cast-nets used are circular, weighted at the edges with lead, and drawn in by a string attached to the centre.

Rights of fishery are usually recognised as ending with

---

[1] The Lhotas draw their daos and challenge the river as though to a contest of strength. The Semas appear to do the same, but do not seem clear about it.

the boundary of the village lands, streams flowing between two villages being fished in by both ; but fishing is very far from playing the same part in Angami life that it does in the life of the Semas, Lhotas, and Aos, and rights to such poor fishing as there is are not regarded with the same jealousy, as a rule. The fishing rights over wet rice terraces, which contain a number of small fish in the rains, are even open to the village though the land is privately owned. It is, however, regarded as theft, and a somewhat serious form of theft, to take fish that have collected in special holes made for them by the owner of the terrace. Here and there a small patch of three feet or so in diameter is left unplanted and a hollow scooped in the mud. Small fish collect here and are regarded, while in the hollow, as exclusively the property of the owner of the field.

The staple food of the Angami may fairly be said to be rice, but meat plays a much more important part in the Angami menu than it does in that of the rice-eating peoples of the plains. There are very few sorts of meat that the Angami will not eat.[1] He does not, it is true, eat worms, but there are few forms of animal life that are on a higher plane than this that come amiss to him. Beef, pork, and chicken are, no doubt, his commonest meat foods, and these are supplemented by mithan and dog on occasions, and even by cats, while all wild animals and birds are eaten, even crows. Kites and hawks are esteemed as a delicacy (their flesh is said to be " very sweet "), and of four-footed game the elephant, though now rarely obtained, is perhaps the most coveted. Except his tusks and skull, all of him is eaten. His bones are buried or hung up in the house and pieces cut or scraped off them from time to time. In this way they will last for years. Together with all the intestines, as in the case of all other animals, the skin too is eaten, unless this is wanted for the manufacture of a war shield. Carrion is eaten without compunction, and elephant flesh

Food.

---

[1] Although frogs form an item in the diet of all Naga tribes, I have met several quite " jungly " Nagas of different tribes who really felt such an aversion and disgust at the idea of even touching a frog, snake, or similar reptile, as one is apt to associate with supersensitive civilised people.

even when almost entirely decomposed, though meat is always preferred fresh. The idea that the properties of animals eaten are liable to pass to the eater is the cause of certain flesh being genna to young men—for instance the flesh of a black forktail with a white head is eaten by the old men, but never touched by the young men for fear that they will become prematurely bald if they eat it. It is possible that the same idea partly underlies the prohibition as to tigers' and leopards' flesh, which may never be eaten by women. It may not be cooked inside the house, but may be eaten by men if they cook it in the porch or outside the house, and provided that they do not take it anywhere near the hearth or the women's beds, and cook it in separate pots kept for the purpose of cooking such food.[1] The Angamis prohibit the flesh of the he-goat to their women, for fear that they will acquire the lecherous propensities of the goat, but in the case of tigers it must be remembered that the tiger is regarded as closely related to man, the *terhoma* (spirit), the tiger and the man having in the beginning been the three sons of one mother, and when a tiger is killed the village priest proclaims a non-working day (*penna*) for the whole village "for the death of an elder brother." In the case, however, of food eaten by the old men and not by the young, it is necessary to distinguish between that which the young men eschew in order to avoid acquiring the properties or supposed properties of the food, and that which they merely refuse to eat because it is distasteful. An Angami was asked if he would eat mouldy rice. "Certainly not," said he. "Not if you were starving?" "No." "What do you do with mouldy rice, then? Throw it away?" "Oh, no, we give it to the old men." The same reply was given when asked what he did with rotten eggs, while the flesh of some malodorous animals appears to be utilised in the same way. Small snakes are not eaten by the Angami, but the python found in the foot-hills is regarded as edible, and I have known Angamis eat with relish the body of a large hamadryad killed near Kohima.

[1] All food *kenna* to women is cooked in these pots.

The other Naga tribes, except the Changs perhaps, are far from being as omnivorous as the Angami in the matter of flesh.

When cooking, meat and vegetables are usually cooked together, while the rice is cooked separately. Millet and Job's tears, though forming the staple food of many Nagas in cold and high ranges, are seldom used by the Angami except for making rice beer. Chillies form an indispensable ingredient in every Angami meal and are cooked together with the meat and vegetables. Of the latter, the principal ones cultivated are beans of one or two different varieties, usually climbers, tomatoes, a variety of spinach, " karela," and pumpkins, of which the young leaves as well as the fruit are eaten. Gourds are grown principally as utensils, but are also sometimes eaten. A very large number of wild plants are used as vegetables—various species of wild spinach, the leaves of the wild " karela," wild yams, which are largely eaten in times of scarcity, though, thanks to the terraced rice fields, scarcity is seldom felt in the Angami country, wild turmeric, sorrel, nettle-tops, ginger, and many varieties of ferns and fungoids. Flesh foods have been already mentioned ; of the smaller fry the grubs of the large blue hornet and of the white ant, the larger grasshoppers, frogs, small crabs, fresh-water snails, and even dragon-flies [1] may be noted. One popular food, and one in which a considerable trade is carried on with the plains, is the highly odoriferous small dried fish imported in some quantity from Cachar and Sylhet to the Kohima bazar. These " smell-fish " are sometimes made locally also. Blood, when eaten alone, is boiled in water to prevent its sticking to the pot and eaten as a sort of soup. Otherwise it is kept raw and eaten gradually, mixing it with other food. Marrow is extracted from the bones when raw, as it easily comes out in that state. Large pieces of meat are smoke-dried and in this condition will last for years. When required, pieces are cut off and boiled. Maize is roasted—the whole head, and

---

[1] Dragon-flies are caught for food by children, who hold out long canes with gummed ends over water or swampy places. The dragon-flies circling round the pool settle on the gum and are caught one by one in appreciable numbers.

a sort of unleavened bread is sometimes made from rice
pounded into flour, but the almost invariable way of preparing all other food is by cutting up and boiling with salt
and chillies, rice being cooked separately. Bits of meat are
toasted on wooden spits, but genuine roasting is unknown.
Food is served on large wooden dishes from which those
present help themselves with their fingers, there usually
being a dish to every two or three persons, the rice and the
curry being served together. Naga food is not palatable
to a European, if only for the excessive amount of chillies
which are mixed with it. The Naga palate delights in this
sort of heat, and an Angami may be often seen chewing chillies
or raw ginger root for pleasure. Pickled bamboo is also
very popular. It is made by cutting up and pounding the
young shoots of the bamboo. These are then steeped by
being placed in a basket, weighted with stones, and drenched
with water (which is drawn off and consumed as vinegar)
and finally spread out to dry. The pickling is then complete
and the product is cooked with curry or eaten raw. All
day between meals, when he is not at work in the fields or
out hunting, the Angami eats appetisers and thirst-raisers
of Naga beans roasted or boiled and mixed up with salt and
an inordinate amount of chillies. This appetiser he carries
about in a little dish or miniature basket held in the fingers
of the hand, on the palm of which he holds the bamboo mug
containing his " *zu*." Sometimes, instead of this, he nibbles
a lump of Naga salt.

The following are the principal food gennas observed in
Khonoma :—

Genna to women.

(1) The flesh of animals killed by wild beasts.

(2) The flesh of monkeys and all tree-living animals
(birds excepted).[1]

The reason given for these two gennas is that it is the
woman who gets the paddy for household consumption
from the paddy baskets where it is stored, and that if she

---

[1] The prohibitions vary from village to village. In Jotsoma, for instance,
women may not eat hawks or things killed by hawks, for the same reason
as monkeys are prohibited in Khonoma.

FIELD REST HOUSE AT JAKHAMA

[See p. 46

EASTERN ANGAMI TERRACED PADDY FIELDS
[Photo by Prof. C. von Fürer-Haimendorf
[See p. 72

WARRIOR'S MEMORIAL AT CHICHAMA, SET UP BY SIDE OF ROAD,
THE GRAVE BEING ELSEWHERE.

[See p. 47

ANGAMI BRIDGE AT JESSAMI

[See p. 46

indulges in the foods named the consumption of paddy will become extravagant and the store quickly used up.

(3) The he-goat—because of his libidinous propensities, which it is undesirable that women should acquire.

(4) The kite—because their livers will swell, if they eat it, like that of the kite, and because they will want to seize upon and bite living things.

Genna to children.

(1) The brains of cows, pigs, dogs, or other animals.

(2) The kite, because its consumption will make them quick to anger and bad-tempered.

(3) A number of insects.

One of these—the edible spider—is tabued because the eyes of children might be affected by eating it and closed up as though by cobwebs.

The following foods are *eaten by the aged but are not eaten by young persons* :—

(1) The white-headed forktail—because the eater will become bald or grey prematurely.

(2) The bodies of the young of domestic animals born dead.

The latter are eaten by the aged provided they have no children or young relations living in the house with them, and therefore, probably, liable to acquire the propensity of having offspring born to them dead.

(3) The flesh of animals killed at the funeral of a *seshoma*, *i.e.*, a victim of *sesho*, or unnatural death—death, that is, by suicide, inflicted by a tiger, or in child-birth [1]—probably, if not certainly, for a similar reason.

The flesh of certain animals, though there is no prohibition on their consumption, is regarded as being unclean—*e.g.*,

---

[1] Such a person is said in the *lingua franca* Assamese of the Naga Hills to have died " apŏtia," and in most tribes drowning and death by a fall from a tree are regarded as " apŏtia." They are probably so regarded in some Angami villages, but not in Khonoma, where, however, an extra ceremony is performed for such deaths which are regarded as somewhat analogous to *sesho*.

Among the Semas a man who has fallen from a tree may be prevented from dying " apŏtia " by pouring water or by merely spitting into his mouth before he expires. The Chang tribe resort to the same expedient.

that of monkeys, crows, and miscellaneous birds " whose
flesh is of unknown quality." These are not eaten by those
who have performed the *Satse* (*Zache, Zhatho*) genna.
Opinions, however, vary as to what flesh is to be included in
this list. Dogs and frogs are sometimes mentioned. It is
genna for a " *kika kepfüma* " or man who has done the
Lishü genna (see Part IV.) to eat chickens. His wife may not
eat them either, though other members of the household
may do so. A " *Kemovo* " is not allowed to eat any of the
game which it is customary to present to him ; he divides
it up between the members of his kindred.

There are no traditions of cannibalism ever having been
practised by the Angami themselves,[1] but there are stories
of the existence of a tribe somewhere to the north-east of
the present Angami country by which cannibalism is or was
practised. The Semas actually give a name to their village,
speaking of its inhabitants as " Murromi." This village,
they say, is situated beyond the Yachumi villages of Kiekho
and Mezachi. The Angamis speak of these cannibals as
" Retsoma," the Lhotas as " Miriri." They are said to
feed up their victims on fattening food and, as in the Solomon
Islands, to break their bones while they are still alive,
killing them when fat. They are credited also with various
magical practices.

Meals are generally taken three times a day—in the
early morning, at midday, and in the evening, but snacks
are frequently taken in between, while *zu* is drunk all day
long. When going to work the midday meal is taken wrapped
up in plaintain leaf and eaten in the fields. Before a meal
a man frequently rinses his hands in water, but this is by
no means invariably done. Wooden dishes are washed out
more or less after use, but the earthen cooking-pots are
only rinsed with a little water poured into the bottom. It
is thought that too much washing is apt to cause breakages,
an attitude reminiscent of, though perhaps more reasonable
than, that attributed by a seventeenth century traveller to

---

[1] It is reported, however, that at the time of Mr. Damant's death and
the consequent punitive expedition some young men of Khonoma tasted
the flesh of a British officer because it looked so good to eat.

the people of Edinburgh, who never scoured their pewter for fear it should wear out the quicker.

There seems to be no particular etiquette with regard to the entertainment of guests at meals.

The drink of the Angami is rice beer. Indeed it is more Drink. than a drink, it is almost the staple article of consumption, the staff of life, and might be reckoned more appropriately as food rather than drink, only if it were so classified there would scarcely be anything left that could be called drink, as the Angami only drinks water in the last resort. "Modhu," or rice beer (*zu*), is of three varieties, "pita modhu," called in Angami *zu-thoh* (= "liquor proper"), "rohi" (*dzü-zu*), and "Saka modhu" (*zu-tseh*). The process of making *zu-thoh* is as follows :—

First the rice is pounded, then put to soak for about an hour. It is then put to dry for two or three hours and pounded again. After this it is mixed into a vat with cold water and left to stand for two to five days, according to the weather.

Dzü-zu is made in a different way altogether, and is a very much more powerful drink. Rice is cooked as though for food. It is then cooled by being spread out in a winnowing tray. After this the yeast is pounded and mixed with it, and the whole mixture, which is a wet one, is put in a basket lined with leaves, and leaves are put over the top of it. It is left thus until the smell indicates that fermentation is complete. The liquid is then allowed to exude, or is pressed, out of the basket, a process which takes place slowly, as the fermented rice may be kept three weeks or more.

When the *dzü-zu* has all been drawn off in this way, water, either hot or cold, is poured through the rice, making the infused beer known as *zu-tseh*. This is usually drunk cold by the Angamis, though most other tribes drink a similarly made beverage hot. It is rather more powerful than the very mild "pita modhu" without having the positively spirituous strength of "rohi."

Distilled liquor, *zuharo*, is made by one or two villages, notably Khonoma, which have learnt the art from Manipur.

Wet rice as prepared for *dzü-zu* is placed in a pot on the fire. Over that a second vessel is placed with a hole or holes in the bottom. Inside this the third vessel, necessarily a small one, is put, while a fourth full of cold water is put on the top of the second. The steam, rising though the holes, condenses and collects on the rounded bottom of the upper vessel and drips back from its centre into the small receptacle inside that into which the steam passes.

The yeast used for making rice beer is sometimes bought in cakes from Manipur. It may also be made from several jungle plants, but the way in which it is ordinarily made by Angamis is from paddy, which has been made to sprout by soaking in warm water or warming when damp before a fire. The paddy in this condition with sprouts of an inch or so is pounded up and used as yeast.

Each family brews its own rice beer, which is made almost daily to keep pace with an unceasing consumption. It does not last very long in any of its forms and in hot weather turns sour almost at once. Although most Angamis will readily accept milk offered to them, none milk for themselves, nor do they show the least desire to obtain milk under ordinary circumstances.

In drinking it is *de rigueur* to set aside something for whatever spirit is concerned. Either a finger is dipped in the cup and touched on the forehead as in Khonoma, or a little of the drink is tipped on to the floor, or both offerings are made. This formality does not seem very definitely connected with any particular deity who can be named. If any definite spirit is associated with it, it is perhaps a man's own *ropfü*, who might be described as combining the characteristics of a familiar demon, a guardian angel, and the notion of a man's individual destiny.

Medi-
cines.

Although not a few substances are used by the Angamis as medicines, magico-religious ceremonies form the chief antidote for ills of all sorts. Panjies are used freely, being put up in a split bamboo so as to point in all directions,[1] and also being stuck in singly over the door. When this is done

[1] This instrument is called *kethi-thedi* and is used for various similar purposes.

a fire is also frequently lighted in the doorway, and faces, made out of bamboo bark or some such material, are stuck up on each side of the door and above it, particularly in the case of infectious diseases.[1] Sacrifices are performed for illness with fowls or pigs. In the former case the fowl's head is cut off with a dao in the middle of the village path, and the village burier places both head and body in the path and leaves them there. Fowls are also killed in this way by a man who has had an unusually heavy sleep.[2] For pains in the heart or chest a live fowl is impaled on a stake in the middle of the road, a purpose for which half-grown chickens are usually used. When a pig is sacrificed its tongue, nose, ears, tail, and feet are cut off and placed outside the village in the path, while small pieces of the animal's flesh are given to the "Kemovo," and to the First Reaper and First Sower, etc. In cases of a lasting illness a man digs where there is no water visible on the surface until he finds water. This he fences over. He then kills an unblemished cock, washes it and cooks it with this water, and when eating this also drinks of this water, which he uses exclusively until well. To find the water a hole is generally dug close to a spring or stream, so that water is found with very little delay. There are other ceremonies as well as these for causing the cessation of illness, and a case of the sacrifice of a cat has already been mentioned, but a considerable number of medicines are prescribed as specifics in certain diseases. A list of the principal medicines used in the village of Kohima is given. They are probably fairly representative of what is known to the Angamis of medicine, though a certain amount of variation undoubtedly exists from village to village. The plants "chipfü" and "püpü-ü" are used for headaches, while for stomach-aches the roots of thatching grass (zoga) and raspberry (romvü) are used as well as the "pirü" plant, and water in which iron has been rubbed. For eye-ache chetho-dzü, the brine from a Naga salt-well, is used, while if the eye receives some injury,

[1] Similar but much more elaborate and terrifying gargoyles are used by some of the Konyak tribes to frighten away the cholera spirit.
[2] He is probably afraid of the loss of his soul.

urine (*pezu*) is applied. For itches, soot (*migo*) and a sort of creeper called *mpe* are used, and for burns earth that has been made muddy by urine (*zupfe*) and the raw gourd (*pfürhe*). For thorns that cannot otherwise be extracted the brain of a certain fish (*khokhe*) or the bile of the toad (*thewü-these*) is applied, and wounds are treated with the plants " *thevo-vase* " and " *nhana-ü*," with the bark of the tree " *sochü*," or with the casts of earthworms (*zochü-bo*). For intermittent fever the crab (*sego*) and the root of the plant " *nyeke* " are used, and the plant " *nutu-prü* " for spleen. Rheumatism is treated with the leaf or root of the " *mezi* " tree,[1] and the antidote for poison is to pluck out the eyes of a living dog and swallow them. When a gland in the groin swells the big toe should be tied round very tight at its root to relieve the swelling, or a thread tied round the ankle. To relieve pain from a cut the spear or dao which caused it should be licked, while the severity of a wound is greatly enhanced if it be touched by one who has recently had sexual intercourse or even if the wounded person be spoken to by such an one. The old adage " a hair of the dog that bit you " holds good among the Angamis as elsewhere. The hairs should be pulled from the dog's moustache and burnt, the ash being applied to the bite. The Semas, who also believe in the efficacy of this remedy, are careful to choose black bristles. The marrow of the serow (*thelu keli*) is also used as a medicine in some ailments, while the gall of the python (*che these*) is not only applied to wounds, but is often mixed with water and taken internally as a remedy for almost any disease. It is looked upon as a sort of panacea, and in the case of external wounds seems really to possess some curative value.[2]

A fractured skull is treated with raw eggs or with raw eggs and chickens' blood, and it is believed that, provided the inner skin over the brain is not broken, the man will live. The writer saw an old man of Khonoma with a circular dent in his forehead caused by a blow from a stone held in

---

[1] I was not able to ascertain the scientific names of these plants, but in the Sema monograph the plants used as medicine or food by the Semas will be found identified for the most part.

[2] See Appendix XIII, p. 454.

the hand of an adversary. The dent was about the size of a shilling and the whole depression about a quarter of an inch below the level of the surface of his forehead. The man claimed to have cured this fracture in the manner mentioned, but the civil surgeon who examined him put it down to " a natural immunity developed of necessity " and to extraordinary good fortune. Dry cupping is practised for severe contusions.[1]

The Angamis, except perhaps the Chakroma, seem to have little knowledge of poisons, though some of the Dayang valley Semas and the Lhotas know some poisonous plants, which are perhaps sometimes used by jealous wives. The only narcotic known is tobacco. The leaf is half dried, pounded, or stamped on and dried again. It is chewed as a rule in the Western Angami villages, while the eastern villages smoke it through water. Generally speaking, each man uses his own pipe, though one man will pass his pipe to another for a pull or two. The bowl is made of a softish grey stone found in several localities, while the rest of the pipe is made of bamboo. The pipe is in four parts, the bowl fitting into a bamboo holder, which again fits tightly into a bamboo water vessel. The smoke is carried down from the bowl into the water by a bamboo tube. When the water is sufficiently foul it is poured off into a bamboo phial which is tucked into the waist belt. Sips of this abomination are taken from time to time when on the march or in the fields, when smoking is out of the question.[2] Plain pipes of bamboo consisting merely of a bowl and a stem in one piece are also used. Cheap cigarettes are everywhere popular.

The Angamis, leading an outdoor life such as they do, Games. would not be expected to have many games of a sedentary nature. One such game is, however, known to them. It is a form of draughts known as *terhüchü*—" Fighting-

[1] The method followed is said to be the same as that used by Lhotas and by the Kukis, a serow's horn pierced at the narrow end being used for the cup, and the vacuum created by suction, after which the aperture is closed by a wet leaf usually of tobacco. The incisions on the skin are made with a hammer-shaped lancet. A set of implements used by the Lhotas may be seen in the Pitt Rivers Museum at Oxford.

[2] Usually it is retained in the mouth for a while and then spat out.

eating," because the pieces of the opposing side fight and
eat one another up. The board is a square one of sixteen
squares (Fig. I) joined by diagonal lines and usually scratched
roughly on a large stone, cut into planking, or merely drawn
in the earth. The pieces, which are bits of stone, move
obliquely or straight along the lines, one going the distance
of one square only at a time unless they are able to " eat "
one of their opponents by jumping over him into an empty
station beyond. As a rule, there are ten pieces on each side,
but the game is sometimes played with eight, in which case
the two outside stations of the forward line are left empty.
A variant form is played with nine pieces on each side, the
pieces being set out as shown in the diagram (Fig. II). In
this form there are triangular refuges into which and in
which pieces may move along any of the lines shown.
Inside these corners the piece may skip one junction of
lines and move straight to the next but one. These triangles
are formed by prolonging all the oblique lines beyond the
square and also the straight lines forming the sides of the
square and those dividing it into quarters. The bisected
angles thus formed are joined up separately.

Some various forms of gambling with cowries are also
practised by the Angamis, one rule being that no gambler
may refuse to go on staking unless the whole sum which he
brought with him to the game is exhausted.[1]

Of active games the Angami is very fond, and several
of his sports are almost identical with our own. His high
jump, *sitse*, is like ours, a wand being supported on two
uprights, while his jumping powers are also tested by placing
a mark in some high position where he must touch it by
jumping with an outstretched hand. This game is called
mabeh. The long jump is either jumped standing, when it is

---

[1] Of course he can fetch more money and go on after that if he likes.
Some villages are particularly given to gambling and men in Khonoma
frequently come and ask for an order to prevent their sons from gambling
away property which does not belong to them at all, but really belongs to
the father. The reason why Khonoma is worse than other villages in
this respect partly is that it understands the art of distilling. Khonoma is
full of stills and there is more ready cash than in most villages, seeing that
Khonoma depends almost as much on trade as on cultivation.

called *chatse*, or in the case of a running jump (*keva*) a large
stone is placed just in front of the jump. The jumper runs,
and leaping on to the stone takes off again from there. The
jump is usually measured, not to the nearest point where
any part of the body touched the ground, as by us, but to
the marks made by the feet where they landed, and a step
back does not discount the length of this jump, which,
however, is in any case poor when judged by European
standards. In the high jump, however, the writer has seen
a Khonoma buck, untrained, and professedly out of practice,
clear 4 feet 8 inches, the height of his chin when tilted, off a
bad take-off and slightly up-hill.[1]

High kicking is a very popular game—a mark is placed in
a tree and the young men kick at it, the mark being raised
when reached. Such kicking with one leg is called *pili*.
When the kicker jumps and endeavours to touch the mark
with both feet together it is called *mh'amesü*. The Angami is
supple-limbed and excels at this kicking game. Putting the
weight, *kechi piye*, is also a favourite game, and is played
with a rounded stone generally about the size of a child's
head. The puts are not remarkable for length. In spear
throwing, *rengu piye*, a spear is set up as a mark and spears
thrown at it with considerable accuracy from a distance of
about twenty or thirty yards. The outside spear range is
about sixty yards, but very few can throw with any accuracy
at this range, while many find it difficult even to throw the
distance. In wrestling (*kenneh*) the opponents grip one
another in a cross-grip, the arms of the one passing one over
and the other under the opposite arms of the wrestler.
Usually the wrestler grips the wrist of one hand with the
other in the small of the back of his opponent, whom he
endeavours to upset ; tripping is allowed. In mock-
fighting, *thedze keya*, boys form themselves into two parties
and arm themselves with a large number of balls made of
leaves and fibre. The two parties line up facing one another
at some distance and sitting down. One man gets up from
each side and the two throw at one another with the balls,
whoever is hit being "killed" and having to sit down,
when another takes his place. This goes on till all the boys

[1] See Appendix XIII, p. 104 .

of one of the sides have been " killed." Peg-tops are spun by boys, being spun so as to knock together and " fight," one upsetting the other. This top, which is made in the form of a double cone with the string round one half, is called *kwüthoh*. The string is of gradually increasing thickness with a loop at the top end through which the finger is passed to prevent the string's going with the top.[1]

The only sort of dancing practised by way of a game, as distinct from ceremonial dancing, is the *Kedohoh* or war dance, in which a young man, armed with spear, shield, and dao, leaps about, spins his spear and utters shouts, in the traditional manner of a warrior challenging the braves of an opposing force. There is a particular step in this dance called *piveh*, which is practised separately as an independent amusement. It consists of leaping into the air and crossing and recrossing the legs (backwards and forwards, not from side to side) two or three times before again touching ground.

Daily Life.

Owing to the saving of labour entailed by the wet culti-vation of rice, the daily life of the Angami is decidedly less strenuous than that of his neighbours who subsist on jhuming, and who have seldom the leisure to loaf about the village all day doing nothing but drink *zu* and eat thirst-raisers, an occupation to which the Angami is much given. The Angami gets up very early, the women usually being the first to open the door and go out. The first thing to do is to blow up the fire, and after this the more cleanly go and wash their faces, the less cleanly their mouths only, while the quite uncleanly start straight away drinking " modhu." The morning meal follows, after which the family go to work in the fields, taking with them rice and curry, wrapped up in plaintain leaves, and numerous gourds of rice beer, while the women carry the babies slung against their backs by their cloths. The midday meal is eaten in the field-house, a small hut built for shelter in bad weather when working at the fields or scaring birds from the crops. Toward

[1] This top is used by most if not all Naga tribes. Among the Semas the young men play at top fighting and top spinning after the completion of the sowing for a couple of months or so. Only the children play with tops all the year round.

dusk the party, which normally consists of the whole household, goes back to the village, often a distance of several
miles, where it takes its evening meal, and so to bed.   When
the husband goes out to hunt or trade the wife and children
go to the fields without him, but on non-working days
(*penna*) the women may sit at home weaving or drying corn,
or doing both together, while the husband, if at home, and
the children loaf about the village, drink " modhu," and
gossip.   In the cold weather the men assemble in the
verandahs of houses, where they sit on planks round a wood
fire made on the ground and tell stories or talk scandal.
On genna days, the day is always begun by taking a little
rice and pretending to heat it at the fire and wrapping it
up in a bit of leaf and fastening it, together with a sip of
" modhu " in a leaf cup, to one of the upright planks of the
partition wall of a house, for the benefit of the spirit or spirits
to propitiate whom they are keeping a sabbath.

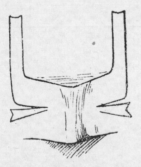

VERY HIGHLY CONVENTIONALISED FORM OF MITHIAN HEAD USED IN
CARVING ON BOARDS ON THE FRONT OF A HOUSE IN CHEKROKEJIMA.

PART III

LAWS AND CUSTOMS

TRIBAL ORGANISATION : THE EXOGAMOUS SYSTEM—ADOPTION
—PEDIGREES—INHERITANCE—LAND—DECISION OF DIS-
PUTES—WAR AND HEAD-HUNTING—POSITION OF WOMEN

PART III

LAWS AND CUSTOMS

TRIBAL ORGANISATION : THE EXOGAMOUS SYSTEM—ADOPTION
—PEDIGREES—INHERITANCE—LAND—DECISION OF DIS-
PUTES—WAR AND HEAD-HUNTING—POSITION OF WOMEN

ALTHOUGH the village may be regarded as the unit of the Social
political and religious sides of Angami life, the real unit of the Organisa-
social side is the clan. So distinct is the clan from the village tion.
that it forms almost a village in itself, often fortified within
the village inside in its own boundaries and not infrequently
at variance almost amounting to war with other clans in the
same village. This rivalry or antagonism of clan with clan
within the village has coloured the whole of Angami life.
In war, even though the village were united, the jealousy
and suspicion of one clan for another would inevitably
be a source of weakness ; in peace the village would from
time to time break out into riot, while it is incessantly
troubled by internal bickerings. In almost every dispute
between two men of different clans the clansmen on each
side appear as partisans and foment the discord. For
certain purposes, however, such as religious observances
and cases of a serious breach of the social code, the clans in
almost any village would be found agreed ; while in some
villages, perhaps most villages, the different clans dwell
normally in peace and unity together, but this is probably
much more the case under British rule than it was aforetime.

The clan has been spoken of as though a very definite
section of society, and so it most frequently is. At the
same time it ought not to be regarded in the light of a
rigid institution incapable of fluctuation or development.
On the contrary, it is always tending to split up into com-
ponent clans, a process which in parts of the Eastern Angami

country has gone very much further than in the Khonoma and Kohima groups. As far as Angami traditions go this tendency has always been manifest. This will be seen most clearly from the history, if it can be called such, of the clan and exogamy since the settlement of the Angamis in their present villages, such "history," of course, being oral tradition only.

The Angami race is believed to be descended from two men, sometimes described as brothers (or cousins) who came up out of the earth. The place is not now known to the Angamis, but, if found, the prints of the hand, knees, and feet of the two ancestors will be seen in front of the hole left by them when they emerged. The Memi point to the great stone at Maikel[1] in the Manipur State as the place where this happened. From the elder of these two sprung the division of the Angami known as the *Kepezoma* (*Kepepoma*), and from the younger the other, the *Kepepfüma* (*Kepepvuma*).[2] The Kepezoma or Kepepoma call their father "*apo*" and their mother "*azo*," while the Kepepfüma or Kepepvuma call their fathers "*apvu*" and their mothers "*apfü*."[3] These appellations are retained by the members of the respective divisions when passing by marriage or adoption from a Pezoma (Pepoma) clan to a Pepfüma (Pepvuma) clan or *vice versa*, so that the daughter, for instance, of a Pezoma man by a Pepfüma wife calls her father "*apo*" and her mother "*apfü*," and on being married herself into a Pepfüma clan will be called by her children "*azo*." The names for all other relations are the same in

---

[1] For the Maikel stone see Hudson's *Naga Tribes of Manipur.*

[2] Compare the descent of the Motu tribe of Melanesians from Kirimaikulu and Kirimaikupe (Seligmann, *The Melanesians of British New Guinea,* p. 43), also the division of the Minyong Abors into Kuri and Kumning descended from two brothers of that name (Sir G. Duff Sutherland-Dunbar, "Abors and Galongs," *Memoirs of Asiatic Society of Bengal,* vol. v, extra number, p. 9) and the descent of the Ahoms from the two brothers Khunlung and Khunlai (Colonel Gurdon, *Short Note on the Ahoms,* p. 5). For Naga parallels see the notes in the Appendix on other tribes. The terms Pezoma and Pepfüma have been used throughout for convenience, but when speaking of a man "*Pepoma*" and "*Pepvuma*" respectively are used in Angami.

[3] The forms *kepepoma, kepepvuma,* are derived, of course, from the words for father, *'po, 'pvu,* while the corresponding terms *kepezoma, kepepfüma* are derived from the names for mother, *'zo, 'pfü.*

Wooden Sitting Place at Kohima

[See p. 48

Angami Bridge at Jessami

[See p. 46

STONE SITTING CIRCLE (*tehuba*) OVER GRAVE OF THE FIRST KEMOVO OF KHONOMA
[Photo by Prof. C. von Fürer-Haimendorf

[See p. 47

ANGAMI MEMORIAL STONES

[See p. 47

the two divisions. In the case of those who are called "father" or "mother" by courtesy the form of the name which belongs to their division is used. In a family purely Pezoma or purely Pepfüma, both parents will be called by their Pezoma or Pepfüma names respectively. This dual system, however, although found existing throughout the Naga Hills, is not evenly distributed. Among the Tengima proper some villages are found entirely Pezoma, others entirely Pepfüma, while others again are mixed ; while the Chakrima Angamis, the most numerous section of the whole tribe, are almost exclusively Kepezoma. The Kezami are sometimes spoken of as being all Kepepvuma, seeing that they call their fathers "*apvo*," but they call their mothers "*azo*," and it may be taken as certain that they are Pepoma (Pezoma), not Pepvuma.[1] We may compare the Lhota practice, where the whole tribe call their fathers "*apo*," the two divisions differing only in having different names for mother, viz., "*aio*" and "*aphu*," and may infer that in the mother's name lies the important point of distinction. It is pretty certain that "*apvo*" is merely a dialectical form of "*apo*."[2] The Memi,[3] again, though divided into Chakrima and Chovoma, seem, conversely to the Kezami, to use the terms "*apu*"[4] and "*apfü*," but present the phenomenon, unique apparently as far as the tribes inside the Naga Hills district are concerned, of a third division of quite a different status to the other two.[5] This division is

[1] Some of the clans in the Viswema group use the same terms for "father" and "mother" as the Kezami, and are reckoned (and count themselves) Pepoma.

[2] It is on account of this variation in the term taken from the male parent that I have throughout designated these two Angami divisions by the words Pezoma and Pepfüma, instead of Pepoma and Pepvuma, as the former pair are constant and can be used unequivocally of the Kezami and Memi. Properly speaking, a male of the Pezoma group should be spoken of as "*Pepoma*" and the female only as "*Pezoma*," *Pepvuma* and *Pepfüma* being similarly used of the other group. I have, however, employed the female terms only for the sake of convenience and perspicuity.

[3] The Memi referred to here and hereafter are Memi only who are resident actually on the Naga Hills District border. The Memi generally have been dealt with by Mr. Hodson in his monograph on the Naga tribes of Manipur.

[4] "*Apu*," however, is pronounced "with the upper teeth on the lower lip," another dialectical form.

[5] The existence of a third group of inferior status seems to be analogous to that of the Chami in the Ao tribe, and to that of a slave clan, whose women have to shave their heads, among the Konyak Nagas.

known as Kachima or Cherhechima and marries with neither
Chakrima nor Chovoma, although it is not endogamous, as
it intermarries freely with non-Memi Angamis and may not
intermarry within itself in the same village. The Cherhechima, it should be added, are regarded as having a
different origin, coming from Pirhetsu Hill, near Maram,
whereas the Memis generally ascribe their origin to a
Tangkhul village called by them Piwhuma ; they are
looked on as inferior and are credited with the evil eye and
other occult powers, which are not, however, necessarily
exercised voluntarily, as they are cursed with some sort of
unlucky emanation.

Of the two ancestors of Angamis, Thevo,[1] who emerged
the first, was the ancestor of the Kepezoma, who are entitled
by virtue of his priority to a precedence in eating over the
descendants of the younger, Thekrono. The Kepepfüma,
however, claim that Thekrono was really the elder of the
two, but that Thevo outwitted him in the matter of
precedence by arrogating to himself priority of birth and
proceeding to eat first on the strength of it, without giving
Thekrono an opportunity to assert his right. However this
may be, a Pezoma man has the right to eat or to start
eating, at any rate, before any Pepfüma man if the two are
about to take a meal in company [2] on ceremonial occasions,
and on such occasions Kepepfüma await Kepezoma and do
not begin eating before them.[3]

[1] The names "Kovoma" and "Chizama" have also been given me
as the names of the two ancestors, but though in this legend applied to
individuals, they appear from their form to be collective nouns. The
termination *ma* used with names seems in all other cases to indicate a
group of men, though the word " tema," of which it is the compound form,
is used for " man " and is the ordinary word for " man " in the singular.

[2] When Thevo emerged from the earth he remarked, " *a thevo mho kecha
keka*," since when the Kepezoma have been ugly but strong, whereas
Thekrono remarked, " *a thekrono a phirimi kezu*," and the Kepepfüma
have since been handsome but weak. The words refer respectively to a
rocky bluff on a mountain spur and to the soap vine.
Compare the division of some of the Fijians into two exogamous *vosa*,
the one called *vosa turanga*, the other *vosa dhauravou ; turanga* meaning
" elder " or " noble," and *dhauravou* " younger " or " plebeian " (*Man*,
vol. xiv, No. 1, January, 1914).

[3] When away from home a party of Angamis eating together wait for
the eldest of the party to begin eating first.

Now some Angamis believe that the two "*kelhu*"[1] or Kelhu. divisions of Kepezoma and Kepepfüma were originally exogamous, marrying mutually into one another, and the pedigrees given at the end of this chapter certainly suggest that, at any rate in the Khonoma group, there existed at least a prejudice in favour of marrying into the opposite "*kelhu*" until a comparatively recent date.[2] It is admitted, however, that at the time of entry of the Angamis into their present country (the first Angami village to settle north of the Mao gap is universally believed to have been Keza-kenoma, to which all Angami villages trace their origin), the Pezoma kelhu had split into Thevoma and Satsüma, the two being admitted as independent communities on the same footing, for exogamous purposes, as the Pepfüma kelhu Thekronoma (or Cherama).[3] The Satsüma, however, were never numerous, and very few exist now outside the villages of Mima, Theniazuma, and of Sachema itself. For practical purposes the two kelhu remained as Thevoma and Thekronoma.[5] The exogamous clans into which these two split up are those which have been mentioned as forming the units of Angami society.[4] These "*thino*," to use the Thino.

[1] I have used this word *kelhu* with some hesitation, and only for want of a better. There is no ordinary Angami word for these two divisions and *kelhu* was given me as the correct word when I pressed for the word and insisted that there must be some word to express such a division. I fancy *kelhu* ordinarily means "generation," and has perhaps acquired a secondary sense like that sometimes apparently attached to "generation" in the Old Testament. It is convenient, however, to use some term, and *kelhu* does as well as another.

[2] For what seems to be a survival of the *Kelhu* in an exogamous condition, see note on Rengmas in Appendix III.

[3] Compare the Lhota organisation, which exactly corresponds (Appendix III.)

[4] These are those divisions commonly designated by the local officers and others "khel." This word "khel" is really an Assamese word signifying the exogamous division of the Ahoms. Its use has been carefully avoided in this monograph, not merely because it is not an Angami word, but also because it has come to have a sense in non-Angami parts of the district which has no reference to tribal division, but only means the part of a village grouped for purposes of administration under a particular headman. This sense has, of course, arisen from the Angami custom of dividing up a village into separate "quarters" inhabited by different "*thinoma*." See Appendix X.

[5] Called Solhima in Chakrima villages.

Angami word, all trace their descent to some ancestor, a member of one of the kelhu, and though going under different names in different places do not forget their relationship with collateral clans in neighbouring, or even very distant, villages. Moreover, these " *thino* " were until comparatively recently undoubtedly really exogamous units, though their place is being rapidly taken by the kindred, and though, in spite of the strong disapprobation of the elders of the clan, who prophesy barren marriages or idiot and diseased children as a result, marriages even within the kindred are not nowadays unknown.

It has been stated that the kelhu is thought to have been the original exogamous division of the Angamis. It is believed that the next stage was to allow intermarriage between members of the same kelhu provided that they were of different villages. This, of course, may be mere conjecture on the part of one or two intelligent Angamis, but there is some support to be found for it in the appended pedigrees as well as a certain amount of inherent probability in the theory, which is strengthened by the customary prohibition of marriage inside the village among the Cherhechima above mentioned. Whether, however, this was the case or not, the inter-kelhu exogamy must have given place to inter-thino exogamy very early among such communities as the Chakrima villages, where not only the majority in the village, but also in neighbouring villages, was of the same kelhu.[1] The story of exogamy in Kohima is an interesting illustration of the sort of development that took place. Kohima was composed partly of a large clan called

---

[1] Occasionally one finds a clan which is half Pezoma and half Pepfüma (see Appendix X). The probable reason of this is either absorption by one group of another smaller group which after its adoption has multiplied out of proportion to the adopting clan, or, perhaps, the amalgamation of two clans at a time of migration. In many instances the former is known to be the reason (see Appendix X), and the fact that Pezoma families migrating to another village usually seem to have been adopted into a Pepfüma clan and *vice versa* is probably to be explained by the original exogamous nature of the *Kelhu*. Thus a Pezoma man would on going to the new village take a Pepfüma wife, and having no clan of his own there would be adopted into her clan, as in the case of the ancestors of Nihu of Kohima, whose pedigree is given below.

Pferonoma, which, though like all other Angamis it hailed from Kezakenoma originally, came more directly from Kigwema, and partly of the Cherama clan coming straight from Kezakenoma. Both these clans were Pepfüma, but, coming from different villages, used to intermarry. Cherama remain intact still, but the Pferonoma have split up into six clans, Hrepvoma, Horotsuma, Chetonoma, Dapetsuma, Pfuchatsuma, and Rosuma. These, though at first perhaps merely kindreds and marrying into the Cherama clan or neighbouring villages, are now exogamous clans inter-marrying with one another. An instance of the thino splitting into what may be called septs may also be seen in the genealogical table of Srisalhu of Khonoma (vide infra), while in the Eastern Angami villages the original clan has become a mere phratry of two or more septs. The use of the word thino for the exogamous sept as well as for the formerly exogamous clan, now merely a phratry, shows just how far this process has gone. A Kohima man of the Cherama clan would answer " Cherama " if asked his thino, whereas no non-Cherama Kohima man would dream of answering " Pferonoma." A man of the Semoma clan of Khonoma if asked his thino will frequently answer " Semoma," but quite as frequently " Chalitsuma " or " Kutsotsuma," according to his sept.

But while the *thino* may still be regarded as ordinarily implying an exogamous group, it must be recognised that the exogamy of the *thino* is giving place to that of its sub-division the *putsa*.[1] The *putsa*, which is really the " kindred," is a more coherent body than the *thino*, and the relative positions in which the individual stands towards the kindred and towards the clan is well illustrated by the few formali-ties and duties that accompany adoption. His per-sonality is so far bound up with his kindred and clan that it is quite in accordance with Angami feeling to hold the clan, and still more the kindred, responsible for the mis-demeanours of the individual. It may be seen from the

Putsa.

[1] The term *putsa*, again, is not perhaps the term most ordinarily used. *Thino* is often used for the kindred as well as for the clan, but seeing that *putsa* (< *apo* 'father', *tsa* 'side') exists with this meaning, I have used it for the kindred to avoid confusion.

accompanying pedigrees that the kindred is on its way to becoming the exogamous group ; even by the Angamis the terms *thino* and *putsa* are not precisely used, and some groups other than large and recognised *thino* of long history are spoken of by both terms, while it is clear that groups now called *thino* have only comparatively recently attained to that status. This is particularly the case among the Eastern Angamis. The annexation, however, of the Angami country by Government has weakened the sanction of the village authorities, and marriages actually within the *putsa*,[1] though very rare and regarded with great disapproval as being " genna," are not entirely unknown. Such marriages are believed to be sterile or to result in idiot or diseased offspring. The word " *saiyeh* " should be mentioned in connection with this subject. Its meaning is vague, and it is used much as the word " family " is used in English, referring sometimes to a small circle of immediate blood relations, sometimes as more or less synonymous with *putsa*, and sometimes perhaps referring to a wider relationship still, such as that between persons of two closely allied kindreds between which no intermarriage is permitted. It should be noted, however, that it never refers to relationship on the mother's side, for which there would appear to be no word at all in the language, blood relationship being, indeed, not recognised through the female line. We thus have a series of groups each split in its turn into more groups, and each, it would seem, losing, as it splits up, its formerly exogamous character. The *kelhu* breaks up into the *thino*, which again splits up into new *thino*, which in their turn lose their exogamous status to the *putsa* into which they are divided. In the present generation the *putsa* would seem to be in the actual process of becoming the real exogamous unit, but has not yet finally become so, as the prohibition, which until comparatively recently applied to marriage within the *thino*, still applies to intermarriage between the more nearly related *putsa*. Thus within the Chalitsuma sept

---

[1] I know of a case in Kohima village where a man married his father's brother's daughter. They have no children. A similar case appears in one of the genealogies given.

of the Semoma clan of Khonoma there are five *putsa*, Vokanoma, Morrnoma, Ratsotsuma, Rilhonoma, and Seyet-suma. Of these the first three, who are descended from three brothers, Voka, Morr, and Ratsa, the grandsons of Chaliu, founder of the sept, are still not allowed to intermarry, but they may intermarry with either of the other two, who may also intermarry with each other. The other two ought properly to be also descended from Chaliu, but their descent is not quite so clear, as the Rilhonoma are not allowed on the ground of relationship to intermarry with two of the four Kutsotsuma *putsa*, the Kutsotsuma, the other sept of the Semoma clan, being descended from Kuthoh, the son of Chaliu's brother Hesennu, and all its *putsa* intermarrying with the first-mentioned three *putsa* of the Chalitsuma. It is probable that the Rilhonoma and the kindred *putsa* of the Kutsotsuma sept represent a second addition to the Semoma clan recruited from the Jotsoma descendants of Semo, and divided between the two septs, an explanation suggested by the genealogist of the Semoma clan.[1]

Kelhu, thino, and *putsa* are all patrilineal and patronymic. They show no traces of Totemism.[2]

Relationship has been spoken of hitherto as being a blood tie merely, but it can also be set up by adoption, though the practice is generally held to be decidedly objectionable.

Adoption.

---

[1] I am indebted to Colonel Shakespear, late Political Officer at Manipur, for the following note on exogamous groups among the Memi and Maram villages :—

"I have not found the division into two main groups among the Mao or Maram people, but it is quite possible that it originally existed. I shall inquire further. At Mao each village has a different system. Shongashon has 4 khels grouped in two exogamous pairs. Kalanamei has 6 khels ; 1 and 2 form an exogamous group and 4, 5, and 6 another ; number 3 inter-marries with both groups. The other 3 villages are divided into khels which are exogamous but are not grouped. Maram has 3 khels which are exogamous and two of them form an exogamous group. In all cases where there are groups the reason for not marrying in the group is stated to be that the khels forming the group are descended from brothers."

For the part taken by the Pezoma and Pepfüma *kelhu* in gennas, see the ceremony of dragging the clan door and the Derochü genna in Part IV.

[2] See Appendix IX on Totemism. It is worth notice that the Angami does not ask " *What* clan are you ? " but " *Whose* clan are you ? " (*no sopo thinoma ?*).

A man with no sons will sometimes adopt some young man to whom he may take a fancy from another kindred, or from another clan, on the understanding that the adopted son entirely forswears the former group and enters the group of his adoptive father, whose property he inherits. Such adoption is rare and almost invariably leads to involved property disputes, as the adopted usually tries to avoid giving up the property rights which may be forfeited by his leaving his own group, while he has to struggle with his new relations for the inheritance of his adoptive parent of which they consider themselves improperly deprived. Adoption within the kindred presents no difficulties and needs no ceremonies, being really not more than an arrangement by which one man looks after another, in return for which he inherits his property under a verbal will, or a larger share of property than he would otherwise have done ; but such an arrangement is not regarded at all in the same light as an adoption from a different clan, and in speaking of adoption among the Angamis the setting up of a more intimate relationship than would ordinarily exist between two members of the same kindred cannot rightly be termed adoption at all, and has no particular significance. Adoption from one kindred to another within the clan is rare, and its significance probably varies with local conditions, being, as it were, a half-measure of adoption, real adoption being adoption from a different clan. The aversion to adoption from another clan arises, no doubt, partly from the property disputes and general ill-feeling caused by the desertion of one group in favour of another, but still more, in the case of the original clan of the adopted, from an intense dislike or even fear of anything that may cause a decrease in the numbers of a clan or of a kindred. The mere idea of the extinction of the kindred or clan is utterly abhorrent to the Angami mind. The feeling which underlies the act of adoption seems to be a desire that the kindred and clan shall not suffer a diminution in numbers by the death of the childless adopter, and for this reason, adoption, properly speaking, is adoption from another clan. There is, however, one kind of adoption from another clan which is looked upon as suitable and

proper. This is adoption by a kindred of a man of another
clan, generally of another village, who has been impelled to
leave his own clan and village owing to enmity. If for some
reason a man incurs the enmity of his village, clan, or kindred
to such a degree that he finds life uncomfortable for him, it
is regarded as quite a proper course of action for him to sell
his land and leave his village and seek adoption by the
kindred of another clan in another village. A change of
clan within the village would lead to clan disputes, but no
one objects to a man in such circumstances leaving his
village and joining whatever clan and kindred he pleases
in another village, except, possibly, the kindred left, who
merely have an additional grievance against him and are no
doubt in some cases heartily glad to be rid of him.

Adoption is attended by a certain amount of ceremonial,
both on the part of the clan which is deserted (having regard
to the individual) and on the part of the individual (having
regard to the clan of his adoption). In the case of the clan
deserted a pig is killed and paid for by a common sub-
scription. It is divided up and all the clansmen eat of it,
the eldest member eating first, followed by others in order of
seniority. A chicken is also released by the oldest member,
who takes it and throws it into the jungle somewhere near
the village, but far enough off for it to be unlikely to find its
way home. The purpose ascribed to this act is the prevention of a repetition of such an occurrence as the desertion of
the clan by one of its members. On his part, the man adopted
chooses to what kindred in his new clan he will belong, if
that has not been already settled beforehand. He then
kills a pig and prepares a large quantity of " zu." The pig
is cut up and every male member of the kindred chosen
receives a share of flesh and a share of the drink, while a
similar share is given to a representative only of each other
kindred in the clan. This, it is said, is a sign that the newly-
adopted member will not treat them as he has treated the
clan from which he has come. The whole clan helps to
fetch the property of its new member and the materials of
his house from its former site, but only the newly-adopted
kindred help in building the new house. Although the

prohibition of marriage within his former kindred is not removed, no intermarriage is allowed between the new member of the clan and kindred which adopts him, though nowadays, at any rate, he and his descendants may inter-marry with the other kindred of the clan. The case given in the pedigree of Nihu of Kohima, in which there appears to be a marriage between the son of an adopted member of the Ramenuma kindred and a woman of that kindred, is explained by the adoption having taken place as a result of the marriage and subsequently to it. It may be remarked with regard to this pedigree that it shows an instance of adoption of a man of a Pezoma clan into a Pepfüma clan. There is no change of *kelhu* in such a case, and Nihu is Pezoma like his forefathers.

Pedigrees   In the following pedigrees the Pezoma lines are shown in italics while the Pepfüma are printed in Roman type. The brackets below the names contain the name of the exogamous clan (the *thino*), and after that, when necessary and obtain-able, the name of the kindred (*putsa*). Where it has been found necessary to give the name of a sept it is given before that of the kindred. Unless stated to the contrary, the village, clan, and kindred of any person in the table is the same as that of his or her first male ancestor in the direct paternal line whose name is given, and marriages into a different village are clearly shown. The names of males are given to the left hand of females in the case of married couples. Where any doubt might arise, sex is shown by the conventional signs.

It may be noticed with reference to the pedigrees in general that, where the clans in a village are all of the same *kelhu*, inter-*kelhu* marriages do not nowadays occur. On the other hand, in the Khonoma group inter-*kelhu* marriages seem to have been almost the rule until the present generation.

The pedigrees here given were obtained after the informa-tion as to the exogamous syst. m in general described above, which was obtained by direct inquiry. They were taken at random and are not selected in any way.

The Pedigree of VISE of Viswema
village. kelhu : Kepezoma. clan :
Rotsoma.

LISANYI *of Viswema*
(*Rotsoma*)
|
VISWELE = Yoéle of Sopvotehema village
| (Taputsoma) [Memi]
|
VISE = Ketselhuwü of Khonoma village
(Semoma).

N.B.—Marriages between Angamis of the Viswema group and of Memi and Kezama villages are very frequent. Vise is bilingual, speaking Memi as well as Tengima.

Pedigree of ZEPULE of Kohima
village.   kelhu :   Kepepfüma.
clan : Hrepvuma (of the Pferonuma phratry).

SOVISEH of Kohima
(Hrepvuma)
|
NGULHU = *Nizhü of Merema village*
| (*Kidütuma*)

KINIZHE = *Chibowü* NI	= Kresawü VIPFELE = ♀
	(*Horotsuma*)	(Cheto-	(Dapet-
ZEPULE = Lolezewü	numa).	suma).
(Chetonuma).		

N.B.—The marriages in this generation only are Pepfüma-Pepfüma ; moreover, they are between the different clans of the Pferonuma phratry. The Horotsuma clan, though a Pepfüma group, contains one or two Pezoma families. It may be observed that Zepule could not remember his sister-in-law's name at the time of questioning, a fact rather typical of the genealogical knowledge of the ordinary Angami. He would, of course, in speaking to her use the title *amiepfü*, and not her personal name.

Pedigree of LHUSELE of Kohima
village.   kelhu :   Kepepfüma.
clan : Hrepvuma (of the Pferonuma phratry).

YACHELE of Kohima
(Hrepvuma)
|
ZELENIU = Gelhuwü of Chedema village
| (Chekronoma)
|
LHUSELE = Zebvüno
(Cherama).

N.B.—The Pepfüma-Pepfüma marriage in the last generation is between persons of different villages. The marriage of Lhusele is outside the Pferonuma phratry. All the clans in Kohima are Pepfüma, the six clans other than Cherama being branches of what was once, no doubt, the clan Pferonuma, but which has long ceased to be exogamous. It used at one time to marry only into the Cherama clan or into other villages. In any case, marriages into the Pezoma *kelhu* are hardly to be expected in Kohima village within the time covered by ordinary Angami genealogical knowledge, although Mozema, a purely Pezoma village, seems to have kept up inter-*kelhu* marriages, by taking wives from Khonoma, but these two villages were always in close touch with one another.

Pedigree of VISANYÜ of Kohima village.
kelhu: Kepepfüma.   clan: Horotsuma
(of the Pferonoma phratry).   kindred:
Lizitsuma.

δ = ♀

of Kohima village
(Horotsuma, Lizitsuma)

LHOZEMO = ♀

LHUTSONYÜ = ♀
  |(Cherama)
KRUSETSÜ

KAWAHE = Nuziwü
Commonly called
Vinyü because he
went to Gauhati to
enlist in the Fron-
tier Police with one
Vinyü, who was
recruited while Ka-
wahe was refused.
After enlisting
Vinyü had a bad
dream and desert-
ed. Kawahe took
his place and
answered to the
name of Vinyü, by
which he was ever
afterwards known,
as the deception
was not discovered.

HIVILHU = Diruü
  (Horotsuma
  Yawütsuma)

LHURUSOH = Sozemowü
  of Jakhama
  village
  (Zema)

SATZELE = Nitsüwü
  (Chetonoma)
  (Sekosenuma)
NIRIHU = Lhulezhewü
  of Dehoma
  village

VISANYÜ = Yavikrü
  (Chetonoma)

VINOLE
  =
Yatsetewü
  (Chetonoma
  Theyonuma)

MHANICHA   Others
  =   Unmd.
Nuboii
(Dapetsuma)

ROGULHUWÜ ♀

KELULHULE δ

KIYAKREWÜ ♀

ZESOWÜ ♀

PFÜMEZA δ

ONILE = Nirutsowü
  (Hrepvoma)

DOPURR = ♀ of Merema village
was banished from
Kohima for accident-
ally killing his brother
and settled at Merema.

N.B.—Visanyü marries his father's sister's son's daughter. Marriages within the Horotsuma clan occur twice in the present generation, viz., in the case of Hivilhu (within the Horotsuma) and Vinole (with the Chetonoma). Marriages, where details are known, are with one exception within the Pepfüma kelhu and with one exception—that of Lhutsonyü—within the Pferonoma phratry, but the pedigree only goes back one generation.

Pedigree of NIHU of Kohima
village. kelhu : Kepezoma. clan :
Puchatsuma. kindred : Rame-
numa.

VISOLE = ♀
of Rekroma village | of Rekroma village
(Kininuma) settled |
in Kohima in the |
Puchatsuma clan |
       PULETHA = Sehuwü
      joined Ramenuma | (Puchatsuma Ramenuma)
      kindred of Puchat-- |
      suma |
           NIHU = Loliü
              (Chetonoma).

N.B.—Here a Pezoma family settles in a Pepfüma clan and remains
Pezoma though becoming one of the Ramenuma kindred and subject to
the same marriage prohibitions as the Ramenuma kindred. Though
accepted as a member of the Puchatsuma clan, Visole's son marries within
it and joins the kindred into which he has married.

Pedigree of TSORIYÜ (♀) of Kohima
village. kelhu: Kepepfuma. clan:
Puchatsuma (of the Pferonoma
phratry).

TUTSÜ = ♀
of Kohima village |
(Puchatsuma) |
      ZESALE = Rilhuwü of Dehoma village
             (Theyonuma)

              Thache = TSORIÜ   MEPO
              A Sema of
              Sanakasami
              village
      VATSÜKRE = ♀
            | (Puchatsuma)
  LUKAHE = Nizenu
        (Rosuma)

N.B.—Pepfüma-Pepfüma marriages (except in the case of the Sema), but
in the last generation between different villages.

Pedigree of NISANYÜ of Kohima
village. kelhu : Kepepfüma.
clan : Puchatsuma kindred :
Rutsanoma.

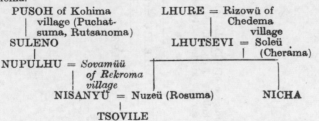

PUSOH of Kohima   LHURE = Rizowü of
  | village (Puchat- | Chedema
  | suma, Rutsanoma) | village
  SULENO   LHUTSEVI = Soleü
  | | (Cherama)
NUPULHU = *Sovamüü*
  | *of Rekroma*
  | *village*
  NISANYÜ = Nuzeü (Rosuma)   NICHA
    |
  TSOVILE

N.B.—Pepfuma-Pepfuma marriages of last generation but one between
different villages.

Pedigree of **VIYALE** of Kohima village. kelhu: Kepepfüma. clan: Puchatsuma. kindred: Rutsanoma.

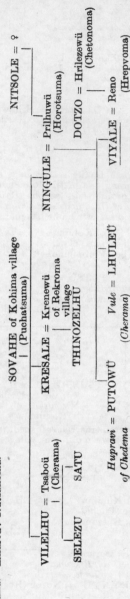

SOVAHE of Kohima village | (Puchatsuma)

NITSOLE = ♀

VILELHU = Tsaboü | (Cherama)

KRESALE = Krenewü of Rekroma village

NINGULE = Prilhuwü (Horotsuma)

SELEZU   SATU

THINOZELHÜ

DOTZO = Hrilezewü (Chetonoma)

Hupravi = PUTOWÜ *of Chedema village*

Vule = LHULEÜ (Cherama)

VIYALE = Reno (Hrepvoma)

N.B.—Vule, though Pezoma, belongs to Cherama, a Pepfüma clan. It is probably a case of adoption.

*Pedigree   of   YALHULE   of
Kigwema   village.   kelhu : Kepezoma.   clan : Kipoma.*

```
        TSUTSONIU = Vakali
          of Kigwema  |   of Mima village
          village      |
          (Kipoma)     |
                   SALHUNIU = Lepulhule
                        |     (Kamima)
                   YALHULE = Viletowü
                                of Mozema
                                village
                                (Pepetsuma).
```

N.B.—The marriage in the present generation is Pezoma-Pezoma, but
between different villages.

*Pedigree of VIDILHU of Mozema
village. kelhu : Kepezoma. clan :
Vihotsuma.*

```
              KOWÜ = ♀
  One of the original colonists |
  from   Kigwema  to  Mozema. |
  Has descendants also in Jot- |
  soma,   Khonoma,   and   in |
  Kohima                       |
                    SOLEHO
                       |
                    RUBA
                       |
                    MATIYU
                       |                              ♂ = ♀ of Mozema
                    RÜPI          of Khonoma            village
                       |          (Semoma)  |        (Vihotsuma)
                    TAIYAO                   |
                       |                     |
                    LHUKWOLE                 |
                       |                     |
                    YEJIHE    =   Krepulewü
                       |          of Khonoma
                       |          village
                       |          (Semoma)
                       |                  KRENIZE = Nihotsowü
                       |                  (Nisonuma) |  of Kho-
                       |                  |           noma vil-
                    VIDILHU = Viriyü                  lage (Se-
                   (Vihotsuma)  (Nisonuma).           moma).
```

N.B.—The first recorded marriage within the Pezoma *kelhu* is in the
present generation.   All the clans in Mozema are Pezoma.

Pedigree of ZELUCHA and
PFETSEHU of Jotsoma village.
kelhu: Kepepfüma. clan :
Thekronoma.

```
                    SONGI
                    | came from Kigwema with the first
                    | colony to Jotsoma; ancestor of
                    | Semoma clan of Khonoma also
              PRILEZHU
            (Thekronoma) |
                    VILE = Rilhuzhewü  LHUWUKRE
                    |  of  Kohima     | (Kwoma)
                    |   village    NITSOLE = Tolhuwü
                    |  (Chetonoma)        |  (Thekro-
                    |                  _____  noma)
                    |                 |          |
                  SOTAMU  =  Tsosewü
                                            |
                                  NGUREZHU = Tsolhuwü
                                  (Toloma)  | of Kohima
       NIPULE  =  Jaleü                     |   village
    of Khonoma |  (Semoma)                  |  (Cherama)
      village  |              PFETSEHU  =  Lhutsolewü
    (Thevoma)  |
       ZUCHALE = Rukriewü    PFUTSOH = Zekrü
             | (Semoma)     (Toloma) | (Tseyama)
    Zenilhuwü (1) = ZELUCHA = (2) Tserreviü
     of Khonoma        ♂        (Toloma)
       village
     (Thevoma)
     [divorced]
```

N.B.—Here there is a Pezoma–Pezoma marriage in the last generation
and a Pepfüma–Pepfüma marriage in the generation before, but in the
latter case between persons of different villages. There are four clans in
Jotsoma—*Toloma, Tseyama, Kwoma,* and Thekronoma.

TYPICAL ANGAMI HOUSE

[See p. 51

OTHER TYPES OF HOUSE-HORN

METSALIMI   KIGWEMA, SHOWING
DUMMY BIRDS

TOP OF POST TO WHICH
ROOF AND TREE IS SECURED

[See p. 51

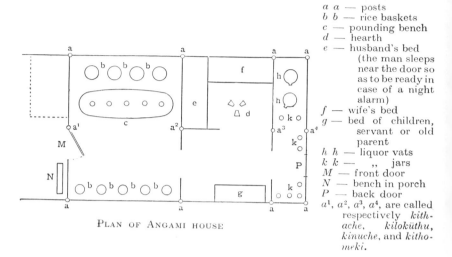

$a\ a$ — posts
$b\ b$ — rice baskets
c — pounding bench
d — hearth
e — husband's bed
(the man sleeps
near the door so
as to be ready in
case of a night
alarm)
f — wife's bed
g — bed of children,
servant or old
parent
$h\ h$ — liquor vats
$k\ k$ — ,, jars
M — front door
N — bench in porch
P — back door
$a^1,\ a^2,\ a^3,\ a^4$, are called
respectively *kith-
ache, kiloküthu,
kinuche,* and *kitho-
meki.*

PLAN OF ANGAMI HOUSE

[See p. 52

KEMOVO'S HOUSE WITH WOODEN SHINGLE ROOF AND TWO PAIRS OF HOUSE HORNS.
TERRACES IN THE BACKGROUND AT MESOLOZUMI

[See p. 52

Genealogy of **SRISALHU** of
Khonoma village. kelhu :
Kepepfüma. clan : Semoma.
sept : Chalitsuma. kindred :
Vokanuma.

SONGI
came with the first colony from Kigwema when Jotsoma was founded
SEMO = *Thewü*
from whom the
clan takes its
name

SOVI

CHALIU
from whom the sept
takes its name

HESENNU

PFÜCHAH

KUTHOH
ancestor of the
Kutsotsuma sept

VOKA
came with the first
colony from Jotsoma
when Khonoma was
founded. The kin-
dred takes its name
from him

MORR
ancestor of
the Morranuma
kindred

RATSA
ancestor of the
Ratsutsuma
kindred

VICHU

KAÄKRE
of Mozema
village
(*Vihotsuma*)

PINIU

VIZÉ
(Merhema)

KRIETSÜ
(Merhema)

KWELHU
(*Thevoma*)

CHEKRIGI

HUTSOH = Zarrü
of Kiru-
fema
village

CHARILE = *Kroniwü*
(*Thevoma*)

LIVI

KESORR = ♀
(*Thevoma*)
SOZEO = *Rekruwü*
(*Thevoma*)
PELHULE = *Varihuwü*
(*Thevoma*)
ZEPURR = *Yakriewü*

VIKILE = Chesonyuwü
of Khonoma village
(Merhema)

DOHAPRE = *Krushehuwü*
(*Thevoma*)

VIZOPRE = Phelhu-
d. s. p. shewü
(Semoma,
Kutsotsuma)

SRISALHU
=
Wokiyü
(Semoma),
Kutsotsuma)

VIRIHU
=
Vilohawü
(*Thevoma*)

VITSELE = *Vilavowü*
of Mozema
village
(*Nisanoma*)

NIKIVI = Zakeméü
(Semoma,
Chalitsuma,
Seyetsama)

Viyezo
(Merhema)
= UTSOWÜ
♀

Two
other
sons

N.B.—Srisalhu, who gave this genealogy, is particularly well acquainted with genealogical matters. Dohapre is the hereditary *kemovo* [1] of the Semoma clan and will be succeeded in the office by Srisalhu, who will again be followed by Dohapre's son Vitsele. The family, however, is [2] unable to exercise its functions owing to the expulsion by Government of the Chalitsuma sept from the original site of Khonoma. The functions are meanwhile performed by Khusapra of the Kutsotsuma sept, which remains on the original site. It will be noticed in this genealogy that Srisalhu's generation is the first in which a Pepfüma–Pepfüma marriage is recorded ; further, that this marriage falls within the Semoma clan, though the parties belong to different septs. In the following generation we find that one of Srisalhu's nephews has gone a step further still and marries within the sept, though into different kindreds. Thewü, wife of Semo, has been shown conjecturally as Pezoma. Nothing is really known about her.

There are three clans in Khonoma—*Thevoma*, Merhema, and Semoma. Violent disputes between these clans may have encouraged marriages within the *thino* during the last two generations.

Pedigree of *Kruzeto* of *Khonoma
village. kelhu : Kepezoma. clan :
Thevoma.*

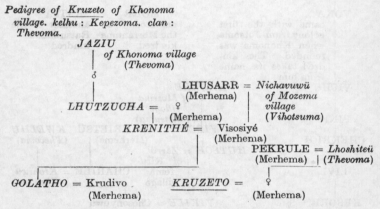

N.B.—All the marriages are Pezoma–Pepfüma and outside the clan. The name of Kruzeto's wife is not given, as it is not usual for a man to mention the name of his own wife " for shame," and being newly married a third person who knew her name was not available when the pedigree was recorded.

---

[1] *Kemovo*, see Part IV.

[2] *I.e.*, at the time of writing. The sept has since been allowed to return to its old site.

Pedigree of *PFÜDILHU o Khonoma village.*   kelhu: Kepezoma.   clan: Theoma.   kindred: Tsüméonoma.

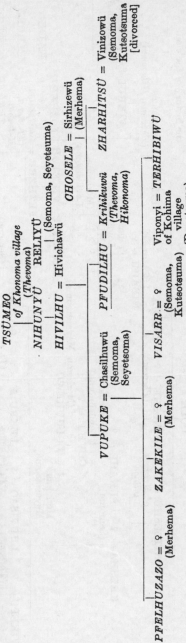

TSÜMEO
of Khonoma village
(*Thevoma*)
NIHUNYÜ   RELIYÜ
| (Semoma, Seyetsuma)
HIVILHU = Hivichawü

CHOSELE = Sirhizewü
| (Merhema)

ZHARHITSÜ = Vinizowü
(Semoma,
Kutsotsuma
[divorced]

PFÜDILHU = Krihikuwü
(*Thevoma,
Hikonoma*)

VUPUKE = Chasilhuwü
(Semoma,
Seyetsoma)

VISARR. = ♀
(Semoma,
Kutsotsuma)

Viponyi = *TERHIBIWÜ*
of Kohima
village
(Dapetsuma)

PFELHUZAZO = ♀
(Merhema)

ZAKEKILE = ♀
(Merhema)

N.B.—Hivichawü and Chasilhuwü are very nearly related, though Pfüdilhu cannot state exactly what the relationship is. Pfüdilhu himself has married within the clan, though into a different *putsa*. He does not know the names of the wives of his brother's sons. Before Pfüdilhu the marriages recorded are Pezoma–Pepfüma, and his nephews follow suit.

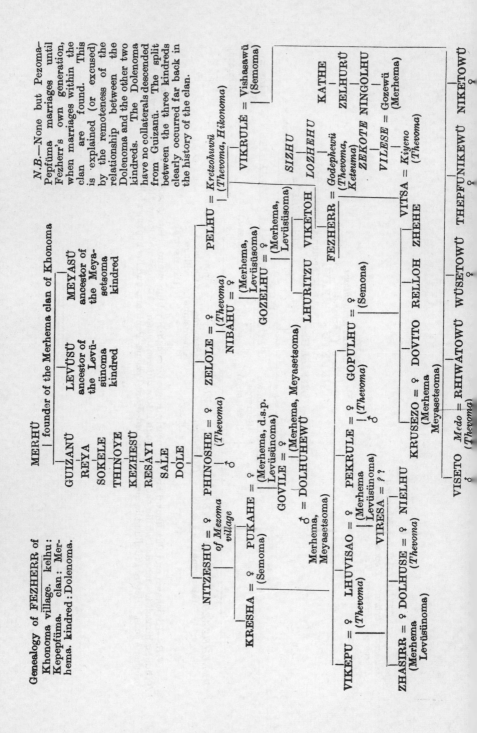

Genealogy of FEZHERR of Khonoma village. kelhu: Kepepfüma. clan: Merhema. kindred: Dolenoma.

N.B.—None but Pezoma-Pepfüma marriages until Fezherr's own generation, when marriages within the clan are found. This is explained (or excused) by the remoteness of the relationship between the Dolenoma and the other two kindreds. The Dolenoma have no collaterals descended from Guizanti. The split between the three kindreds clearly occurred far back in the history of the clan.

MERHÜ
| founder of the Merhema clan of Khonoma

GUIZANÜ
REYA
SOKELE
THINOYE
KEZHESÜ
RESAYI
SALE
DOLE

LEVÜSÜ ancestor of the Levüsünoma kindred

MEYASÜ ancestor of the Meyasetsoma kindred

PELHU = Kretzohavü (Thevoma, Hikonoma)

ZELOLE = ♀ (Thevoma)
NIBAHU = ♀

PHINOSHE = ♀ (Thevoma)
♂

NITZESHÜ = ♀ of Mezoma village

KRESHA = ♀ PUKAHE = ♀ (Semona)

PUKAHE = ♀ (Merhema, d.s.p. Levüsünoma)
GOVILE = ♀
♂ = DOLHUHEWÜ (Merhema, Meyasetsoma)

Merhema, Meyasetsoma

GOZELHU = ♀ (Merhema, Levüsünoma)

LHURITZU VIKETOH

FEZHERR = Godephevü (Thevoma, Keteuma)

VIKRULÉ = Vishasawü (Semona)

SIZHU
LOZHEHU

ZEKOTE NINGOLHU
VILESE = Gozewü (Merhema)

KATHE
ZELHURÜ

VITSA = Kiyeno (Thevoma)

VIKEPU = ♀ (Thevoma)

LHUVISAO = ♀ (Merhema Levüsünoma)

PEKRULE = ♀ (Merhema Levüsünoma)
VIRESA = ♀♀

NIELHU

GOPULHU = ♀ (Semona)
♂

KRUSEZO = ♀ (Merhema Meyasetsoma)

DOVITO RELLOH ZHEHE

ZHASIRR = ♀ DOLHUSE = ♀ (Thevoma)

VISETO   Medo = RHIWATOWÜ ♀   WÜSETOWÜ ♀   THEPFUNIKEWÜ ♀   NIKETOWÜ ♀
(Thevoma)   ♂

Pedigree of NITZORE of Khozama village (Chakrima). kelhu: Kepezoma. clan: Venomi. kindred: Lohekoma.

```
                    KETHO = ♀ of Thevopetsima village
        of Zogazumi (Nagvema)
        village settled in Khozama
                        |
                POSEKÜ = Thakule
        of Khozama village | of Zogazumi village
                           (Zogazu Nasama)
                    TSELHU = Kileoii
                           (Lhokatsiikoma)
                           |
 ┌────────────┬────────────┬────────────┬────────────┬──────────────┐
Kagho =      Lhutsoni =   Mecho =      NITZORE =    DEHOMA       ZUMOLHO
DISAHILE     LHIZHULE     METANILE     Nipule
(Lhokat-     (Lhokat-     (Verekoma)   of Khetsa-
siikoma)     siikoma)                  peoma
                                       village
Kikwii =
SATAHILE                                    MELHOPI = Sakwile
(Venomi,                                    returned to   of Zogazuma
Lohekoma)                                   Zogazuma
                                            [divorced]
```

N.B.—All the marriages are Pezoma-Pezoma, as is inevitable in the Chakrima country, but the earlier ones are between different villages. In the present generation Satahile has married into her own *puesa*, a fact deprecated by Nitzore, who gave the pedigree. "Melhopi" would be known as "Melhutsii" in the Kohima dialect.

There are four clans in Khozama divided into many kindreds.

Pedigree of SOTZÜZHÜ of
Purobama village (Chakrima.)
kelhu : Kepezoma. clan : Seka-
mutsomi.

<pre>
          ZEËNÜ   JOVISA
       | of Purobama | (Telentsomi)
       | village |
       | (Sekamutsomi)   VAKRÜ
   NGORRENN = Hoizile |
       | (Pogwenumi)   ZÜSANN = Sazele
       | | (Pogwe-
       | _____| numi)
       | |
    SOTZUZHU = Edutsüle
       | (Telentsomi)
    LHONIRÜ
</pre>

N.B.—Generally speaking the Chakrima villages are composed mainly of Pezoma clans.

Pedigree of TAHEMO of Keza-
bama village (Kezama). kelhu :
Kepezoma. clan : Senomi.

<pre>
     MECHIMM
     | of Kezabama
     | village
     | (Senomi)   MESHOKO = Etsulhiü
   EDILO   (Lekomi) | (Wetsami)
     | |
   HILLO = Zutheniü   GWEGHELO = Metetsele
     | (Lasumi) | (Senomi)
     | _____|
     | |
   TAHEMO = Gweseniu
            (Lekomi)
</pre>

ANGAMI TERMS OF RELATIONSHIP.

N.B.—Where the terms used by the Kepepfüma differ from those used by the Kepezoma the former are given in italics. The terms are as used in the Khonoma group. A few variations used by the Kohima group are given in brackets.

Father . . . . . . 'Po, *'pvu.*
Mother . . . . . . 'Zo, *'pfü.*
Son . . . . 'No.
Daughter . . . . . 'Nopfü.
Elder brother (m.s.)[1] . . 'Dzereo.
Younger brother (m.s.) . 'Siezeo.

[1] "m.s." signifies that the word is used in address by males only, "w.s." that it is used in address by women only.

Brother (w.s.)	.	. .	'Pru.
Sister (m.s.)	.	. . .	'Üpfü ('lupfü) (if necessary to distinguish the seniority, phi-chüpfü, ' elder,' and nhi-chupfü, ' younger,' are suf-fixed as required).
Elder sister (w.s.)	.	. .	'Dzerepfü.
Younger sister (w.s.)	.	.	'Siezepfü.[1]
Father's elder brother	.	.	A-po, *a-pvu* (in address). 'po dzereo, *'pvu dzereo,* in speak-ing to third person.
,, younger brother		.	'Nyie (or 'nyiedi).
,, brother's wife(m.s.)			'Thi (or 'zo, *'pfü,* in address).
,, ,, ,, (w.s.)			'Ni (or 'zo, *'pfü,* in address).
,, sister		. .	'Nye, 'nya.
,, sister's husband		.	'Mi (followed by personal name.)
,, ,, son		. .	'Chu, 'chuno (followed by per-sonal name).
,, ,, daughter		.	'Chupfü (followed by personal name).
Mother's brother	.	. .	'Mi, 'miyu.
,, brother's wife		.	'Thi ('zo, *'pfü,* also used by courtesy).
,, sister		. .	'Zo, *'pfü* (in address). 'Zopfü, *'pfüpfü* (in speaking to third person). 'Pfüzo is also used.
,, sister's husband		.	'Ni (followed by personal name). If the man addressed is older than the speaker's father the terms apo, *apvu,* would be used for politeness' sake.
Younger sister's son (m.s.)		.	'Chu, 'chuno.
Younger sister's daughter (m.s.)	.	. . .	'Chupfü.
Sister's son (w.s.)	.	. .	'No.
,, daughter (w.s.)		.	'Nopfü.
Father's father	.	. .	} 'Putsao, *'pvutsa.*
Mother's ,,	.	. .	

[1] Terms of endearment *aloö* and *kechi* are also used as for any child, the latter for a female child with the suffix *no—kechino,* while with the suffix *bu* for a male it might be used by a woman for her younger brother— *kechi-bu.*

Father's mother	{	'Zotsa, *'tsapfü* (or *'pfütsa*).
Mother's ,,		(Though *'tsapfü* is strictly a Pepfüma term, it seems to be used sometimes for Kepezoma as well.)
Grandson		'Chuno.
Granddaughter		'Chupfü.
Husband		'Nupfü.
Wife		'Kima.
Wife's father		'Mi.
Wife's mother		'Nye.
Husband's father		'Mi.
Husband's mother		'Nye.
Wife's elder brother		'Thi.
Wife's elder sister		'Thi.
Wife's younger sister		'Siezepfü (in address; in speaking to a third person and wishing to be explicit, 'Kima siezepfü would be used).
Husband's elder brother		'Thi.
Husband's elder sister (older than speaker)		'Ni (personal name used if younger).
Son's wife		'Miepfü.
Daughter's husband		'Na.
Elder sister's husband		'Thi.
Younger sister's husband		'Na.
Elder brother's wife (m.s.)		'Thi.
Younger brother's wife (m.s.)		'Miepfü.
Elder brother's wife (w.s.)		'Ni.

The following relations are addressed and spoken of by the personal name (unless it is necessary to specify precisely, when the exact relationship is indicated, *e.g.*, " My mother's brother's daughter " = *A-mi u-nopfü*) :—Father's brother's child, mother's brother's child, mother's sister's child, wife's younger brother, husband's younger brother, husband's younger sister, younger brother's wife (w.s.), brother's child, elder sister's child (m.s.), wife's brother's child, husband's sister's child, wife's sister's child, younger brother's wife (w.s.), wife's sister's husband, husband's brother's wife.

A child's wife's parents are addressed by name or by the term *reshema* = " a connection," a very vague term of relationship applied to relations or connections by marriage who are not of the same exogamous group as the speaker.

The term *ryano* is applied to one another by men whose wives are sisters, or by women whose husbands are brothers.

N.B.—The relationship denoted by the terms apo (*apvu*), azo (*apfü*) may be to some extent gauged by the fact that a man when trying to speak of his uncle or his aunt in Assamese, instead of saying " My father's elder brother " (or " younger brother "), etc., speaks of his ' big father ': or his " little father," as the case may be.

The question of inheritance[1] has been already mentioned in dealing with that of adoption. A man cannot, as a rule, without causing considerable indignation leave his property to any person outside his kindred, or at any rate his clan, except in a very modified degree to his daughters and their children. But, except in the matter of leaving land to daughters and in the reservation of one-third of the deceased's personal possessions, including land, for the widow, all customary inheritance can admittedly be modified at will by the verbal directions of the bequeather,[2] and a verbal bequest to a stranger would be admitted as valid and would probably under ordinary circumstances be respected, and indeed the writer has himself benefited by such an one. Within the kindred, provided no special directions are given, the next male heirs inherit ; subject, that is, to the widow's third, while among the Kezama the widow gets all the movable property. Only males can permanently inherit real property, and the males of one generation share alike. That is to say, if a man leaves no sons but several first cousins, these will divide the property equally. But in the case of sons inheriting from their father this is not so. The usual custom is for a man to divide the bulk of his property during his lifetime. When his sons marry and set up house, each receives his portion of inheritance from his father, and on the death of the latter the youngest son, even though he

Inheritance.

[1] The inheritance rules given here must be taken as general rules only. Custom varies slightly from village to village, though the general principle, is the same.

[2] See Appendix XIII, p. 454.

may have already been given his portion, inherits all the property, including the house, which is retained in his father's hand at the time of his death, though he has to give the best field to the eldest son, taking another in exchange. This rule, however, may be modified and frequently is modified by verbal directions, while in one or two villages all the sons seem to inherit equally, though this, if actually the case, is unusual. Among the Memi the eldest son gives his portion to the youngest son and takes that which his father had retained. In the Khonoma group the son who inherits the house-site has to drag memorial stones to commemorate his parents and set them up in or near the village.

The property of any son dying without male children during his father's lifetime reverts to the latter, but after the father's death it goes to the youngest son, who can keep or share it with his elder brothers as he pleases, while in the case of the younger son himself dying without a son his elder brothers share his property equally. Should there be neither father nor brother living, uncles or first cousins would inherit, then second cousins, and so forth, brothers among the inheritors sharing equally. In case of no relations being found, the kindred inherits, and failing any kindred the clan. Under this custom, the death, when it does take place, of the last member of a kindred in any village who has left no verbal directions as to the disposal of his property may raise claims from villages at a great distance and based on involved descents from a distant and almost legendary ancestor. The death of a man in Samaguting, which was originally a composite village containing colonists from Khonoma, Mezoma, Sachema, Kohima, Merema, and other villages, produced claims to inherit from some kindred or other in nearly all the Angami villages west of the Chakrima and Kezama groups. Fortunately for the settlement of the question, someone was found in Samaguting willing to take oath that he belonged to the same clan, and being resident in the village he succeeded in establishing his claim to the property. The inheritance of an adopted son would normally be determined at the time of adoption, and if no verbal instructions were left the adopted son would probably

be expected to take oath that the deceased had intended him
to inherit as a son.   As regards the portion given by a man
to each of his sons during his lifetime, it should be noted that
the gift is nullified, or may be regarded as nullified, by any
disobedience of the father by the son.   Thus, if a man find
that his son is gambling away his portion and will not desist
when told to do so, the father may revoke his gift, or, if he
prefer, may merely put a prohibition on sale of the land.
A revocation, however, during life would not prejudice a
son's rights of inheritance after death failing explicit directions.   Among the Memi the eldest and the youngest of
the sons of a man dying before he has given them portions
take larger shares than the rest.

It has been stated that a man cannot leave real property
to his daughters.   Failing sons, however, it is the practice
among the Memi for the daughter to take all land purchased
by her father during his lifetime.   Except for this case
among the Memi, a man cannot leave land in perpetuity to a
daughter, and no woman can permanently inherit land of
any sort, be it terraces, jhum land, building or garden land,
or fire-wood plantations.   Nevertheless, a man can leave
as much land as he pleases to be enjoyed during the lifetime
of the daughter to whom it is left, the property reverting
to the male heirs after the death of the daughter.   Personal
property, including cash and cattle, is bequeathed to
daughters absolutely.   A woman's own property goes to
her children, her personal ornaments always to the
daughters.   Failing children, her property goes to her
father's heirs, who take all the ornaments of a woman dying
without a daughter, even if she has a son.

In this connection, too, we have to deal with the difficult
question of *mengu*, the custom governing the point varying
between the Tengima and Chakrima villages most markedly,
while minor variations occur from village to village.   In
the matter of *mengu*, the Dzuno-Kehena group mostly
follow the Chakrima custom, as do the Kezami and probably
the Memi.

Among Tengima *mengu* = the return given by a man to
his wife's relations in recognition of the fact that he has

become rich through her help. Such a return is not compulsory unless the woman on her death-bed directs that it be given, but a small complimentary *mengu*, consisting of the dead woman's hoe and some paddy, is usually given by the widower to her father's family (*cf.* the Sema custom by which a bridegroom presents a hoe to his bride's mother).

Among the Chakrima *mengu* = the return by a woman's descendants to her paternal family of land, etc., bought with such items of her dowry as would, if unsold, have ultimately returned to her father's family. The return takes place after the death of the woman's children. [Under a standing order of the Deputy Commissioner Naga Hills claims must be made within six months of the claim becoming admissible by Angami custom. This limitation is not a part of the Angami usage, but has been found necessary for the purposes of courts of justice.] This system is applied to personal property given or bequeathed to daughters as well as to real property, but it is rarely that a full return of the bequest is expected or even asked. Indeed by the time two generations have elapsed from the date of the donor's death it is exceedingly difficult to say exactly what was given to the original beneficiary, and very often a merely nominal sum is asked for in recognition of, and settlement of, the claim. Even where the identical land which has thus passed into the female line has been retained, the claim of the male heirs for the return of the land is often waived in consideration of a money payment representing a good deal less than the real value of the land. At the same time there is no definite proportion of the original sum which the male heirs are bound to take in satisfaction of the claim, and it is always open to them to insist on return of the original bequest in full, and though rarely if ever insisted on in the case of personal property, a full return of land is frequently required. The mere fact that a full payment of *mengu* is neither made nor expected, except in the case of land, frequently causes a great deal of dispute as to what is a suitable amount to be given, in view of the property acquired by the original daughter, as the views of the male heirs vary, while those who have inherited from the daughter frequently attempt to avoid any sort of payment at all. Sometimes, of course, exorbitant demands are made, and the writer has not only known a case in which all the numerous offspring derived from a single cow were claimed as *mengu* in return of the aforesaid single cow which a man had given to his daughter two generations before, but also a case in which the half of a large property in land, cattle, and cash was claimed as *mengu* on the ground of the physical and mental abilities of the claimant's great-grandfather's daughter. This estimable lady had received no portion from her father at all, but such was her frugality and industry that though she and her husband possessed practically nothing when they were married, they left a great deal of property to their children. Needless to say the claim for *mengu* did not in this case prove successful. It would be possible, on the other hand, to mention rare instances to the contrary where a sum of Rs.20/– or so has been accepted as *mengu* for terraces worth perhaps Rs.120/–. The custom of *mengu* has been treated here under the head of inheritance, but at the same time it should be noted that it is inextricably involved in the question of dowries given with girls in marriage. Of course, when a man gives his daughter in marriage he usually gives property with her then, if he is going to give her property at all ; and this property is subject to *mengu* like all other property given during life or after death by a father to his daughter in those villages in which the Chakrima custom of *mengu* obtains. Thus, as the bulk of the property given by fathers to daughters is given at the time of marriage, *mengu* comes to be associated in thought with tne dowry *quâ* dowry. *Mengu*, however, is really only a charge on dowries inasmuch as they are transfers of property to daughters. The Angami mind draws no fine distinction between gifts of property during lifetime and after death, still less between property given at the time of marriage and property given at some other time.

Not unlike *mengu* is the custom relating to *yīpē*, that is, a " panikhet " (or other property, " jhum," cattle, etc.) given among the Kezama to a bride by her parents or to a bridegroom by his. It remains the exclusive property of the recipient, but failing direct heirs returns to the donor's family. In the case of cattle given as *yipe* young born after the marriage of the recipient become the joint property of husband and wife. *Yipe* may be sold, and this extinguishes all hereditary or reversionary rights in it except when the proceeds of a sale of *yipe* are used to buy fresh land, in which case this land becomes *yipe* in place of the original gift.[1]

Land.

The question of property in land has been covered, at any rate as far as buildings and terraced land and plantations are concerned, in dealing with inheritance. There are, however, one or two questions that have not arisen. In the first place, it has sometimes occurred that prisoners of war, though in the first place occupying practically the position of slaves in the household of their captors, have been given land to cultivate and have been received into the clan. In such cases the land has in course of time become regarded as the property of the descendants of the original prisoner. Still, should these descendants wish to return to their own village, they would have, according to strict Angami custom, to give back to the clan, the kindred, or the descendants of the original owner all the property acquired by them, however rich they might have become in the meanwhile. Such a case occurred recently in Kohima village, the descendants of a runaway Memi, who had been bought from his captors and received into the Dapetsuma clan, selling all their property and returning to their ancestor's village after five generations. In this instance the claim of the clan was settled for a money payment. A second point arises in connection with jhum land. Terraced fields, wood plantations, gardens, building sites, and the greater part of jhum land is individual property and, subject to life interests, mortgages, etc., may be sold or otherwise disposed of at the will of the owner, though when selling an ancestral field the vendor retains a small fragment in nominal ownership lest he die or suffer misfortune. There is, however, in several Angami villages a certain amount of jhum land which, like land reserved for thatching grass

[1] *See* Appendix XIII, p. 455.

or for the preservation of cane for bridges, is the common property of a kindred or a clan or of the whole village. The cultivation of land of this sort is settled either by a system of general consent, arrived at after much discussion and many searchings of heart, or by a system of grab under which the man who wishes to cultivate goes and sets a mark on the land of his choice, and provided no one else has been there before and that he has not attempted to get so much land as to deprive the other members of the clan of an opportunity to obtain a similar amount, his claim to cultivate that year and the following year is admitted. A series of cultivations by the same man in the same place appears to set up a private right to the particular plot, and it is no doubt in this way that private rights in land have arisen. In some trans-frontier villages all land is still common property of the village. Of course, in jhuming it is the practice for the village, or at any rate the clan, to jhum together, as collective jhuming saves a vast deal of labour in fencing . and scaring birds. Indeed, a solitary patch jhumed by one household in the midst of surrounding jungle would stand a poor chance of surviving the depredations of birds and beasts. It is also not infrequently arranged that jhuming operations shall be carried on on one side of the village, while cattle owners may graze in the opposite direction only. In such an event the man who wilfully went and jhumed in the wrong direction would have no claim to compensation from cattle owners for damages to his crop by cattle. Jhum land that has not yet become the subject of private rights cannot, of course, be sold except by the clan or kindred owning it, though with their consent it might be possible for a man to sell his share in the common rights. Jhuming, however, is of quite secondary importance[1] in the Angami country, the Chakroma villages excepted. In these latter jhuming is practised almost to the exclusion of irrigated terraces.

Property other than land is not subject to customary

---

[1] And for this reason common rights in land still survive. Where jhuming is the normal form of cultivation, private rights have superseded common rights, as among the Semas and Aos.

restriction except in so far as weapons and ornaments worn by men always go to male heirs.

Settlement of disputes. The annexation of the Angami country has probably affected but little the internal arrangements of villages for their own ordering and governance. The Pehumas or chiefs, such as they were, seem to have had very little more authority than the " Gaonburas " nowadays appointed by Government, and that is saying very little. There occurred in some villages cases of the chieftainship passing on by inheritance. Stories are still remembered in Khonoma of two redoubtable chiefs, Dopule and Pelhu, who held sway over Khonoma, and the latter of whom is at present represented in the person of Fezherr, one of the Gaonburas of the Merhema clan. It is most unlikely, however, that the hereditary nature of such chieftainships depended on anything more than the influence, wealth, and intelligence of the chief's son's enabling him to retain the position afforded him by that of his father. At best the chief's position probably gave him no power except on the warpath. Nothing can be well managed by a debating society, but war not at all, and although a definite leader might be unnecessary for small head-hunting raids, pitched battles, such as sometimes took place, and expeditions on a large scale would necessitate someone's taking the lead, while leadership in war would doubtless give influence, though not authority, in the village in times of peace. Major Butler writes[1] : " The authority or title of the chief of a village is hereditary. The eldest son, on the death of his father, or even before his death if very infirm, succeeds to the dignity. In most villages there are generally two chiefs[2] (representing the two ' kelhu ' ?), but their authority is nominal. Their orders are obeyed so far only as they

[1] " Travels and Adventures in Assam," p. 146.
[2] He is probably referring to Kemovos, not chiefs. The Kemovo is hereditary, and there are usually two of them, but they are not chiefs, nor necessarily leaders in war, *pehuma*. A French writer on the subject catches the Angami attitude very well : " Ils n'ont point de chef : ' Voilà notre maître ! ' disent-ils en fichant leur javelot en terre (" Nouvelle Géographie Universelle," Vol. VIII, p. 398.)

HOUSES IN KHEZAKENOMA

[See p. 53

PAINTED FRONT OF A RICH MAN'S HOUSE

[See p. 55

CONVENTIONAL
MITHAN HEAD.
See page 66.

POSITION OF THREADS. See page 61.

A *Breast-rod*
B *Shed stick*
C *Lease-rod*
D *Bram*
K *Heddle*

DUG OUT BEER VAT

[See p. 66

accord with the wishes and convenience of the community."
Captain Butler writes : [1] " The Naga Peuma is, in fact,
simply *primus inter pares*, and often that only *pro tem.*"
The Gaonburas of the present day hold very much the
same position. They are not ordinarily hereditary, being
appointed by the Deputy Commissioner, more or less on
the nomination of the clan, but they are certainly without-
any more authority than the ancient " Pehuma," and more
often than not are compelled to disgorge for the benefit of
their clan the small sum which they are paid yearly as
commission on their collection or house-tax. Of course,
the personal element is always present, and Gaonburas
may be found now and then commanding no little influence
and respect, but as an institution not much attention is
paid to them, except when the villagers, or a party of the
villagers, wish for their services as a go-between with the
local officials. Before the Deputy Commissioner's Court
was available, disputes, when settled at all, were probably
settled by a sort of informal council of elders, who would
discuss the matter under dispute with one another, the
parties, and the general public at great length, until some
sort of agreement was arrived at. Regular customs with
regard to the manner of dealing with offences certainly
existed, and in the absence of any higher authority there
is no doubt but that the elders managed to arbitrate
after some fashion or other in most disputes. At the same
time those who know the Angami will have some difficulty
in realising how any except the most trifling disputes ever
did get settled within the village, at any rate with any finality
at all.   To quote Captain Butler again : " Every man follows
the dictates of his own will, a form of the purest democracy
which it is very difficult to conceive of as existing even for
a single day ; and yet that it does exist here is an undeniable
fact."

In deciding disputes questions of customs would be, and
still are, referred naturally enough to the old men of the
clan, and, as even the Angami has some respect for his
elders, the decision of old men in regard to matters of custom

[1] *Journal of Asiat. Soc.*, Pt. I, No. IV, 1875.

is more or less final, though it sometimes happens that a young man will snap his fingers at custom and defy his fellow-villagers to do their worst. Questions of fact are

Oaths. usually decided by oath, and an oath, at any rate if the lives of others are made responsible for its truth as well as the life of the swearer, is usually accepted by either party, and is usually, provided always that it embraces a fairly large number of lives, say those of a kindred, evidence that the swearer and the others whose lives are offered believe in the truth of their case.[1] Angamis are not usually willing to risk their lives by pledging them to the truth of a state-ment of a relative unless they are fairly well satisfied that the statement is true, for a false oath is held to entail death or at least misfortune as the result of it. Cases are every now and then quoted by Angamis in which So-and-so died as a result of taking a false oath. In a dispute involving a large tract of land between the villages of Keruma and Sihama a man of Keruma took an oath (as to the boundaries lying in a certain place) on the lives of all the village. When he fell ill the same year of a mysterious disease accompanied by horrid swellings and pustules over his whole body (such swellings are particularly associated with false oaths), his son went hurriedly to the spot where the boundary stones had been placed as a result of the oath, and destroyed the cairn set up by Keruma, in the hope of saving his father's life by a renunciation of the claim, which was, however, reasserted a few years later. The chief difficulty in settling disputes by oath is in finding the actual facts to the swearing of which both parties agree. In some cases there is naturally not much question about what these are to be, but it usually happens that one side wishes to insert some clause, often more or less, perhaps wholly, irrelevant, to which they know the other party cannot swear; when, however, the facts to be sworn are agreed upon, the oath is administered, usually, but not necessarily, by a third party, to the swearer, who repeats the sentences after the administrator of the oath as couples being married repeat their " troth " in the Anglican ritual after the priest. The swearer turns his cloth so that the seams are outwards[2] and

---

[1] *See* Appendix XIII, p. 455.

[2] As in the case of warriors on the warpath. *See* p. 151.

undoes the knot in his back hair ; often but not always he " touches wood," holding in his right hand a twig or piece of stick, perhaps as a symbol that the false swearer may wither like a dead twig.[1] The various sentences are usually each emphasised by a downward motion of the right arm and hand both by the administrator and the swearer of the oath. After stating the facts sworn to and the number of lives responsible for their truth, the oath concludes with the formula : " If I lie in what I now say, then betwixt heaven and earth, let me not grow like other men, but let me become as ruin, as burnt out fire, as rotted twine."[2] The Memi form of the oath contains the expression " huchi jukharhe nakhu "—" bury me between the inverted heaven and earth," and a man wishing to swear a false oath tries to substitute for this phrase, or for part of it, the expression " huchu nari " (= " cock's genitals "), making nonsense of the whole oath, and it is said that this fraud every now and then succeeds in deluding the other side, and no doubt it is occasionally successful when the other party are of another group ordinarily speaking Angami, Kezami, or some other different dialect and not fully conversant with the Memi language. Some forms of oath, not now in general use among Angamis, are mentioned

---

[1] See Appendix XIII, p. 455.

[2]
A che de kepuko	ketidzü puro	ti kidzü-nu donu
My now words spoken	false speak–if	sky earth–from between
lhu me metu-meta	kenyepfu	keka kemhe
grow men equal–other	let me be forbidden	ruin burnt-out-fire
kerri kerro	tsü towe	
twine rotted	let me do.	

A Sema oath runs:—" As the aiyeshu rots, as the gourd-vine rots, let me. rot; let earth from a man's grave choke me." (Aiyeshu keghashi, apukhi keghashi, ighapeni; akumo ayeghi-namo ipahakhi.) This would be accompanied by the biting of earth and a piece of the swearer's own hair on the blade of a weapon. See Appendix XIII, p. 455.

The oath on the village water is one of the strongest known to Semas, and prevents the person who takes it falsely from eating fish and crossing streams. An oath on the Dayang river, which has a similar effect, is one of the most powerful in the Naga Hills, at any rate among the Lhota and Sema villages near the Dayang. An oath on the Tizu water has a similar power in the neighbourhood of that river.

by both Major and Captain Butler [1] ; the severing into two parts between them of a dog, fowl, or spear-head held by each of the two parties, or the pulling in half of a live fowl by the two parties, one holding its head and the other its leg, "intimating that treachery or breach of the agreement would merit the same treatment" ; the holding or biting a gun-barrel, spear-head, or tiger's tooth with the declaration, " If I do not faithfully perform this my promise, may I fall by this weapon," or animal [2] ; and the standing within a circle of rope or cane and repeating a formula to the effect that if the swearer breaks his oath he may be caused to rot away as the cane rots. Captain Butler also mentions that one oath, "generally voluntarily offered after defeat, is to snatch up a handful of grass and earth, and after placing it on the head, to shove it into the mouth, chewing it and pretending to eat it, one of the most disagreeable and literal renderings of the metaphorical term 'eating dirt' I have ever witnessed." This last oath mentioned by Captain Butler is probably the oath of peace taken at the conclusion of hostilities, of which the formula ran :—

" If any man of my village break this peace first, then, so long as water flows in my spring and so long as the sun and the moon remain in the heaven, shall my men be defeated ; and all the forest and red earth shall not be enough to cover my corpses and much blood shall flow on my side."

Major Butler also mentions that on the taking of an oath between two villages a large stone would be erected as a monument with the words " as long as this stone stands on the earth, no differences shall occur between us."

[1] Major Butler, op. cit., p. 154. Captain Butler, "Rough Notes on the Angami Nagas," Journ. Asiat. Soc., Pt. I, No. IV, 1875.

[2] This form of oath is frequently used by the Semas and Lhotas, a piece of earth, frequently from a grave, or in a land dispute from the disputed land, and a bit of the swearer's hair being added to the gun, spear, dao, or tiger's tooth and bitten with them. The strongest form of an oath known to a Sema is that on his own flesh, and I have seen a Sema, to attest his innocence, snatch up a dao and chop a joint of the finger almost off, biting through the remaining flesh and swallowing the fragment of his finger. In this particular case the oath was undoubtedly false, but the question was one of murder.

With regard to oaths, it should be noticed that it is genna to take an oath on days between moons, non-moon days being known to the Kemovo. Angamis are also, generally speaking, exceedingly unwilling to take an oath as regards the future. If asked to do so they will usually reply that they do not intend to do anything contrary to the desire of the person asking them to swear, but that they might inadvertently do so under the influence of liquor or of some deity and thus unintentionally render themselves liable to the consequences of a false oath. In small matters, however, such as in the assessment of a village, it is possible to make the headmen less inclined to deception than they usually are by insisting on their expressing a solemn desire to be caught by a tiger or bitten by a snake should they tell a lie or conceal any person who should be assessed to revenue.[1] Should an oath be taken as a result of agreement that an oath should be administered, the truth of the swearer's statement would ordinarily be assumed, and if the oath were false he would have to abide by the consequences of perjury, whatever they might be. In the case, however, of an oath taken on several ives, any one of the persons responsible may at any time withdraw their life, in which case the oath is null, and to obviate this it is often agreed at the time of swearing that, in case of such a withdrawal at any future date, a fine of so many rupees will be paid by the swearer, or the land will revert to the other party, or that some other such penalty shall be forfeited. Should the oath prove manifestly false, the other persons

---

[1] Compare the oath of the Dusun of British North Borneo :—

" I swear by Kenharingan above and by In-the-earth, that I will speak the truth, if I do not do so, may a crocodile eat me, may a tree fall on me in the jungle," etc. (*Journ. R. Anthrop. Institute*, Vol. XLIII, 1913, p. 439.)

The formula of a tree falling on one in the jungle might easily be used in a Naga oath and would be in absolute consonance with the idea contained in the being eaten by a tiger or in other forms of unnatural death. Among the Lhotas and Semas death by the falling of (or from) a tree entails the same prohibitions as to the property of the deceased as being killed by a tiger. Man-eating crocodiles are, of course, unknown in the Naga Hills, though the Semas have a legend of a huge fish that climbs up out of the water to eat man, and which can be speared by lying in wait near a baby in a basket, the monster being attracted by the crying of the child.

whose lives have thus been placed in jeopardy will on their part claim compensation from the false swearer, and might in serious cases expel him from their community. An outbreak of small-pox in one of the Sopvoma villages in the Memi country three or four years ago was put down to the taking of a false oath and followed by the expulsion of the perjurer from the village.

Punish-
ment of
offences.

In a case in which a person accused of any crime against the social code failed to take an oath, he would be punished according to the customary rules. There are among the Angamis customary punishments for most faults, and no fine distinction is drawn in the punishment of offences between a purely social sanction and a definitely magico-religious sanction. Offences such as the breaking of genna would probably be punished with a fine paid to the village fund or to the clansmen, unless the circumstances were aggravated by some untoward consequence, when banish-ment, a favourite punishment with Angamis, for a longer or shorter duration of time would be inflicted. Rape was punished by the beating of the raptor by the kindred of the woman and by his expulsion from the village for three months. Theft was always punished by exacting from the thief seven times the value of the property stolen, the fine being paid to the victim of the theft, whose property was also returned to him if recovered. If the thief were so poor as to have no property with which to pay the sevenfold damages, he was beaten by the kindred of the victim, and it is said that his own kindred, if a different one, would not interfere. Further, the labelling of a man " *Kerüguma*," " thief," inflicted great shame on the culprit.[1] The same

[1] Among the trans-frontier Semas theft is still occasionally punished with death. In 1912 Ghokwi, chieftain of a Trans-Tizu Sema (Zümomi) village, had a complaint from a Tukomi Sangtam village tributary to him that one of his own villagers had committed theft in this tributary village. Ghokwi sent for the man and, finding the story true, speared him out of hand. Among the Changs, not only is the thief himself killed on the third offence (he is let off twice), but his wife and children are killed as well, an effective way of stopping hereditary tendencies to crime. It is a common and, as far as my experience goes, a true saying among Nagas, that the child of a thief will grow up a thief himself. Kohima jail at the moment of writing contains a Chang thief for whose blood half-

holds good of the term "*Themu*," "murderer," which conveys excessive ignominy. Three degrees of homicide were recognised. Homicide by accident was punished by seven years' banishment from the village,[1] and sometimes by confiscation of all land as well. This was sold by auction, though in the case of homicide by accident the bidding would not go high and the offender's relations would be allowed to buy in the land at a price below its real value, while the offender might take away all personal property, including cattle. In the case of homicide in a fight a public meeting was held to decide on the facts. The guilty man was punished by the auction of all his property and seven years' banishment, and called "*themu*." Viselhu of Khonoma, who was convicted in 1914 of causing the death of a man of the Thevoma clan in the Thevoma-Semoma riot in 1906, asked for seven years' imprisonment in preference to seven years' banishment, on the ground that the latter would in this case have entailed the stigma of being called "*themu*." In such cases the descendants or relatives of the murdered man would not be allowed to take revenge on the "*themu*" after his return, on pain of similar treatment in their turn. The most heinous form of homicide was that by stealth or treachery, perhaps in revenge for some real or fancied wrong, but not in open

a-dozen trans-frontier villages are thirsting. He fled from one village to another, thieving in each, and in his last trans-frontier residence he ran matters so close that his wife and child were killed and he himself barely escaped with a split face. His wife's relations are also waiting for him as being the cause of her death. I heard of a case of a woman thief among the Changs, the sister of the man just mentioned, who was rolled in a mud-hole and stamped upon in the mud in order to punish her for her theft without doing her serious injury since she was a woman. Her husband's property was also sold up entirely, but then the woman had stolen from the village cemetery, a very serious offence. The Lhotas used to sell their thieves to the Aos, who cut up the men and kept the women as slaves.

[1] For injuries not amounting to death the Lhota tribe expels for a lesser period. Quite recently a man named Mangethang was expelled from Phiro at the instance of the village for three years for causing a fellow-villager to fracture his leg. He threatened him so that he fell from a 'machan.' The Lhotas also used to deal most effectively with troublesome persons by putting their foot through a hole in a log and wedging it there so that they could only move about with difficulty.

fight. It was dealt with as homicide in a fight, but not only the murderer but his whole kindred were expelled for seven years, and in some villages even for a whole generation. All these punishments refer, of course, to homicide within the village community, within which it is genna to kill, though what happened in the case of adultery, which is said by Angamis, and which is recorded by Captain Butler,[1] to have been punished with the death at any rate of the guilty wife, in the days of Angami independence, it is difficult to say. Adultery nowadays is punished by divorce, the woman being deprived of her usual one-third share of movable property. In the case of infidelity on the part of the husband, divorce may follow, but the husband is not in any way penalised in such a divorce, which is treated as divorce by mutual consent, the wife taking one-third of the joint personal property. Probably in any of the cases above mentioned the general rule of expulsion would have been difficult to enforce as between different hostile clans in a village divided among itself. The murder of a man of one clan by another in such a village as Khonoma, Jotsoma, or Viswema would much more likely lead to fighting between the clans than to the murderer's expulsion. In cases of difference between private persons of different villages, the vendetta, on which Major Butler lays so much stress,[2] would, of course, be the only and the inevitable method of settlement. Such a vendetta, entailing blood for blood at least until the tale of lives were equal, or perhaps with more likelihood, *ad infinitum*, each side wishing to be ahead of the score of the other, would probably embrace at least the kindred of the two parties. It would not, however, necessarily extend beyond the clan, and it would be quite possible for all the other clans in both villages to be friendly, while the clans of the respective parties to the vendetta were on head-taking terms.

From a vendetta of this sort it is but a short step to definite war. War, however, among Angamis when independent, as among the unadministered Semas to-day, contained elements of formality and even of a pomp and circum-

---

[1] *Loc. cit.* [2] *Op. cit.*, p. 156.

stance by no means associated with mere head-taking. The
proper proceedings, preparatory to war, opened by the War.
sending of a messenger to the village with which there was
a dispute, or with which the challenging village desired a
trial of strength. This messenger would probably be a
man well versed in the dialect of the other village and
known to them through trading operations if possible.
He would challenge the village to do battle and would name
the day, saying, " The men of my village will come on such
and such a day. Our spears are very long, come out and
try if you can eat them," or giving some such message.
Not a few such challenges have been sent in the past to
Government Officers in charge of the Naga Hills District.
The messenger might send the message through a third
village or might go in person to the village challenged.
In the latter case he would always run some risk of having
his head taken for his impertinence, in which case informal
hostilities would commence, but if his challenge were
accepted the challenging village would come out to meet
the challenged on the day named, both parties being in
full dress and armed with shield, two or three spears each,
and dao.

Major Butler [1] mentions that before setting out on a war
expedition " the chief appointed to command the party
consults the usual omens, which proving propitious, a
fowl is killed and cooked, and all partake of it." These
omens would be taken in the ordinary way by slicing a
piece of the " *chiese* " plant, after which the fowl mentioned
by Major Butler would be strangled and the usual omen
taken from the way it crossed its legs in death. For a
good omen the right leg should cross over the left.

Warriors going out to war may not carry their spears
pointing back over their shoulders, the ordinary way, but
must carry them pointing forwards or straight upright ; nor
must they wear their clothes inside out (*i.e.*, with the seams
inwards).

The opponents would halt at about a spear's throw
apart and start to argue, then to abuse each other. This

[1] *Op. cit.*, p. 149.

would be probably followed by a shower of stones from
one side or the other till someone started throwing spears.
By the time the two sides were thoroughly worked up the
weaker spirits on both sides would have run away, and
eventually one side or other, finding itself lacking in numbers
or in courage, would take bodily to flight, often throwing
away its weapons in the panic. Casualties would probably
not be very heavy on either side, unless one was seized with
a panic early in the proceedings, so that the other side was
able to pursue in large numbers. After this the war would
become a mere series of head-taking raids with no formality,
carried on by both sides according to impulse and
opportunity. Of course, war among Nagas, as among
civilised nations, is by no means necessarily prefaced by a
formal declaration, and more often than not would start
by an ambush or a raid on the part of one of two villages.
It is a well recognised fact that the village which gets the
first blow in this manner scores heavily, as it gets perhaps
twenty heads or more by taking the enemy unawares,
whereas after both sides are on the look-out for raids it is
difficult to get more than two or three at a time. At the
same time, formal battles on a large scale have taken place
on many well-known occasions. The challenge of Kekrima
to Captain Reid has already been mentioned, and there is
another case related by Khonoma of their defeat by Kekrima.
As the account comes from the defeated party, it may be
received with a certain amount of confidence, and it is
particularly interesting as showing a certain use of tactics,
which are not usually associated with Naga operations.
Mr. Hodson[1] describes war among the Naga villages as
" at its best a blind struggle between mobs of individuals, without guidance or coherence, never a
conflict of well-organised masses with a view to
intelligent co-operation," but in the case of the Kekrima
victory over Khonoma, a village renowned for warfare, the
success of Kekrima is ascribed to the studied disposition of
the Kekrima forces. The Kekrima centre was formed of
the usual type of Angami warrior armed with spears and

[1] " Naga Tribes of Manipur," p. 113.

shield, who advanced in the usual manner dancing, shouting, and spinning their spears. This main body, however, was supported on the right wing by a party of light infantry, so to speak, armed with daos only, and on the left wing by a party armed with the wooden mallets used for breaking clods of earth. The Khonoma forces were fewer but awaited the Kekrima advance in a compact body with entire confidence, strong in the possession of twelve Tower muskets, a very formidable battery. The Khonoma artillery did succeed in repulsing the main body of the Kekrima attack, but the wings rushed in at a critical moment, probably when the redoubtable muskets were being reloaded, and did so much damage that the Khonoma braves were forced to retire precipitately from the field with considerable loss, the enemy capturing some of their guns, a victory notable in the βατραχομυομαχια of Naga warfare. Another episode likewise memorable among these " battles of kites and crows " was the assault on the Lhota village of Phiro by five Rengma villages helped by Jotsoma and Mozema. The allies are related to have tried to carry the defences of Phiro by assault, no easy matter, as they consisted of a twenty-foot ditch surmounted by a wall, the whole bristling with well-seasoned panjis. The repulse of the assault was followed by a sortie and Phiro added 100 heads to the collection in the village tree. The figures, however, come from Phiro itself and must be well salted before consumption.

It has been mentioned before that the Angamis do not poison their weapons. Poisoning wells, however, has been practised by them. Major Butler [1] relates how the village of Chephama " bruised and steeped a poisonous root in the water " of their well, with unfortunate results on the sepoys camping at the village. He adds that " the Naga prisoners said that while the root was fresh its effects were what had been experienced (dizziness and heaviness of the upper eyelids) ; but if allowed to rot, it would kill all who partook of it in three or four days." It is worth noticing that on one of the " Mozungjami " expeditions, the Chang village of Tuensang poisoned its well by collecting and

[1] *Op. cit.*, p. 113.

depositing in it the dung of dogs, pigs, and fowls, and a number of sepoys and coolies contracted dysentery. Also during the siege of Kohima in the Angami rising the Khonoma braves put the head of a sepoy they had killed into the spring from which the garrison drew their water in order to poison them, or to prevent their use of the well.

Prisoners taken in war were usually killed. It was, however, genna to kill any prisoner who had succeeded in touching with his lips the arm of any one of his enemies. Such a prisoner would be held to ransom, kept as a servant, or simply released. In the latter event peace, or at any rate a truce, would follow almost as a matter of course, the released prisoner intervening and affording an excellent excuse for a cessation of hostilities. Prisoners seem to have been frequently kept as servants, particularly women, but slavery as an institution and involving a trade in slaves, though existent, seems to have affected only a very small proportion of the population. Children were sometimes kidnapped and sold, and so were women. One of the interpreters now on the Deputy Commissioner's staff was a Rengma taken as a child by Angamis and sold to Kacha Nagas as a slave. There is a Lhota woman in Pongithung who was sold as a child to Kukis and has returned recently to her village at the age of about sixty. Most slaves, however, seem to have been exceedingly well treated and eventually received into the community which they served, and the practice of selling slaves for execution and distribution of their flesh, which prevails among the Konyak tribes north of the Dikhu and among the Rangpang[1] Nagas, and which was occasionally practised by the Aos, did not apparently obtain among the Angamis.[2] Major Butler notes the value of slaves as estimated by Angamis: " A male slave is worth one cow and three conch shells, a female

---

[1] See " Human Sacrifice in Ancient Assam," Gait.

[2] Among the Phoms a small boy of about ten years old will fetch from three cows to two mithan. Men will even sell their nephews or brothers at times, but not as a rule, unless they are thieves. When sold to Konyak villages they are usually cut up, but the Phoms themselves do not count killing a slave as taking a head, or say that they do not.

SKETCH
OF THE
HILL FORT KONOMA
ANGAHMEH NAGAH HILLS
Taken by Troops
Composed of the 1st & 2nd Assam Lt Infantry, Local Ar

Under the Command of Major Hy. Fo
with Capt.n D. Reid Commanding Artillery, Lieuts Campe
D.r A.M.cLean in Medical Charge, under the Superinten
J. Butler Principal Assistant Agent Governor
December 11th 1850

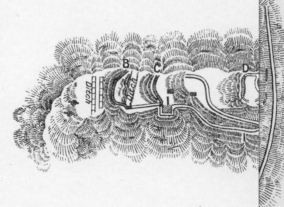

A

A *Position of Mortars at 600Yds distance. East side o*
  On south, high Mountains.
B *First Moorcha of stone 36Ft long, strengthened wit*
  having a command of 20Ft above outer edge of
  broad and 14Ft deep and entirely covered wit
  4,6, and 3 inches long, driven pointing into groun
C *A stone Moorcha of earth, stone and wood 7Ft*
  of 10Ft above the defence at B and a deep
  these two Moorchas, cut out of the rock, (whic
D *A stone defence to protect the houses from*
E *Earth and stone defence with a command of*
  and deep ditch cut out of rock.
  Ascent up a ladder.
F G *Stone defences with ditch.*
  H *A very strong Moorcha 35Ft long and 9Ft thi*
  loopholed, with a communication leading in
  covered way extends all round the Fort
  standing. Traverses at weak points.
  I *Loopholed planking defences. Extreme lengt.*

  Ltd. Edin.

slave is worth three cows and four or five conch shells." [1]
The torture of prisoners occasionally took place, though
very very rarely. It is related that a party from Rekro-
Kezama once caught a man of Kigwema alive and tied him
up and kept him for a month, stoning him and clubbing
him from time to time until he died. The torture of the
Lhota warrior Chakarimo by Savi, chief of the Angami
village of Phekekrima, has been already mentioned. The
unfortunate Lhota was tied to a stake and had pieces cut
from him by the bucks and boys of Phekekrima village.
When he had been cut into 312 pieces he died, and the spot
where the torture took place, between Phekekrima and
Chekrama, is still called "Chekarimo Zhikenu." Major
Butler mentions [2] the execution of a Jotsoma coolie by
Kacha Naga warriors of Lakema, who tied the man to
a tree and used him as a target for spears. But on
the whole torture seems to have been the exception, and
rarely indulged in by Angamis. [3]

The Angami precautions against the assault of a village
were elaborate. Most of their precautions have been noticed
in describing the village, and it is enough to add that when
anticipating attack they would escarp the sides of the hill
on which the village stood, protect by pits and panjis all
possible routes of approach, remove at night the poles which
served as bridges for ditches and ladders for walls, and
collect large masses of stones, both for rolling down the
hill on to the approaching enemy and for use as missiles
proper. The remarkable lengths to which a powerful
village might go in elaborating its defences may be gathered
from the map of Khonoma made by Major Butler after its
capture in 1850. [4]

[1] *Op. cit.*, p. 157.   [2] *Op. cit.*, p. 169.

[3] I am inclined to think that these stories of torture are always open to
grave suspicion. A gruesome tale of the torture by a Yachumi village of
a Sema prisoner was recently brought to me in Mokokchung which proved
to be a pure invention. A Sema raider having been wounded by the
enemy and having hidden in the jungle, his friends came home and related
how his hands and feet had been cut off, and he had been dragged round
the village and tortured to death by the enemy. Two days later he
turned up alive.

[4] *Op. cit.*, p. 199.

While war might be occasioned by a varied number of circumstances, a private feud, a land dispute, mere lust of blood, anything, in fact, from a rude remark to the taking of a head, the general cause usually ascribed to the outbreak of war by Angamis is increase in male population. War is regarded as the certain accompaniment of an increase in the number of the village bucks, and the conclusion of peace as the no less certain result of a marked diminution in the same. After the opening conflict a state of war must usually have meant no great drain in population, but merely the taking of occasional heads. It would ordinarily be ended by one side's happening to lose heavily either in raiding or by an epidemic of disease, or perhaps by a common desire on both sides to cultivate in safety. The oaths taken at the conclusion of peace have been given above, and the cessation of hostilities would be symbolised by the blunting of a dao, hammered upon a stone till the edge was destroyed. Among some of the Angamis the making of peace was also marked by the sacrifice of a cat.[1] In many cases one side would agree to pay annual tribute to the other, the tribute being either merely a nominal one of a few beads or a substantial payment in mithan or salt. The contingency of conquest does not usually occur, though some of the Kacha Naga villages seem to have been entirely dominated by settlements of Khonoma Angamis who superimposed on them their own customs.[2]

Head-hunting. Head-hunting as an accompaniment of the blood feud and of war has been mentioned, but so much significance has been attached to the practice that it possibly deserves some special notice. Some recent writers on the tribes of North Borneo[3] have sought for an explanation of the

---

[1] The two Phom villages of Hukpang and Ourangkong are often at war. When they make peace they kill a slave and hang up his head in the place where the fighting began.

[2] This, no doubt, was partly due to the razing of Khonoma village and the dispersal of its population after the Angami rebellion. It was some time before the population was allowed to return at all, and many seem to have remained for good in Kacha Naga, and some Memi, villages.

[3] "The Pagan Tribes of North Borneo," Hose and McDougal, 1912.

practice in a desire for the hair for the ornamentation of
the shield and the sword-hilt, or in the custom of killing
slaves to accompany a dead chief beyond the grave.
Neither suggestion seems to hold good of the Angamis.
The first would, at any rate if applied to the Angamis or
other Naga tribes, appear as an inversion of cause and effect,
while the second practice is not known in the Angami
country. Head-hunting in one form or another is a widespread practice, and whatever the various incidents of
head-hunting in various quarters of the globe, the ultimate
reason of its existence in any particular spot must probably
be sought in some deep-rooted and innate characteristic of
human nature.[1] Among the Naga tribes, at any rate,
head-hunting, though associated with a vague idea of the
benefits accruing from human sacrifice, must also be
connected in no small degree with ordinary, everyday
human vanity. What man, or at the least what Naga,
who has killed his enemy does not want to boast about it ?
And unless he can show the body, where is the proof ?
Most savages are somewhat economical of truth ; at any
rate the Naga is when it comes to his exploits in war and
the chase. If the slayer can produce the body of the slain
his statement is likely to be accepted as true, and since
retrieving the body would be a laborious, not to say often
dangerous, proceeding, the head is the natural part of it to
bring back as testimony, as it gives a definite assurance that
the foe has been killed, not scotched. This at any rate is
the Angami explanation.[2] Moreover, if it can be retrieved,

[1] It is worth quoting from Mr. O. Henry :—
"Truly the . . . merry head-hunter . . . reduced art and philosophy
to a simple code. To take your adversary's head, to basket it at the
portal of your castle, to see it lying there, a dead thing, with its cunning
and stratagems and power gone—Is there a better way to foil his plots,
to refute his arguments, to establish your superiority over his skill and
wisdom ? "

[2] Among the Lhotas any human flesh brought into the village on
return from an expedition is "vetted," so to speak, by a board of old
men, who sit and hold a sort of inquest on the flesh produced to make
sure that it really is what it is stated to be by the bringer. And until
the trophy has been passed by this board no ceremony can be performed
for the success. I am indebted to Mr. J. P. Mills for having drawn my
attention to this point.

the Angami does prefer the whole body, and if the whole body is not available he will take the arms, hands, legs, and feet of the corpse as well as its head.[1] And in this connection it must also not be forgotten that the Naga does not fight in the open country and under the eyes of his fellows, but in heavy jungle and in raiding parties of small numbers from one upwards,[2] where none can observe his deeds of daring. Nor does the Naga make so very radical a distinction between human heads and heads of game. Man is the biggest game and the most dangerous game, and his pursuit is therefore attended with precautions which may be unnecessary in the case of smaller game, but he is still game. There is, after all, not so much to separate a sportsman's desire for, say, a fine buffalo head and a Naga's desire for the head of a man. Most Britishers are head-hunters at heart, and to a Naga every sort of head is welcome. All the skulls of larger animals killed by him are religiously kept, from that of an otter to that of an elephant, while even the heads of small birds may often be seen nailed to his house. As the Naga kills primarily for food, he recognises no differences in sex or age, and although he undoubtedly takes a pride in killing, say, a sambhar with a fine head, yet the heads of does and fawns are hung up as trophies beside it. So it is with his human heads. He recognises no distinctions between human heads provided they have cut their teeth ; if they have not cut their teeth they are not taken.

Up to a certain point then, and with the exception that the flesh of most animals is eaten and man's is not, the distinction between the pursuit of man and of animals is one of degree rather than of kind.[3] It is true that the successful hunting of man is followed by genna, but so in

---

[1] In any case cuts are made in the arms and legs of the victim in order to entitle the slayer to the armlets and leggings that form part of the warrior's *insignia*.

[2] Small and stealthy raids for heads are called " *Rüzutsü* " in contradistinction to " *Rüdise*," a war expedition. The omens are taken in the same way for the former as for the latter already described.

[3] See, in particular, the gennas for head-taking and for successful hunting in Part IV. The similarity is striking.

ANGAMI WOMAN CARRYING GOURD OF *zu* IN A BASKET
(*thĕkrākor*)

[See p. 65

ÜBO. See page 70.

DECORATIVE CLAY MODELS

[See p. 67

TEHUBA AT MOZEMA

[See p. 48

varying degrees is that of animals. A strict genna precedes the robbing of bees' nests—a somewhat more dangerous game than ordinary hunting ; a genna follows a successful chase of a tiger or leopard. Again the killing of a man entitles the killer to certain distinctive articles of dress, but so does the killing of a leopard or tiger. Among the Angamis this only goes as far as the shield on which the skin may be worn,·but among the Semas it entitles a man to wear a boar's tush collar, one of the recognised signs of head-taking, and among the Rengmas and some of the Lhotas to a distinctive cloth also usually associated with the killing of man. Of course, Naga tradition associates man and the tiger very closely together. It may be noticed in this connection that among the Konyak tribes it is common for a slave to be bought for the chief's son to kill in order that the boy may wear ceremonial dress without risking the dangers of war. The wretched slave is tied up and the boy kills him with a dao, pieces of his flesh being distributed throughout the young men of the Morung. This custom brings us nearer to another idea which underlies head-taking, and that is the idea of sacrifice, the notion that the killing of a human being is conducive to the prosperity of the community or of the crops. Here again we find among the Lhotas a parallel between head-taking and fishing, as the yield of the harvest is connected, in some villages at any rate, Changsang, for instance, with the success or failure of village fish-"poisonings." The idea, however, of the benefit conferred by human flesh, or the taking of human life, is a very strong one among Nagas, though it is perhaps disappearing under the present *régime* of peace. Major Butler [1] mentions the sale of a Kachari boy by some Angamis to some men of a Lhota village : " A man of the village having died immediately after the purchase, it was considered a bad omen, and that ill-luck had befallen them on account of this captive child. They, therefore, flayed the poor boy alive, cutting off his flesh bit by bit until he died . . . then divided the body, giving a piece of flesh to each man in the village to put into his ' dolu,' a

[1] *Op. cit.*, p. 189.

large corn basket. By this they suppose all evil will be averted, their good fortune will return, and plentiful crops of grain will be ensured." It is no doubt partially with the same notion that Naga coolies taken on trans-frontier expeditions so carefully save up little bits of "meat" to put in the Morung when they return, and to divide among their kindred. Only quite recently some Lhotas of Chingaki were punished by the Deputy Commissioner for going across the frontier and buying some flesh of a person killed in a head-taking raid, and selling part of it to another village after their return. The Angamis too had a custom, to quote Major Butler, "of cutting off the heads, hands, and feet of any one they can meet with, without provocation or pre-existing enmity, merely to stick them up in their fields and so ensure a good crop of grain." Finally, the late Mr. A. W. Davis, writing in 1898[1] as Deputy Commissioner of the Naga Hills, says,

"There can be no doubt that all the tribes in this district consider that by killing a human being in certain cases they are doing the most effectual thing towards averting the displeasure of some particular evil spirit (*terhoma*). Amongst the Angamis especially this idea is very prevalent, and there have been two cases of murders committed within the last five years near Kohima, the only object of which was to propitiate an evil spirit. I will describe these cases in detail.

"(a) Kigwema case.—In the autumn of 1891, small-pox, which was very prevalent, attacked the two lower *khels*[2] of Kigwema village, and a large proportion of the inhabitants died. The two upper *khels*, the people of which all had been vaccinated, remained free of the disease. As, however, Nagas had at that time but little faith in vaccination, the people of these two *khels* determined to make themselves as safe as possible. A village council was therefore called, and it was decided that four men should be sent out to bring in a head as offering to the ' *terhoma* ' in order that the plague of small-pox might be averted. Four men were accordingly sent. They went and lay in wait by the cultivation path of a neighbouring village, and killed a

[1] Gait, "Human Sacrifices in Ancient Assam."
[2] *Khel* here is the part of the village inhabited by a clan—*thino*, and the clan occupying it.

woman, a small boy, and the baby he was carrying as they were returning alone from their fields. The baby's head and an ear each from the other two were cut off, carried away, and buried in the vicinity of the murderers'[1] village. This murder was, from the Naga point of view, eminently successful ; the angry deity was appeased, and the two upper *khels* of Kigwema remained exempt from the disease, which decimated the two lower *khels*. A similar case under exactly similar circumstances is said to have occurred at the village of Jakhama near Kigwema during the previous epidemic of small-pox which occurred about twenty years ago.

" (*b*) There is a very general superstition among the Angamis and Semas that to kill a human being and place a small portion of the flesh in the murderer's fields is a specific to ensure a good crop, and this is said to have been the reason that prompted certain men of Purobami to murder two men, a woman, and a child near the Sijju River towards the end of 1895. The two men were partially scalped, while the child was taken away alive and killed outside the village. Murders like these partake of the nature of sacrifices, as their object is to avert disaster and so to ensure good crops.

" Before we annexed their country, the Aos were great slave owners, and these slaves were occasionally made use of for a semi-sacrificial purpose, *e.g.*, two villages are at war and are desirous of making peace. It is found that one side has taken more heads than the other. To make things equal, and as a sacrifice to the spirits of the dead who have gone unavenged, an agreement would be arrived at that the village which had taken the fewest heads should receive one or more slaves from the other village.[2] These slaves were bound and left at a spot agreed upon beforehand. There they were found by the young men of the receiving village, who killed them and carried off their heads in triumph. Thus were the spirits of their dead restrained from troubling the living. A case of this kind, in which Kanching gave, and Ungma village received, slaves, occurred not very long before we took over the Ao country.

" I have been frequently told by Aos that human

[1] The ringleader was that Kasakre of whom a sketch by Colonel Wood-thorpe is reproduced in this volume.

[2] Longsa when they attacked Kanching, lost many heads, and Kanching only one, but when making peace Longsa are said to have given Kanching a slave to kill in place of the man they had lost.

sacrifices are not infrequent among certain of the Trans-Dikhu tribes.   The method is said to be as follows : When the village jhums are ready for firing, a slave is tied up in the middle of them.   The jhums are then lighted, and the slave is burnt to 'death.   A sacrifice like this ensures a good crop."[1]

As regards the disposition of heads, we find one frequent difference between the treatment of those of animals and those of human beings. The heads of domestic animals are, it is true, set up in the fields where they have been sacrificed by those tribes who sacrifice in the fields, but the heads of animals killed in hunting are invariably hung up in the house of the hunter, with the exception usually of the skulls of tigers and leopards.   On the other hand, heads taken from human beings are, by the Lhotas, Rengmas, and Semas, always hung up in a tree, usually somewhere near the edge of the village.   The skull is bored and hung up by a cane string.   It has been suggested that the practice of hanging captured heads in a tree is a survival of tree-burial, but it is to be noticed that the Aos and the Konyak tribes, which regularly practise tree-burial in the ordinary way, do not put the heads they capture in trees, but hang them in their houses or their " Morungs," or in the house of their chief,[2] while the heads of animals killed in the chase are often put up in the " Morung " also.   The Angamis bury the heads taken from their enemies face downwards in the earth.

It has been remarked that the Naga knows no distinction between heads.   That does not mean to say that he does not pride himself on the killing of a redoubtable enemy, as distinct from killing women and children, though his rather bloodthirsty omnivorousness in slaughter may be gathered from a report by Mr. Carnegy, Political Officer in the Naga

---

[1] I have made many inquiries, but so far failed entirely to locate or find any trace of this practice. I am of opinion that the report was incorrect, and an Ao invention. The Aos are very particular liars where their enemies are concerned.

[2] The Changs and Konyak tribes divide the head, the " second spear " taking the top or back of the skull, or, if there are three in at the death, the left half of the face, the top or back piece being then given to the third spear.

Hills, of an incident in 1876 : " In the middle of July a party of forty men of Mozema went over to Kohima and were admitted by one of the khels (clans) friendly to them, living next to the Puchatsuma quarter, into which they passed and killed all they could find, viz., one man, five women, and twenty young children. The people of the other clans made no effort to interfere, but stood looking on . . . one of the lookers-on told me that he never saw such fine sport (i.e., the killing of the children), for it was just like killing fowls ! " Still it would seem that heads taken by deliberate treachery as opposed to surprise, i.e., by inviting a man to partake in some friendly act and then killing him unawares, were reckoned as different in some way from heads taken in the ordinary raid, as they are said to be represented on the warrior's shield by inverted heads. Also as regards heads taken from women and children there is some reason to believe that under certain circumstances they were more highly valued than those taken from men, provided, in the case of children, that the teeth were cut. Hodson mentions this point,[1] and Colonel Shakespear throws doubt on it, but there is a case worth recording which goes far to substantiate its truth.[2] In 1911 Captain Porter, of the 17th Infantry, then quartered at Kohima, went on a shooting trip into the Lhota country.

---

[1] " The Naga Tribes of Manipur," p. 114 and note.

[2] I am indebted to Captain Porter for this incident, which was related to me by him shortly after it took place. Since writing the above another fact has come to my notice which seems to clinch the argument. The Semas have a regular formula of praise which they sing for a man whom they wish to honour, saying that he has taken the head of a *girl* of such and such a tribe or village. For instance, I heard the following sung in answer to a request for a Sema song :—

O Sakhalu no Abor-limi i pu ghü	ihoh, ihoh, ihoh-ü.
O Kohazu asa likighü	ihoh, etc.
O Ilheli alho ve	ihoh, etc.

i.e., " Sakhalu took-and-brought-back (the head of) an Abor girl, Kohazu cut-off-and-put-in-his-ear (a bit of her) hair ; Ilheli was pleased." This formula is applied to anyone else, substituting another tribe or village for Abor, the name of the hero's younger brother for Kohazu, and of his wife for Ilheli. The Sakhalu, it may be noticed, here mentioned, went on the Abor expedition as a scout and took six *male* heads, but the use of " *ilimi* " (a girl) is constant.

Accompanied by some men of Phiro he was benighted near
the Rengma village of Infoma. The Gaonbura only admitted
him and his Lhota companions to his house with great
reluctance and flatly refused to feed the Lhotas. Afterwards, on inquiring the reason of this unlooked for lack of
hospitality, Captain Porter discovered that there was an old
enmity between his host and his " shikari." In the days of
their youth there had been a very pretty girl in Phiro, all
suitors to whose hand had been rejected. At last her
mother said that she should marry whichever of her suitors
would bring her the ears of an Angami girl. The ears were
brought ; the "shikari" with Captain Porter was the eartaker
and successful suitor ; the wife of the headman of Infoma
has no ears ; *Hinc illae lacrimae.* The reason given to
Captain Porter for the specification of an Angami *girl* was
that the warriors worked at the cultivation furthest from the
village, above them the young men, then the old men, then
the old women, and then nearest to the village the young
women and children, and to get a pair of ears from the latter
meant penetrating the enemy's ranks at the risk of the
aspirant's head, both going and coming back. Infoma is
not really an Angami village, but it contains an admixture
of Angami blood, while it is possible that the headman's
wife may have come from one of the neighbouring Angami
villages, as most tribes are bilingual along their marches
and intermarry freely. Of course the heads of women
and children were often taken under less romantic circumstances than these, a favourite method being to lie up at
dawn by a neighbour's well, to take the head of the first
woman or child coming to draw water, and to decamp
with all speed, setting panjis to delay pursuit. And additional
reasons for special value being attached to a woman's
head are probably to be found in the greater amount of
long hair to be obtained for the purpose of garnishing a
warrior's insignia, and most of all in the inevitable reduction
the killing of a woman would effect on the birth-rate of the
hostile village. Surprise was essential to a head-taking
raid, and if a party found a village prepared for them the
valiant warriors would almost certainly turn back home

again. It is agreed by all Angamis, as well as by other Nagas, that head-taking was essential to marriage in so far that a buck who had taken no head, and could not wear the warrior's dress at festivals, not only found it exceedingly difficult to get any girl with pretensions to good looks or to self-respect to marry him, but was held up to ridicule by all the girls of his clan.

Among the Angamis the good old days of head-hunting have gone. Girls who wish to marry cannot now afford to be so particular. The distinctive marks of the successful warrior are assumed on the fictitious grounds of having thrust a spear into a corpse or even of having gone as a coolie upon an expedition on which killing took place.[1] But though the flesh is withheld the spirit is willing. Surreptitious heads are still sometimes brought back from punitive expeditions, on which a crowd of interpreters and Naga coolies follow in the wake of the sepoys, uttering loud yells and transfixing with their spears the corpses of the slain. It is related that at the taking of Makware village a Naga clerk of the Deputy Commissioner's staff, educated in speech and civilised in dress, having failed to provide himself with a spear, was seen dancing in vociferous triumph over the corpse of an enemy and with horrid yells plunging his umbrella again and again into the wounds.

But it is not everyone who is so fortunate as to accompany, armed even with the humble umbrella, a trans-frontier expedition from which to bring back bits of scalp, or ears, or toes, while the desire to perform the ancient ceremonies comes to many, and among the Semas, Rengmas, and Lhotas, if not the Angamis, it is a favourite expedient to cut off the tail, or some of the hair of the tail, of a neighbour's mithan or cow, and to follow up this feat of chastened valour with the genna performed for the taking of a head. As an animal treated in this way loses at least half its value—it can no longer be slain for any ceremony—the

---

[1] In the Konyak village of Auting, annexed about five years ago, the young men have already taken to wearing ceremonial dress with the *insignia* of the head-taker after spearing a wooden dummy, since the real thing is no longer obtainable.

almost invariable result is a case in court, and the culprit is not infrequently detected by his too hasty eagerness to perform the rites, though he sometimes waits until he thinks the affair has blown over so that he can celebrate in safety. Thefts, too, are sometimes regarded as fit occasions for the performance of the genna. The Ao regards stealing from the plains as a meritorious action, while the Sema is apt to take a similar view as regards the Ao, whose cattle serve the double purpose of giving him an excuse for a genna and the wherewithal to perform it. A lock of hair from the head of a living person is also made to serve as a substitute, at a pinch, for the head from which it is cut, and almost all Nagas except those in service are most unwilling to cut their hair, except in their own villages, as, of course, the utilisation of a lock of their hair as a substitute for a head would entail, as a result of the genna performed by the taker of the hair,[1] death, or at least dire misfortune, to the man from whose head it was cut.

The taking of heads in this life, however, does not seem to have any connection in the Angami mind with life in another world, except in so far as the headless man cannot get to the abodes of Kepenopfü, whence the great unwillingness of all Nagas to allow the heads of their killed to be taken by the enemy, if it can possibly be helped. The Konyak tribes fight in pairs, so that if one man is wounded or killed the other can drag away his body and save the head. Losses also seem to be by all Nagas counted primarily in heads rather than in lives. The tale of a warrior's heads is recorded on his grave, but then so is that of the tigers he has killed, and it does not seem likely that he would wish to be accompanied and served by tigers in the life beyond, while the same principle, if applied to the tale of his *liaisons*, which is likewise recorded on his tomb, would cause a confusion among deceased Angamis seventyfold greater than that suggested in the famous riddle of the

---

[1] Among the Changs a man who loses his way in the jungle cuts off a bit of his hair, and puts it in a stick as an offering to the spirit (believed to be that inhabiting the python) which has ensnared him, after which he never fails to find his way home. Semas similarly placed cut off a bit of the fringe of their cloth for the spirit of the forest.

Sadducees, of the woman who had married seven brothers, at least if the deceased's own count were accepted. There is nothing in the Angami eschatology to suggest that he believes his victims in this world will accompany him into the next.[1]

The position of women among the Angamis would at first sight appear to be but a low one. By the Tengima proper and Chakroma she is debarred from inheriting land at all, while among the Eastern Angamis she can only inherit subject to the reversion of the property to the male line on the death of her sons, or to a substantial payment in lieu of such reversion. At the same time she is, of course, free to purchase and possess land and transmit purchased land to her posterity absolutely. Again, not only is relationship through the female side not recognised, but its very existence does not seem to be realised, and a man who can enumerate his male ancestors for fourteen generations cannot name his grandmothers for four. As for his collateral relatives on the female side, he knows nothing whatever about them. Mr. Davis, writing of Naga women in general, goes so far as to say that after marriage they " become mere household drudges."[3]

Position of Women.[2]

With this latter proposition, however, we can in no wise agree, at any rate not in so far as Angami women are concerned, nor for that matter Sema women either. However low the legal status of the Angami woman may seem, her position in the household makes it true that in the Naga Hills, as elsewhere, " women are a very strong folk." The husband expects absolute fidelity from his wife, but, at any rate in the case of the ordinary villager, he renders a fair measure of it himself in return, and while in all domestic matters the wife is an equal partner, consulted by and consulting with her man, a woman is, in Tengima villages, usually the holder of the village office of First Reaper (*Lidepfü*). While hunting and warfare fall to her husband's lot, as weaving and cooking to hers,

---

[1] *See* Appendix XIII, p. 455.

[2] *See also* under " Marriage ", Part IV of this book.

[3] Assam Census Report, 1891, p. 250.

agriculture and, in some degree, trade are carried on by both together. When a guest is to be entertained the wife assumes the *rôle* of hostess ; in family quarrels she is usually to the fore. In the question of the marriage she is allowed a freedom of choice that will easily bear comparison with the freedom of choice which she exercises in the most civilised of nations. Her parents, it is true, may resort occasionally to a good deal of persuasion in regard to matrimonial projects. They never resort to force, and cases of girls married against their inclinations are exceedingly rare. In the last resort she is always able to evade a distasteful alliance by conveniently dreaming dreams of ill-omen at the critical point. Polygamy is not practised, and Hurukhe of Kohima, formerly head interpreter to the Deputy Commissioner, is the only Tengima Angami known to have had two wives at the same time, though there is nothing to prevent their having a number in succession. The Memi do have two wives at the same time more frequently, but they too look on the practice with a good deal of disfavour. Among most Angamis the price of a bride is merely nominal, a few chickens, a couple of pigs, and a spear, but in some of the Chakroma villages, Chephama for instance, sums of from twenty to a hundred rupees are paid. Divorce is easy to obtain ; incompatibility of temper is a quite sufficient reason ; and unless she is herself divorced for adultery the woman always obtains a third of the joint property exclusive of land. As a widow, though entitled to nothing but her third (except in the Eastern Angami villages, where, if childless, she gets the whole of the property other than land), she is usually provided for by her husband's relations, that is, if the husband before death has not given directions for provision for her, which he usually does. She can also remarry where and when she pleases, provided only that she may not remarry from her deceased husband's house. She must go back to the house of her father or of his male representative. Mr. Davis remarks, " It is wonderful how soon after marriage a Naga woman loses her good looks, if she ever had any.

As soon as ever she has had a child she takes no further care about her personal appearance." As far as the Angami woman goes this is absolutely true of most, and it possibly indicates the strength of her position.

The Angami woman before marriage is given a very great deal of liberty, though the extent to which she takes advantage of this has possibly been exaggerated. Mr. Davis, speaking not of Angamis in particular, but of Nagas generally, says : " I should say that it was very rare for a girl not to have at least one lover."[1] Customs, however, differ in this respect in a very great degree between different tribes. While the Ao girl is bound to admit men to the girls' houses at night, chastity before marriage prevails among the Semas, where the marriage price of a girl is reduced at least 50 per cent. by the fact of her having had an intrigue. The Angamis would seem to fall somewhere between the Ao and the Semas, for while separate girls' houses do not exist in Angami (Tengima) villages, though they are found in Memi villages,[2] girls are not looked after with the same jealousy as that with which a Sema girl is watched until her marriage. Accurate information as to the precise degree of chastity observed by Angami girls is very difficult to obtain. When asked about it, Angamis usually admit that it is common for a girl to have a lover, but they deny that it is the rule, and say that some do have one and some do not. It is also usually averred by them that public opinion is against it, and that a girl who is found out is subjected to a great deal of ridicule, while a girl believed to be fickle or known to have transferred her affections from one lover to another finds it very difficult to get anyone to marry her. Mr. Davis, still speaking of Nagas in general, has said that a girl's lover " would as a rule belong to the girl's own *khel* (*i.e.*, *thino*) and would be a man whom it would be impossible for her to marry

[1] Assam Census Report, 1891.

[2] In some Memi villages the girls share the same morung as the young men, the boys sleeping on an upper platform, the girls on a lower Publicity is probably an efficient bar to flirtation.

in any case."[1] In the copy of Assam Census Report for
1891 which belongs to the Subdivisional Office at Mokokchung, the late Mr. Noël Williamson, a careful observer,
made the following marginal note against this statement :
" I think that this is rarely the case.   Incest before marriage
is as abhorrent to these people as that on marriage."   As
far as the Sema, Chang, Lhota, and Ao countries go, Mr.
Williamson was undoubtedly right.   An Ao girl, although
bound to admit any other man in the village, may not
admit to her house a man of her own exogamous group.
If she does so she is held jointly guilty with the man.   The
Lhotas have the same dislike of any *liaison* within the
exogamous group.   With the Angamis what appears to be
really the case is that while a girl *might* take a lover from
her own clan,[2] she would at any rate be rigidly forbidden to
take one from her own kindred, which is regarded as entailing
great misfortune.   As the kindred is now becoming the
real exogamous unit of the Angamis, their practice in this
respect is much the same as that of the Lhotas and Aos,
only in the case of the Angamis the clan as a social unit has
not yet disappeared, as it has done among the Lhotas, and
in some villages still remains a more or less exogamous
body.   A theory of the origin of exogamy and marriage
was advanced by Mr. S. E. Peal,[3] who suggested that

[1] My own opinion is that among the Angamis, as among other Naga
tribes, the lover would as a rule be a man whom it *would* be possible for
her to marry.   It very frequently happens that a girl does marry her
lover.   Indeed, it is probably the rule rather than the exception.   Possibly
Mr. Davis was misled by the change in the exogamous unit from the
original *thino* to its subdivision.   Premarital intrigues and the subdivision
of exogamous groups are in a way not unconnected, as it is certain that in
a large exogamous group living as a community there would be many
intrigues inside the group, if its members were Angami or indeed of
almost any other Naga tribe.

[2] But see the account of the origin of the Chetonuma clan of Kohima
in Part VI under " Kohima."   Here a girl runs away from her village
as the result of an intrigue with a fellow clansman.

[3] *Vide* Gait, Assam Census Report, 1891, p. 122, note.   Among some of
the Ndreng Lhotas it is common for a man going on a long journey to
allow a near relative of his own kindred to cohabit with his wife during
his absence.   Such cohabitation, however, is usually only allowed by a
definite arrangement, and only to a man of the husband's kindred.   The
Sema villages of Seromi and Tichipami have told me that they were

within the tribe all women were common property and that no single man could claim an exclusive right to any woman of the tribe, but that such a right was recognised in the case of women captured in war from other tribes. This theory, of course, would provide an explanation of the freedom of sex intercourse before marriage, but if we accept it, the prohibition of intercourse between unmarried members of the same kindred must be regarded as a comparatively recent growth, or as an extension to the kindred of a prohibition which formerly affected only the family.

The licence allowed to unmarried girls raises another question. What of their children ? Here again accurate information is exceedingly difficult to obtain. Illegitimate children are very rare, and Mr. Davis remarks that " it is impossible to resist the conclusion that they are made away with immediately after birth, or that abortion is procured before the birth of the child." The practice of infanticide is denied by Angami men, but they admit that some method of procuring abortion may be known to and practised by the women, although they, the men, do not know about it. In Kohima illegitimate children were born in private and killed by their mothers ; in the Eastern Angami country illegitimate children were forbidden by the village to be reared. Girls about to become mothers used to, and probably still do, though, of course, it is denied, procure abortion by twisting and squeezing the abdomen. Should a child be born it was invariably killed, though not in any particular manner, and the soles of the infants' feet were pierced all over with thorns to prevent their returning to haunt their mothers' dreams. It was believed that if they were allowed to grow up the village would be without success in war or hunting. Of course it is denied that this custom still prevails, and in support of such a denial the Kezabama Gaonburas point out a man born out of wedlock who is said to have been allowed to grow up as a

allowed free intercourse with any of the women in the Sangtam village of Charr, as the men of that village wished to improve the stock by an admixture of more warlike blood, Charr being rather an inferior village with warlike neighbours. Seromi and Tichipami go there regularly to trade.

result of the village's having been taken over by Government. It is, however, to say the least of it, curious that they should only point out one. The Kacha Nagas are related by Khonoma to kill children who are born with the " placenta " adhering to the neck by pouring boiling water into their mouths, and it is said that a woman of Lakema was sentenced to three years' imprisonment for killing her child in this way when Mr. Porteous was Deputy Commissioner. The Aos undoubtedly procure the abortion[1] of illegitimate children, and, as Mr. Davis suggests, it is only fair to assume that for every case of abortion or infanticide that comes to light "many happen of which nothing is heard. The custom being one that is approved of by all Nagas, it is impossible to expect them to give information of the occurrence of such cases."[2]

It is probable, however, that among the Angamis proper, at any rate, illegitimate children were not *necessarily* killed, as there is at present a definite custom with regard to their disposal. Male children go to the father when weaned, but no proper ceremony is performed for their birth. The women probably perform one on their own account in secret, but the men do not know what it is, as the father does not take part. He merely provides food and drink for the woman, who comes to his house to fetch it. This provision is tantamount to an acknowledgment of parentage, and a refusal to provide the food and drink according to custom gives great offence to the girl and her relations. The mother herself is not allowed to grow her hair and must remain shorn like the other unmarried girls. If she insists on growing her hair, no one is allowed to marry her except a man of the very poorest condition and of the lowest standing in the village.

---

[1] A method used in the Ao village of Nankam is to feel from the outside for the child's head a few days before birth and catching hold of that part of the mother's body together with the head of the child inside to give a sharp rap on it with a stone, which causes the child to be born dead. This method is said to be known to certain old women who practise it in privacy.

[2] Assam Census Report, 1891. See also Part IV of this book, under " Birth."

Although Angamis do not admit that there is absolute freedom of intercourse between the unmarried, they readily admit that widows, unless quite aged, are in no way restrained in this matter, even by public opinion, which seems to be the only real check upon girls, while in some of the Eastern Angami villages there are regular prostitutes. This class appears to be sometimes recruited from unmarried girls as well as from the younger widows, and is most numerous in rich Eastern Angami villages like Kezabama. These women frequently acquire a good deal of land and take their fees in work. One of them died just after the Makware expedition, a number of days' labour on her terraces being owed to her by different clients. Captain Butler, in his enthusiastic encomium on Angami women, is quite wrong in saying " prostitution is a thing unknown here. . . . A Naga woman would scorn to barter for her person "; but he was doubtless speaking of the Tengima villages, where it is not known except in so far as it has been introduced round Kohima. He also adds that " the foul diseases that follow in its train are evils to which Naga flesh has not been born an heir." If this is so, they have unfortunately been inherited since Captain Butler wrote. Part, however, of his encomium may well be quoted :

" As with the men," he says, " so with the women, I think they are certainly taller than the average of other hill women, and their features more regular. They are chaste, faithful, merry, and, unlike their brothers, never to be seen idle. Their duty it is to fetch the wood, draw the water, cook the food, brew the liquor, besides working in the fields and weaving cloth at home. It will be observed that among the characteristics of the woman I have placed chastity, and it may be as well perhaps for me to explain that by this term I do not for a moment mean to say that they are exactly chaste according to our ideas, but simply that they are true to, and act up to, their own principles with regard to that virtue. . . . Young men and maidens mix together with almost all the freedom allowed by nature's law. Incontinence on the part of the married, however, is rare, and an unfaithful wife is a thing almost unheard of, but then the penalty is *death*."

The rather sentimental relations of the sexes may be

gathered from the well-known song *Nichu nikri* [1] sung in Khonoma at the Thekrangi genna :—

We in childhood were united ;
Let there be no parting ever.
By the pathway do I linger,
From afar continue gazing
At that fairest of all maidens.

When her hair grows long in marriage,
When her hair is bound and braided,
Let her not forget our friendship,
But go with me to the rice fields.
I will wait for her at daybreak,
Take her on beyond the others
And return alone by Sŏrŏzhŭ
(Following that devious footpath
So that no one shall remark me).

Without her I shall be lonely ;
Go and tell her I am lonely.
In the sky the moon has risen
And the god, the Sun, has set ;
Now the moon is looking on me,
On that pleasant village pathway
We so oft have trod together,
But can tread no more together
After death has come upon us.

Loitering by the stone of Ketsorr
Let us pluck the heads of wormwood,
Pluck the tall heads of the grasses,
Snatching leaves and light caresses—
So shalt thou be mine, Belovèd.
Each our separate cups of modhu
Into one gourd will we empty,
And will quench our thirst in common.

We will go before the spiteful ;
We will let them see our friendship.
If in going to the rice fields
We should fear to go together
Men will notice our aloofness,
Notice and remark upon it.
Whether we go down together,
Or remain aloof in going,
Still the envious will accuse us.
Be not angry, Pesekriewü !

[1] For Angami version and verbal rendering, see Part V. *Sorozhu* is a distant grazing ground, while the name *Pesekriewü* means " she-who-will-be-lamented-when-dead." The stone of Ketsorr is a memorial stone on the outskirts of Khonoma village.

KOHIMA VILLAGE FROM S.E. SHOWING PREFERENCE (more or less) FOR EASTERN ASPECT FOR FRONT OF HOUSE

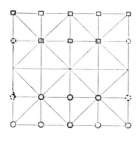

FIG. I.

TERHÜCHU

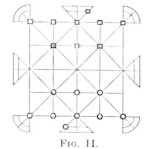

FIG. II.

[See p. 101

IMPLEMENTS

1 Rake (*tsaro*)
2 Axe (*sidure*)
3 Handle for using axe blade as *adze* (*kecheh*)
4 Rain Hat (*tserre*)
5 Hoe (*kedzü*)
6 Rain cloak (*perrhyoh* or *atikru*)

[See p. 78

PART IV

RELIGIOUS BELIEFS, CULT, WORSHIP: GENNA, *KENNA*, *PENNA*, *NANU*—CEREMONIES ATTENDING EPISODES IN THE LIFE OF THE INDIVIDUAL—BIRTH, NAMING, MARRIAGE, DEATH, ACQUISITION OF SOCIAL STATUS, ETC.—MAGIC AND WITCHCRAFT—OMENS, DIVINATION, DREAMS

PART IV

RELIGIOUS BELIEFS, CULT, WORSHIP: "GENNA," *KENNA*,
PENNA, *NANU*—CEREMONIES ATTENDING EPISODES IN THE
LIFE OF THE INDIVIDUAL—BIRTH, NAMING, MARRIAGE,
DEATH, ACQUISITION OF SOCIAL STATUS, ETC.—MAGIC AND
WITCHCRAFT—OMENS, DIVINATION, DREAMS

> "My Brother kneels . . . . in heathen-wise,
> But in my brother's voice I hear
> My own unanswered agonies.
> His God is as his fates assign,
> His prayer is all the world's—and mine."

IN approaching a subject such as the religious beliefs Religious
of the Angami, one is met at the outset by an obstacle of beliefs
very great difficulty. In common with other savage races
the Angami regards the supernatural in general from a
point of view that is sublimely vague. So vague is his
idea of the deities and spiritual beings in which he believes,
that he makes no attempt whatever to reproduce in carving
or in picture the mental image which he forms of them, if
indeed any clear formation takes place in his mind. Poly-
theist, pantheist he may be, but he is no idolater. Far,
very far, is he from saying with Evarra :

> "Thus Gods are made
> And whoso makes them otherwise shall die " :

though, on the other hand, he is very definite as to the
manner of their service. He has a very clear idea of how
gods should be served, and that whoso serves them otherwise
shall die, if not physically, at least socially. And this,
although much of the service which he offers seems to be
proffered to no god in particular, to no definite personal

177

beings, but is associated merely with such supernatural forces as may influence his destiny or his daily life. At the same time, while he does not, like the civilised man, naturally classify and departmentalise his notions of the supernatural, he does recognise some sort of distinction between, on the one hand, souls of the dead (and perhaps of the living), and, on the other, deities ("*terhoma*") of a more or less definite nature, ranging from deities with certain functions and individual names to vague spirits of the jungle, stone, and stream. All these latter are clothed to his mind with some hazy cloak of unity, but have so much entity as to be capable of propitiation, singly or collectively, or, if occasion warrant it, of challenge and defiance. Captain Butler records the case of an Angami chief who lost his son by an accident when serow hunting. When the news was brought to him he seized a shield and spear and leaped forth wrathfully challenging whatever spirits had caused his son's death to come and fight him that he might take vengeance. Similarly, although "*terhoma*" are, generally speaking, invisible and intangible, they, or their jealous or malicious influences, may be arrested by the use of panjis set up as a "*kethi thedi*" already described. It is not necessary, however, for these panjis to be particularly sharp, and it is conceivable that the idea underlying their erection is similar to that which induces the Dusun of Tempassuk, in British North Borneo, to put up spears outside their villages to keep off small-pox, the intention being that the spirits of the spears fight with the spirits of the small-pox when the latter attempt to enter the village defended by the former.[1] It is noticeable also that houses visited by sickness are protected by rough masks cut out of bamboo bark to represent a face, holes being made for

[1] *Journal of the Anthropological Institute*, 1913, Vol. XLIII, p. 455. See also Colonel Gurdon, "The Khasis," p. 108 (new edition). The Angamis, by the way, conceive of the spirit of small-pox as sowing the disease, as it were seeds, over all entering in at the village gate. Accordingly when a village is visited by the small-pox the inhabitants give up using the gate and go in and out some other way, climbing over the wall or ditch or through jungle. They give no personal name to the spirit of small-pox, but speak of it as a *terhoma*.

the features, a rude device seen among the Konyak tribes
in the much more elaborate form of regular faces, painted
and grotesque. It is perhaps a matter for speculation as
to whether these faces were originally intended, like the
gargoyles of Mediæval Europe, to frighten away evil spirits,
or whether it was intended that the spirit of the mask should
wrestle with the spirit of sickness, or whether the mask
was first put up that the sickness might seize the mask
instead of a human being. Ordinary panjis are put up over
the door of the house together with the masks, and a fire
is lighted in the centre of the doorway. These precautions
are believed to prevent those who go in and out from taking
infection from the sick man. Evil spirits and bacteria
seem to be much the same thing. In any case they can
be deterred from attacking the person by the device of
carrying in the hand, or licking and sticking on to the
forehead, a bit of wormwood (*chena* or *pina*) leaf, which is
apparently most obnoxious to the spirits of disease. Children
are particularly susceptible to attack, and a woman travelling with an infant in arms protects it by carrying a reaping
hook held in front of her to the haft of which a bit of
wormwood also is often tied—as a sort of disinfectant, in
fact.[1]

Disease may also be averted by offering a substitute in
the form of old cloths, live chickens, eggs, etc. During
the influenza epidemic of November 1918, which was very
severe in the Naga Hills, the paths round Angami villages
were littered with odds and ends of clothing and ornaments
offered in this way, and with eggs laid in the path for the
same purpose, while very many chickens were turned
loose in the jungle. Chickens freed and driven away in the
jungle to serve as a substitute for the person turning them
out (or perhaps merely as an offering for the spirits of the
jungle, or, it may be, to carry away the element of sickness
or misfortune that attaches to the persons who devote
them to this purpose) are called *chĕsü* and regarded as
accursed.

Among Nagas generally we find plenty of animatism,
particularly as regards stones. The Sema village of Lazemi

[1] *See* Appendix XIII, p. 456.

boasts a pair of stones, male and female, that breed and
produce offspring yearly, while similar beliefs may be found
among all Naga tribes. Somewhat similarly, an animal,
a snake for instance, may be regarded as an embodied
spirit which it is not advisable to injure, and any particular
and known animal which for a long time successfully evades
its pursuers is credited with supernatural qualities. Such
an one is the great boar of the Dayang Valley below
Gariphema, whose tracks are reported to be a foot long,
a worthy successor to him of Cosa's fen.[1] As in Europe,
supernatural beings are sometimes to be controlled by the
possession of something that belongs to them ; the story
of the Ladies of the Well, one of whom was at last captured
by the mortal who abstracted from her the head-band used
by women to carry loads,[2] is a familiar theme in our own
folklore.

Cult.   Of the spirits revered by the Angami there are a number,
both of persons and of kinds. Nor are their qualities by
any means so malicious as they have been painted. The
missionaries in their blindness teach the Angami convert to
regard all *terhoma* as evil, and mission-taught Nagas are
in the habit of translating the generic *terhoma* into English
or Assamese as " Satan." All of these " satans," as they
call them, are, however, very far from having those qualities
which we traditionally associate with the Devil, and the
qualities of some of them are definitely benevolent. Chief
of all of these is Kepenopfü, usually spoken of with the
possessive [3] suffix as *Ukepenopfü*. This spirit is sometimes
spoken of as a creator, but it would seem that this is rather
in the sense of the creator of living beings than as the creator
of the universe. The word *kepenopfü* literally means
" birth spirit," and Kepenopfü, indeed, is the ancestress
(or ancestor) of the human race, and since the two ancestors
of the *terhoma* and tigers were of one birth with the ancestor

[1] The white serow at Seromi in the Sema country is another. No trap
can catch it nor any hunter shoot it. I had a barking deer of similar
qualities in my garden at Mokokchung until it was shot.

[2] See Part VI—specimen of Angami language—the story of Jessu.

[3] Of the third person: Sir G. Grierson says that the Angami suffixes are
remains of a pronominal adjective. See Part VI.

of man, Kepenopfü might also be regarded as the ancestress
of all spirits and the larger cats. Other animals were, at
any rate according to one legend, supplied to men by one
of the *terhoma* associated with the Terhengi genna, so that
they too are indirectly traceable to Kepenopfü. Kepenopfü
has been called the ancestress of men, rather than the
ancestor. Many Angamis, it is true, think and speak of
Kepenopfü as a male being, but the termination *pfü* is a
feminine termination, and always carries a feminine sense,
and, when made to reflect on the point, most Angamis
admit Kepenopfü to be a female being,[1] and it is as such
that she appears in the legend of the diverse origin of the
Naga and the plainsman (*vide* Part V), in which she appears
as the ancestress of men and has a mysterious husband of
superhuman attributes. On the other hand, in the story
of the Angami Tower of Babel [2] Kepenopfü causes the men
who are building a tower up to heaven to speak different
languages, because she is afraid that she will have to give
them all gifts if they succeed in arriving, and this would
seem to suggest the male sex, as under ordinary circumstances gifts would not be expected of a woman. The
dwelling-place of Kepenopfü is always located in the sky,
and the souls of those who have lived good lives, according
to the Angami standard, that is, go to the sky after death
and dwell with her. Kepenopfü is not credited with any
activities malicious or ill-disposed towards human beings,
but is always regarded as beneficent. Kepenopfü it was
who gave to men of old time the stone axe as an instrument,
but man in his stupidity being unable to use it, she withdrew
the gift, and to this day when an axe falls from heaven in
her lightning, the worthless part only remains to be found
by mortals, the valuable properties of the stone returning
to heaven again with the flash.

Whether or not Kepenopfü should strictly be reckoned
among the *terhoma* is a doubtful point, but her attributes

---

[1] The conception of Kepenopfü in the Angami mind is apparently at
present undergoing a process of change from female to male, and indeed
the word is used by Christian converts for their anthropomorphic conception
of God the Father.

[2] See Part V.

are similar to those of other *terhoma*, and the Angami mind undoubtedly associates her with them as one of them. Among these others we find *Rutzeh*, the evil one. He is the giver of sudden death. If a man die unexpectedly, blood issuing from his mouth and nostrils, no illness having preceded it, his death is ascribed to Rutzeh. *Maweno* is the Angami goddess of fruitfulness. She keeps pebbles and paddy in her bag. If a man meet her and ask for anything, she gives him one gift, never two, a pebble or a grain or two of paddy. If she gives it to him for his fields he will have good crops, if for his cattle, many calves. *Telepfü*, on the other hand, is a mischievous being. She carries people away—men, women, or children—and hides them. She does not kill them, but renders them senseless, though if their relations succeed in finding them again they recover consciousness. *Tsükho* and *Dzürawü* are two spirits, male and female, husband and wife, represented as dwarfs, who preside over all wild animals ; they are not inimical to man, but send him game in answer to his prayers when he goes a-hunting.[1] *Metsimo* guards the approach to paradise, a sort of Angami St. Peter.[2] *Tekhu-rho* is the god of tigers. He is held responsible for the loss of missing persons lost in the jungle, etc. A genna is done to him for their death. He is also believed to avenge the death of tigers or leopards killed by men, if the dead animal is not prevented from telling him the name of the man who killed him. This may be done by wedging open the mouth of the dead tiger with a piece of wood and putting the head into a running stream at some distance from the village. When the tiger tries to tell the *Tekhu-rho* who has killed him, all that the spirit can hear is a meaningless gurgle in the water. *Ayepi* is a sort of fairy that lives in men's houses and brings them prosperity. Few men see her, but sometimes her tracks are seen like little human footprints in the stored paddy or on the dusty floor.

[1] See the story of Chikeo in Part V.

[2] The form he takes among the Memi is that of Pekujikhe (see Part VI, specimen of the Memi language), who seems to be also invested with the attributes of Kepenopfü's husband (see Part V, *Legends ; "* The Naga and the Plainsman ").

Kechi-ke-rho is the spirit, or rather the species of spirit, which inhabits stones. *Temi* is a ghost. It proceeds from the corpse of a man drowned, or killed by an enemy, by any kind of evil spirit, or by his own hand. It cannot kill men, but threatens them and frightens cowards.

This short list is not intended to be in any sense exhaustive, but merely to include some of the more prominent *terhoma* and to indicate the ideas with which they are associated. *Terhoma* are legion, and probably every village could tell of several quite unknown to the villages adjoining it. The majority of *terhoma* are unknown by name, unspecified, vague inhabitants of the invisible world. There is, too, a female spirit called a *rhopfü*,[1] attached to each man or to men in general, it is difficult to say which ; a mysterious spiritual force which seems to combine the attributes of guardian angel, familiar spirit, Destiny, and in some cases it would seem even of man's own soul. The description is vague enough, but the danger to be avoided in transcribing any Angami ideas upon the supernatural is, above all, the danger of distinguishing what is vague, of giving form to what is void, of defining what is not finite. If an Angami is asked what the sun is he will probably answer that he does not know, " perhaps it is a *terhoma*." And to *terhoma* generally most natural phenomena, such as earthquakes and eclipses, are ascribed, though actual worship of nature in the sun, moon, fire, or other of her manifestations is absent.

The Angami conception of godhead being such as it is, we should hardly expect to find any definite code of morals dependent upon it ; morals, of course, there are, even a code of morals, but the sanction on which it rests is social, not religious. Theft, for instance, as also homicide, while very serious offences when perpetrated by an individual against another of his community, are proper if not praiseworthy actions when perpetrated against a member of another community. At the same time, there is a vague

[1] The Irish *bean-sidhe* is a precise translation of *rho-pfü*, but the idea attached to " banshee " in English has become more or less identified with a particular manifestation.

idea in Angami eschatology of a distinction between the sheep and the goats, for whereas the former go to a heaven, located somewhere in the sky, to dwell with Ukepenopfü, the latter go down beneath the earth, where they pass through seven existences. The first of these is usually described as that of a butterfly,[1] but it cannot be definitely stated what the other six are, though butterflies, bees, ants, and other insects are mentioned, butterflies in particular. If asked whether any of these existences may be passed in human form, the answer given is, "Who knows?" One thing, however, is clear, and that is that at the conclusion of the seventh the existence of the soul becomes extinct, "leaving his rib on (the roof of) his house." The rib in this case is said to be the rib of whatever being the soul inhabited in the seventh state, and the house is explained, when an explanation is asked for, as being the dwelling of whatever sort occupied in that existence. It is probable, however, that, until asked to explain, the mental image formed is one of a human being and a human house. The seven existences are described as taking place in seven spheres of the under-world, one below the other.[2]

The ideas as to the sort of existence experienced in heaven by the soul which qualifies for the domains of Kepenopfü are considerably vaguer than those on the future existence already described, which must await the vast majority of Angamis. A notion, however, is expressed by some that life with Kepenopfü will be a sort of improved edition of life on this earth with the more unpleasant incidents expunged, with hunting, perhaps with head-hunting, and doubtless with unlimited " zu " drinking and feasting.

[1] Hodson, "Naga Tribes of Manipur," p. 159, mentions a statement that the Angamis do not kill a certain butterfly because it is occupied by the souls of the dead. I have not been able to find any such practice among the Angamis, though the Memi sub-tribe state that if *children* kill the great white swallow-tailed moth they are liable to go mad. I have not been able to extract any specific reason for this belief, but it is not unlikely that these huge and rather ghostly insects are associated with the souls of the dead. Grown men, however, kill them without compunction and pin them up on the fronts of their houses.

[2] Possibly this belief in seven spheres of the under-world is connected with the unluckiness which in Angami opinion attends the number seven.

The principal qualification for the abode of Kepenopfü is that one should have performed the *Zhatho* (or *Zache* or *Satse*) genna and should have thereafter eaten no unclean meat. Unclean meat is usually described as the flesh of monkeys, dogs, frogs, and " birds whose flesh is of unknown quality." One sometimes hears it said that no Angamis who have eaten unclean food can go to the abode of Ukepenopfü, but if this is so Kepenopfü must lead a singularly solitary existence. Perhaps she (or he) prefers this. Every Angami, male at any rate, who goes thither has to enter along a narrow way on which he must meet the spirit called Metsimo and struggle for a passage. If Metsimo overcomes him, he is cast into limbo and remains a wandering spirit between heaven and earth, in the company, it would seem, of the souls of infants stillborn or who died before the conclusion of the birth genna, and of warriors killed in battle whose bodies and heads were not recovered for burial, unless burial by effigy, which is performed in such circumstances, is an effectual precaution against such a doom. It is apparently with a view to this struggle that an Angami warrior is buried with his weapons.

The souls of the dead, however, are perhaps not entirely cut off from the former existence, as a dead man's drinking horn is frequently, if not usually, hung up in the place where he usually kept it filled with liquor in case he may return for refreshment, and in some cases the horn is occasionally refilled, until the memory of the dead has faded away. It may be added that the average Angami troubles his head very little as to what is in store for him after death. He looks on death as the abhorrent end of everything that interests him, and neither pretends to know nor cares what comes after.

The beliefs of other Naga tribes on the subject of a future existence contain interesting parallels to the Angami theories, which are worth notice in passing. The belief in the narrow path to paradise seems universal among Nagas. The Lhotas and Western Semas place it along the ridge of the Wokha hill (whence may often be heard the wailing of dead children crying for their parents), from north to south, and on reaching a depression just north of the summit the soul descends over the cliff on the eastern face of the rock by a cane rope to a cave of the Dead which is believed to exist there. It is at the point of descent that the struggle with the guardian spirit takes place. A line in the strata of the cliff face, which can be seen from a distance, is also pointed out as the Path of the Dead. The Semas of the Tizu valley place this path on the Naruto hill between Yezami and Aichi-Sagami overlooking the Tizu river, and the Aos[1] on a long ridge sloping up from west to east, which can be seen clearly from most of the villages on the Longbangkang range, somewhere beyond the frontier to the east of the Dikhu Valley and apparently in the Phom country. The Changs have a future world underground. The Semas also state sometimes that the good dead go to some village of the dead towards the sunrise, and the bad towards the sunset. Every dead Lhota has a bead or a cowrie tied on to his wrist with which to propitiate the spirit who guards the path. The Cave of the Dead at Wokha is visited in sleep by the Lhota dream-women, who can foretell the future, particularly of a hunting expedition, as a result of their conversations with the souls of the deceased.[2] Semas, Changs, and Lhotas also hold a concomitant but contradictory theory of the entry of the souls into insects after death.

Worship.   The worship an Angami village renders to its deities, if worship it can be called, is directed by certain officials, who, though in some cases of no importance socially, perform functions which from the Angami point of view are extremely important to the community. The most important of these, at any rate in most villages, is the *Kemovo*.[3] The

---

[1] The Aos sometimes say that the souls of the dead enter " mithan " ; that they are therefore reluctant to sacrifice too many, and that they do gennas in the places where " mithan " have been killed, as soul-occupied places. According to one of many Chang beliefs, human beings are the " mithan " of the sky spirits and a man dies whenever the sky spirit kills a " mithan."

[2] Mr. Mills tells me that the Lhota soul is heard groaning on its way to the Hill of the Dead as much as two or three months before the body dies.

[3] Memi—" *Mohvo*."

Kemovo must be an occupant of one of the original house
sites of the village, and is normally a descendant in the
direct line of the founder of the village or of the founder,
in the village, of the clan' for which he acts as Kemovo.
The Kemovo directs all public ceremonies and fixes the
days for them, and as the office is hereditary, he is also
the repository of the genealogical and historical traditions
of his village, clan, and kindred. The office, while descending from generation to generation, remains, however, in
the hands of the old men of the family, so that the second
brother will succeed the elder, and the third perhaps the
second, the office going back in the next generation to the
eldest son of the eldest brother, to this eldest son's brother
after him, and back again as before to the eldest son's son.[1]
When a new village is built a man from one of the original
house sites of the parent village, preferably, of course, the
Kemovo himself, must go and select the site for the first
house of the new village, and whenever a new house is built
in any village, the village Kemovo has to perform a
ceremony before building starts. The person of the Kemovo
is regarded in a limited way as sacrosanct, inasmuch as it
is thought very unlucky indeed to kill the Kemovo of another
village even in war.

It should be added that the term Kemovo has a treble
significance, as, apart from the magico-religious functions
of the Kemovo and his hereditary office, the status of
" Kemovo " may be acquired by a man performing in
completion the full series of personal gennas which determine
social standing, while the Kemovo is among the Eastern
Angamis the occupier of the first house site of the village.
In the Eastern Angami country the Kemovo is normally
Kemovo in the treble sense of the word, the Kemovo being
a man selected from among persons otherwise properly
qualified by descent and genna-status to occupy the first
original house site of the village. But while in the Khonoma

---

[1] This is the descent in Khonoma. Eastern Angami villages seem less
particular about the succession of the elder line. A Kemovo must be a
married man, bachelors and widowers are disqualified. There is no
reversion to an elder line passed over once for some deficiency. There
are normally two at least in a village.

group he is Kemovo in the first or official-hereditary sense
and perhaps in the third sense, in the Kohima group the
term Kemovo bears only the second or social significance,
and carries no particular functionary duties, though the
term is applied in any case to the holders of the other three
village offices mentioned below. Here, in the Kohima
group, the functions which are performed by the Kemovo
of the Khonoma group are performed by the *Pitsu*, a term
not used in Khonoma, who also combines with those of the
Kemovo the functions of the Khonoma "*Zhevo*." Except
in the Kohima group, the Kemovo is the official repository
of genealogical lore. The *tehuba* or sitting-place in front of
the Kemovo's house normally contains the graves of
deceased kemovos and is regarded as a very sacred spot.
It is used for dancing in at gennas.

In Cheswezuma, and probably in other Eastern Angami
villages, there are two kemovo, as one of anything would
be unlucky, a pair, as in the case of husband and wife, being
the natural unit. These kemovo are more or less hereditary
as described, and a man who was blind or deaf would have
to be kemovo if there were no other available member of
the family, and might be so in any case, but it would be
regarded as most unlucky. In addition to the kemovo there
is also one *pitsu*. This is always the oldest man in the
village, irrespective of any other consideration. When he
dies the next oldest man becomes *pitsu* in his place. He
has no regular ceremonies to perform, but is sometimes
called on to officiate on special occasions, *e.g.* if it is
necessary to observe a special *penna* because the crops are
doing badly, or because an insect pest has attacked them.

The *Zhevo* is indispensable to the personal gennas performed by the Angami, and he directs these gennas much
as the Kemovo directs the gennas of the community. He
goes to the house of any person performing a genna and
blesses the man and tastes before anyone else the liquor
and the meat used, and receives from the person doing the
genna a large piece of raw meat and some of the blood of
the animal killed. His offices are needed in all personal
gennas of whatever nature, and he is thus almost always

called upon in the case of sickness to advise as to what sort
of genna should be done. In the Kohima group, as has
been already noticed, the function of the Kemovo and the
Zhevo are combined in the person of the *Pitsu*, who is
entitled to wear a special cloth called " *hredi* " or " *pitsu-pfe*."

Particularly connected with agricultural operations are
the " *Tsakro* " (*Chikrau*) and the " *Lidepfü*." The Tsakro
is the old man whose duty it is to begin the sowing ; until
he has formally inaugurated the sowing of the crop it is
genna for any man to sow. Some villages keep one Tsakro
for the rice crop and another for the millet, or one for wet
cultivation and one for jhuming, but practice differs in
this respect. In Jotsoma the first sower of millet is a
young man who is changed every two years or so owing to
the irksomeness of the food tabus which· he has to observe.
The Lidepfü is the old woman who in a corresponding
manner inaugurates the reaping of the crop.[1] Some,
particularly Eastern Angami villages, appoint an old man,
called in this case " *Lidah*," and not a woman for this
purpose, but the appointment of an old woman is the rule
among most Angami villages. The Lidepfü in Sachenobama
was in 1913 a young girl. For both the Tsakro and the
Lidepfü it is genna to work in their fields for thirty days
before the ceremony of first sowing or reaping as the case
may be. Each of them receives a sort of payment in paddy
and at the appointed time sends four or five men of the
clan to which he or she belongs to collect a contribution of
a small basket of paddy from every house in the clan.
The Tsakro collects his after the Terhengi, the genna which
follows the harvest, the Lidepfü hers after the Sekrengi
genna which precedes the sowing. Both are forbidden to
eat or even to touch rats, mice, squirrels, and animals
killed by birds or beasts of prey. This genna is also extended
to the Pitsu.[2]

Acts of worship have been spoken of as " gennas " Genna.

[1] There is possibly some significance in this selection of a man for
sowing and a woman for reaping. Is it connected with the " spending "
and " storing " functions which have been attributed to the male and
female in nature respectively ? Weininger (" Sex and Character ")
speaks of them as " the ' liberating ' and the ' un·ting ' impulses."

[2] *See* Appendix XIII, p. 456.

because there is no suitable English word which describes them, and the word genna, though by derivation from the Angami "*kenna*," signifying "forbidden" merely, has become regularly used in the Naga Hills for the various incidents of a magico-religious rite. These may suitably be dealt with under the three heads which are in casual speech lumped together under the expression "genna."

Kenna.
First of all we have "*Kenna*" (or "*kenyü*"), that is to say, "prohibition."[1] Now this word "*kenna*" is used without any reference whatever to the sanction on which the "prohibition" rests, and it is for this reason that the word "*tabu*" has been rather avoided, since there is nothing in the Angami word to suggest the reason of the prohibition. So loose is the use of the word "*kenna*" that it may refer not only to the breach of the strict rule of a magico-religious observance or to the breach of a social law, theft for example, but to the most trivial matter of pure utility. An extreme instance of the latter came before the notice of the writer. One of his interpreters had shot a monkey and going on ahead had jestingly propped it up in a lifelike attitude against a fence. The writer coming along with a village headman inserted into the open mouth of the dead animal the stump of a Burma cheroot[2] which he had been smoking. The Angami with him remarked at once "*hau tsü kennawe*," "it is forbidden to do that." On being asked how such an act could be *kenna*, it was explained that it was highly improper to waste so precious a luxury as the stump of a cheroot. Leaving out of account, however, extreme cases of this sort of use, it is possible to distinguish classes of *kenna* according to the intention underlying the prohibition. A good example of such a distinction may be seen in the prohibitions associated with the use of wood. On the one hand the burning for firewood of the wood of trees used for building is *kenna*. Of course it is just possible that the reason underlying this may be a fear that the use of this wood as firewood might make the timber of houses more liable to conflagration, but the simpler and accepted explanation, that the object of this *kenna* is to preserve the

---

[1] Lit. = "it is forbidden." In Memi—*chino*.

[2] *See* Appendix XIII, p. 456.

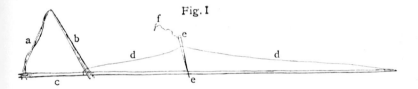

Fig. I

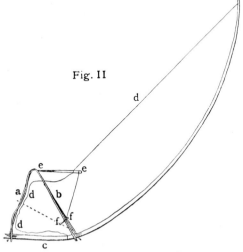

Fig. II

KESHEH.   I. THE SNARE UNSTRUNG.   II. THE SNARE SET

a, b, c, the triangle, *b* being the double side and *c* the bamboo
 slat forming the base.
d, d,   the thong.
e, e,   the wooden spike.
f,   its peg.
The dotted line . . . . . in Fig. II. represents the twig by which
 the peg *f* is kept in place.

Fig. III.

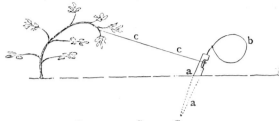

SNARE FOR SMALL GAME

[See p. 87

Angami terraced fields [See p. 72

Angami putting the weight [See p. 103

building material from waste, is perhaps more likely to be
the true one. On the other hand, and, whichever be the
explanation of the *kenna* on timber trees, differing from it,
is the *kenna* on the use as firewood of the tree " *hetho* " from
which are made the wooden images substituted in burial
ceremonies for the unrecovered corpses of those slain in
battle. While it is *kenna* to burn the wood of the tree
" *mela* " at weddings, because if burnt at weddings or touched
by the bride or bridegroom it causes barrenness and necessitates a divorce. The story which explains the prohibition
against burning *hetho* wood is told as follows :—

"The wood called ' *hetho* ' is not to be burnt or brought
to any dwelling for this reason : a man was once lost and
no trace of him or of how he disappeared could be found.
His relations wanted to perform the ceremonies for his
death. It was much discussed as to how this should be
done. At last it was decided to make a wooden image of
the dead man, and an old woman " (she would be the dream-
woman of the village) " was consulted as to what wood
should be used. She conversed with a spirit in a dream and
the spirit advised her to make use of a thorny tree so that
in future all should be afraid to touch it. Then the *hetho*
was chosen " (it has thorny bark and crimson flowers.
Its Assamese name is *Mădăr* [1]) " as it was sufficiently large,
soft, and thorny. Since then the *hetho* has not been burnt,
as it is considered in some sense a man. When a man dies
at a distance from his home, his companions cut off some
hair and bring it home, and making a figure of *hetho* wood,
affix the hair and perform the funeral ceremonies, substituting this figure for the corpse."

In the matter of dress we may compare the *kenna* which
forbids a man who has not taken a head to wear the hornbill's
feather, the insignia of the successful warrior, with the
kenna which prohibits a man from not merely putting on
but even laying across or against his body a petticoat which
has once been worn by a woman. The fact that there is
not the least objection to a man's putting against his body
a new and unworn woman's petticoat shows that it is not

---

[1] It is the বহ মদাব of the Assamese, *Erythrina fulgens.* Cf. p. 229
infra. It is perhaps significant that this tree is preferred by the Garo
for the pyre on which the dead are burned. See Playfair, *The Garos*,
p. 109.

the nature or meaning of the garment itself which, as in the case of the warrior's insignia, is the reason of the prohibition. A *kenna* similar perhaps to that against burning timber trees for firewood may be seen in the prohibition against cutting the stubble from the reaped field until the whole harvest of the village is gathered in. The idea here would seem to be that until the really valuable part of the harvest is gathered a man who has reaped his own grain should aid his neighbours. Delay would not hurt the straw, and it would not matter much if it did, whereas grain quickly spoils if unreaped and is of vital importance to the community. But perhaps the best instance of a purely utilitarian prohibition is the one by which a village in which there is some epidemic is put " out of bounds " by the neighbouring communities purely to avoid risk of infection.[1]

It should be added that by the word *kenna* used hereafter without specifying any particular act prohibited is meant a prohibition laid on persons or households from holding intercourse of any sort by word or by deed with others. This, in fact, is perhaps the commonest use of the word, and its corruption " genna " has sometimes been used in this sense exclusively, though now usually having a much vaguer significance. *Kenna* in this sense is, however, subject to degrees. It may refer merely to speech, though it usually refers to all communication whatever. A bunch of green leaves is affixed to the front of a house when its inmates are *kenna* in this sense.

Penna.

While *kenna* is the prohibition laid on a unit of the community, *penna*[2] is the prohibition laid on the whole community. It includes the idea contained in *kenna* and goes further. Besides entailing on the community a *kenna* towards strangers in a greater or less degree and for a longer

---

[1] Compare also the *kenna* against taking paddy out of the " duli " except in the morning and with the doors shut. The woman must do it if there is one in the household, and a stranger is absolutely prohibited from touching the paddy in the " duli." The object is purely utilitarian —to prevent the too rapid use of the rice supply, but the process of thought on which the tabu is based is less clear.

[2] Memi — *mani.*

or shorter period, *penna* entails entire abstention from work in the fields by the community as a whole, when such abstention is proclaimed by the Kemovo or Pitsu. The essence of it is that the individual should not leave the village to go to his fields or cultivate. It does not necessarily prevent the man's going out hunting or his wife's weaving or performance of household duties. The power ascribed to the observance of *penna* may be gathered from the effect which their observance with a definite object is believed to have upon the individual. For instance, two Sachema women went to catch snails in the Jotsoma terraces when the paddy was ripening, and some Jotsoma men, annoyed at the possibility of damage to their crop, threw mud at the women. They were not even struck by the mud, but when some of their fellow villagers threatened to do a genna consisting in this case of a day's *penna* (that is with *kenna* as regards strangers) " for the loss of two heads," the two women, fearing that they would die as a result of such a genna, hurried into Kohima to get orders against its observance. A precisely similar effect was ascribed to *penna* in the case already alluded to of the man of Nerhema who sacrificed a cat for illness, and instances might easily be multiplied. From time to time certain days (*e.g.*, those on which there is no moon either new or old, those on which eclipses occur, etc.), at the instance of the Kemovo or Pitsu, are observed as days of *penna* as opposed to " *li-chu* " (= " field-go "), much like the " dies nefasti " of the ancient Roman Courts. In most Angami gennas a certain number of days are observed as *penna* and the rest as *nanü* merely without prohibitions other than that against going to work in the fields. *Penna* really is *kenna* applied to the community instead of to the individual. The word *kenna* would probably be hardly, if ever, applied by an Angami to a communal prohibition, at any rate when speaking of the community, though it might be used of the incidence of the communal prohibition upon an individual.

Supplementary to *kenna* and *penna* in magico-religious Nanü. observances we find in some degree or other *Nanü*, the whole rite, the active side of the observance as well as the negative

and passive sides exemplified in *kenna* and *penna*. *Nanü*
is also used as the term for a whole genna in which *penna*
is observed by the community or by the individual
(accompanied by *kenna*) and followed by a period of similar
abstention from work in which *penna* has not been actually
proclaimed by the priest. The ceremony implied by
nanü is at its minimum the offering of a little folded leaf
containing a few grains of rice and a sip of liquor which is
hung up in the house on all days of *penna*, the grains of
rice having been held for a moment at the fire by way of a
pretence at cooking it. Perhaps even the offering of a
little liquor shaken from the cup or touched on to the
forehead before drinking on all occasions might be held to
be *nanü* at its minimum. At its maximum *nanü* consists
of sacrifice of flesh, part of which is set aside for the spirits,
wearing of ceremonial dress, dancing, singing, and the
pounding of dhan, together with the total abstention from
work in the fields involved by *penna*, and complete *kenna* to
intercourse with strangers. But while offerings in a lesser
or greater degree accompany all observances, they may
amount to a mere drop of liquor set aside on the morning
of a genna day, or may be the head and entrails of a chicken
or the snout and feet of a pig killed in case of illness. In
the latter case parts of the animal killed are given to the
Zhevo and sometimes also to the Kemovo, Tsakro, and
Lidepfü. In the case of a genna conferring social status
a number of cattle, more or less fixed according to the
particular genna, are sacrificed and the whole clan, or at
least the kindred, is feasted. The wearing of ceremonial
dress accompanies some of the village gennas, but practice
in this respect varies a good deal and is anything but a
criterion of the importance of the genna. Different villages
attach varying degrees of importance to different gennas,
and it thus happens that a genna kept with great ceremony
at one village is comparatively insignificant at another
village which makes a great deal of a genna barely observed
in the first. Dancing, singing, and dhan-pounding as a
rule go hand in hand with ceremonial dress. Dhan-pounding
at a small genna is done inside the " *theka ki*," which is the

house of some rich man who has a large pounding table and which is always used for this purpose at gennas ; at a big genna it is done outside in the open, a large number of tables being collected for the purpose. Pounding is done in full dress and by both men and women, and in some cases, *e.g.* the Thekrangi genna at Khonoma, the girls and young men pound at the same trestle, standing on opposite sides of it and using the long straight pestle. In the Terhengi genna in Kohima the men doing gennas of social status pound separately, using a hook-shaped pestle.

Dancing as practised by the Khonoma group is a very serious affair. It consists of a solemn procession of young men in full dress which moves at a slow pace describing circles, eights, and similar figures and splitting into two lines which work in and out of one another serpent-wise. The motions of the dancers are stiff and there is a certain amount of posturing with the arms and hands, the upper arms being kept close to the body and the fore-arms and open hand being moved up and down from the elbow, but not from side to side. Free movement is much restricted owing to the weight, cumbrous dimensions, and instability of the head-dress worn. In the Kohima group, where the rather fragile wheel of hornbill feathers is not worn by the younger men, who wear less cumbrous erections of bamboo and paper, the movements of the dancers are freer, while in the Viswema group the dancers work up a gradually increasing pace, ending up by running very fast and leaping. In this ceremonial dancing the old men take little part, following for a time at the end of the line and directing operations generally. They do not trouble to put on full dress, but carry weapons and any marks of particular distinction to which they are considered entitled.

Both dhan-pounding and dancing are accompanied by singing, the nature of which has already been described. The songs sung include both particular songs traditionally associated with the occasion, and sometimes in archaic language not fully understood except by those skilled in them, as well as songs in common use which may be fancied by the singers.

Prayer.   The idea of prayer, as we understand it, is perhaps not foreign to the Angami mind, as witness the prayer offered to Tsükho and Dzürawü by persons going out hunting : " In your name have I come out, and in hope of your aid, I pray that ye will discover and give unto me of the animals in your keeping." In some cases, however, what would seem at first to be a prayer has probably degenerated and is repeated rather as a charm, and as such the traditional formula must be observed.

Commu-
nal cere-
monies.   The following is a list of the principal gennas in the Angami year. The dates are approximate only, as the actual beginning of the genna depends partly on the state of the crops, and in some cases, e.g. that of the Titho genna, the Angami villages wait for the Memi villages,[1] and the Kemovos of each village take their cue from the villages to the south-east or south of them as far as Mekrima, which is generally regarded by Angami villages as the authority in these matters. The order in which these gennas are observed, moreover, is not the same in all villages, and as two gennas are often coupled together in their observance, and differently coupled by different villages, it is difficult to give a lucid statement of the calendar. The order given is that in which the gennas are observed in Khonoma, or at any rate approximately so. The Sekrengi is put first because it seems naturally to fall into that place ; Angami opinion, however, is divided on this point between the Gnongi, Sekrengi, and Terhengi gennas as the first genna of the year. It is related that once two men got so heated in a dispute as to whether the Terhengi or the Gnongi was the first that they fought over it and killed each other. The Terhengi, however, marks the completion of the agricultural year, while the Sekrengi has for its object the preservation of health in the coming year. The claims of the Gnongi are based on its marking the beginning of fresh agricultural operations. The Gnongi and Terhengi are generally treated as the two most important gennas of the year in the Kohima and Khonoma groups, but practice

[1] The *Mohvo* of Mekrima is the one from whom the other Memi villages take it in the first instance.

varies in this respect, and among the Eastern Angamis the Titho or its equivalent holds perhaps the most prominent place of all. The gennas conferring social status, though performed at the Terhengi in the Kohima group, are performed at the Sekrengi in the Viswema group. The Kezami and Mémi gennas given as corresponding to those in the Khonoma list are those which seem to correspond most nearly in the purpose, time, and manner of their performance, but it is difficult to be precise, as Angami opinion on the matter differs considerably and is sometimes quite at variance with all apparent probabilities. In most cases, of course, no opinion is formulated on such points until it is asked for, when the person questioned is taken by surprise, answers at random, and invents reasons afterwards to justify his answer. The list of gennas is followed by additional details in regard to the Sekrengi, Thekrangi, Thezukepu, Titho, and Terhengi gennas, which are fairly typical of the observance of gennas in general.

ANGAMI GENNAS.

1. *Sěkrěngi.*—Falls on the second day after the full moon of the month Keno[1] or of the month Kezi. When falling in Keno, it falls sometimes on the fifth day after the full moon. Five days' kenna and penna and five more nanü only are observed; ceremonial dress is worn, at any rate in the Khonoma group. The ceremony is to ensure the health of the community during the coming year. The men have to eat separately, taking their food away from the hearth

---

[1] The Angamis divide the year into twelve months :—

Thennye (approximately)	October.	Kera	. . . .	April.
Zipe or Viphie	November.	Ketsü	. . . .	May.
Rede	December.	Chachü	. . . .	June.
Doshü	January.	Chadi	. . . .	July.
Keno	February.	Chire	. . . .	August.
Kezi	March.	Reye	. . . .	September.

An intercalary month, called *Revü krenhye*, is inserted about every fourth year to correct the mistakes which have arisen from calculating twelve lunar months to the year. It is difficult to see how the insertion of a full month would do so, but probably it merely affords an opportunity of starting again in the right place. The reckoning is done by old men, who are not explicit on the point. The average Angami knows nothing about it.

and remaining chaste for at least three days. Dogs are eaten in large numbers.

This genna is not usually regarded by the Tengima as one of very great importance. It perhaps corresponds to the Kezami genna called *Zātsü*, and to the Memi *Süpra*. The Memi have also an important genna called *Thoni*, at which vegetables are tabooed, which falls about the same time as the Sekrengi, while the Sālēni genna of the Memi which I have given as corresponding to the Tsungi contains features associated with the Tengima Sekrengi.

2. *Gnŏngi.*—Falls on the third day after the full moon of the month Kera ; marks the completion of the sowing of jhum land. Twelve to fourteen days' *penna* are observed in the Khonoma group, but in the Kohima and Viswema groups only five days'. This genna is the most important of all, after the Terhengi, to the Tengima Angamis. The *kenna* is very strict.

This genna seems to correspond to the Kezami *Yĕkĕnge* and the Memi *Rüprā.*

3. *Thĕkrăngi* (called by Kohima *Kĕrŭngi*).—Falls on the day of the full moon of the month Chachü or else twenty days later, according to the state of the rice crop ; marks the transplantation of the paddy seedlings into the irrigated terraces ; three days' *penna ;* ceremonial dress worn by Khonoma (but not by Kohima) for dhan-pounding, singing, and dancing ; seems to correspond to the Memi *Düni.* A death in the village within a week or so of the Thekrangi genna causes its postponement for at least a day.

This genna is regarded as of comparatively small importance.

4. *Tsüngi* (called by Kohima *Chādăngi*).—Falls in Khonoma about seven days after the new moon, or, if the crop is backward, at the full moon of Reye ; in Kohima nine days after the new moon of the preceding month Chire. Khonoma observe five days' *penna*, Kohima seven, and Viswema fifteen. The village roads and graves are cleared. No animals or bamboo shoots for pickles may be taken through the village paths, and no one is allowed to speak to any one of another village. This genna corresponds to

the Kezami *Ětsǔngě* and Memi *Sālēnī*, which is regarded by the Memi as of particular importance and is the occasion of the commemoration of the ancestral dead. *Cha-da-ngi* = " path-clearing genna."

5. *Thězǔkěpǔ.*—Celebrated by Khonoma with the Tsungi ; has for its object the preservation of the rice crop from field-mice and rats. One day's strict *penna* is observed, followed by a day's *nanü*, on which no work is done. *Thezukepu* = " the sung mouse."

6. *Lǐkwěngī.*—Kept by Khonoma thirty days after the Tsungi, and by Jotsoma with the Lideh (see *infra*, No. 9). Not observed at all by the Kohima or Viswema groups ; marks the beginning of the millet harvest ; three days' *penna* observed. *Likwengi* = " bird (or rather " field ") scaring genna."

7. *Thēwǔūkǔkwǔ.*—Kept by Khonoma with the Likwengi, but by Viswema with Vateh (see No. 10), which is the first day of a three days' genna, Thewüukukwü taking up the last two, and the whole combination falling later than the Thewüukukwü in Khonoma. In Jotsoma the Thewüukukwü marks the cutting of the " ahu dhan." *Thewüukukwü* = " giving the toad his share," in explanation of which it is related that the man, the rat, and the toad once found some rice together. When discussing its division, the rat (alluding to the Naga method of carrying loads slung on a band across the forehead) said, " My head is pointed ; I cannot carry it, let me eat in the edge of your field as my share," while the toad said that he did not want his share, but that the man might offer him some every year in his (the toad's) name. Thus it is that the rats eat rice in the fields and the Thewüukukwü is performed annually.[1]

At this genna the converse of the Sekrengi is observed, women having to eat separately from different dishes and taking their food from leaves or baskets but not from the platters in regular use ; they have to eat away from the

[1] For a possible explanation of the connection between the toad and the rice crop see " Golden Bough," Vol. VIII, p. 291. The Semas connect the toad with *Latsapa*, the spirit responsible for the rice harvest, and also, apparently, with thunder and lightning. See the Monograph on the Sema Tribe.

hearth, and are generally under the same restrictions as regards men as men are under as regards women at the Sekrengi.

This genna seems to correspond to the Kezami *Būtsütŏh* and the Memi *Baulŭtōwē*, at which women take liquor only —no cooked rice or meat—for two days, and have to eat apart from the men and from new dishes and using a new hearth, which are put aside when done with and not used again. The Butsütoh and Baulutowe, however, are kept after No. 8 and not before it, resembling Viswema in this respect.

8. *Tithŏ* (or *Tīchū*).—Kept by Khonoma five days after the Likwengi, has for its object the protection of the ripening crop from hail (*Titho* = Sky-ceremony). *Penna* is observed for five days by Khonoma and Kohima, by Jotsoma for ten days, by Viswema and by the Memi villages for at least thirty days. It is said that this genna used to last from one to three months, according to date, as it still does more or less in some of the Memi villages.

No trade is allowed during the duration of the genna and it is absolutely *kenna* to introduce into the village by way of trade or otherwise any white material such as salt or cotton or even rice.

The genna corresponds to the Kezami *Ĕngŏngē*, at which also no new clothes may be taken from boxes for fear of causing wind storms, and during which it is genna to kill chickens, and to the Memi *Mūni* or *Chīrāsō*. The genna is regarded with particular importance by the Eastern Angamis.

9. *Lĭdĕh* (called *Bĭngī* by Viswema) is performed in Khonoma three days after the new moon of Zipe ; by Jotsoma it is combined with the Likwengi. This genna marks the opening of the rice harvest and lasts two days. On the first day, called " *Bĭlipfŭ-lĭdĕh*," *penna* is observed by everyone except the Lidepfü who goes to the fields and cuts a few heads of paddy. The second day, called " *Mĕsĭ-lĭdĕh*," is *penna* for everyone, and on the following day it is open to anyone in the village to reap as he pleases.

This genna seems to correspond to the Kezami *Metsa*.

10. *Tĕkĕdĕh* (called by Kohima *Vātĕh* or *Kĕvā kĕtĕhā*).—

Kept by Khonoma three days after the new moon of Rede,
but by Kohima five days after the first moon following on
the completion of the harvest, so that it falls sometimes in
November and sometimes in December. The Viswema
group combine the Thewüukukwü with this, the Tekedeh
occupying the first day of the combined genna, and the
Thewüukukwü two days more. In Khonoma this genna
lasts five days and celebrates the completion of reaping.

11. *Tĕrhĕngĭ.*—Kept by Kohima eleven days after Vateh
and with considerable circumstance, ceremonial dress being
worn and dhan pounded. Khonoma wears no ceremonial
dress for this genna, but then the personal gennas of Zhāthō,
Lĕsü, and Kĕtĕshĕ are not done by Khonoma. The genna
lasts ten days and celebrates the harvest-home for the year.
The Angamis proper, particularly Kohima, attach great
importance to this genna. It corresponds to the Kezami
Ărrĭnghē, at which men must remain chaste for three days
as at the Angami Sekrengi, and to the Memi *Ădhōnĭ.*
Terhe-ngi perhaps = " spirit-genna " (<*terho*).

The following story is told in Kohima of the origin of the
Terhengi gennas. Once upon a time an old woman lived
at Merema village with an unmarried daughter. One day,
when going home from her fields a *terhoma* called Zīsō
followed her and put his hands over her eyes from behind.
The old woman said, " Who are you ? Go away ! " But
Ziso said, " I will not let you go unless you promise me your
daughter in marriage." So she promised and was released,
but looking round saw no one. A few days later the same
thing happened again, and again she promised, going home
very sad at heart.

Now one day the daughter went with her companions to
work in the fields, and as she was coming home she lagged
behind the others. Suddenly Ziso caught hold of her and
took her to his lair and she lived with him as his wife.

A year later she came back to her mother's house and said
to her, " My husband is a very handsome and wealthy man ;
come with me and ask of him whatever you will, and you
will receive it. But I tell you this now : there is a small
basket hanging on the right-hand side of the middle room

of his dwelling, in which all kinds of animals are kept. Ask for nothing save only that basket." Then, taking some husks of corn, they set out for the daughter's house, dropping husks along the road for fear of the old woman's losing her way home again.

After staying some days with her son-in-law, the old woman said she must go home. Then Ziso said, " Tell me, mother-in-law, what you would like, and I will give it." And the old woman answered, " Many things I would like, but I cannot carry them, so I will only ask for that little basket hanging in the middle room, for me to keep my yeast in." But Ziso was troubled at her saying and said, " Mother-in-law, do not ask for that but ask for something else." But the old woman answered, " I am an old woman. I cannot carry heavy things." Then Ziso gave her the small basket, saying, " Don't open the cover in the road or anywhere until you reach home. Then put a fence about it, and shut the door when you open the basket, and don't go out for five days." So the old woman started home with the basket.

But about halfway the old woman found the basket very heavy, and herself longing to open it. So she took off the lid, and behold! Animals of every·kind, mithan, boars, birds, mice, and every sort of beast and flying thing, and those which were able to fly or run swiftly came forth and fled, and those unable to get away were again shut in by the old woman as she put back the lid. Then she came to her house and shut the door and opened the basket, and the animals which remained—mithan, cows, pigs, dogs and fowls—came out of the basket, and she kept them in the house with the door shut for five days and they all became tame. These animals are called " the woman's share " (thĕn-yūma rī) and may be given by a man to his daughter[1]; the wild beasts are spoken of as " the man's share " (thĕpvŭma rī).

The following year the old woman's daughter and son-in-law came to visit her and found her house filled with

---

[1] As opposed to land, which may only go to the male heirs. See Part III under " Inheritance."

domestic animals. And Ziso said to the mother-in-law,
" Kill these fat bulls, and eat them in my name." And so
this festival is kept every year and called Terhengi
(*Terho-ngi*, " the spirit's feast "), for Ziso was a spirit.[1]

With regard to the wearing of ceremonial dress at gennas
it is noticeable that in Kohima it is *kenna* to wear hornbill
feathers between the sowing of millet and reaping of the
rice, a prohibition which rather discounts the celebration
of gennas in dress, as most of them, indeed the greater part
of the year, fall into this period. In Khonoma, however,
there is no such prohibition, as the Thekrangi is a full dress
affair. Ceremonial dress, however, is never worn by the
kindred [2] of persons who have recently died ; they take
part in the genna wearing ordinary clothes.

The Sekrengi genna,[3] which has for its object the prevention of illness during the coming year, begins, as all gennas
do, by the taking of a little rice and pretending to cook it
by holding it for a moment at the fire. It is then wrapped
up in a plantain leaf and together with a similar miniature
leaf cup of rice beer tied to the central post of the partition
wall between the two main rooms of an Angami house.
This, on the first day of the genna, is followed by a visit
on the part of all men to the village spring, where they wash
themselves, their weapons and tools and clothes in fresh
water, the spring having been watched on the eve of the
genna by boys, no doubt to prevent defilement. On
returning, every male who is old enough to do so kills an
unblemished cock, but must kill it by throttling it with his
hands alone. The position of the legs at death is watched,
and if the right leg is passed over the left and excreta passed,
the omen is good. If, however, the omen is bad another

---

[1] Almost precisely the same story is recorded by Soppitt as a Kachari
story. See " An Historical and Descriptive Account of the Kachari
Tribes of the North Cachar Hills," by C. A. Soppitt. Shillong, 1885.
Reprinted with an introduction by E. C. Stuart Baker, 1901, pp. 56–57.

[2] Where the kindred is a large one this would only apply to the nearer
relations.

[3] This account is of the Sekrengi genna as observed in Jotsoma. Details
vary from village to village.

and another cock is killed until one dies with its legs in the right position.[1] Each man after killing his cock makes a fire, which he must light from a fire-stick and nothing else ; matches or burning brands must not be used to light this fire, and in the lighting of the fire another omen is taken. If the spark is first produced to the right of the stick the year will be a good one for men, if to the left for women. The cock killed is cooked on the fire made, and eaten by the man who killed it. Beef and pork may also be eaten, but it is the custom to eat dogs' flesh in particular at the Sekrengi genna. In the Khonoma group, where this custom is particularly well observed, many households eat several dogs during the Sekrengi. No reason is given for this canine diet except that it is the custom, much, one may suppose, as turkeys are eaten at Christmas in England. The Lhotas, however, who eat dog in a precisely similar way at the genna by which they propitiate their evil spirit Tsungram (? Tsungram = Sekre), say that they sacrifice and eat dogs because the dog being the most cunning of all beasts is preferred as a sacrifice by the evil one to all other animals. It may be noted, however, that the Angamis regard dogs' flesh as an excellent tonic and pick-me-up for anyone who is in poor health.[2] This probably has a good deal to do with the dog diet at the Sekrengi, which is observed to secure good health in the coming year.

The strangling of cocks and the Sekrengi genna generally is the occasion on which male children leave the " women's side." In Jotsoma and Khonoma the boy old enough to strangle a cock may no longer sleep on his mother's bed, and if he does not sleep on a third bed will sleep on his father's. In the Kohima group the boy has to leave his parents' bedroom entirely and sleep in the outer portion of the house, and generally speaking he begins to associate with the other boys of the village rather than with his mother.

During the whole of the first two days of the Sekrengi genna all men are *kenna*. They have to eat separately and the women may not approach them, and may not even

---

[1] In Khonoma this is done at intervals of one month. In Kohima not at all.

[2] *See* Appendix XIII, p. 457

draw water for them as on other days. On the fourth day
of the genna the young men put on ceremonial dress and
go to the jungle, from which they fetch in pith, sticks, and
wood, from which they make gigantic reproductions in the
traditional colours and type of the largest kind of bead
necklaces worn by men. These they string up in a large
house in which they congregate after the evening meal and
sing. This house is called the *theka ki* and seems to be selected
for its size and general convenience. It is also the custom
during this genna for the young men, more particularly in
Eastern Angami villages, to go out into the jungle armed
with pellet-bows and to bring back numbers of birds,
lizards, mice, etc., which they tie to long bamboo poles
and set up in front of their houses. Prosperity in general
and in particular success in war in the coming year
depends on the number of small birds and animals taken.
The village is strictly *penna* for the first five days of the
genna, work of any sort being forbidden, and, of course,
all coming and going to or from the village. In addition
to this, during a further five days of *nanü* no work is done
in the fields.

It is at the end of this genna that the Lidepfü collects her
fees for opening the harvest, sending four or five men of
her clan to collect paddy—a small basketful from each
house. The fact that the First-reaper collects at this
genna while the First-sower collects after the harvest genna
is noticeable. Taken in conjunction with the fact that
performers of these offices are usually old and poor and
have little or no cultivation of their own, it possibly
suggests the existence of a fear lest the acts of beginning
the sowing or reaping should bring some ill consequence
upon the crop of the first sower or reaper, and that it is to
avoid associating themselves with some such misfortune
that the rest of the village delay contributions until another
agricultural year. It is possibly intended, however, to
make the First-sower " reap what he has sown " and suffer
(in his contributions) for a bad crop.

The Thekrangi genna is marked by dancing and singing
on the part of the young men, boys, and girls who are

unmarried, or married but who have no children. In the afternoon of the second day they turn out in full dress and pound dhan and sing in the *theka ki*, the girls and men being on opposite sides of the pounding trestle and singing staves alternately. This is followed by a procession round the courtyard of the house, the men carrying mithan horns of rice beer and the girls carrying leaf cups, while the procession is headed by a man carrying a veteran's spear, covered with tresses of human hair, but deprived of its iron head, for which a point of rolled plantain leaf is substituted, for fear of someone's getting injured if the iron head were retained. In the rear of the procession one of the young men carries a pair of the shield-horns adorned with human tresses that are worn on warriors' shields. The two horns are tied together and carried over the shoulder ; sometimes, however, a second spear is carried instead. On the approach of a similar party from another clan in the village (the cases witnessed by the writer were at Khonoma), both parties go to the *tehuba*[1] outside the house of the Kemovo and " dance " and sing there, the songs being sung by the men until the conclusion, when the song is finished up with the assistance of two girls specially picked for the part. Each clan occupies the *tehuba* in turn, returning from it to the *tehuba* of the clan and thence to the courtyards of their *theka ki*. The *tehuba* regarded as the village *tehuba* must be visited first. The dancing consists of going solemnly in a procession round the circle, the lines sometimes dividing into two, so that one goes one way and the other the opposite way ; the girls are told off as partners to the boys and move in a sort of second rank on the inside of the boys. This goes on for a couple of hours or so, the parties eventually, after singing for a short time inside the *theka ki*, breaking up and going to their homes for the evening meal. It is

[1] For *tehuba*, see Part II. Each clan in a large village like Khonoma has its own Kemovo with a *tehuba* outside his house, but one of these Kemovo is regarded as the village Kemovo and takes precedence of the others. In Khonoma the village kemovo is the Kemovo of the Thevoma clan, the only Pezoma clan in the village, though whether the village kemovo is always Pezoma in a genuinely mixed Pezoma-Pepfüma village I cannot say.

PLAYING ONE OF THE BEAN GAMES

[See p. 103

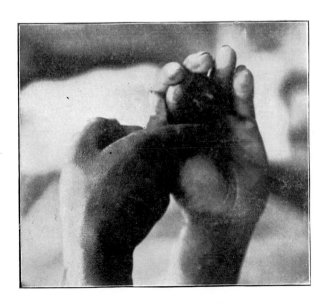

PHOTOGRAPH SHOWING METHOD OF PROPELLING THE BEAN

[See p. 103

NIHU OF KOHIMA

[See p. 123

VISARE OF KHONOMA

[See p. 129

unlucky for rain to fall during the singing and dancing in the *tehuba*. It is regarded as an omen of death, and, unless very slight, necessitates the abstention from all ceremonial during the observation of the genna in the following year. Heavy rain, of course, stops proceedings at once, as it would ruin the ceremonial costume of the men in no time.

In the evening each party meets again in the *theka ki* of the clan to sing. The men arrive first and sit down in two opposite rows on benches placed ready at the two ends of the big front room cleared for the occasion and with a fire lit in the centre. The huge head-dresses are reduced to possible dimensions by taking out all but the centre feather spoke and bringing up the two little spokes at the back to close on each side of it, giving a sort of *fleur-de-lys* effect. The men sit as close to one another as they can in exactly the same attitude, with a mithan horn of rice beer, from which they do not drink, held in the right hand, the right arm resting on the right knee. The girls turn up a little later and sit down on benches along the two sides of the room, but leaving passage room along the side on to which the doors give, which is crowded with spectators as thick as they can be packed. The girls keep their eyes fixed on the ground, for they are regarded as most immodest if they look about them at all—at least in public—on such occasions. In the privacy of the outer darkness a good deal of flirtation probably goes on. The singing is in alternate verses in some cases, but men's songs are also sung by the men only and women's songs by women. The subjects of some of the songs are considered particularly appropriate to the occasion, *e.g.* the song given at the end of Part I of this Monograph, while in other cases they may be any songs current in the village; one, for instance, of those heard by the writer told how the young men had hunted a sambhar for a very long distance and been benighted in the jungle, while another was a request from a wife to her husband to bring her back two flowers from the jungle when he came home, one for her and one for the child. This singing in the evening takes place on all three days of the genna and lasts most of the night, but only on the second and third days is ceremonial dress worn, and then not always on the third day. If there are enough unmarried boys and girls to form a procession by themselves, this procession takes place on the second day without dhan-pounding or the carrying of spear or shield-horns, and sometimes mere children take part, while the older unmarried and the young childless married persons perform the genna as already described on the third day instead of the second. If, however, the number of eligible performers be few, the genna is performed as described on the second day. Platters of pork, sprinkled with salt, are also carried in the procession and given to each married girl taking part, the bride's mother giving a chicken to the bringer in exchange. Dhan-pounding and the carrying of spears, etc., in the procession is definitely connected with the participation of married persons in the genna, which seems to be intended to promote the fertility of the crops and of newly married couples.

The Thezukepu is in some ways perhaps the most interesting of all the Angami gennas. It is not regarded as having the importance of the Gnongi, the Terhengi, or the Titho, but the first two of these at any rate are not marked by nearly such intriguing details as the Thezukepu, " the Sung Mouse."[1] The account of it given here is the genna as observed in Jotsoma. On the eve of the first day of the genna the young men of the village look for a sort of field-mouse called " *Zukrano*," and catching one alive and putting it into a section of bamboo, place it outside the house which does duty as the Morung. After the evening meal the young men assemble at this house and choose one of their number who is to throw the mouse.[2] The mouse is taken from the bamboo, and its ears are bored and cotton-wool put in them as though it were a man. It is then placed in the hand of the man selected to throw it away ; the young men gird up their loins, and the man living in the most outlying house of the village is called to, but does not leave

[1] Or possibly " telling off the rat " would be a more correct rendering.
[2] He is called *thĕzŭkĕseō* = " (the one) who throws the mouse."

his house. The mouse-thrower, stripped naked, then runs as fast as he can through the village, from the bottom towards the top, and outside, and throwing the mouse away down the village path tells it to go to such and such a village, naming some remote village of the Eastern Angamis, Semas or elsewhere. The thrower is accompanied meanwhile by a dozen or so other young men, who run along with him snatching sticks from the fences and beating upon the ground, singing and shouting to frighten away the mice. The thrower runs back to the Morung house and jumps up upon the machan used for sleeping, and is not allowed to step down to earth again for twenty-four hours. Meanwhile, from the time when the man in the furthest house of the village has been called, all the older men and the women staying in their houses stamp and shout as though driving the mice out of the village, and from the moment that the first sound of this stamping and shouting is heard no one may eat or drink again that night, and those in the middle of a meal must stop it. On the following day the village is *penna* and no one may pick vegetables. This day is called "*Thezukepu.*" On the next day, called "*Reddeh,*" a pig is sacrificed in order to make the rice in the houses last well.

The origin of the Titho genna is said to have been the destruction of the crop year after year by hail. At last the people asked a wise man what to do, and he told them to do a genna or they would always lose their crops. Accordingly a six days' genna is done every year by Jotsoma, who do this genna rather more thoroughly than the other villages of the Khonoma, Kohima, and Chakroma groups. At Jotsoma two or three panjis are placed by the Kemovo on each side of the village path and an unblemished cock is released into the jungle. This is done twice, once at one side of the village, once at another. No other villages of the Khonoma or Kohima groups, however, still observe this custom. But the Memi village of Mekrima, from which the Tengima villages derive their observance of this ceremony, actually release a calf at this genna. This calf must be pitch black without a white spot. It is hobbled with thin creepers for five days, and if during these five days it escapes in spite of the hobbles, hail is certain to fall. In Sopvoma the black calf is tied to a certain stone for a whole day, and if it remains silent the omen is good, if it lows to one side or the other bad hail may be expected from that quarter. All Angami villages prohibit the export or import during the genna of rice, salt, cotton, beads (particularly white beads), wooden dishes, ivory armlets, or any other white material.

It has been already stated that the object of this genna is to avert hail. Hail constitutes a very serious danger to the Angami rice crop when the latter is ripening, and in the higher hills about the Barail range is of by no means uncommon occurrence. The reduction in the duration and in the importance of the genna among the more northerly and westerly villages of the Angamis is no doubt the result of the lessened danger from hail, while the prohibition laid on white materials is probably based on the theory that their whiteness will cause a fall of white hailstones. In some of the Naga villages in the Manipur State the genna is observed from the time when the crop begins to ripen practically until the harvest, as will be seen from the following notes, for which the writer is indebted to the kindness of Colonel Shakespear :—

"Mao. *Chijira goshür* genna, for just under three months no trading allowed in the thirteen villages which obey the Mohvu[1] of Pudugnamei.[2] It begins eight days before a new moon and lasts two whole months and eight days into the next, which is the new moon of November."

"Maikel. The Maikel Khullakpa[1] can declare a genna called *Kapâni*, which lasts two months and sixteen days. A cow is tied up, and in which direction it bellows, hail is feared. Trading is stopped. This is the same as Chijira goshür. The first day of the genna extends to Kohima."

"Purun.[3] *Uchijiragashur*—a genna for a month in October. Purum, Oinam, Theba Khulel, and Khuno and Koide keep this genna. It is prohibited to bring fowls, cows, salt, pigs,

---

[1] *Mohvu* is the Memi word = Tengima *Kemovo*, to which *Khullakpa*, a Manipuri word, also corresponds. "Maikel" = Mekrima.

[2] *I.e.*, Sopvo-terhema.

[3] A Khoirao village, but with probably a strong Memi admixture.

dogs, into another village boundaries. Stone-pullers must remain chaste. The genna is only kept for a month by these villages, but they take the word for it from the Mohvu of Maikel."

The gennas above enumerated are clearly connected with the agricultural year, or at any rate with the agricultural interest of the community. Other communal gennas there are, however, which though of infrequent and irregular occurrence cannot be entirely passed over. Such an one is the genna at which war dancing is indulged in. This is a genna of little importance and occurs only now and then —once perhaps in about seven years or more, and at no fixed interval. It is proclaimed by the Kemovo when the number of young men in the clan is unusually large. Possibly in the days of Angami independence it may have been followed as a rule by a military expedition, but nowadays it consists only of a day or two's *penna* and the putting on ceremonial costume by the young men, who dance war dances before the assembled clan or village, to the great gratification of the other sex.

Another is a genna observed, if not yearly, at any rate frequently, and often in consecutive years, by the clan as differentiated from the village. This consists in paying a visit to the members of a friendly clan in another village. Many clans have long-standing ties of friendship with particular clans in other villages and the memory of such ties is preserved and kept green by these visits. The visits take place on invitation, and a day is fixed on which the male members of the invited clan put on ceremonial dress and go in a procession with no little pomp to the village of their hosts, where one or two days' *nanü* is observed, both parties dressing ceremonially and indulging in much dancing, feasting, and merry-making. These visits are often paid between clans of distant villages, villages some-times two or three days' journey apart, as when the Thevoma clan of Khonoma visited the Kipoma clan of Kigwema, sleeping one night at Jotsoma on the way, or when one of the clans of Razama paid a visit to a friendly clan in Kohima, three days' journey away. In such a case the whole journey is performed in ceremonial dress and rain is a serious disaster. These visits are paid about the month of March and at no other time of the year. The clan which issues the invitation is occupied for several days in preparing a vast quantity of liquor, and numbers of animals are killed for the feast. Males of all ages take part in the visit and the dancing.

In addition to these and other recurrent gennas, any untoward or unusual occurrence may call for the observance of a genna by the village or clan, as, for instance, the fall of any earth on to a genna stone (*kipuchie*) or the dragging of a new door for the village gateway. The latter ceremony is performed at Sachema as follows :—

The door is dragged up beforehand to within half a mile or so of the village. This is done without ceremonial dress and is not attended by genna. On the day of the ceremony the Kemovo takes some new " pita modhu " and a cock and goes early in the morning to the stump of the tree from which the door was cut. The cock is fed and let loose, while the " modhu " is poured into a plantain-leaf cup. A little " modhu " is also poured on to a plantain leaf and offered to the cock. If the cock takes the " modhu " it is regarded as a good omen. The Kemovo then goes to the door itself, taking with him the Zhevo and Tsakro. The two former take grass (*kurhi*) and touch the door with it, addressing the door in the following terms :—

" You must not stay here but go to the place appointed for you. Men shall be more in number, paddy and cultivation shall be more prosperous, cattle, dogs, etc., shall be more plentiful."

The Kemovo ties two thin strings to the door and drags at and breaks them. Then two boys, who have never had sexual intercourse, one Kepezoma and one Kepepfüma and both naked, the former on the right and the other on the left, tie on two string ropes, which must on no account subsequently break, and pull them. Then all the men may take hold of the ropes, and they proceed to drag up the door towards the gateway. On the way up the door is stopped and blessed by the Tsakro, the Zhevo and Kemovo having done so before as already described.

No one is allowed to follow or get behind the door ; and all spectators and women have to get inside the village walls before the door arrives at the gate. The clan to whom the door belongs drags the right rope and the other clan or clans drag the left rope. Every male in the village (including small boys) has to have his hand on the rope, though the dragging is really done by a dragging party.

On arriving at the gate, the draggers being inside, the clan to whom the door belongs first drop their rope and go in procession to the *tehuba*. When they have all left, the others follow. Then the Kemovo, the Zhevo, and the Tsakro take a fowl and touch the door with its beak and repeat the blessing. The fowl is then killed with a piece of wood in the house of a man near the gate, where the "modhu" for the genna has also been made, and it is eaten that night by the Kemovo only off plantain leaves.

A dance called *sovi* follows.

A large amount of a compound called " *hinu* " is prepared from maize, Job's tears, rice, beans, chillies, salt, and " *kenya.*" This is the only food to be eaten that day after the dragging of the door until the evening meal.

All the men wear dancing dress (without arms), except those who have had a death in the house, and they wear ordinary clothes, as at all gennas at which ceremonial dress is worn. Before the ceremony strangers are not allowed inside the houses where the preparations for the genna are going on.[1]

Should the clothes and miscellaneous stuff left on one side by persons working in the fields get burnt while they are doing so, a *mi-penna* (*mi* = " fire ") is kept by the whole village. One was observed in Kohima village on March 25, 1919. Should the stubble catch fire at harvest time, too, a *mi-penna* is observed, while if the wind should overturn the mat used for threshing and winnowing the grain a genna called *Thekrelhāpe* is observed.

The gennas which attend the life of the individual Angami fall roughly into two divisions : the gennas which are more or less inseparable from his existence in the community, Individual Gennas

[1] *See* Appendix XIII, p. 457.

gennas, that is to say, which attend all ordinary individuals, at his birth, his marriage, and his death, and the gennas which are more or less optional and which determine his status in the society. It is perhaps simplest to deal first with the gennas that attend all individuals and afterwards with those that are not essential.

An Angami woman when about to deliver [1] a child breaks the strings of beads that she is wearing, letting the beads fall about the floor, and throws off all her clothes except a single cloth wrapped round her body like a shawl. She delivers her child hanging by her hands to a head-band (for carrying loads), which is fastened to a beam in the house, her knees being clear of the ground.[2] The genna that follows is the same whichever the sex of the child. The mother is kept separate from the rest of the household, her bed being separated, and a separate hearth being built for her, though in the same room as the general hearth. Immediately after the delivery and before the cutting of the navel-string,[3] she is fed on rice-beer, rice, and the flesh of a hen (never that of a cock) which has been touched by the child. For five days, for ten in the case of her first child,[4] the mother is fed exclusively on this food, a second hen being killed if the first is not enough, and during these five days her husband is kenna, and in some villages the whole household is kenna. The household is kenna in any case on the day of birth,[5] as it is if any domestic animal gives birth to young.

When the five days have expired the mother is allowed to

[1] The Kezami Angamis when a birth is about to take place put all eatables and drinkables outside the house. The Kacha Nagas do the same, but not the Tengima Angamis.

[2] See Appendix XIII, p 457.

[3] Among the Memi, at any rate, this is done by the mother herself with a bamboo knife. I think the Tengima bury the placenta in the house. Certainly the Memi do.

[4] It is after the birth of her first child that an Angami girl removes from her ears the white shells that she has worn from infancy. She gives them to her husband. Similar shells are worn by the Ao girl, who, however, parts with them when she is tattooed, a ceremony which takes place as soon as she is considered old enough to be be married and usually after her betrothal, or what practically amounts to such.

[5] The Kacha Nagas remain kenna for thirty days after a birth.

go out, but by the back door of the house only, and if there
is no back door one has to be made for the purpose. No
one must see her going out, she goes out by stealth, taking
all the cooking, eating, and drinking utensils of the household
with her, and when no one is looking she throws them away
behind the house. Her husband opens the back door for
her and keeps a look-out to see that there is no one watching,
but he must not look at his wife as she is coming out to
throw the things away.

The baby is washed with warm water on the day of its
birth, and this washing is followed by the cutting of the
navel cord, but it is not washed again till the five days'
genna have expired. On the sixth day, after throwing
away the cooking utensils, the mother takes any child of
her husband's kindred and of the same sex as her baby and
goes with this child to the village water-hole. The child
draws water and gives it to the mother, who carries it back
to the house and washes her baby with it without heating
the water. The mother also on her way plucks two or three
sprays of the plant called " *tsoheh*," which she brings back
with her. She puts a drop of water and then a twig of this
plant on the babe's forehead and adjures it to become strong
and hard like the *tsoheh* plant. At the same time she tears
the twig in two.[1] This ceremony she repeats on the right
and on the left hand of the infant. On the eighth day she
carries the child who accompanied her to the well to the
house of one of her husband's kindred who is newly married
and has suffered no misfortune. For this purpose the
house of a married man whose children are all alive will also
serve. The wife of this man places a little rice beer on the
child's lips and gives the child a little rice and a little rice
beer in a diminutive gourd, after which the mother of the
newly-born baby again carries the child back to her
house.

The infant, when it grows up, stands in a particular
relation to the newly-married man to whose house the
child was taken. He or she must call him " father " and

[1] Is this in order that the virtue of the plant may leave it and so pass
into the child ?

his wife " mother," and neither must on any account behave aggressively toward the other.

On the ninth day the father and the mother, taking the baby[1] itself, go to the fields, and after pretending to do a little work they eat and drink and then return home. Sometimes they do not even go to their fields, but go out of the village and dig some ground anywhere at all. When returning home they bring back two pieces of alder tree. This concludes all birth ceremonies.

If the child be born dead, or die before the completion of the five days' genna, one day's *kenna* is observed, nothing more, and the child is buried inside the house. The father must be present when it is buried, and if he is away from home the burial of the body is put off until he returns. A case occurred in Jotsoma during the Abor expedition of 1912 in which the wife of a man who was with the expedition gave birth to a daughter which died. The body was kept unburied in the house for two months until the father returned to his family—and they living in the house all the time.

If a woman die in childbirth or before the completion of the five days' genna, she is taken out, not by the door, but through a hole made in the side of the house, and buried with all her property. Her baby is taken out and buried with her, if it die as well. Should it live it would normally be brought up on rice pulp, but cases of gynecomastism seem to occur occasionally.[2] There is at the time of writing a girl in Jotsoma whose mother died when she was an infant and who was suckled by her father Niselhu, also still living, who first let the child suck at his breast to comfort it, but after a time was able to give it milk. In the Lhota

---

[1] In one version of the birth ceremonial given me it was the baby itself which was fed in the house of one of the husband's kindred, while it was a boy or girl from the husband's kindred who was taken out of the village to dig.

[2] See Haeckel, " Evolution of Man," p. 114.

In Yampi, a Chang village, there is a noted warrior named Yenso, who is said to have breasts like a woman, while in Yuonyar there is an hermaphrodite named Chualan Abaja. Cases of the suckling of orphaned children by quite old women seem to occur from time to time among the Lhotas.

village of Longsa a girl named Pontselo, still living, is said
to have been suckled by her father Chiathang from the
time she was fifteen days old, when her mother died. Angami
children are usually suckled until they are two or three
years old. One may frequently see a woman with a baby
and an older child, both of which she is suckling. Children
whose father dies remain in the custody of the mother or
her relations until weaned, after which the father's heirs
have the custody of them.

Infanticide used to be practised in the case of children
born of unmarried girls. In such cases delivery had to
take place in the jungle, and the child was killed ; the
Kezami women used further to pierce its feet all over with
thorns to prevent its visiting and haunting the mother in
her dreams. It was believed that if it was allowed to grow
up the village would have no success in hunting or in war.
Nowadays an unmarried girl who is pregnant is turned out
of her parents' house before delivery, and gives birth in the
cow-house of someone else's porch or some similar place,
and the presence of any second person at the time of delivery
is *kenna*. Whether the mother performs any ceremony is
not known.

Twins are uncommon, but the occurrence of twins is
not disliked [1] and if both are boys it is a matter for con-
gratulation ; their mother is under an obligation to give
them flowers of the same variety and cloths of exactly the
same pattern.[2] Triplets are very rare indeed. One case is
remembered to have occurred in Mozema, but all three died.

The Angamis have no ear-piercing ceremony, the ears of
girls being pierced when they are from six to twelve months
old, and those of boys as soon as they can speak. Also,
in the case of the majority of them, no naming ceremony is
performed. A ceremony, however, is sometimes performed
on the fifth day after birth, when the omens are taken in
the usual way by slicing pieces from a stick of the shrub

---

[1] It is regarded as extremely fortunate by the Memi.

[2] *Cf.* " Nigerian Notes. (III) Twins," by N. W. Thomas, *Man*,
Nov. 1919, No. 87. In the cases mentioned from Nigeria one of the twins
dies if whatever is given to the elder is not given to the younger also.

Name.

called *chiese*, and dropping two pieces parallel, and other two on the top of them. If the second two stay on without falling off, the name suggested is chosen.[1] This name is, with the Angamis, a name of abstract significance suggesting the presence of good qualities or good fortune, such as Kevise, " arriving at a good time," Vinile, " keep good," Viyale, " let your share be good," Rhichale, " long living " (or " long let him live "), Visanyü, " want more good," Zelucha, which might be rendered " Companion on the Long Road."[2] The root *vi* (" good ") is particularly common, as in Vibile, Visopra, Visatsü, Viponyü, and a host of others. There are, however, certain circumstances under which a child is given a second name. Should he be born under conditions of unusual distress or affliction his mother will give him a suitable name of precisely an opposite nature to that of the names mentioned.[3] This name is in some villages kept secret[4] and told to no one but the child himself

[1] A child is called at first " *Kechibu* " or " *Kechino*," according to sex, until someone, usually one of its parents, gives it a name. The husband's relations are sometimes, but not necessarily, consulted.

The Aos take the similar omen with the fire-stick, when they take one at all.

[2] This rendering is perhaps a little fanciful. An English-speaking Angami translated it to me as meaning " long comfortation," but this does not give the full idea either. The word contains the ideas of companionship, consolation, and road, duration, or distance, and was given because his parents had lost two or three sons born to them previously and hoped to be comforted by Zelucha into their old age.

[3] The Sema nomenclature (Monograph on the Sema Nagas) may be compared.

[4] Precise information on this point is almost impossible to obtain. Many Angamis have told me that no such custom as that of giving a secret name, or even a second name, exists at all, yet I was told about the custom by an intelligent Angami of Jotsoma, whose information on other points proved most reliable and who would have been most unlikely to mislead me deliberately. Further, it is very difficult to see how he could have invented the existence of such a practice. It may be that it is only known to those who have second names, of whose number my informant may possibly have been one. In Kohima village second names are given which are not secret, but which are only known to a few intimates and relations. Visanyü of Kohima (see Part III, " Genealogies ") informed me that he had a second name, *Miacho* = " little flesh," *i.e.* " tiny," given him by his mother at the time of his birth because he was so puny, but not used and only known to a few.

when he is old enough, and the very existence of such a second name and of the practice of giving one is stoutly denied. In other villages the second name, though not a secret, is not generally known and is not used. The Angami has an objection, still strong in some places, although not insurmountable and now rapidly dying out, to mentioning his own name himself. If he does so he is liable to be mocked at by his fellows as an " *huthu*," *i.e.* an owl that is always calling out its own name, while every Angami is averse to mentioning the name of his wife. In the case of a newly-married man nothing will induce him to do so. Women likewise are very reluctant to mention their own names.

When about four to six years old a boy leaves his mother's side (till then he may sleep on his mother's bed) and goes to his father's side of the house. This takes place at the Sekrengi genna, when the child strangles a fowl according to custom. From that time forward he definitely belongs to the male community and no longer remains with the women at gennas, when the sexes are separated. In the Kohima group he is no longer allowed to sleep in the same room as his parents. There is no ceremony on attaining puberty or on assuming man's clothes.

Bad language must be avoided while a child's first cloth is being woven, as if bad language is used under such circumstances the child that wears it will be affected for the worse.

The Angamis, as has already been noticed, are monogamous Marand exogamous. One case of bigamy, but only one, is riage.[1] known to have taken place among the Tengima Angamis, and although it is somewhat commoner among the Memi, it is looked on by them also with disfavour. The marriage by a man of two sisters concurrently is forbidden, and the second marriage is usually a non-ceremonial one. There are among all Angamis two forms of marriage, one celebrated with ceremony and formality, and one without, and although both forms are equally binding and the informal marriage confers no social stigma or disability on the wife or on her

[1] See also Part III, " Position of Women."

issue, the ceremonial form is preferred by persons aspiring to the respect of themselves and their fellows. It entails, however, a certain amount of expense, though that is little enough, and a certain amount of formality, which is sometimes perhaps irksome.

The informal marriage consists merely in a man's taking a girl to his house, where they remain *kenna* for one day. Where it takes place it is usually the outcome of an intrigue between the two, or is necessitated by the poverty of the parties.

The ceremonial marriage is very much more formal. A man who intends to get married employs or gets his father to employ an old woman as a go-between with the girl's parents. She makes all the arrangements and there is no intercourse between the parties. First omens are taken by strangling a fowl and watching the position assumed by its legs as it dies. If the right leg crosses over above the left the omen is good. Then both the man and the girl must note their dreams on the same night. Dreams of weeping, of excretion, or of the sexual act are bad, but if the man's dreams have been good, the old woman goes and asks the girl what hers were like. If hers have also been good, the marriage price is discussed by the old woman with the girl's parents. The marriage price consists normally of a spear,[1] two pigs, and fifteen or sixteen fowls. The man will buy a spear, pigs, chickens, and keep them in his house, while the girl starts making rice beer in readiness for the ceremony. At this point in the proceedings there is frequently some delay, but when everything is satisfactorily and finally arranged, young men of the girl's family and of her own age go on the day fixed to the bridegroom's house and carry off, as though by force, the spear and the pigs and chickens, which they kill and eat at the bride's house,

[1] Whatever its significance here, the presentation of a spear is usually regarded among Nagas in general as in some sense the tribute of an inferior to a superior, or as signifying the recognition of some obligation under which the giver lies in regard to the recipient. It is commonly given by one village to another when the former cultivates land on sufferance from the latter, and it often forms part of the penalty paid to an injured husband by his wife's paramour.

and all the girl's kindred go and eat and drink there. One
basket is filled with small pieces of flesh ; one leg of pork is
set aside ; and four or five gourds are filled with liquor and
set aside. At dusk two men take this meat and drink and
take their places in a procession which goes to the bridegroom's house. This procession is thus composed : First
the bride, next one boy and three girls from among her
companions, then the two men carrying meat and drink,
and finally a number of young men of the bride's kindred
and clan, singing. Inside the bridegroom's house are the
bridegroom and his parents, no one else. When the procession arrives the first seven persons mentioned as composing
it go inside,[1] but only the first five of these remain, and all
talking must be in a whisper. First of all the bridegroom
eats of the meat and drink brought by the men, while the
bride eats a little piece of liver and of rice, which she has
brought with her, and drinks liquor brought by her in a
little " lao " and poured into a small leaf cup likewise brought
by her. Then the bridegroom's parents eat and drink, and
then the rest ; after they have all eaten the bridegroom goes
to the " morung " house and sits on the " machan." Next
the bridegroom's kindred present the bride's escort with a
big fowl and give one fowl each to the two who brought the
meat and drink, after which all go away to their houses
except the one boy and three girls, who spend the night in
the bridegroom's house, the groom staying in the " morung."
Next morning one of the bridegroom's kindred gives a fowl
each to the boy and to the three girls. Then the bridegroom's mother gives the bride liquor in a leaf cup, which
she drinks up. The bride must not leave the house before
sunrise, after which she takes a pitcher and fetches water
and cooks for the household.

This day the household is *kenna*, but on the following
day the bride and the bridegroom go to the fields and work

---

[1] A Kacha Naga bride has to step into the bridegroom's house with her
right foot, placing it upon a piece of iron (a rupee is often used nowadays)
laid on the threshold of the house. A Sema bride carries a dao in her
hand which she gives to her husband. She also has to step across the
threshold with her right foot first. She always spends the night after
arriving at her husband's house with her parents.

together on the part given to them by the latter's parents. They eat together in the fields. For the next three days they are confined to their own village and its lands, not being allowed to visit other villages, but after these three days the ceremony is complete. There is usually, however, no consummation of the marriage for at least two or three months, and it is said that this is delayed sometimes for as long as a year " for shame," during which time the bridegroom sleeps at the " morung." In the Khonoma group a delay of several months is normal.

The marriage rites as performed by the Eastern Angamis are more elaborate, and an account of the Memi ceremony follows. It is taken from an unpublished note of Major Kennedy made during the Assam Census of 1901.

" The young man or his parents send an old man or woman to the girl's parents with a proposal of marriage. If the latter agree to the match, an answer is sent to that effect, and then both the girl and young man consult their dreams. Dreams of water, a tiger, dhan, etc., are considered lucky, while dreams concerning pigs, a dead person, etc., are unlucky. If the dreams of one party are bad, and those of the other party good, they consult their dreams again at the time of the next new moon. Should the dreams of both sides be auspicious, negotiations regarding the property to be contributed by each are entered upon. The girl is supposed to contribute at least half as much property as the man. Her dowry consists of dhan, cattle, fields, and beads. When this is settled, a day is fixed for the wedding. On that day, an old woman of the husband's ' khel '[1] is sent to bring the bride. The old woman takes two hoes as a present to the bride's mother. The old woman then brings the bride to her husband's house, the girl being unattended by any of her own people. The bride takes with her two laos of dzu and a seer or so of rice, together with her own clothes in her khang (basket). When the bride reaches the bridegroom's house, the old woman who accompanies her gives the bridegroom and bride a piece of plantain leaf, of which they make cups. The old woman then fills the cups with dzu from the bridegroom's house. The bride and bridegroom, without drinking the dzu,

---

[1] " Khel " in this note means " clan," the Angami " thino."

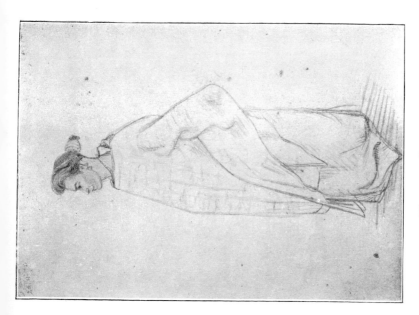

WUZELE OF KHONOMA

WUZELE OF KHONOMA AND HIS NEPHEW SRISALHU

[See p. 127

KHONOMA GATE AND WALL

[See p. 155

exchange the cups of *dzu*, which they then place in crevices of the wall, the man on the right side of the entrance door, and the woman on the left side thereof, inside the house. Any number of young girls belonging to the bridegroom's 'khel'[1] are assembled, except seven, which is considered by the Memis, Angamis, and Kezhamas as an unlucky number. These girls consume the *dzu* brought by the bride. That night a young girl of the husband's 'khel' sleeps with the bride. The bride is not allowed to eat food cooked in her husband's house. That night the bridegroom sleeps in the young men's dormitory till about midnight, when he returns to his house, and calls the young girl who is sleeping with his bride, and conducts her back to her father's house. He then goes back to his house, and makes a noise at the door, on hearing which his father and mother and all occupants of the house, except the bride, leave the house. The bridegroom then enters and has connection with the bride, after which he returns to the young men's dormitory, his parents, etc., returning to the house. Next day the bride and bridegroom bathe at separate springs, the bride being accompanied by the girl who slept with her the night before, and her ablutions being performed in the morning. The bridegroom spends the whole of that night at the young men's dormitory and does not visit his wife. On the third day, the bride and bridegroom are not allowed to see each other, the bride remaining in the bridegroom's house and the latter at the house of a friend. That day the bridegroom selects three stones to form the fireplace, and makes two or four wooden spoons. These he sends to his house by a messenger, who gives the spoons into the hands of the bride, and leaves the stones in the house. That night again the bridegroom sleeps in the young men's dormitory and does not visit his bride. Next morning the bridegroom returns to his own house, when the bride makes a fireplace of the three stones sent the previous day by the bridegroom. She then cooks food for the bridegroom and herself in new utensils, and they eat the food together. That day the bride must remain in the house and do no work, but the bridegroom may work if he likes. That night they sleep together. On the following day in the early morning, the bride and bridegroom go to the fields together, and do a little nominal work, and then drink the *dzu* and eat the food which they have brought with them. They each bring back one small piece of firewood with them, which they burn that day. This concludes the actual marriage ceremonies. A few days after this, the bride goes to her father's house and brings from there two ' khalsis ' of *dzu* and 100 pieces of pigs' flesh. The bridegroom then first entertains his father-in-law with the *dzu* and flesh so brought, and then feasts his own friends. As among the Angamis, it is customary for the bride's friends to bring flesh and *dzu* to the house of the newly-married couple during the next succeeding Salegni (Angami Sekrengü [1]) or Chitegni (Angami Terhengi) genna. In the morning the newly married couple go to the bride's father's house, and return from thence, the bridegroom carrying a piece of flesh, and the bride a ' khalsi ' of *dzu*, followed by the bride's friends with their offerings. It is customary for the bridegroom's friends to bring kodalis to the feast, which they present to the bride's friends, who have contributed the food and drink. When the first child is born, the wife takes it to her father's house, where all her relatives present her each with a fowl, a cock if the child is a boy, and a hen if the child is a girl. These fowls are taken back and are kept shut up till they are by degrees killed and eaten, it being considered most unlucky if one should escape. The above ceremonies are those observed in the case of persons previously unmarried. No part of the ceremony is more essential or binding than another, all being necessary to constitute a marriage between persons not previously married. If a man takes a second wife, without divorcing the first wife, the full ceremonies are observed, if the girl has been previously unmarried. Widows may marry, but they must obtain the permission of their late husband's heirs before doing so, else they lose their property brought as dowry. A widow can marry her husband's younger brother, but is not compelled to do so. She cannot marry her husband's elder brother. In the case of the remarriage of a widow, the ceremonies for the first day are the same, but the bride and bridegroom sleep together that night, and next day the new fireplace is constructed. The couple go to the fields on the following day for nominal work. It is not the custom for the presents of food and drink to be made by the bride's father and relatives after the marriage.

"Divorce is allowed and is common. Incompatibility of temperament is the chief reason. There is no ceremony. A woman, however, cannot leave her husband until more

---

[1] I think Major Kennedy is possibly wrong in saying that the Saleni and Sekrengi gennas correspond, but it is always difficult to be certain. *Vide supra* Tsungi genna and also Sekrengi genna.

than five days after the marriage have elapsed. If she does so her husband can keep all her property. Otherwise the woman takes her property away with her, unless she is unfaithful or makes arrangements to marry another man, while under her husband's roof, in which cases she forfeits the property brought as dowry. Infidelity on the part of the man is not a ground for divorce, but if a man arranges to marry another woman, before divorcing his wife, the latter is entitled to a cow and a dhuli of dhan as compensation. When a man wishes to take a second wife without having divorced his first wife, he must first obtain the latter's permission. Divorced persons can marry, the ceremony being the same as that for the widowed persons."

By some Naga tribes the work of burying the dead seems Death to be regarded with a certain amount of repulsion, but the Angamis do not, like some others, relegate this function to a particular individual in each village. The office is usually performed by the deceased's male relatives. In the case of *seshoma*, however, only old men take part in the burial (*vide infra*).

The first office performed after death is the washing of the corpse by a child of the same sex as the deceased, while the latter's most intimate friend, by no means necessarily a man of the same clan, brings flesh, rice, and rice beer to the dead man's house. After the washing the dead man is laid out upon the bed and covered from the eyebrows to the feet with his own cloth. His ceremonial dress is piled about him, and above his head a " kang " (carrying basket) is placed containing seeds for wet rice, Job's tears, millet, and every other kind of grain and eatable, together with a lao of " zu " and the dead man's own cup. A share also of the flesh, rice, and " zu " brought by his best friend is put into this " kang," while the remainder is given to the living occupants of the house, who may on that day eat nothing provided from their own household. Next day the young men of the deceased's kindred bring cattle, including those of the dead man, or some of them, if he had any. The Zhevo or Pitsü, as the case may be, makes a wound in each beast, after which it is killed by the young men, who, after setting aside the heads, livers, and certain other portions, divide the flesh as they believe the deceased would have done had he been alive ; that is to say, large portions are given to those with whom he was specially intimate, and who during his lifetime received much from him, and *vice versa.* In Khonoma, men of the Thevoma or Semoma clans consider it obligatory to eat up any share they may receive within two days, provided they are of the same clan as the dead man, though if of a different clan they may keep it as long as they like. All this time the family of the dead man maintain a doleful howling. The young men of the kindred make the coffin, which is of wood and lidless. When it is ready the deceased's father-in-law, if he have one, if not a friend from another clan, or usually from another clan, enters the house of the dead man and stands on the left-hand side of the body. He then places a spear at the right of the corpse if a man's, a black cloth if it is a woman who has died. He also cuts off a lock of hair from the head of the corpse. Then the coffin is brought inside and a little thatching grass burnt inside it, after which the body is laid in the coffin. The grave is dug during the day, either in front of the house or alongside one of the village paths, and the corpse, covered with a cloth and lying in the coffin, is placed in the grave at dusk. With the body in the coffin are buried a fire-stick (" *segōmi* "), one or two spears, a dao, and a young chicken alive, and the bitter seed called " *gàdzōsī* " (it is used for killing leeches) is placed between the teeth. The object of the *gadzosi* is that the soul may be eating it when he meets with the spirit Metsimo, who guards the path to paradise. When Metsimo sees the dead man eating *gadzosi* he lets him pass by, but if the dead man has no *gadzosi* in his mouth, Metsimo makes him eat a monster nit from his (Metsimo's) head.[1] If *gadzosi* or a leaf of the plant is not obtainable, any leaf will do, but it must be spoken of as " *gadzosi.*" In the case of a woman, a few beads are buried with her, her cloths

[1] Someone has reported of Angamis that they make wounds in the bodies of dead warriors so that they shall go to the next world as though killed in battle by an honourable death, but I have never met with the custom.

and a new under-petticoat and a reaping hook, with the chicken and the *gadzosi* as in the case of males. Then the coffin is covered with flat stones, and on to the stones that cover the lower half of the corpse the contents of the " kang " mentioned above are poured. Then the earth is heaped in and the grave levelled, to the accompaniment, in the case of males, of the firing of many guns, and to the howling and shrieking of the women, who beat upon the ground with their cloths, having tried to hold back the coffin as it was lowered into the grave. Mr. McCabe quotes in one of his diaries the cry raised at the disappearance of the coffin :—

" Do not be afraid, do not mourn. You have only followed your parent's custom. Although you have died, let us remain happy. Although God has not been kind to you, and you have died, fear not ! "

On the next day the kindred of the deceased with someone from another clan come together at the deceased's house and eat of the meat previously set aside, except the livers. Ceremonial dress is worn and the men shout and leap by the grave, challenging the spirit that has carried off the dead man, asking him where he has hidden, and bidding him come that they may spear him and kill him.[1] They then put up the skulls of the slaughtered cattle over the grave together with the shield, ornaments, clothes, weapons,[2] eating and drinking utensils, and other such personal possessions of the dead man, a gourd of *zu*, and the empty flasks which contained the powder fired on the previous day. On a woman's grave a little basket is placed, containing her spinning and weaving utensils, and a diamond-shaped frame on which different coloured threads are stretched. They also build up over the grave a stone tomb. In the case of the Chakrima villages, a wooden effigy almost of life-size dressed in the ceremonial dress of the dead is set up over the tomb, which is by most Tengima merely hung with the cloths, skulls, etc., while in Viswema large white cloths stretched upon bamboo frames are erected high up off the

[1] See Butler, " Travels in Assam," p. 150, and compare Owen, " Notes on the Naga Tribes in Communication with Assam," p. 24. Owen's notes refer to Konyăk tribes.

[2] See Appendix XIII, p. 457.

ground to advertise the death of rich men cut off in the prime of youth. Food is then again taken at the house of the dead man, the livers of the cattle killed being cooked by members of a different clan. When cooked, a piece of liver with salt and chillies is given to each member of the deceased's family, who, without speaking, throw their pieces outside the house some yards away. After this everyone goes back to his own house.

On the second day after the burying seventeen portions of cooked rice with a little salt are tied up in plantain leaves. These are buried outside the house on the fourth day. On the fifth deceased's platter and drinking cup are suspended by a string inside the house, the string being undone and thrown away after thirty days, when the cup and platter are given to one of deceased's intimate friends ; about ten days later the deceased's family kill a cock and divide the flesh equally and eat it, the funeral ceremonies being then finished.

This does not always entirely complete the ceremony. Sometime between the Tsungi and Terhengi gennas of the year in which the death occurs, or of one of the first two or three years following, one or two pigs are killed and the tomb built up with more solidity than at first. This additional ceremony is not essential, but if at any time the tomb breaks a pig must be killed and repairs executed ; but this can only be done between the Tsungi and Terhengi gennas,[1] and it is only between these gennas that a grave may be removed (graves are occasionally removed for the sake of convenience to a different site), or that a man's bones may be brought from another village for interment, as is done when a man dies away from home. The grave of a Kemovo is particularly sacred, and is only disturbed with extreme reluctance, at any rate in the case of the original founder of a village. There is no particular orientation of the dead, but if two persons are buried

---

[1] This rule is stated more precisely as follows :—

Graves may only be repaired or moved : (1) between the end of the millet harvest and the beginning of the rice harvest ; (2) between the end of the rice harvest and the sowing of the millet ; *i.e.* between the reaping and sowing of the millet crop, except whilst the rice harvest is in progress.

at the same time and place they are given the same
orientation.[1]

In the case of persons killed in war, or whose bodies are
for some similar reason not recoverable, a wooden image is
made of the wood called " *hetho* " and, if obtainable, a
piece of the deceased's hair affixed to the head. This is
substituted for the real corpse and the ceremonies performed
as usual.

Persons killed by wild animals, or dying in childbirth,
and suicides are not allowed to be buried within the precincts
of the village, but the rites are the same subject to the
proviso that the flesh of the cattle killed at the funeral
and the beads worn by the dead may be taken only by the
old man who buries the body, and may not be sold in the
village, while the flesh is *kenna* to all young men. Such a
death is called " *sesho* "[2] and the victim of it " *seshoma.*"
Death by a fall from or by the fall of a tree is regarded as
akin to *sesho*, but though some extra ceremony is performed,
the ordinary ceremonies are not affected as in the case of a
genuine *seshoma*. Suicide, it may be noted, is not common.
The writer has only heard of three cases among the Angamis.[3]
One of these was the result of debt. A man of the Semoma
clan of Khonoma, being heavily in debt, bequeathed his
terraced fields to his sister, dined unusually well, and went
off saying that he was going to work on the railway. Next
day he shot himself. He is said to have made himself more

---

[1] See Appendix. Some villages lay the feet towards the east.

[2] The word commonly used in the *lingua franca* of the district is *apotia*
(<Assamese আপদ = accidental or causing misfortune).

[3] I have also known of one case among the Aos, a man who tried to
spear himself, according to his own account, at the dictation of an evil
spirit, but this man seemed to be more or less demented ; and of one
case of a Kacha Naga who hanged himself in the jungle, under the impression that he had killed a man, though in point of fact the man was only
severely wounded and recovered. I have heard of other Nagas hanging
themselves, and suicides by Lhotas are more frequent. I knew of one
who speared himself after committing a murder, and of several cases of
persons taking poison. The Lhotas know of the bitter root of a creeper
which can be mixed with liquor. This is drunk in some quantity and
intoxication ensues, followed by death while in that state. Lovers who
for some reason cannot marry each other not infrequently make use of
this way out of their troubles.

or less drunk before he actually did the deed. The second case was that of a man of Chephama who committed suicide by poisoning himself with the herb " *kwethi*." The third was in Viswema, where a man hanged himself in June 1918. Mourning is observed by the deceased's near relatives not wearing ceremonial dress should a genna involving its use occur shortly after the death.

Social Gennas.

Gennas which confer social status among the Angamis form, as it were, a series of steps, each one more costly than the preceding one. It does not seem to be obligatory upon anyone to perform these gennas, but in point of fact they are usually performed by anyone who can afford them, and in the case of the first three may be and are repeated at any time. These first three, in fact, form a sort of preliminary series to which comparatively small importance is attached. Three of them are mentioned, since this is the number in Khonoma, but it probably varies a good deal, and the names given in different villages likewise.

The *Kreghaghi* is performed by anyone who reaps a harvest more than usually plentiful, or who obtains from his fields a hundred or more loads of paddy. It is not performed once only, but whenever occasion occurs. It merely entails the killing of a cow and the feasting of friends on the flesh, a portion being set aside for the *Zhevo*. The performer of the *Kreghaghi* is entitled to brush his hair straight down behind instead of tying it into a knot.

The *Kinoghe* consists in the sacrifice of a cow, shares of which are given to all the members of the clan, house by house, and to personal friends outside the clan.

The *Pichiprele* consists merely in feeding four *Zhevos*, who bless the votary.

Anyone who has once performed each of these preliminaries may proceed to the performance of the four great social gennas. These are usually performed at the same time as either the Terhengi or the Sekrengi gennas, the practice varying in different villages, as do the names of the gennas performed. The names given here are the Khonoma names, the Kohima names being given in brackets. The standard of sacrifices is the Kohima standard, which is given here because the Khonoma standard cannot be given completely, for in Khonoma *Lesü* and *Ketseshe*[1] gennas cannot now be performed, as the necessary details have been forgotten as a result of the expulsion of the village from their site on more than one occasion owing to differences of policy between the village and Government. The gennas in question are as follows :—

Thesa (*Chesa*).—Two " dhulis " [2] of paddy, four bulls, and two pigs suffice for this. Ceremonial dress is not worn. The performer of Thesa may put some thatching grass in split bamboos and put up one on each side of the front of his house as a sign that he has performed the genna, and may also fence in part of his porch. Before proceeding to the next genna, Thesa must be performed at least twice, and may be performed thrice.

Zhatho (*Zhache*)[3] is performed, by those who have completed Thesa, with three dhulis of paddy, eight bulls, and four pigs. Ceremonial dress is worn while pounding the paddy. As a sign of the celebration of this ceremony two planks are placed as barge-boards (*füsi*) on the front gable of the house and the cloth called *Zhavakwe* is assumed. This genna must be performed twice before proceeding to Lesü.

Lishe or *Lesü* (*Lichü*) is performed with six dhulis of paddy, ten bulls, and five pigs. This is the minimum, but the genna need only be performed once. Ceremonial dress is worn while pounding the paddy, and while dragging through

---

[1] A stone-pulling genna is done in Khonoma by sons who inherit their parents' houses, but this is not the genuine *Ketseshe*.

[2] The *dhuli* is the Angami *Chu*, the large basket for storing grain mentioned in Part II. The measure is roughly as follows :—

12 *Zharha* [a small basket holding about a seer (2 lbs.) of rice. (*Zha* = day > daily wage)] = 1 *Utsa*.
  2 *Utsa* = 1 *Zhazhō*.
  2 *Zhazhō* = 1 *Bé* (about a maund).

One " *Chu* " contains from 15 to 20 maunds ; a load is about 60 lbs. 1 " maund " = 82⅔ lbs.

[3] I think that this is the genna also called by the Angamis *Temoza*, the corresponding Memi genna being *Mozü*, performers of which (among the Memi) may not eat game for a year. A man under such a prohibition who kills game gives a feast at his house to the old men of the village, who, while present at his house, may drink from leaves only, not from cups.

the village two wooden posts, one of them forked, named with the names of the husband and wife performing the genna.[1] The performer of this genna is entitled to replace the plain barge-boards of the performer of Zhatho by barge-boards crossing at the point of the gable and elongated into a pair of great horns which are usually pierced with one or more large round holes, said to be made for the purpose of lessening the danger of destruction by wind. These are called *Kika* (= "house-horns"), and the man who has done the genna *Kikakepfüma* ("house-horn-bearer"). He and his wife are prohibited from eating fowls, a prohibition which among the Memi extends not only to the *Kikakepfüma* and his wife, but also to any of their children living in the house both during their occupation and after their death. However, it is sometimes evaded by the children, who may eat chickens cooked at a different hearth, provided they wash their mouths afterwards.

Ketseshe (Chisü), i.e. " stone-pulling," is performed by those who have done Lesü. Eight dhulis of paddy, twelve bulls, and eight pigs are required. Ceremonial dress is worn for pounding paddy and for the pulling in from the jungle of a large stone (*chisü* = " stone-pulling ") which is set up to commemorate the genna in some conspicuous place. This stone-pulling is performed by all the young men of the clan, or of the whole village, of the person performing the genna. In Memi and Tengima, and nowadays in most Chakrima villages, it is usual to pull and set up two stones, one for the man and a smaller one for his wife.

The stone, which often has to be dragged from a long distance, is levered on to a sort of sledge made from the fork of a tree, to which it is lashed with canes and creepers. Rollers are placed in the path of the sledge, which is pulled up to the village by sometimes several hundreds of men hauling at long ropes of cane and creepers, with singing and dancing.[2] A hole is dug for the foot of the stone, which is

---

[1] See Appendix IX.

[2] The Lhotas have an alternative method in which a huge wooden framework is made and the stone lashed to the middle of it, when the carriers lift it and carry it by the surrounding framework, which is made of tree-stems lashed together like gigantic trellis-work, and admits of men carrying together to the number of six or more abreast and twelve or more deep.

tilted into it from the sledge. The earth is filled in and beaten down round the foot of the stone, on the top of which some leaves are placed and some liquor poured, the feast following the ceremony. Stone-pulling is practised by the Lhotas and Rengmas as well as by the Angami tribes, and is believed by some Semas to have been originally practised by them as well, though they have forgotten the details of the ceremony accompanying it and no longer practise it. On the other hand, it is not practised by the Aos and the tribes more nearly related to them (see Appendix). It is the monoliths pulled at this genna and set up in or near the village to commemorate the giver and the giving of the feast which are such a noticeable feature of the Angami country.[1] Monoliths are also erected in some cases to perpetuate the memory of the dead,[2] but the genna stones just mentioned are not cenotaphs, and the Chisü genna with stone-pulling may be performed as often as a man has means to do so. A man who has performed the Chisü genna once may, in the Kohima group, call himself Kemovo and roof his house with wooden shingles instead of thatch. Among the Memi, however, the Chisü (called " Shoh " by them) entitles to " kika " only, and not to shingles.

In all the above ceremonies the paddy is used to make rice beer, being pounded by the kindred and friends of the performer of the genna, the cattle are slaughtered, and the meat and drink are used to feed the community. The occasion is made one of general festivity, and sports of various sorts are indulged in by the young men. The performer of the genna may not cut his hair for thirty days after it is finished, and is never allowed to make pots.

Of the miscellaneous gennas performed by individuals Gennas upon various occasions, the majority are not unnaturally for illness. aimed at the prevention or termination of illness. This gives rise to frequent rites, rites which vary from place to place and from time to time, and are probably often invented by the Zhevo for the particular circumstances which call for some genna. The Nôsōtsā consists in the sacrifice of a

---

[1] Cf. Col. Gurdon, " The Khasis," p. 149 (second edition).

[2] E.g. in Khonoma by the son inheriting his parents' house-site. They are erected in or near the village, not as a grave-stone, but as a monument.

small cock to cure a child's peevishness ; the *Terho-rogi*,
to take another instance, is performed for a man who is
very weak from illness. A chicken with big strong feathers
is selected, and together with the bark of the tree *tsŏmhō*,
ginger and salt, is taken by the *Zhevo* outside the village
on to the village path. The Zhevo then says, " Whatever
the cause of the illness, whether defilement contracted from
women or other cause, it must go with the life of the fowl."
He then kills the fowl by piercing its neck with a sharpened
bamboo, watching the fall of the drops of blood and the
crossing of its legs for omens. The *Kirupfezhe* again is a
specific for the stomach-ache. Any man as a substitute
for the sick man takes an egg and divides it into eight
sections by marking it with a burnt stick.[1] He then takes
the egg and throws it down on the village path outside the
gates, where nearly all such gennas are performed, and in
throwing away the egg throws all the illness away likewise
This, however, cannot be done by the sick man himself.
The *Derochü* [2] is performed in the case of any illness or by
reason of being talked about, either for good or for ill. A
pig is killed and two chaste unmarried boys, one a Pezoma
and the other a Pepfüma, are sent into the jungle to bring
a bit of tree, to make a wooden hearth, some firewood, and
some wormwood. They make a new fireplace and make
fire with a fire-stick, the Pezoma boy being the first to work
the stick. If he fails to get fire the owner of the house
works it. The pig is beaten to death with sticks (this is
the ordinary way of killing pigs and is most expeditious),
the first blow being given by the Pezoma boy. The pig is
singed on the fire until its hair and outer skin are singed off.
It is then washed and cut up, the Pezoma boy giving the
first cut. A piece of the liver is then cooked (boiled) with
ginger, chillies, and salt in an earthen pot. Before the
cooking, a small piece each of the flesh is given as usual
to the Kemovo, Zhevo, Tsakro, and Lidepfü, and also to
the " morung " and the *tehuba*, being taken by the two boys,
while the tongue, nose, ears, tail, and feet are cut off and
placed by the village path. After his wife has cooked the

[1] Thus: ⊕ .   [2] Called *Thevo-noroto* in Jotsoma.

piece of the liver, the owner of the house severs off two
little pieces of it with his nails and throws them away.
He then makes a cup of leaves and puts *zu* into it
and drinks it, and gives his wife to drink and his family
likewise in order of age. He first eats a bit of the flesh,
and then the others as they have drunk. He puts the meat
in his mouth while he has the *zu* still in it.

Before this no one may eat or drink ; afterwards they
may do as they like. The two boys eat with the household
and observe the same *kenna*. None of them may speak to
any new arrival in the village or anyone who has left and
returned to the village that day.

In the evening the two boys are allowed to go, after which
the family may not eat or drink till cock-crow next morning.
The door is shut and they do not go out except to ease
themselves.

The two boys each get one leg, the Kepezoma a hind-leg
and the Kepepfüma a fore-leg (or half each of the meat
unconsumed at the end of the day), and a pot of *zu* each,
in their own pots. The family must consume the whole of
the flesh (except the legs given away) on the genna day.

The piece given to the " morung " is placed in the cane
binding of the *Kitache* (the middle front post) inside the
" morung " house and the *tehuba* piece is thrown on the
sitting-out place and no one eats these.

When the Zhevo gets his share he says " *Kevi u cheto* "
(" It shall be well "), and on departing the Pezoma boy
says " *Keche kenia che ke keniatowe. Keshe keje che te showe.
Che kemesa watewe.*" (" Sickness is forbidden—Death must
not occur—It is all clean.")

For a man who is ill, or who has had an unusually heavy
sleep, a chicken's head is cut off with a dao in the middle
of the village path by someone who usually helps to bury the
dead, while for pains in the heart and chest a live chicken
(usually quite a small one) is impaled on a stake in the
middle of the path. In case of lasting illness, a man digs
in a dry place for water until he finds it. He fences it
over, kills an unblemished cock, washes it and cooks it in
this water, and when eating it also drinks of this water.

A typical prevention genna is that by which immu..ity from stings is secured by persons taking bees' nests. From the day on which the expedition after bees' nests is arranged, the men who are going must abstain from sexual intercourse. On the actual morning of taking the nests they are *kenna* and may not speak. They make a charm of the casts of earth-worms and bits of the plant *rena* and throw them behind them. In absolute silence they go and make the ladders and take the comb. Under such circumstances, they do not get stung by the bees, though any mistake leads to fearful stinging.[1] The bees' nests taken in this way are those of a large black rock bee, which stings very badly.

Rain-making.

In Khonoma it is said that no genna for producing rain is known, and no one who knows Khonoma will be surprised, as it could never conceivably be needed. There is, however, a genna for stopping rain which has results out of all proportion to its simplicity, if indeed the full rite is revealed, which is perhaps unlikely. All that is said to be necessary is for a man who has had no children to take a dish of water and evaporate it out of doors by boiling it. When dry, he must say " Let the days be fine like this," and no rain will fall for seven years, a result which ought to be quite enough to prevent this genna's ever being performed. In Kohima village a genna called the " *Tikopenna* " is observed if there should be a drought. It lasts one day and the whole village is *penna* and barred to strangers.[2] In case of shortage of rain in the spring, rain can be obtained by a genna called " *Theza*," which is performed only by a dozen or so families called *Kiruse Prütsü* of the Rutsanoma *putsa* of the Puchatsuma clan, though it was formerly also performed by the Belhonoma *putsa* of the Chetonoma clan. When the

[1] Srisalhu of Khonoma, who described this genna to me, says that he has often taken bees' nests after doing it without being stung at all. The probable explanation is that persons believing in the genna gain absolute confidence and hence are able to go about the business with slow, steady, deliberate movements, which, I understand, are far less likely to irritate bees than the nervous and hasty movements of persons afraid of being stung. The effect of contact with an unchaste person as enhancing the severity of a wound has been noted in Part II under " Medicines, etc."

[2] The Memi also obtain rain by observing a strict *penna* for the whole village.

village wants rain, they have to ask the members of this
putsa, who, when asked, have to perform the necessary
genna (it *must* be asked for in case of drought), which is
done as follows :—

A relation of any man of the *putsa* who has died since the
last rainy season goes to the village spring in the early
morning without speaking to anyone. He takes a very
small quantity of water in a new gourd and goes to the grave
of the dead man, where he pours it out into a leaf of the
chiese plant, saying, " *Ti apvu, Kidzü apfü, a ngumezhedi
mhidzü-tu a de süche*," which being interpreted is, " Sky,
my father, Earth, my mother, show mercy on me and let
your tears fall for me." Having said this, he will drop
water twice from the leaf on to the grave. From that time
he is *kenna* for five days, being unable to speak to anyone
and obliged to remain day and night upon his bed. He
may not set foot to earth, and if it is necessary for him to
get down he must tie two bits of wood or bark to the soles
of his feet to prevent their touching the ground and on
going outside the house must cover his head with a winnowing fan. He may drink *zu*, but must not touch any other
food during those five days.

This rain-making genna is said to have had the following
origin. There was a man of the Puchatsuma clan of Kohima
called Kerutsa. This man went to a king in the plains
and asked for a *Bakechüguo*, a charm which would enable
him to get food without doing any work, (lit. a " Sit-and-eat
charm "). The king told him that he was a lazy fellow not
fit to live, and gave him some obscene gifts and a cow
buffalo. After some highly improper behaviour [1] he died,
and his death was followed by a drought and consequent
famine both in the plains and the hills. Eventually the
king sent a messenger to the hills to say that a hillman
had died in the plains, where there was a famine because
the corpse had not been taken away. Meanwhile, owing
to the loss of Kerutsa's body, no rain had fallen in the hills
and cultivation in Kohima was suspended. The Kohima

[1] Primum bubalam futuit. Deinde, bubalâ ob fututionem illam mortuâ,
ad libidinem satiandam mentulâ harenam pertundebat. Sic obiit.

people consulted a *themuma*[1] in a Kezama village, who told them the reason of the drought, and further that it would not rain that year unless they went to look for the corpse of Kerutsa. Accordingly they determined to go and to look for it and agreed that whichever clan did not go to help in the search should be called " *Solhima*," *i.e.* " alien." In the end the six clans Rosuma, Puchatsuma, Dapfetsuma, Chetonoma, Hurutsuma, and Hrepvoma went to fetch the body, but the Cherama clan refused, and so was called *Solhima* by the other six clans.[2] The six clans went down to the plains and brought back the bones of Kerutsa, and as soon as they reached the Dzüdza (Zubza) river, which is the boundary of Kohima land, they saw a little cloud in the sky, and before they reached the village it started raining heavily. When they arrived at Kohima village they all washed their hands and cooked food at their hearths and ate it, but the Belhonoma *putsa* of Chetonoma and the Rutsanoma *putsa* of Puchatsuma built new fireplaces and cooked their food on them before eating, and therefore it is that when rain is wanted the village insists on one of these *putsa* doing the genna described, provided someone of the *putsa* has died during the year. The Belhonoma *putsa* of Chetonoma has evaded liability to the performance of this genna by a trick. The heirs of a dead man of Belhonoma gave all his utensils to the deceased's sister, who was married to a man of the Chalenoma kindred of the Mekhuma clan of Kigwema, and told her to do genna for five days. They performed no gennas themselves and thus evaded future responsibility for the rain genna, which is now performed by the Chalenoma kindred of the Mekhuma clan of Kigwema. The genna is also said to be performed in the Chakrima village of Theniazuma and in some of the Kezama villages.[3]

Head taking.

Of the personal gennas, that for taking a head (called " *Sha* " in Kohima) is one of the most interesting. The successful warrior on returning to his village waits outside the gate. There any one of his family may bring him food,

[1] For " *themuma* " *vide infra* — " Magic and Witchcraft."

[2] Cherama were, of course, separate in any case. They came from a different village (*vide supra*). All Pepfüma clans seem to be called " Solhima " by the Chakrima.

[3] See Appendix XIII, p. 457.

[Photo by Mr Butler

ANGAMIS DANCING

[See p. 195

DHAN POUNDING AT SOCIAL GENNAS DURING THE *Tĕrhĕngī* GENNA IN KOHIMA VILLAGE

[See p. 195

while he awaits any who may come to pierce the flesh of the slain enemy. After that he enters the village escorted by the men of his clan singing and shouting, and goes first to the "*Kipuchie*," the genna stone, of each clan in the village, and deposits at the foot of it the flesh of his enemy or enemies, shouting, "*Wo, ho . . . . wu !*" for each man killed. Then he goes to his own house and deposits the head, limbs, or whatever flesh he has brought in front of the house, and his wife goes to make *zumho*. This is prepared by steeping rice in water, pounding it, mixing it with water in a gourd, and adding a double quantity of yeast. His wife pours this *zumho* on to the head or flesh, saying, "Let the enemy be lazy and sleepy ; kill them and let me do this again ! "[1] Then each successful warrior (if there be more than one) takes the usual omens from the sliced *chiese* plant and the crossed legs of strangled fowls, and kills a pig, the meat of which must be consumed that evening. Before eating or drinking, however, he must have washed both his hands and his mouth and have thrown away not only the water used in so doing, but also all the water to be found in his house at the time.

Early the next morning the warrior goes to the spring with spear and shield and bathes. On his return he must taste the leaf of the plant *gatsei* and some rice beer, after which he can eat of food cooked by women. The women then go out and catch the small fish called *khuorüho*, which is cooked and eaten that night. For the next five days it is *kenna* to go to any other village, both for the warrior and for all who have pierced the flesh of his victim, while the whole village is *genna* for one day.

The foregoing genna is that observed by the Khonoma group. There are certain differences in the observances of the Kohima group which are worth recording. The successful warrior after he has entered the village goes to the *Kipuchie* of the clan only, where he places the flesh of

---

[1] The Sema puts the plant *aghu* (used for yeast) on to the head of the man or animal and walks six times round it, calling on the whole tribe of the dead to turn silly and come and get killed. This *aghu* is also burnt at peace-makings.

his foe and the spoils of victory, shouting, " *Ao, huo . . . whi !* "
for each enemy killed. After going to his house, the *zumho*
is not poured on to the head by his wife, but by the man
himself. His wife or any female relative brings the gourd
of *zumho* and pours it out, the warrior receiving it in a cup
of the plantain leaf called *pfenuonyü* and pouring it on to
his enemy's head, saying, " Let my enemy be lazy and sleepy,
and let creepers make him fall, and let me kill him with my
spears and dao." That night he will take omens from the
legs of a chicken, and the next day a pig is killed in some
older warrior's house, and eaten there, both warriors
remaining indoors. On this day the veteran puts a feather
of the red bird called *sokrosokro* on the younger warrior's
head and " blesses " him with the words : " Your mother,
and your father's-younger-brothers and your father's-sisters
and your father's-elder-brothers allow you to wear (this
feather) ; wear and be most fortunate ! "[1] That evening
the flesh of the enemy is buried outside the gates of the
village, the head being buried face downwards.[2] Strictly
speaking this genna should be done twice before the warrior
can assume the hornbill's feather, after which he may wear
a feather for every man he kills.

Hunting.   The genna performed for success in hunting is most noticeably similar to that performed for the killing of an enemy.
The hunter must eat outside the village, for after he enters
and goes to his house he can take *zu* only. When he reaches
his home he deposits the head of the animal inside the door
and his wife or some other woman brings *zu* in a gourd and
pours it into a *pfenuonyü* cup held by the huntsman, who
pours the liquor over the animal's head with the words
" That magical animal has been killed, let me kill more."[3]
Then a piece each of the flesh of the animal is given to the
Kemovo, Zhevo, Tsakro, and Lidepfü, and the remainder is

---

[1] " *N'pfü, n'nima chiu n'nye n'dima n'ou pfünushe ; pfüdi kevi-u tsüleche.*"
I have given the translation as given to me by an intelligent Angami, but
would point out that *'nima* might equally well mean "mother's-sisters'-
husbands," while I have never come across *'dima* in any connection but
this. (*Vide supra*, Part III, "Terms of Relationship.")

[2] I am inclined to think that some of the Eastern Angamis put the
skull in a tree.

[3] See Appendix XIII, p. 458.

cooked by the hunter's kindred in front of his house and eaten by them. The hunter himself keeps only the skull, though after he has killed a hundred and fifty animals he too may eat of the flesh.

The use of the term magic here is not intended to suggest any very clear distinction in the Angami mind between the magical and religious rites. There are, however, practices directed against persons with intent to work them harm to which the term may perhaps be not inaptly applied. Magic in this sense may be practised by the community in certain cases. The observation of *penna* or *kenna* by the village may cause the death of a person named as its subject. This has already been made clear, and one or two instances mentioned of gennas kept by the village which were held to affect individuals. One of these was a case of inverted cause and effect. In the case of the Sachema women who had mud thrown at them in Jotsoma, it was because Sachema followed this mud-larking by observing the genna for the loss of a head or heads that the lives of the two women were endangered. In the other case mentioned, that of the Nerhema man who sacrificed a black cat, the village actually observed a day's *penna* with the hope and intention of making his illness worse. There is, however, a procedure more effective than the mere holding of a *penna* alone. On the day of *penna* a sort of Commination Service may be held to curse some unfortunate who has given offence. The Kemovo gets up before the assembled clan, all the children being present, and announces that So-and-so has done such-and-such a deed, whereon the people answer " *Sa, Sa,*" " Let him die, let him die ! " This curse is believed to be a powerful one, and to strengthen it still further a branch of green leaves is put up to represent the person cursed, and everyone hurls spears of wood or bamboo at the bough with such expressions as " Let him die," " Kill So-and-so," and every sort of abuse. The spears are left where they lie, the bough withers, and the subject of the curse dies likewise. This performance is also held to be effective even when the name of the culprit is unknown, and the writer has known it resorted to in a

(margin note: Magic and Witchcraft.)

case where a man of Cheswezuma was thought to have died
as a result of poison administered by someone unknown.
So too a ceremony of this sort sometimes spoken of as *The
Cat Genna* is observed among Chakrima in cases of theft
where the thief is unknown :

The owner of the stolen property assembles his kindred
before the morning meal and taking a cat, or kitten, ties
up its legs and mouth and impales it on a bamboo stake
which he plants in the ground outside the village gate beside
the path. He then goes with his kindred to the *tehuba*
and curses the thief that he may suffer as the cat suffers.
The kindred confirm the curse, shouting " *Ho ! ho !* "
In a case of this genna performed at Kekrima by a man who
kept suffering thefts of corn and fowls the curse took the
following form :—

" *A lha regurr teyopono chize keche kerri titowe* " (" May
the thief of my paddy perish to-night "). To which the
kindred made answer " *Hooooo.*" " *A vo regurr teyopono* "
. . . etc. (" May the thief of my fowl," etc.). To which
the kindred made answer as before, the curse being repeated
with "Ho, ho-ing" for each theft.[1]

The practice of this sort of magic by individuals does not
vary in principle from that resorted to by communities.
To spear a wooden effigy, or an old gourd painted like a
face, and then to do a genna for having taken So-and-so's
head has the effect of causing the death of the person
named, and it is open to anyone to practise witchcraft on
this wise, as also to cause illness or loss or even death by
the world-wide device of a wooden or clay figure into which
thorns or bamboo spikes are stuck. There are, however,
forms of divination and witchcraft demanding more
specialised knowledge, the people who practise them being
private practitioners and not public functionaries. They
are known as *Themuma*.[2] There is, for instance, a particular
species of pebble, difficult to obtain, which, if merely thrown

---

[1] See Appendix XIII, p. 458.

[2] *Themuma* are persons who are recognised more or less on the strength of
their own assertions as possessed by a god (*Terhoma*). They are not in any
sense appointed by their fellow villagers. Their powers vary from merely
dreaming dreams to the practice of genuine black magic. The Themuma is
often able to divine only when in a trance or some such non-normal condition.

at a man when he is not looking, brings illness upon him.
Nor is it necessary that the stone should strike him. It is
enough to throw it in his direction. The Semas attribute
a like power to the berry of a certain tree which need only
be concealed in a person's clothes to poison him.[1] A
knowledge also of poisons that can be given in food or drink
is regarded as an attribute of witches, but it does not seem
to be much practised by Angamis. A knowledge of poisons
is commonest, perhaps, in the Chakroma group, though
probably rare there, and the use of them is more often
attributed to women than to men. Legerdemain, also
regarded by the Angamis as a form of magic, seems to be
rare among Angamis, but men who practise it are said to
exist.[2] Still rarer are the "*Zhumma*," or invulnerables,
who cannot be harmed by spear or bullet. One such is
believed to have fought against Government at the time
of the Manipuri rising. Less rare perhaps were the
Kihupfuma, men or women born unlucky and gifted with
occult powers causing illness and misfortune to men and
animals not only voluntarily but also involuntarily by virtue
of an evil influence emanating from them at the waning
of the moon. Lycanthropy is believed in but not practised
by the Angamis, though their neighbours and perhaps
near relatives the Semas are inveterate lycanthropists.

Like all Nagas, the Angamis believe in some village
away to the East peopled solely by lycanthropists, but they
also believe in the existence of a spring [3] sometimes said to
be of blood, from which whoso drinks becomes a were-tiger
or were-leopard. The people of that neighbourhood are
said to know and shun this spring, but the danger to
strangers is believed to be great. No personal transforma-
tion takes place in the drinker, but the soul of him becomes
bound up with the body of some particular tiger into which

---

[1] Semas do not do this themselves, but accuse the Eastern Angamis of
doing it to Sema guests and strangers who may happen to pass through
their villages.

[2] I have known of several such persons in other tribes. If consulted
as to an illness or hurt they will reply that there is a stone or a tooth or
some such thing in the body of the sufferer and then proceed to extract it.
See the Sema Monograph under *thumomi*.

[3] *Cf.* S. Baring Gould, "The Book of Were-wolves," p 145.

it enters from time to time, and when the tiger dies the man dies also. Such a tiger is spoken of as *mavi* and has five toes (a tiger with dew-claws might be said to have five toes and I have seen a leopard with dew-claws identified by Rengmas as a were-leopard). When children are peevish and keep crying the people of that country dip a blade of thatching grass into the spring and give it to the child to suck. It stops his wailings but he grows up a tiger-man. This spring is believed by some Angamis to be found in the Sema country. The projection of the man's soul into the tiger is particularly liable to occur between the expiry of the old and the rising of the new moon.

Divina-
tion.

The *Zhumma* and *Kihupfuma* belong to the past, but of seers and dreamers there are still many to take omens and reveal the unknown by divination and dreams. Omens that may be seen or heard by anyone and of which there is a recognised interpretation are legion. The short rainbow is regarded as a sign of death by fighting or by fire or on a journey, probably within the month in which the rainbow is seen. The song of the bird *Koshotiatsu* foretells famine, and there are several birds whose call is lucky if it comes from the left, but unlucky from the right. Major Butler [1] mentions that the crossing of the path by a deer was a most unlucky omen for an expedition and relates that he has known a large war-party turn back immediately in consequence ; he also says that the call of a tiger from behind is regarded as unlucky, while it is very lucky if heard from the front. An eclipse of the sun or moon is believed to have been formerly quite enough to turn an expedition back from the war-path, though later, at the time of the British occupation, an eclipse was regarded as an omen of success. Such omens as these are necessarily fortuitous, but omens of many sorts may be taken on various occasions.[2] Major

[1] *Op. cit.*, p. 155.

[2] One Angami form of divination is said to have existed, and possibly is still attempted but is apparently obsolete, in which after keeping some sort of genna the diviner thrust his hand out through the wall of his house. If, when drawn in, blood was found in it, the omen is one of unnatural death (*sesho*), if grain, then of riches, if dew, poverty. My informant, however, could not say in what manner the genna used to be kept, nor could he tell me of any case in which it had been resorted to.

Butler notes that the measure of success likely to attend
a raid may be learnt from the flight of a cock, which if
strong and far is auspicious. Fire and the fire-stick, as
already described, are used at the Sekrengi genna, while
omens taken from the position of the legs of a strangled
fowl are used on the same and other occasions, the omen
being favourable if the right leg crosses above the left.
The taking of omens by the slicing of the *chiese* plant and
watching the fall of the slices is the commonest form of all
and may be seen every day in the Angami country. This
method is used in hunting, warfare, in choosing the name of
an infant, and on every kind of occasion. The writer has
been told by Dr. Rivenburg of Kohima that he has seen a
whole village turn back from an expedition owing to the
inauspicious fall of the slices, but his own experience is
that very little faith is put in this method of getting omens.[1]
The writer has often seen them taken at the start of a
hunting expedition, but never heard anyone propose giving
up the expedition for a bad omen of this sort, an event which
the sanguine Angami usually accepts with the very true
statement that no faith can be placed in them at all. When,
however, the omens are taken by someone with a particular
reputation for getting true results, probably more reliance
is placed on them, and enough belief is placed in some seers
for men to resort to them to find out the whereabouts of
stolen property or the name of the thief. In these cases
divination by looking into a bowl of *zu* or other liquid is
sometimes resorted to, but the divination of theft is
nowadays in bad odour, as the seer is apt to get punished
by authority for fixing guilt on innocent persons. Palmistry
of some sort or other is known to the Angamis, though it
is not often practised.

There are also women who answer questions from trances.
They are called *Terhope* (= " god's bridge ") and they go
into a trance occasionally (particularly in the house of a

---

[1] I fancy the village that turned back from their expedition for the
reason given were never very enthusiastic in the first place, and were rather
pleased to get an excuse for substituting some less risky amusement—
" Fugacissimi ideoque tam diu superstites."

man who has just died), falling down suddenly. From the trance they answer questions asked them, though they remember nothing on their return to consciousness. Before she can answer any question, however, it is necessary to force open the Terhope's mouth and put into it new *zu* and yeast. The trance usually lasts about half an hour to an hour, and as in the case of lycanthropists in the Sema tribe, the body aches severely on its return to consciousness. A Terhope in Jotsoma called Whelalhuwü, who was questioned when in a trance (December 1914) as to the cause of illness in the village, answered that the old Naga bridge over the Dzüdza (Zubza) river should be rebuilt. This would have entailed a bridge almost alongside the existing bridge on the Government cart road.[1]

But of all forms of second sight dreaming is the favourite and the best. The Angamis have almost a science of dreaming, and it is practised in particular by old women, who take fees for dreaming. One pice is the usual fee, and in return for this the woman foretells the result of a hunting expedition, a trading venture, or whatever it be that her client proposes to do. These dream-women have most repute for their prophecies in the case of hunting, but every huntsman is also his own dreamer, and their dreamings, as far as the writer's experience goes, have a curious way of coming true. After nightmares or unusually bad dreams, offerings consisting of the feathers and part of the intestines of a fowl are placed outside the village gate on a plantain leaf, the dreamer, who stays *kenna* that day, eating the remainder of the fowl. Nightmares are believed to be caused by the visit of the wraith of a sleeping friend which

---

[1] There is a well-known dream-woman named Lobeni in the Lhota village of Phiro. She told Captain Porter, of the 17th Infantry, that he would not kill the proclaimed elephant he had gone out to look for in the ten days of his leave, but would get it if he stayed on two days longer. Captain Porter got the elephant, but was unable to get back to Kohima by the expiry of the allotted ten days and actually reached it two days late. My own experiences with Lobeni were less successful, but then I sent out to consult her from Kohima, and, although provided with the pocket handkerchief she asked for, she complained that she could not reach me in her dream, but was turned back every time she tried as soon as she got to the old rifle range near Kohima.

is stronger than that of the dreamer. A story is told of
a man who kept having bad nightmares, and so took to
sleeping with his " dao " under his pillow. When the
nightmare came he tried to kill it with his " dao," and,
getting up to pursue it, saw a butterfly fly into his friend's
house. The next morning this friend told some neighbours
that he had been horribly frightened in the night by dreaming
that a man had tried to kill him with a " dao."

It is believed that to dream of flying or of falling down is
an indication of the growth of the body during sleep. To
dream of being bitten by a tick, which cannot be pulled out,
is an omen of approaching death, while to dream of a man
dressed entirely in new clothes is a sure premonition of the
death of the man thus seen. A curious instance of this
came within the writer's own experience. He left Kohima
for a tour in the Kezama villages on September 8, 1913.
At the moment of leaving, his own interpreter, Zelucha of
Jotsoma, came up to say that he was not feeling very well
and would prefer to join later after two or three days, so
another interpreter, Vise of Viswema, was taken in his
place. Mao was reached on the 10th, Kezakenoma on the
11th, Razama on the 13th. At Razama Zelucha was
expected to arrive, but another interpreter, Solhu of
Kezakenoma, came instead, saying that Zelucha was ill.
On hearing this Vise remarked that he knew it already, and
that Zelucha was going to die. When asked how he could
possibly say this, as Zelucha had been quite well a few days
before and had not been really ill when Vise last saw him,
Vise said that he had dreamt of him on the night of sleeping
at Mao, and had seen him dressed entirely in new clothes.
This, he said, left no doubt. The news of Zelucha's death
reached camp at Tekhubama on September 16.[1]

---

[1] I have a very vivid recollection of the details of this incident, which
occurred just as has been recorded. I noted the dream and its interpretation in my tour diary (now in the Deputy Commissioner's office in
Kohima) when it was mentioned to me, and before Zelucha's death had
actually occurred. He died, I think, on the 14th. He had been of great
assistance in collecting the information given in this monograph and the
loss was a personal one.

PART V

FOLKLORE—ANGAMI SUPERSTITIONS, TRADITIONS, LEGENDS, " CONTES "—SONGS

PART V

FOLKLORE—ANGAMI SUPERSTITIONS, TRADITIONS,
LEGENDS, "CONTES"—SONGS

To enumerate the various superstitions of the Angamis
would fill a book in itself, even interpreting the word superstition in what is perhaps the narrowest sense in which we
can use it, that is to say, as designating the detached beliefs
regarding natural objects and trivial actions encountered in
ordinary life which do not form an obvious part of any system
of belief and have not on the face of them any reasonable
explanation, as designating, for instance, such a practice
as that of "touching wood" among ourselves. The Angamis'
belief that whoever approaches the foot of the rainbow will
die is explained by their saying that the spirit of the rainbow
will kill the person, but no reason is given for the belief that
it is dangerous to plant hedges of "cactus" (i.e. *Euphorbia
antiquorum*) because they cause storms, or for the belief
that a man's stomach aches when someone at a distance is
molesting his property. These are typical superstitions.
More picturesque is the belief that marriages should not be
made in the month in which the swallows come, for girls
married in that month will not stay with their husbands,
but will run away back to their parents' houses. New
superstitions, or old superstitions in new forms, seem easily
assimilated. There is a belief in many Angami villages
that it is dangerous to be photographed, as if the photograph
be taken to the plains the person photographed will gradually
decline and die, while in some villages it is practically
impossible to photograph young girls, as they regard the
camera as some diabolical contrivance for revealing their
pudenda. One interesting belief is that in the unluckiness

of the number seven. No party of seven persons will ever leave the village together for any purpose, even to cut jungle, as something unfortunate, such as the death of one of their number, is certain to happen to a party of seven. If seven men were to go trading together at least one-seventh part of the capital taken would be lost.[1] The belief in the power for evil of praise or blame and protection by *kethithedi* has been already described.[2] Angami superstitions, however, are legion.

Some of the prophecies current among Angamis are worth mentioning. There is a belief in Khonoma and other Angami villages in the return of a king who will drive out the British and rule over "all who eat from the wooden platter," *i.e.*, all Nagas. This king is believed to be sleeping, as Barbarossa sleeps, in a cave in the Kacha Naga country. He may be identified with the Kachari king Bhim Raja, of whom such a story is told, and it is probable that this Naga prophecy is of Kacha Naga or Kachari origin. Another prophecy is that of *Chüsénu*, "Armageddon," when everyone will fight and men will become so small that they can climb up chilli plants and their ears will grow the wrong way on and wooden pestles (for pounding paddy) will put forth leaves ; at that time the dead will rise and the stored grain will fly in the air and men will run about to catch it for their food, and every family in the tribe, indeed in the whole hill country, will have a dispute. It is suggested sometimes that this prophecy was fulfilled when Khonoma was taken by the British troops, as wooden pestles are believed to have put forth leaves at that time. The belief that " men will become so small that they can climb up chilli plants " is interesting, because the Khasis not only have the same belief, but state it in precisely the same words. With regard to the folklore stories that follow, it should be said that

---

[1] This belief may perhaps be connected with the Pleiades, of which the Angami see seven, who are said to have been seven men who went out to dig bamboo rats but got ambuscaded and killed.

[2] See under Agricultural Implements, and also House Building. The writer had an Irish wolf-hound of exceptional size which attracted a great deal of attention from Nagas. When it died of distemper its death was ascribed by Nagas of all tribes to the number of conversations and remarks of which it had been the subject.

they have been collected mostly through the medium of interpreters in the bastard Assamese which forms the *lingua franca* of the hills, and not directly in the Angami language. Many of them have been told on the march and round the camp fire as the result of some chance question, of the associations of the locality, or of some incident of the day. They have been arranged in three groups, which, even if there is no very clear line of demarcation, will perhaps serve to distinguish roughly the different classes of stories. First of all come such traditions as have a more or less historical complexion—stories of village feuds like that of Kohima and Puchama already recounted, in which the supernatural plays little or no part, and which, subject to a somewhat liberal discount for exaggeration, we may well believe to be true. The legends which follow the traditions are stories of the early history of villages or of the race in which the supernatural figures largely—stories like those already given in Part I of the founding of Sohemi, or of the dispersion of the tribes at the Kezakenoma stone. Finally, the stories classed as " *Contes* " are those which seem to be told, not for the explanation of any custom or the handing down of any record, but simply and solely for the sake of the story itself. Here are fairy tales, animal stories, and cynical observations of human foibles. The Angami is an omnivorous collector and retailer of stories, and some of those included under " *Contes* " undoubtedly contain a foreign element, and one at least seems to be of foreign origin. It is not impossible that some future collector of Angami folklore will find Angami versions of the stories from " Uncle Remus," with the leopard as " Brer Fox " and the barking deer as " Brer Rabbit," on which the writer has sometimes relied for his own contribution to an evening's entertainment.

The folklore is followed by a few typical songs[1] in Angami

[1] I am, unfortunately, no musician, and cannot give the notation of the singing, but one or two of the songs have been recorded on the phonograph and the records sent to the Pitt Rivers Museum at Oxford. These are poor illustrations of the real thing, as it has been possible only to get the effect of one or two voices on the instrument, whereas it is of the essence of most Angami singing that there should usually be a number of voices of differing qualities singing together, not, I understand, strictly speaking in harmony, but at differing pitches, which gives an effect of harmony.

and English taken quite at random. Like almost all Angami songs, they are nearly sentimental enough to suit an English drawing-room.

TRADITIONS

MEZOMA AND THEMOKEDIMA

Themokedima was at war with Cherema (Natsimi) and asked aid of Mezoma, promising to pay annual tribute. Mezoma took five heads off Cherema and were [1] paid five cows, and Themokedima refused to pay any more. Consequently Mezoma called Nerhema and Tofima to their aid and raided the Themokedima fields, killing a large number of women and children, about 150. Then when Themokedima got news of Mezoma's coming a second time they ambuscaded them and took them in the rear. Mezoma were accompanied by Nerhema, Chichama, and Tofima, about 700 or 800 in all, of whom about 50 were killed. The next year Mezoma was [1] cut up by the British Government for raiding a Kachari village.

KHONOMA AND MARÁM

At Khonoma there is a place called " Viyakiricha," i.e., " the place of the dream-stone." After taking omens on chickens, men, if the omens are favourable, go and sleep there, and, if the dream is good, they send word and are fetched back by the village.[2] Now the men of Marhema (Marām) got to hear of this custom, and, sending messages to the men of Khonoma to come to the dream-stone to fetch some one or other, took many heads. A man of Khonoma, therefore, known as Phuyi, led a raid on Marām and took

[1] Words ending in ma are plural or collective nouns indicating the men of such and such a village (ra); thus Mezoma = the men of Mezo; Mezora = the village Mezo. It is, however, customary among foreigners in the Naga Hills to use the form in ma to indicate the actual village as well as the men who live in it, so that one may be excused for using sometimes a plural and sometimes a singular verb with the name of a village.

[2] Folklore (vol. xxv; p. 85) compares the practice of dreaming on the stone to that of sleeping (ἐγκοίμησις) at Greek shrines, referring to Sir J. Frazer, Pausanias, 1898, vol. ii, 476 iii, 243, also to J. C. Lawson, " Modern Greek Folklore and Ancient Greek Religion," 1910, p. 61.

AN ANGAMI GRAVE (*mekra*) (The grave of Zelucha, Interpreter of Jotsoma)

[See p. 225

STATUE OF DEAD MAN ON HIS GRAVE, SHOWING BY THE STONES AT HIS FEET A TALLY OF SUCCESSES IN WAR AND LOVE. THE STONES WITH FACES CARVED ON THEM REPRESENT ENEMIES SLAIN, THE PLAIN STONES BEHIND THEM THE WOMEN HE LOVED

[See p. 325

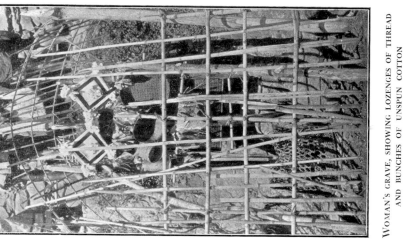

WOMAN'S GRAVE, SHOWING LOZENGES OF THREAD AND BUNCHES OF UNSPUN COTTON

many heads, and made moreover a song upon Marām. But the men of Marām made as though they were not angry, and said the song was a pretty song. Khonoma then went upon a second raid, crossing over Japvo to Marām, but on Japvo much snow fell and the men of Khonoma became numbed. Some men who heard the shouting and calling of the Khonoma men in this condition went and gave the news in Marām, who came up and cut up 140 men ; only fifteen (including Phuyi himself and one Viya) got away, for Khonoma could not use their spears for numbness. One Shetzu was taken prisoner and ransomed himself by promising a mithan yearly as tribute, and this tribute was paid for two years. The first year Khonoma sent a good mithan, the next year a little one, which Marām at first refused to accept, but Khonoma said they could have that or nothing, so Marām merely replied that they would not have peace with Khonoma if a proper mithan was not paid the next year. But the third year, instead of giving the mithan to Marām, Khonoma gave it to Jotsoma, and these two villages, joining forces, went up against Marām and took many heads. And again a second time 20 or 30 men from the two villages went up and got two heads from Marām, but the 15 men in the rear lost their way in the cane jungle on the way home and could not find their way back. After 50 days the only four men who survived starvation got back to Khonoma on the point of death, and two of them ate heavily and died, but Chasamo of Khonoma and Navüno of Jotsoma, eating very little, were saved by their cunning. And after this Khonoma, realising that fate was against them in the matter, left Marām alone.[1]

A NAGA JUDITH

Akhaji of the Marhema (Marām) village killed a man of the Samuma village who had a sister named Inyapfükuvura. When she heard that Akhaji had taken her brother's head,

---

[1] The Marām version is that their Mohvö put a spell on Khonoma, causing the snow to fall and the men to be numbed.

Inyapfükovura prepared much food, and wrapping it in a cloth went to Akhaji's house. She told Akhaji that she had brought food for him, and asked him whether he would eat first and then enjoy her, or *vice versa*. Akhaji said he would eat first, and, having eaten, he fastened the door and took Inyapfükovura to his bed. But Inyapfükovura had a dao concealed in her petticoat, and when Akhaji was expecting it least, she cut his throat, and having cut his head completely off, she hid it in her petticoat and took it home.

On the way she met Akhaji's father and mother, and they said, "Have you seen Akhaji to-day?" And she said, "I gave him to eat." And they said, "Where is that blood dripping from, and what is it? It has dripped all along the path behind you." But she said, "I am much ashamed, but what can I say? I let Akhaji lie with me and I am defiled." So they let her pass by. And when she reached her own village, she put the head down outside the village gates, for it is tabu for a woman to carry a head through the gate. So she went in and fetched her elder brother and told him, but he would not believe. "You are a woman," said he, "how could you take Akhaji's head? You are lying to me." And when she asseverated, he replied thus many times. But at last, weary of her importunity, he went out with her, and she showed him the head and he knew that her words were true, and taking up the head he carried it into the village in triumph.

LEGENDS

KOHIMA

The following account is given of the origin of Kohima village :—

There are seven clans in Kohima—Rosuma, Hrepfüma, Dapfütsuma, Cherama, Hurutsuma, Puchatsuma, and Chotonoma. All these clans bear the names of men who were their ancestors. Rosuma, Hrepfüma, Dapfütsuma, and Cherama came from Sopvoma in the Memi country. Rosu first selected a site at Kohima and went back to

Sopvoma and fetched the other three clans. The man
Puchatsu was at Chimokedima (Samaguting). Rosuma
and Dapfütsuma went and fetched him to Kohima. Hurutsu
came himself from the direction of the Kacha Naga country.
While Hurutsu was cutting trees in his " jhum " he heard a
voice come like an echo from a hollow tree : " O-lo ! ho ! "
He went to the tree and found a man. At first the man
could not understand what Hurutsu said, but after staying
with Hurutsu for a long time he learned to understand his
(Hurutsu's) language. Hurutsu called him " Lezechu,"
i.e., " jungle-cutting generation," and from him is descended
the Lezechunoma *putsa* of the Hurutsuma clan. The
Chotonoma are descended from a bastard child of a man of
the Semoma clan of Khonoma. A girl of that clan fell in
love with one of her fellow clansmen and became pregnant.
Overcome by shame, she ran away to Kohima and lived
in Rosu's house. One day Rosu saw blood on the girl's
calves and said to her, " What is the matter with you ? "
She answered that she had been out because she had
diarrhœa. Then Rosu went to the spot and found a child
crying there. He put the child under his cloth and brought
it back. On the way someone said to him, " What are you
carrying under your cloth ? " and Rosu replied that he was
carrying a cucumber. For this reason the child was given
the name " Chüto," *i.e.,* " cucumber." When the child
grew up Rosu gave him a sow and other goods, and chose a
house-site for him where the Chotonoma clan now live.
One day Hurutsu stole his sow. Chüto came and told Rosu
about it, and said that the thief was eating the flesh in the
jungle and coming back at night. Then Rosu and Chüto
went out together and lay near the path, one above it and
the other below it, and they tied their toes together with a
string so that they would wake up when the thief tripped
against the cord. Then they went to sleep. Later the thief
came by and stepped on the string, and both the men woke
up and seized him, and were going to kill him ; but the
thief, who was Hurutsu, requested them not to kill him but
to take compensation, so Rosu ordered him to give seven
sows to Chüto, and he gave them. So the rule is followed

to this day that if anyone steal anything he is mulcted in seven times its value.

N.B.—Another and possibly less legendary account of the origin of the Kohima clans says that Cherama came straight from Kezakenoma to Kohima, while the other six clans, which are grouped together as Pferonuma and said to have been originally six *putsa* of one clan, came from Kigwema, where they had settled first after leaving Kezakenoma. Kezakenoma, to which all Angami villages trace their origin, is only a few miles from Sopvoma. The Lezechunoma *putsa* is also otherwise derived from a man who ran away from Jotsoma, a descent which only in 1913 gave rise to a claim to a large area of jhum land. The claim was, moreover, successfully established.

Marriage between Cherama and Rosuma is not allowed. The reason given for this is that the founder of the Cherama clan married Rosu's sister. This reason is unique, and so contrary to all the Angami theory and practice of exogamous marriage that one cannot help thinking that it is a purely fictitious reason. The otherwise invariable reason given for prohibition of marriage between two clans or kindred is that they are descended from brothers, and it is possible that the reason given for the prohibition on marriage between Cherama and Rosuma is an attempt to explain a prohibition, the real reason of which was unknown, in a case when genealogy and traditions excluded the " two brothers " explanation.

KEZABAMA

Now Kezabama was founded by a man and his family who went along from Kezakenoma way with a cock, a dog, and a mithan, waiting for them to give a sign. Although they reached suitable places for a village the cock would not crow, nor the dog bark, nor the mithan bellow. But at last, just below Swemi village, the cock crowed, the dog barked, and the mithan bellowed, so they asked the people of Swemi, who were, as they are to this day, Semas, for land. And they gave it to them.

Swemi was then a very big village of 700 houses and the fields stretched so far that women with children could not get to work in the fields. So to avoid having children the men did with the women as Onan did unto Tamar.[1]

THEROCHESWEMA

Therocheswema was not always on its present site. When it was on the old site one day a barking deer ran into the house of the Kemovo. And from that day onward the men of Therocheswema became as ogres, eating double the amount of rice eaten by ordinary men. So the village was threatened with starvation.

At last the people removed to the present site of the village, after which they reverted to their human condition.

YASABAMA

The Yasa road is only two feet wide, and is very high, and they say that one day an old woman stole a basket of rice from another village and a tiger killed a bullock on the other side, and the two—the tiger with the bullock and the old woman with the rice—met in the middle of this road, and both were so frightened that the tiger dropped the bullock and jumped right over the old woman to get away, while the old woman threw down the rice and ran for her own village.

THE UNIVERSE

The sun is as large as a field. He is male[2] and the moon is female. The sun only comes out by day because he is afraid to go about at night. When he does come he is so ashamed of his cowardice that he flashes up and comes out like lightning. Originally when he did not come man went and called him, but he came not. Then the bull went and called him, but he came not. Then the pig and after him the dog went and called the sun, but still he did not come.

[1] Book of Genesis, ch. 38.
[2] This is not the normal Angami version which makes the sun female and the moon male. Probably the inversion of the sex in this account is due to the teller's having been sophisticated in a school.

Even when the fowls called him he would not listen. So the cock said, " Oh, very well, I will come and look for you, and if anything touches me I shall crow, and you will have to come." Since then the sun has always come when the cock crows for him. The cock also told the sun he was not to go away, but he said he was afraid of the dark, so the cock said he would tell and he did so.

In the moon there are nettles and a cotton tree. Like the sun, he moves about while the earth is still.

The sky is really smaller than the earth. In the beginning the sky said to the earth, " You are so big, I cannot cover you, wrinkle up your feet." So the earth wrinkled to let the sky cover it, and that is why there are hills and valleys in the earth while the sky is smooth. But even by wrinkling, all the earth could not get covered, and one place got left outside. This place is called Whedzura. There is no sky in Whedzura, and so they never see the sun there, but they have a stick which is very precious by which they tell the time, and the light there is like a sort of moonshine. The air in Whedzura is very strong and so people get old very quickly. They marry off their children one year and cannot even recognise them the next. If a man would go there he must start when he is born, it is so far, otherwise must he die of age before he reach there, growing old upon the road.

The Naga and the Plainsman

Ukepenopfü was the ancestress of all men. Her husband[1] had a big moustache and a long beard reaching to his feet,[2] and he was very wise. If his children had seen him they would have been frightened and have run away without learning his wisdom, so he lived hidden in a vessel waiting till his two sons should grow up. But one day some people asked the boys whether they had ever seen their father, and they said, " No, we have no father." Then

---

[1] Apparently this personage is sometimes identified with the spirit Metsimo (Memicè *Pekujikhe*) who guards the way to the land of the dead.

[2] See specimen of the Memi language in Part VI. The beard is a distinctive feature as it is very rare among Nagas. See also Appendix II, para. xxix.

they answered, " Yes, you have. He has a long beard and
hides himself in a big wooden vessel. Go and say to your
mother that unless she shows him to you you will kill her."
Now Ukepenopfü could not deny the existence of the
boys' father, so she said to them, " Very well, I will show
you your father, but he who gets frightened cannot get his
father's knowledge and wisdom." And the boys agreed.
Then she took them to the vessel and showed them their
father. And the elder boy, who became the ancestor of
Nagas, got very frightened and ran away, but he who later
begat the Indians (*Teprima*) wished to go to his father in
the vessel. Then the father came out and took up this
son to his bosom and said to his wife, " I had thought to
teach both my sons all my wisdom, but now my elder son
has run away. If I stay here he will not return. My wife,
take care of him and he shall take your name with him."
Then the old man went to the plains with the younger boy,
and that is the reason why the Nagas are poorer in knowledge
and cunning than the men of the plains.

Another version of the origin of the Naga and the
Plainsman tells how two brothers each took a different
path, but while one blazed his path on all the *chomhu* trees
the other blazed his on *chemu* trees. Now the blaze on a
chomhu tree remains white for several days, but that on a
chemu tree turns black very quickly. Consequently most
of the followers of these two brothers followed the first
and emerged into the plains, while the few who followed the
second stayed in the hills. This story is also told by the
Lhotas. .

TIGERS

Now the Angamis tell this story, that man, the tiger, and
the spirit were three brothers, the sons of one woman, and
whereas the man tended his mother carefully, washing her
and bathing her, the tiger was always grumbling about the
house, snarling at anything and giving everyone trouble.
The man ate his food cooked, the tiger ate his raw, and the
spirit just had his smoke-dried. One day the mother, who
was tired of the family squabbles, made a grass mark and

set it up in the jungle, and told the man and the tiger to race for it, saying, "Whoever touches it first shall go and live in villages, but the other must go and live in the dark jungles." Then the spirit said to the man, "I will shoot the mark over with an arrow when you call out, and then you can say you touched it first." So when they had run a little way in the jungle the man called out, "I have touched the mark," and at the same time the spirit drew his bow and struck the mark with an arrow, so that it trembled, and the tiger coming up while it was still shaking was deceived, and went away, angry, into the jungle.

After this the man sent the cat from the village to say to the tiger, "After all, you are my brother ; when you kill a deer, please put a leg on the wall for me," but the cat muddled the message and said, "When you kill a deer put it on the wall for the man," and the tiger, thinking that a whole deer was meant, was angry and hated the man. All the same they are brothers, and to this day, if a man kill a tiger, he will say in the village, "The gods have killed a tiger in the jungle," not "I have killed it." As if he did all other tigers would say, "This man has killed his brother," and would go about to devour him. But the tiger is afraid of man because he (the tiger) cannot carry stones, while he sees the man take up stones as great as a basket. Therefore, thinking that man is very strong, he is afraid.[1]

[1] The Semas have this story in an almost identical form, the Rengmas and Lhotas also. *Cf.* also Appendix II, paras. XXIX. and XXX. Among the Angamis, at any rate, old men, and nowadays young men too, eat tiger or leopard flesh, but a Sema will not touch it, as he looks on men and tigers as of one blood, and the Angami still has to cook it outside the house or in the porch and may not bring it near the women. When an Angami kills a tiger or a leopard the kemovo proclaims a *penna* "for the death of an elder brother." (*Cf.* the practices of the *Mosá-ároi* clan of Kacharis and the *Mashá-aröi* clan of Meches, which go into mourning for the death of a tiger. Endle, "The Kacharis," pp. 25 and 82.) At the same time the killer of the animal puts its head, with the mouth wedged open by a bit of stick, into running water, so that when it tries to tell the *Tekhu-rho* who killed it, all that can be heard is an inarticulate gurgling in the water. Changs do the same, while Semas stuff a stone into the dead beast's mouth (to prevent its ghost from waylaying them in the next world) and wedge the mouth open with a stick as well. See also Appendix on the Memi.

THE DOUBLE-SKINNED (AND THE ORIGIN OF CHOLERA)

They tell also of a tribe of men whose skin is double ; these men were aforetime of the Naga race, but separated from them because of a quarrel they had over drying rice on the stone [1] whereon one load of rice set to dry in the morning becomes two loads by dusk. And after the quarrel the double-skinned tribe fled away to another place, and though men shoot them they die not, save they be shot when belching or loosing their bowels. And they say that two Angamis travelled by this country and were well and hospitably entreated, and when they would return to their own village the double-skinned gave them a pipe of hollow bamboo, telling them not to open it on the road, but when they should reach their home ; and they also offered them their double skin, but the travellers would take it not, lest there were some bad thing in it, and after that they had returned, they opened the bamboo, and the double-skinned had put Cholera therein, and it came forth and destroyed many men of that village.

AMAZONS

Now the Angamis tell this story : There is in a certain place a village of women only, and if a man go there they drive him away by shooting at him with war bows, and they raise not any males save one only, and when other male babes are born they boil water and put them therein to kill them. These women, moreover, do no hard work, but eat great store of starch and oil to make them strong to battle.

Others say that when a man go there, the women that be there be so eager for him that in striving to possess him they tear him to pieces utterly.

Note.—The Semas place the Amazons in a village east of the Patkoi-Barail range.

Folklore refers to a large number of versions of this widespread myth, viz. : The Male and Female Islands described by Marco Polo (ed. Sir H. Yule, 1871, vol. ii, p. 237 *sq.*).

---

[1] *I.e.* the Kezakenoma stone (see Part I).

The Country of the Western Women described by Hiuen Tsiang (S. Beal, " Buddhist Records of the Western World," 1884, vol. ii, pp. 240 *sqq.*, 270).

The Tibetan kingdom of women, the existence of which has been asserted by E. T. Atkinson (" Gazetteer of the Himalayan Districts," 1884, vol. ii, p. 458) and by C. H. Sherring (" Western Tibet and the Borderland," 1906, p. 338).

The Islands of Daughters of the Gods in the " Jātaka " (Cambridge trans., I, 110).

One of the villages in Mang Peng, Northern Shan States, Upper Burma, said to be at the present day inhabited exclusively by women (J. G. Scott, " Gazetteer of Upper Burma and the Shan States," 1901, Part II, vol. ii, p. 201).

The island recorded on the west coast of Africa by the ancient geographer, Mela (III, 9).

The tale of the " City of Women " recorded by Major A. J. N. Tremearne (*Folklore*, xxii, p. 60).

The " Voyage of Bran " (Kuno Meyer's trans., I. Nutt, 30).

A tale of the Tami Islanders off the coast of New Guinea (Neuhass, " Deutsch New Guinea," Berlin, 1911, vol. iii, p. 550).

A Gazelle Peninsular tale (I. Eneier, " Mythen und Erzählungen der Küstenbewohner der Gazelle-Halbinsel, Neu-Pommern," Munster-i-W., 1909, 85, 89).

A tale of the Tonga Islanders (" Tonga," Edinburgh, 1827, vol. ii, p. 116).

Early accounts of Spanish discoveries in America, and the finding of Matinina or Madanino by Columbus (Arber, " The First Three English Books on America," Westminster, 1895, 30, 99, 189).

It is probably with the Tibetan or Shan States version that the Angami account is most likely to be connected, and if the actual existence of these places is a fact the Naga accounts may be ultimately derived from some contact with such a village at some remote period in the history of the race.

KOPPELBURG

There was once a chief, a mighty man, who built him a strong house and digged a deep ditch thereabout, and put water therein to keep him from his enemies. But a stronger than he came. So the strong man fled to a little hill wherein he made him a hole to hide, and the door of that cave was strong and hard and none could open it except the owner willed it. Being yet a young man he led away Naga boys to that hole in the hillside by singing and making manifold music, and the parents of these boys sought them, but found them not again.

With reference to this story *Folklore* remarks :—" This is the Koppenberg of German tradition." For the " Pied Piper of Hamelin " see *Folklore*, vol. iii, p. 227 *sqq.* ; *F. L. Journ.*, vol. ii, p. 206 *sqq.* ; J. Grimm, " Household Tales," 1884, vol. ii, p. 412. For the Indian version of the pipe which causes everyone to dance, see C. H. Tawney, " Katha-Sarit-Sāgara," 1880, vol. i, pp. 338, 577 ; vol. ii, p. 309. A negro version is given by Miss Mary A. Owen, *Journal American Folklore*, vol. xvi, p. 58. Also see Sir John Rhys' learned discussion of Lucian's account of Ogmios, the Gallic Hercules—" Lectures on Celtic Heathendom," Hibbert Lectures, 1888, p. 13 *sqq.*

Tower of Babel

Ukepenopfü was the first being. Her descendants are very many. Instead of dying she was translated into heaven. Later on her descendants thought to communicate with her by building a tower up to heaven, up which they would go and talk to her. She, however, knowing their thoughts, said to herself, " They will all expect presents and I have no presents for so many men. The tower must be stopped before it get any higher." So she made all the men working at the tower to talk different languages, so that they could not understand one another, and when one said bring a stone, they would fetch water or a stick, and so forth, so that all was confusion, and the tower abandoned, and hence the different tongues of the various tribes of man.

There was once a country under a powerful chief with great armies and the people thought they would mount up to heaven by building a ladder of wood. So they builded a stair, and made the stair very high into heaven. Now the men who were up at the top asked for more wood and the men who were below made answer, " There is no wood, shall we cut a piece from the stair ? " So the men at the top not understanding what they said gave answer, " Ay, cut it." So they cut it, and the ladder fell, and great was the fall thereof, and they that builded it were killed.

Note.—Folklore in commenting on these two stories quotes one almost identical with the second from Sikhim (" Gazetteer of Sikhim," Calcutta, 1894, p. 42) and a number of legends very similar to both stories from the Chin Hills. Mashonaland. Mexico. and the Chocktaw Indians of Louisiana. For a very close parallel to the Angami version, see "Men of the Trees", by R. St. Barbe Baker, ch. xiv. The story is told by the Akikuyu of East Africa.

"CONTES"

CHIKEO'S GIFT

A man used to go every day to scare birds from the fields and he noticed that every day someone had been before him and had sharpened his dao on a stone, having wetted the stone. So one night he sat by the side of the river, and at dawn Chikeo came and began to sharpen his dao. He was wearing a rain-coat. The man seized Chikeo. Chikeo said, " Don't kill me and I will give you what you wish for." He agreed to this, and Chikeo whistled, and all the animals came out of the forest and gathered together. Then Chikeo said, " I will go up the hill. You may kill which animal you choose. When I get to the top of the hill I shall call and you will not then be able to have it." Chikeo went up, and the man looked over the animals to see which was the best, and could not decide. Chikeo got to the top and whistled and all the animals ran away. A jungle cat got trodden on by one of the animals and was killed, so the man took that and ate it.[1]

THE FIG-TREE

Once a man was travelling to another village and could not reach it that day. After it got dark he killed a ghost with his spear, and he slept that night under a great stone in the shelter of a fig-tree and ate its fruit, for he had nothing else to eat. And after he had laid down there came many ghosts with torches calling their friend who was killed, and they called out in a loud voice, " Chu'o, Chu'o, Shen gatila " (that is, in Angami, " Keso'u jutiahe," for the ghosts spake in Kacha Naga). And the great stone answered them back, " Even if he have died (*i.e.* the man who killed him) he has not come to me to-day." So the ghosts took up the dead body of their friend and went away.

After this the man heard another tree call out to the fig-tree to come and do genna to heal him (for the tree was

---

[1] I am indebted to Mr. Barnes, Deputy Commissioner of the Naga Hills, for this story. Chikeo is the dwarf-like spirit, a sort of leprechaun, who presides over animals mentioned in Part IV as " Tsükhǫ."

sick), but the fig replied, " I cannot come to-night to do genna for I have a guest." A few minutes later the tree that had called out fell down, and the fig-tree told the man that this tree had had fever for a long time and died that night.

And the next morning the man got up and ate up the ripe fruit of the fig and was filled, and he went to the village and told them all that had happened, and therefore do our Angamis say that the fig is the chief priest of the trees.

BATTLE OF THE BIRDS AND SNAKES

Once upon a time the lizard and the smallest bird made a well. ,But whenever the lizard went to get water in his water-pot he dirtied the water, so the smallest bird said to the lizard, " Don't make the water dirty every time before I draw my pitcher full." But the lizard would not listen. So the smallest bird asked him again the second time, and the lizard said, " You go and call all your birds together and I will go and call all the reptiles together at the foot of that tree," so they each called their people and the two sides fought. And the birds came down and carried off snakes, but they were afraid to catch the biggest snake. And the crow flew down to catch the snakes' " gennabura," but as it was carrying it up it dropped it back into the middle of a stone, and the snakes began to increase. If that snake were taken the others would all die, but the crow had failed and the other birds were afraid. Then the smallest bird went and found the biggest bird and asked it to come and kill the biggest snake, which has a comb like a cock, and the big bird said, " But there is no one to feed my young." So the smallest bird said, " I will feed your young." Then the big bird went and flew high up in the air and stooped and dropped and killed the snake.

Note.—Folklore suggests that this is possibly a reminiscence of the destruction of the snakes by the bird Garuda, the Garula of the *Jātaka.* The Semas, however, have a version of this story which is used to account for the colouring of different species of birds. I very much doubt the likelihood of any Hindu influence having started these stories, though conceivably the Hindu tale and the Naga tale might be ultimately derived from a common source.

SNAKES

Once upon a time a girl went to work in the fields. On her way she met a snake in the path, and the snake would not let her pass until she said " Do not bite me and I will marry you." So at last she said it and the snake let her go. Afterwards he married her. Then the snake bit her in the breast and she got breast ornaments and he bit her in the leg and she got cane leggings. Another girl saw this and afterwards met a snake. So she said to the snake " We will marry," and she took it up and put it into her basket, but the snake said nothing. It bit her in the arm and her arm swelled up and she died.

THE SHREW-MOUSE

The shrew is the pig of the " *terhoma*." One day a man was fishing, but when he put his traps into the river nothing would go near them except a shrew, so he drove the shrew away, and soon he saw many fish come near, but the shrew drove away the fish. Then the fisherman killed the shrew, and many fish came to his trap and he lifted them out on to the bank and killed them and put in his trap again, and a second time came many fish, and again he took them out and killed them. And as it was too late for him to go home he slept under a large stone called Tsurnga on the river bank. And a *terhoma* came up the river and called out from the water to the stone Tsurnga and said, " Did you see any bad man to-day ? " And Tsurnga answered, " No, why do you ask ? " And the *terhoma* said, " My pig has not come home to-night and probably some man has killed him." So the man was very much afraid and fished in that place no more.

They also say that a man married a woman of the *terhoma*, and his wife took him to live in the sky and he had three sons by her, and one day he went out to hunt, and the *terhoma* with him said, " A wild boar is attacking our brother-in-law," and he looked down and saw a shrew-mouse and he killed the shrew-mouse, and that night all the *terhoma* came with their pots and their dishes to him and the man roasted the shrew for his sons and the *terhoma* to eat.[1]

THE MOUSE

Men first found rice growing in the middle of a pool, and as the water was deep they could not get at the rice, so they sent the mouse to fetch the rice and the mouse fetched the rice. Then the man said to the mice, " Come, take your share," but the mice said, " No, we cannot carry it as our heads are very small, please let us eat a little of your rice every day instead." So the man promised to let the mice do so, and so the mice continue to eat the rice of men.[2]

THE DOG

Now the dog had no hole to live in. So he went to the tiger to live with him, but when they went a-hunting the dog barked. But the tiger did not like this, so he would not have the dog with him, as he could not hunt with a barking dog. Then the dog went to the elephant, but the elephant said, " If you bark the tiger will find us," and sent him away. Then he went to the wild dog, and he and the wild dog hunted small animals together all day and ate them, but the wild dog hunts in silence and the dog barked much. Therefore the wild dog left the dog, and the dog went to the barking deer, but he wanted to devour the deer's young and he barked too much withal, so the deer left him. And so, at last, the fifth time he went to man, and man taught him to hunt and found his barking useful, so he kept the dog and cherished him.

THE WILD DOG

Now the Kacha Nagas say that formerly the man and the red dog lived together and the man sent out the red dog to hunt and kill for him, and when the red dog killed he brought his kill to the man.

[1] The Semas tell a similar story of the wild boar, which they, like the Lhotas, call the pig of the spirits—*teyhami* (= Angami *terhoma*).

[2] See note on " Thezukepu " genna.

But one day the man beat the red dog with a stick and sent him out to hunt, and when he got out of reach he called out to the man, " If I kill I will not come back, but I will put a leg in the road for you." And the man answered, " Don't put a leg in the road but bring it to the house." And the red dog called back, " All right then, if we kill we will leave you some of the animal's hair on the road in our fæces."

And so when wild dog kill and eat, the animal's hair may always be seen in their fæces on the path. This is the story the Kacha Nagas tell.

N.B.—This story, though actually told by a Kacha Naga, is the one commonly told of the wild dog by the Angamis.

THE BEAR

The bear is a stupid animal. He builds a platform in a tree and goes to sleep on it. When it rains he wakes up and says, " I must have made a mistake. This is not my house, as I built my house so well that the rain could not get through." So he climbs down the tree, and when he gets to the bottom examines the tree and looks up. Then he says, " This is very funny. It is my own house right enough. I had better go back." So he climbs up and again goes to sleep on the top. When the rain starts again he gets wet and repeats exactly what he did before.

This story is told likewise by the Semas and Lhotas.

BOILED CRAB

One day a little bird went to work at his fields and she called her friends to help her, and the crab came among them. About midday the little bird called her friends from the field and they all came into the field house. When they had all collected, the little bird put a pot on the fire and she perched on the rim and laid an egg into the pot for each of her friends to eat.

The next day they went to the crab's fields to work and the crab brought nothing to eat, for he had seen what the little bird did and meant to imitate her. So at midday he

STONE BOUND TO THE SLED READY FOR PULLING

[See p. 232

MEMORIAL STONE (*Jakhama*)

[See p. 232

ANGAMIS OF KOHIMA VILLAGE PULLING A STONE ON A SLED FOR ERECTION

[See p. 232

went to the field house to cook the food, and he made the
fire and put on the pot and he climbed on to the rim of the
pot and tried to lay his egg, but while he was trying he
fell backwards into the pot and could not get out again,
so he cooked himself and thus died.

Meanwhile the crab's friends went on hoping that he
would call them to eat, and as the afternoon wore on they
got very hungry, and one of them came to the field house
and then he saw the cooked crab in the pot. Then the
friend went and told the others that the crab had died in
the cooking pot, and the other friends came and took him
out, and as they were feeling hungry they ate him.

THE TRAVELLING COMPANIONS AND THE GRATEFUL DOE

Once upon a time a man called all his fellow villagers and
went with them to hunt, and he had a gun and shot many
animals and never missed and so hunted every day. But
the other villagers, although they never killed anything
themselves, would not give the huntsman his share. So
one day, when he saw a big doe barking-deer, he refused to
shoot it.

After this he went to travel, and as he was going along
a snake came out on the road and it turned into a beggar
man and asked him where he was going. He replied,
" I am going to travel," and the beggar straightway
answered, " I also. Then we will go together." And as
they were going along a frog came out in front of them and
became a man and also asked where they were going.
" We are going to travel," said they, and the frog man went
along too. Then as they were going along the doe turned
into a very nice girl on the road, and was washing her hair
in the river, and she called out to them " Where are you
going ? " and they said " We are going to travel," so the
girl said " I will travel too " ; so they called to her to come
along with them, and the girl joined them.

And when they reached a country the hunter man and
the girl married, and the hunter man went to a Sahib, and
the Sahib said to him, " If you don't make a water-field

and make rice grow in it in one day, then I will kill you with only an hour's grace," and when the Sahib said this the man became very sad and he went and told his wife, and his wife said, " All right, I will do it. Please cut off my head with your dao." But the man refused. But at last she prayed him so often that he cut off her head, and when he had done it he was very sorry and wept much. But his wife made the field and grew the rice and went back to their lodging and cooked their food and waited for her husband, but he did not come. So she sent the beggar man and the man who had been a frog to call him, but he did not come. And after that they went and hauled him to his wife's house, and when he got there and went in his wife said, " Why did not you come ? " And the man said, " I killed you just now, and you are here again ! " And she gave the man his food, and the beggar and the frog man. And when they had eaten she said, " Well, now let us go to our own country. Once upon a time you saved my life by not shooting me and I have saved yours from death now," and having spoken thus she became a doe again and went away into the jungle. And the man who had been a frog became a frog again and went into water, and the beggar turned back into a snake and crept into the bushes, and the man went alone to his own home.

Note.—*Folklore* refers to J. A. Macculloch, " The Childhood of Fiction," pp. 225 *sqq.*, for numerous variants of the friendly animals which assist the hero.

The Rat Princess and the Greedy Man[1]

Once upon a time a man was going to his fields and on the way he caught a rat. When he went home he took the rat with him and put it in a box. A few days later he opened the box to look at it, and behold, the rat had turned into a very beautiful girl. When he saw the girl he thought about her, " If I could marry her to the greatest man in the world I should become a rich man myself," so he made up his mind that as he had come by a very beautiful girl, he would marry her to the greatest man in the world. Then he went to the king and asked him if he would marry her,

[1] *Cf.* Bompas, "Folk-lore of the Santal Parganas", LI.

saying that the king was the greatest personage that he knew of. But the king replied, " Oh, my friend, I should like to marry your daughter, but if you say that she must marry the greatest that there is, then know that I am far inferior to water, for if I go into the river where the stream is flowing fast, it very easily carries me away. Therefore water is greater than I."

Then the man went to water and spoke to him as he had spoken to the king, but water also answered him, " I am not the greatest ; for when I would be still then comes wind and blows me into motion. Therefore wind is greater than I."

So the man went on to the wind and offered his daughter to him in like manner, and the wind too replied, saying, " I am not the greatest. The mountain is stronger than I and greater. All other things can I blow upon and move, but I cannot stir the mountain."

So again the man went to mountain, but the mountain answered him, " Yea, I am greater and stronger than some, but even a rat can pierce my side whenever he please. Thus for his work's sake the rat is greater than I."

Then as the man had nowhere else to go and knew of no other great one he returned home, and behold his daughter was turned into a rat even as she had been.

MATSŪO

Matsuo used to rob the children of their food every day, so at last the children told their parents. Then the parents took counsel to kill Matsuo, and they said, " What shall we do with him ? " Matsuo said to them, " Shut me in a box and push me into the river, that will kill me." And they said " We will do so." But when he was in the box in the river he'saw two girls fishing and said, " If you let me out I will fill your baskets full of fish." Then the girls let him out, and as they were going back to the far bank he defæcated into their basket and said " Take." Then the girls, seeing what he had done, told it in the village, saying, " Matsuo deceived us." And Matsuo came back again, robbing the children of their food once more, and the children again told their parents.

Then as the parents were taking counsel Matsuo came to them again and said, " Pile a lot of thatch on the top of me and burn it, that will kill me." And the men did so to him, and the whole village got burnt, but Matsuo escaped, and lived to plague his fellow villagers in many other ways.[1]

[1] The two stories that follow are also stories of Matsuo.

THE INGENIOUS ORPHAN

Once upon a time there was an orphan boy, and he was very poor. And he went to the king's[2] village and heard that the king's daughter was of an age to be married. So he went to the king's house and he said to the king, " How dark your house is," and the king said, " What is yours like ? " And he answered, " My house is transparent. I can see the sky from anywhere in my house." And when the king was eating, he said, " Have you only that one dish ? " " Yes, I have only one dish," said the king, " what of yours ? " " When I have eaten, I throw away the old dish and eat from a new one every time," said the orphan. And then, " Have you only these cows ? " " How many cows have you got, then ? " asked the king. " My house is so full of cattle," he answered, " that some must stay outside." And the orphan saw the king's grandmother riding on a horse.[3] " Do you let your grandmother get so cold ? "said he. "What do you do with your grandmother ? " said the king. " My grandmother," he answered, " is always warm, keeping by the fire."

After hearing all this the king gave his daughter to the orphan in marriage, and he took her to his home. But when the king's daughter reached her husband's house she marvelled, and she laughed at her husband's house and said, " This isn't transparent ; we can't see the sky from here."

[2] King—Angami *kedi*, a word used for foreign potentates, such as the Maharaja of Manipur or, indeed, the Emperor of India. (*See* Appendix XIII, p.

[3] Query, an exotic touch ? The horse is an animal unknown to the Naga, and his word for it, *kir* or *kwirr*, is almost certainly a corruption of the Assamese " ghora." Though it is also said to mean " hornless."

" Oh yes, we can," said he. " Look there " (pointing to the leaks in the roof). Then she said to him, " What are your plates like ? Please tell me," and he said, " I have no proper dishes, I make one of leaves every time I eat." " And how many cattle have you ? " said she. " Only one," says he, " but it is lying half inside the house and half out." " And your grandmother ? " " My grandmother is underneath the fireplace," [1] he replied.

Then his wife wrote to her father not to come and visit them for seven years, for she was ashamed.

Then she sent her husband to her father to borrow money, and he got the money and travelled to another country and bought rags and rubbish as manure to trade, and he collected it in his house. Then his wife said, " What is the use of that ? What did you buy that for ? " And he replied, " This is very good for a certain thing," and he went again and borrowed money from his father-in-law and bought more. This he did three times, but the third time he did not buy rags and rubbish, but gold.[2] And he made round pellets with the earth and rags and rubbish like those which are made for a bullet-bow,[3] and he melted the gold and put in pellets, covering them with gold. Then he sold these gilt pellets to the people from whom he had bought the rubbish.

Now these people, when they found mud pellets inside the gold, went and complained to the king, and the king sent for him. " Did you sell gold with mud pellets inside it ? " said he. " Yes," said the orphan, " I did. Do what you will with me, O king. I borrowed much money from you, and when I came to these people to trade they sold me earth and rags and rubbish. Therefore I too sold them mud

[1] Alluding to the Angami saying " *Ti a pvu, kije a pfü* " (" The sky is my father and the earth my mother "), as a Naga hearth is made of three large stones planted into the earth so as to make a rest for the pot under which fire can be placed.

[2] Another exotic touch. Gold is not known to the Nagas except to those in places which have considerable intercourse with plainsmen, and even then it is not prized by Nagas at all for decorative purposes.

[3] This weapon is made and used like a bow, having two strings, which are joined in two places about one inch apart in the middle, making a socket of an inch square, in which the pellet made of hardened clay is put.

pellets in the gold." Then the king said to the man who had complained, " Did you sell earth and rags and rubbish to this man ? " And he answered, " Yes, we did sell him earth and rags and rubbish." Then the king was unable to find any fault in him and so punished him not at all. And in time the orphan became very rich.[1]

THE MAN WHO TURNED ASHES TO RUPEES

Once upon a time a man went riding along a road and he put a lot of ashes under his saddle, and then he came up with a man and his mother. And the old woman, being very tired, said, " Please lend me your horse to ride on," and her son said too, " Please, if you are not tired, lend us your horse to get home." And the horseman answered, " I am not tired, but when your mother rides on this horse all my rupees will turn to ashes." But the old woman and her son, disbelieving this, said, " Oh, if they do, we will pay back your rupees. How much have you got in the horse ? " And the man replied " I have so many." Then the son said, " All right, if necessary I will sell my rice-fields and my houses and pay you." So the horseman said, " Very well, I will lend you my horse." And when the old woman got on the horse the ashes flew out. So she and her son straightway sold their rice-fields and paid the owner of the horse, and he, returning to his village, told the villagers that he had exchanged the ashes for the rupees. They accordingly all burnt down their houses and gathered the ashes to sell, but no one would buy them. And he used to deceive his fellow villagers in this way at other times.

Now the way the man had got the ashes to put under his saddle was this :—

His elder brother was a king and he himself kept cattle— a large number. One day all his cattle fell over a precipice and were killed. So he went and stripped off all their hides and hung them on the branch of a great tree and made

---

[1] The exploits of this orphan form the subject of a large number of Angami stories, of which the one given above is typical. It seems, however, to have been influenced by contact with other people, as does the story following, which also introduces a horse. Possibly Manipur is responsible for the foreign element, or it may come from a Kachari source.

a fire underneath to dry them. And it was very cold, so some men who were passing by brought a lot of money to count it out by the fire, but the branches of the tree broke, and these men were frightened and ran off without their money, and the man who was drying his hides took the money and told his fellow villagers that he had killed his cattle and sold their skins for this money, so that the credulous villagers killed their cattle too and flayed them and tried to sell them, but nobody would buy. Then they came back and burnt the deceiver's house, and he, gathering the ashes, mounted his horse and deceived the old woman and her son in the manner described.

And after the villagers had been again deceived about the sale of ashes they took the man and tied him up preparatory to throwing him in the river ; but leaving him alone for a while, he started to sing. This attracted another cowherd, who set him free that he might sing the more easily, for he wished to hear the song, but as soon as he was free he tied up the cowherd boy in his place, and the villagers coming back, threw the boy into the river. So cruelly did this man entreat his fellow villagers.[1]

THE MONKEY AND THE JACKAL

One day a monkey and a jackal met in the jungle, and the jackal said to the monkey, " I wish I were a monkey, as you can climb trees and get at any fruit you like." But the monkey retorted, " I wish I were a jackal, as jackals can go to men's houses and get rice and meat and fowls and anything they want." Then the monkey said, " I will bring the best food I can get, and you bring the best food you can get, and we will taste and see whose is the better." " All right," said the jackal, and went off to get food, and the monkey did the same. When they returned the monkey said, " Please give me your food first." So the jackal put

---

[1] *Apropos* of this story, *Folklore* points out that " the story of the deceiver who is ultimately caught, but escapes by cunning and puts his enemies to confusion, is found in many savage tribes," and gives some references to similar stories. One of which is recorded by Bompas from the Santal Parganas (op. cit., LXII, p. 189).

References to horses or gold or kings probably suggest that these stories may have been borrowed from Manipur or the Kacharis.

it in the monkey's hand and the monkey ran up to the top of a tree and ate it all, and would not give the jackal any fruit. And the jackal was very angry and went away, saying, " All right, I will punish you for that." So he went and hung about a thicket of wild " taro," and the taros looked tender and very large, and when the monkey came by he called out to the jackal, " What are you doing there ? " So the jackal answered, " Oh, I am only eating the Sahib's sugar-cane, as it is very sweet." Then the monkey said, " Please give me some " ; but the jackal answered, " The Sahib will be angry." " Oh no, he won't," said the monkey. " All right then, come and take it yourself," said the jackal. " Go and cut one, peel the skin, and eat it." So the monkey cut a wild taro and peeled and began to eat it, and his throat itched and his mouth swelled up so that he could not even talk. Then the monkey went off to a bees' nest and he said to the jackal, " Don't bite that," and the jackal wanted to bite it, but at first the monkey would not let him. Then he said the jackal might as soon as he (the monkey) had gone behind a hill. So when the monkey was out of sight the jackal bit and the bees poured out and he got badly stung. Then the jackal went off to a pool that was overgrown with tank-grass so that the water could not be seen, and he sat down and waited. Then the monkey came along. " What are you doing ? " said the monkey. " I am watching the Sahib's clothes," said the jackal. " I am coming to join you," said the monkey from the tree. " You mustn't," said the jackal. " I shall jump down," said the monkey. " All right then, jump down if you must," said the jackal, so the monkey jumped down into the water and was drowned.[1]

[1] There are no jackals in the Naga Hills except at the edge of the plains and round the civil station of Kohima. This story reads like a garbled version of the Kachari story of the Monkey and the Hare, in which, however, the hare scores all through. There are no hares in the Naga Hills. On the other hand, the story is known also to the Aos and to the Lhotas, the Aos telling it of a jackal and a bear. It does not seem to be known to the Semas, who are not in touch with the plains. In the Ao version the bees' nest is described as a drum which the bear is invited to beat, in this point following the Kachari version more closely than the Angami story does. The Kachari story is given in Mr. Endle's monograph on the Kacharis.

The Deaf and the Blind

Now there was a deaf man and a blind man. The deaf man had very good sight and the blind man had very good hearing, and the two were friends. One day the deaf man said to his friend, "Let us talk. My friend, I am very much attracted by your condition. I wish I were you." And the blind man answered, "Why do you find my condition so attractive?" "It is true," said the deaf man, "that you do not see anything, but you can hear any noise whatever." And the blind man said to the deaf, "You would very much like to be me, and why is it that I should so much like to be you? The reason is that though it is true you can hear nothing, yet you can see anything in the world." And with that they fell to catching sparrows with lime.

The Ogress (Kacha Naga)

Once upon a time there were two boys whose parents had died. The boys did not know how to till the fields, and lived by snaring birds, and an ogress ate the birds' heads. One morning the boys kept watch to see who ate the birds' heads, and when they saw the ogress they said, "Oh, old woman, why do you eat our birds' heads?" She answered, "I had forgotten you. Come and live with me and I will cherish you dearly." Now the country of cannibals[1] is surrounded by a broad river, though the old ogress had a charm by which she crossed it. When the three of them came to the river she said to it, "Please let me pass now," and the water parted and they walked over.

When they reached the ogress's house, she left the elder boy outside, and, taking the younger one in, put him in the room where she kept her charms. The ogress took great care of the two boys, and the younger slept with her in the house, but the elder slept in a different house.

Now when the little boy had gone to sleep the ogress's husband said, "We will kill and eat," but the ogress felt

[1] The Semas say that there is a village beyond the Yachumi tribe where children are bought and fattened for food.

This story is also told by Khonoma Angamis, who may, however, have taken it from the Kacha Nagas.

the boy and said, " He is not fat enough, we will not kill him yet." And this happened for many nights and the boy overheard it several times. So one morning he said to his brother, " Her husband wants to eat us, he must be a cannibal." But his brother answered, " Oh, they like us very much, they probably won't kill us." Then his brother answered, " You say to her husband that your stomach aches badly, so that you cannot sleep in the other house." So that night the elder boy slept with the ogress. But he did not go to sleep, he only feigned to sleep, and he heard the ogress say, " Oh, the elder boy is not fat, but the little boy is ready to eat," and next morning he said to his brother, " Your words are true, but what are we to do ? As for the river I can get across. But I do not know the way, so what can we do ? " The other said, " I can manage that " ; so they took the cannibal's charm and thus got across the river, and the ogress came after them, but she had no charm and could not cross the river, so the boys escaped.

Note.—Folklore quotes a number of instances of the crossing of water by persons with supernatural powers, and gives a story of the Ntlakapamux, or Thompson River Indians, which has a close resemblance to the above story (Teit, " Traditions of the Thompson River Indians," Boston, 1898, pp. 93, 119), mentioning at the same time that the adventures of children among cannibals is a well-known theme among the tribes of British Columbia, and that some of them resemble the Naga story still more closely then the one mentioned.

HUNCHIBILI

We Lhotas[1] call the wild boar the pig of the gods. Once a wild boar kept eating the fields, and a man at last managed to wound it and tracked it by its blood to a cave and went in. Inside there was a god who asked what the man wanted and whether he had wounded his pig. The man was afraid, and so he said that he had come to ask for the god's daughter in marriage. Then the god showed the man his two daughters, one ugly, but dressed in fine clothes, and the

[1] The version given is a Lhota version, but the story is common to the Angamis, Semas, and Lhotas, and may fairly be given here as an Angami story.

other pretty, but dirty and naked ; but the man chose the latter and took her away in a basket.

When the man got to the village, he left the basket by the water-hole and went into the village to call his kinsmen. Meanwhile a woman named Hunchibili came up and looked into the basket. Then she took the girl and threw her into the stream and got into the basket herself, pulling the lid on after her.

The man came back with his relations and they opened the basket and everyone was disgusted with Hunchibili's ugliness and laughed at the man for having told them that he had brought back a beautiful wife. The man himself could not understand what had happened, but believing Hunchibili to be the girl whom he had brought back from the cave, he married her.

Now the real wife, who had been thrown into the water, turned into a bamboo plant, out of which a young shoot sprang up ; and the husband saw the shoot and cut it and took it to his house and had it cooked. But when it was boiling on the fire it kept quite quiet until the man came in, and as soon as he came in it kept crying out from the pot, " Hunchibili ! la, la, la, la ! Hunchibili ! la, la, la, la ! " and the man became afraid and threw it away. Then when he had thrown it away, it turned into an orange tree and the man cherished it. Then a single orange ripened on the tree, and when Hunchibili came out on to the platform at the back of the house this orange swung as far away as it could, but when the husband came it bent down towards him quite close. At last he picked it and put it into a basket. And then he forgot all about it.[1]

After this, when the man went with Hunchibili to the fields, they used to find on their return that the husband's bed was swept and garnished, but that Hunchibili's bed was

---

[1] In a Sema version of the story the orange is picked by an old woman, and the girl when she comes from the orange keeps tidying up the old woman's house until she is caught by her, after which she recognises her husband by spinning a top which only he can pick up.

I have also found this incident of a girl coming out of an orange and tidying up the house daily when its owner is away in a story current among the Khasis.

covered with dirt and filth and dung. This happened every day. At last, being unable to find out who did this, as all his neighbours denied having done it, the husband lay in wait in the porch of his house, and when Hunchibili had gone to cut wood, he saw the god's daughter come out of the basket and sweep and clean his bed and throw dirt on Hunchibili's bed. Then he ran in and seized her and she told him the whole story. So the man took a dao and sharpened it, and when Hunchibili came carrying wood she said, "Father, come and help me off with my load." So the man came and he cut off her head with one stroke of his dao, and the "kachu" plants, which Hunchibili was carrying with the firewood, got soaked in her blood, and from that time forward red kachus have made men smart.[1]

ANGAMI SONGS

The following songs are taken from Khonoma village, where songs are divided into ten or more classes. The ones given are recorded as nearly as possible in the dialect in which they are sung, and which is apt to vary from the ordinary spoken dialect in being archaic.

The following classes of songs are recognised, the classification of a song depending on the nature of the tune, the number of the singers, or the circumstances under which the song is sung.

1. *Tsali.* Sung particularly at gennas (such as the Thekrangi Genna).

2. *Chakrü.* Sung in the village or in the fields.

[1] The Semas add a sequel to this in which from the body of Hunchibili also springs up a tree, which the hero cuts down and makes into a ladder for his granary. When his wife is with child he insists on going out on a head-hunting expedition in spite of the girl's prayers, and orders her on no account to go to the granary before his return. As he is coming back victorious his parents insist on the wife's going to get grain for him, and the Hunchibili ladder shakes her off, so that she falls and is killed. The husband goes to the cave to seek for her, but the god puts him off with a girl made of beeswax, who melts away one day in the sun, after which the husband again goes back to the cave, but though the wife wishes to go back with him, the spirit refuses to let her go with a man who has twice let her get killed.

3. *Lhipecha.*   Sung when "dancing" in the *Tehuba* or similar place at gennas.

4. *Pithucha.*   Sung when pounding dhan.

5. *Likwino.*   Sung rather fast (comparatively, that is) and pitched fairly high.

6. *Lhipisu.*   Sung by two men. The words are those of *Chakrü* or similar to them, but the tunes different.

7. *Wüpese.*   Sung by boys sleeping in the morung when they are on the machan.

8. *Sheli.*   Sung in the jungle only. It is *kenna* to sing *Sheli* in the village.

9. *Keli.*   Sung by quartettes of two men and two women taking alternate versicles.

10. *Lideh.*   Sung very slowly and pitched very low.

In the songs given here, the indication of the speaker before a line or verse does not mean that there is necessarily any change in the singer, but is given to show the meaning of the song. The English renderings are very free, as it is almost impossible to make a literal translation intelligible, the construction tending to go on the lines of

> Little boy, pair of skates,
> Rotten ice, Heaven's gates,

while, on the other hand, the repetitions and vocal interpolations required by the singing have been omitted in recording and translating alike.

Tsali	*Free rendering*
"*Adzü Gwe ü*"	
Man. Adzü gwe ü ukeri tagwe.	M. I will marry my love.
Woman. Keri nyeri terhöpfü medoh.	W. Marriage is by the will of the spirits.
Man. Toh loi mü yu kemvü kechü.	M. Of that comes happiness.
Woman. Mia ketha u she kenyü mewa	W. You are one who runs after other girls.
Man. Mhiare tomu a she shiale.	M. If you go away I am sad.
Shelihuwü mewa upokrü	No one else has bought your life, Shelihuwü,
Piezhü mo mu mia ri pi sheni.	And since not, why do you fear other men ?

This song is sung by young men to the girls they wish to marry. The latter, if willing, sometimes take up the woman's responses. The singing of this song is the form taken by a proposal of marriage. Shelihuwü is a girl's name.

Tsali

" Dozhü "

A girl speaks.	*Girl.*
Thiwürüri Dozhü atikru.	When it rains, Dozhü is my rain-shield.
Chipfü ledi Krutzeze renu.	I will take it and go to Krutze's Pond.
No reliche, Dozhü meniu.	Go slowly, Dozhü, dearest.
Dozhü speaks.	*Dozhü.*
Che lavorri, aketawü.	Now we have reached home, darling.
Dozhü's Wife speaks.	*Dozhü's Wife.*
Avokino ri rhotero	If we two are divorced,
Avo peino sekose ketse	If we divide our children between us—
Ngu ke mema mhochemachawü	But we should not do what our enemies would like !
Memi rhise rosiwü rese	(? No more) plucking flowers and fruit,
Hanaso hanaiyano.	My younger brother's share and my share.
No peyu, a bikeye.	You have reached your prime, I am past my youth.
Thebi kesa serhe toghowü.	You can associate with the young.
Akeshowü thenupvü süche.	It was my misfortune to be a woman.

This song is known as " Dozhü." Dozhü, a married man, has a flirtation with a girl. He returns home and threatens to divorce his wife, who argues with him. Krutze's Pond is said to be the name of a pool on Kohima land, Khonoma having learnt the song from Kohima.

Lhipecha

" Kidzü Tsohpru "

Men.	*Men.*
Kidzü tsohpru tsia wü lhunu zhü.	Seeds are in the earth and keep falling thereto :
Zuwa derri lhule lo voh ü.	They take them away, but still they spring up.
U tema sa lhule mo a ru.	If man die he riseth not again.
Women.	*Women.*
Thenuma wü ba cha soïchie.	Girls delay not too long (to marry) !
Haï tha pfü haï tsü rei gü,	When your hair grows long you will grow old ;
Tieh tei mu u rrli keseh.	When that cometh to pass life is at an end.

Men.
  Khrü wü jü rei la le lovoh ü.
  A ni rrwü jüroh la mo le.

Men.
  The moon waneth and waxeth again,
  When I have lost my beloved there
    is no more meeting.

This song is sung at the Thekrangi Genna in Khonoma, and also when sowing jhum fields.

Lhipecha

" *Nichu Nikri* "

Nichu nikri va kemela nu.	From youth on let there be no parting.
Tsuranumo chaza prirano	I will wait by the path to watch ;
Lhumetso vapi tero gü.	I gaze at that fairest one from afar.
Mathakeji zepfü aserhe	When her hair is long and bound up, let her remain my friend and go to the fields with me.
Tozholemu ti keso zizhe	Then will I wait for her at dawn.
Zeppepile zemegu peki	I will take her beyond the others.
Alheno tsu Sorozhu chakro	I will return alone by way of Sŏrŏzhū.
Kemozhu lechu vo nitso.	Then am I lonely by myself. Send her word of it.
Tigi khrü pre, terho-naki krü	In the sky the moon is rising, the sun-god has set.
Kevilhe nu ovate nihoh	The moonlight is shining down on me,
Urrahuri zu kevi cha	On our favourite path through the village ;
Lhato memo seya huteru.	After death we can tread it no longer.
Ketzorü no tsie keseranu	By the stone of Ketsorr
Premezüzu bidoh keyukri	Let us pluck off heads of grass and caress one another.
Ketianuwü u kethapü che.	Thus shall I possess her.
Uhi wadi kehreledi nu	We will pour our cups into one gourd,
Sevü u ngu kemü meya-modzü	We will go ahead of the spiteful,
Thelojiche zekevakiwe.	We will not hide our love.
Serhemoü mewe ogipu.	If we do not go to the fields together, men will remark on it.
Kemokiri votso tenihoh.	Whether we do or we do not, they will accuse us.
Pesekriewü a-ge jahelo.	Don't be angry with me, Pesekriewü !

This is sung in the procession round the *Tehuba* at the Thekrangi Genna. Sŏrŏzhū is the name of a distant grazing ground. The stone of Ketsorr is a memorial stone put up to the memory of one Ketsorr. Pesekriewü is a girl's name meaning " She-who-will-be-lamented-when-she-is-dead."

Likwino

" Hoiyi Olle "

Sodzü huri uthu ho kerhe	Though the villages are separated the herds graze together.
Chaziu gi pre che kedi gi nu	Upon the ridge there is a great stone to sit on.
Nirivole heri votate.	Do you go there ! I will go too.
Nishi seko tudzü luranu	Your three suitors are at the well ;
Ketsie sese pitsa se kedoh.	They are picking up stones and dancing.
Thiahu derri setsoh pfüinoh	Of all women you are the most beautiful ;
Vimejile sajie da kerri.	Your skin is fair and there are brass earrings in your ears.
Nichuma krö kiche vo kehu.	The little boys are gathered in the morung.
Meni matse siwü ni mele	But you have your true-love's name ever on your lips,
Bale hu mu chare de nu	And I am ashamed to remain in your presence.
Lozorewü levi metseu	All men love you, Lozorewü,
Mezhe jüra memi mo chade.	Every part of your person is beautiful.

This is a song put in the mouth of an unsuccessful suitor of a girl called Lozorewü. It is to be noticed that brass earrings are not worn by women in Khonoma nowadays, though they are worn by Chakrima girls and in some of the Dzünokehena villages. The writer heard this song sung by a quartette of two men and two girls of the Semoma clan of Khonoma. The title " Hoiyi Olle " refers to the tune of the song, which entails the singing of these two meaningless words in a repetitive refrain between the lines of the words.

Sheli

Ketsa nu lerr-ro udi krehewü	When we go into the jungle hide no word.
Repu hudi kezoro viho.	To speak all that is in the heart and be friends, is well.

Sheli

Khonhye wü ri küzü tsanu tsu	We have never been into the forest together.
Mheye lipi a niuko shümolie	I have never plucked wild herbs to fill my love's basket.
A renumoho.	For this I am sad.

SEKRENGI GENNA BAMBOO WITH SMALL BIRDS ETC., TIED TO IT

[See p. 205

PHOTOGRAPH SHOWING METHOD OF CARRYING IN STONES FOR MEMORIALS BY LHOTAS.
THE STONE IS BUILT INTO A HUGE FRAME OF SCAFFOLDING, AS IT WERE, WHICH IS
CARRIED BY MEN FIVE OR SIX ABREAST AND TWELVE TO TWENTY DEEP

[See p. 232

PHOTSIMI (SOUTHERN SANGTAM) WAR TROPHY
OUTSIDE MORUNG: AN ENEMY'S HAND PINNED
TO A POLE

Sheli.

Man.
Thenumewü thepeso hilo.
Thapfüliro larr ukezomoho.

Man.
Do not tease a girl.
When her hair is grown she will no
longer be my friend.

Woman.
Hi tse u thapfü larr ukezomo ro

No wü leshü pi che.

Woman.
Whether I don't come back and be
your friend after my hair is grown,
You wait and see.

It is *kenna* to sing *Sheli* except in the jungle. In the
last song the man means that the girl will forget about him
when she is married. She replies that she will leave her
husband to come back to him.

PART VI

THE ANGAMI LANGUAGE

PART VI

THE ANGAMI LANGUAGE

THERE is a Naga story, current in different versions among the different tribes, to the effect that in the beginning the Deity gave the knowledge of reading and writing both to the Nagas in the hills and the plainsmen of Assam, but whereas the latter were given stone or paper on which to record their writings, the Nagas were given a book of skins which came by an early end owing to its edible qualities.[1] Hence the Nagas have no written language. As one might expect, however, of men without the art of writing, the language of signs has reached a high state of development —a development no doubt fostered and maintained by the recurrent necessity of communication between members of neighbouring villages speaking dialects or languages totally incomprehensible to one another. To judge how highly developed is this power of communicating by signs, etc., it is necessary only to experience a Naga interpreter's translation of a story or a request told to him in sign language by a dumb man. Not that there is any stereo-typed method of signs—there is no more an universal sign language than an universal Naga language, and the signs used depend on the genius and personality of the speaker, but the natural aptitude for their use is such that from one Naga to another their meaning is rarely obscure. Indeed the writer has known a dumb man make a long and detailed

[1] A similar story is reported by Sir G. Duff Sutherland Dunbar as current among the Padam Abors.

complaint of an assault in which nothing was missing except proper names, and even these were eventually identified by means of the dumb man's description of his assailants' dress and personal appearance.

Besides being used for communication, signs are used with considerable effect to emphasise the spoken word in every sort of circumstance. Of this use no better instance can be given than by quoting Captain Butler [1] :—

"They (the Angamis) have a singularly expressive manner of emphasising messages. For instance, I remember a challenge being conveyed by means of a piece of charred wood, a chilli, and a bullet, tied together.[2] This declaration of war was handed on from village to village until it reached the village for which it was intended, where it was no sooner read, than it was at once dispatched to me by a special messenger, who in turn brought with him a spear, a cloth, a fowl, and some eggs, the latter articles signifying their subordination and friendship to me at whose hands they now begged for protection. It is perhaps scarcely necessary for me to explain that the piece of burnt wood signified the nature of the punishment threatened [3] (*i.e.*, the village consigned to flames), the bullet descriptive of the kind of weapon with which the foe was coming armed, and the chilli the smarting, stinging, and generally painful nature of the punishment about to be inflicted. And only the other day a piece of wood, with a twisted bark collar at one end and a rope at

---

[1] "Rough Notes on the Angami Nagas," *Journ. Asiat. Soc.*, No. IV, 1875, p. 317.

[2] By the Semas a challenge to war is sent in the form of a broken panji. I myself had a challenge to personal combat sent me accompanied by a splinter of wood thrust into a chilli, signifying that if I did not accept I was fit only to be impaled like a dog or chicken killed for some genna. The message purported to come from the Yachumi village of Saporr, but probably was sent by its neighbour Sotogorr, of the same tribe, in the hopes of getting Saporr into trouble. During the Kuki rising of 1917–18 the hills were full of this sort of symbolic message.

[3] In the case of a Kuki message sent to Khonoma in 1917 the burnt wood was said to signify the simultaneity with which the Kukis and Nagas should rise against the Government.

the other, used for tying up dogs with on the line of
march, was brought to me with another prayer for protection.[1] The explanation in this case is, of course,
obvious, namely, that a dog's treatment was in store for
the unfortunate recipients of this truculent message.
Two sticks cross-wise, or a fresh-cut bough, or a handful
of grass across a path, declare it to be closed. But of
such signs and emblems the number is legion, and I
therefore need only remark that it is curious to observe
how the ' green bough ' is here too, as almost everywhere,
an emblem of peace."[2]

The crossed sticks or fresh-cut bough mentioned by
Captain Butler are familiar to everyone who has spent any
time in the Naga Hills. The writer once tested their
efficacy by putting a couple of branches across an obvious
and well-worn short cut to the village to which he was
marching when several of his Naga servants had fallen
behind. These men carefully avoided proceeding along
the usual path and took the alternative route three times
its length. This device of sticks and boughs is noticed by
Colonel Woodthorpe[3] as being also used to turn aside the
small-pox demon in his approach to a village.[4]

With regard to the spoken language of the Angamis
something has already been said in the earlier pages [5] of
this monograph, and for a proper account of the language
the reader is referred to the Angami Grammar by McCabe

[1] I had just such an one brought to me by Bakema (Yangkhunou),
who had it from the rebel Kukis in 1918.

[2] It is also an emblem of *kenna*. Green boughs are put up on houses,
the occupants of which are *kenna*, while a man who is *kenna* (among the
Aos) wears a bit of green stuff in his ear.

[3] *Journ. Anthrop. Instit.*, Vol. XI (1881), p. 69.

[4] Smoke signals are used by Semas, but are very simple, consisting
merely in making a smoky fire so that the smoke may be seen at a distance
and convey information previously agreed upon. The only case in which
I have actually seen this method used was when five or six villages agreed
to fish the Tizu on a given day together. The further villages sent up
smoke signals when they started for the river, so that the others should
know when they ought to set out.

[5] Part I.

and Vol. III, part ii, of Sir George Grierson's "Linguistic Survey of India." Sir G. Grierson has classed the languages of the Angamis proper, the Chakrimas, and the Kezamas in the sub-group "Western Naga," and that of the Memi in the sub-group "Naga-Kuki," of the Naga Group. As has been already noticed, the linguistic grouping of the Naga tribes does not seem to be absolutely conterminous with what may be styled their racial grouping, as the Memi are in every respect but that of language very intimately allied to the other Angami tribes.

As regards the language of the Angamis proper, Sir G. Grierson distinguishes several dialects, but it should be made quite clear that these are not really more than local divergences of the Angami language which are found in every village, and the dialect of Jotsoma, for instance, differs every whit as much from the dialect of Kohima as does, say, the "*Dzuna*" dialect mentioned in the "Linguistic Survey." McCabe's Grammar is based on a sort of amalgamation of the dialects of the Khonoma group of which Jotsoma, Khonoma, and Mozema are the principal villages, and the dialects of these villages are, generally speaking, simpler in vowel sounds than other Angami dialects. It is very much to be regretted that, since the publication of McCabe's Grammar, the Kohima dialect, with its impossible diphthongs and double vowel sounds, has been adopted as the standard for the Angami country and used in schools in transcribing Angami in Roman letters.

McCabe's Grammar contains a valuable introduction in which he shows how the vast diversification of Naga languages and dialects has in part arisen. His vocabulary, however, contains a number of words given to render abstract nouns in English. These must be accepted with caution, for though Angami is possibly richer in abstract ideas than Sema and other Naga languages, abstract notions are, on the whole, utterly foreign to the Naga mind, and many of the Angami words given as abstract nouns in McCabe's vocabulary are in reality adjectives or parts of verbs. Some adjectives, too, are rendered by verbs in Angami.

"*Chileto*," " will do," to give one instance, is used to render " able."

One point in the Angami vocabulary is worthy of notice. Whereas other Nagas readily borrow new words from Assamese or Hindustani and assimilate them into their own tongue (this is particularly noticeable in Sema), the Angami invents a word of purely Angami form. Thus an Angami speaks of a steamboat as *mi-ru*, literally " fire-boat," while the Sema, who on the Angami principle could perfectly well coin the word *ami-shuka*, would never dream of using anything but *jahaz*, even when speaking in his own tongue to other Semas. Similarly, while the Angami always speaks of a gun as *Misi* (= " fire-stick "), the ordinary word used by the Sema is *alika*, which really means the cross-bow used by his Chang and Sangtam neighbours, or *masheho*, which seems to be borrowed from the Angami word.[1]

The tonal nature of the Angami language is noticed by McCabe (pp. 4 and 5), and a short list of instances is given in which the meaning of the Angami word varies according to the pitch of the voice. This list might be vastly amplified, and other Naga languages resemble Angami in this respect. The tables of comparison between Angami and Ao, Angami and Chinese, and Angami and Nepali are taken from McCabe, and a further table is added by the writer, of Angami, Sema, Chang, and Burmese, for the Burmese words in which he is indebted to Captain Hensley, sometime of the Naga Hills Military Police. The subsequent remarks on the Angami language are taken from the "Linguistic Survey," where, by the way, Sir G. Grierson gives a complete bibliography of authorities. The story illustrative of the Angami language and the tables showing variations in dialects come from the same source. For the intimate relation between Angami and the other Naga languages, as well as Manipuri, Grierson should be consulted.

---

[1] Some Angamis who went with the Naga Labour Corps to France saw aeroplanes for the first time, but were at no loss at all for a word, dubbing them *kepronya* (= " flying machines ") without hesitation.

COMPARATIVE TABLES OF ANGAMI AND OTHER
LANGUAGES[1]

English.	Angāmi Nāgā.	Nowgong Nāgā.[2]
Ant	Mhāche	Machā
Blood	Tezā	Azü
Egg	Dzü	Tsü
Fire	Mī	Mī
Horse	Kwirr	Korr
House	Ki	Ki
Salt	Metsā	Matsü
Water	Dzü	Tsü
Thou	No	Nā
He	Po	Pā
Two	Kennā	Annā
Five	Pangu	Pangu
Nine	Tekwü	Taku
Ten	Kerr	Tarr
Twenty	Mekwü	Matsü
To-day	Thā	Tā
Eat	Chi	Chijong
Laugh	Nü	Mannü
Go	Tsu	Tsu

The Nowgong Nāgā has been taken from Hodgson's "Note on the Aborigines of the Eastern Frontier," published in *Asiatic Society's Journal*, 1849.

The following table compares a few Angami Naga and Chinese words :—

English.	Angāmi Nāgā.	Chinese.	Types.
Three	Sê	San	Nankin
Thou	No	No	Mānyak
This	Chi	Cheko	Nankin
Which	So *or* sopo	So	,,
Here	Chiki	Cheli	,,
Now	Ché	Cheshi	,,
To	Ki	Kih	,,
Day	Kinhi	Kinjih	,,
		(to-day)	
Yes	Si (know)	Shi	,,
Ear	Nie	Nitu	Shanghai
Cultivation	Ti	Ti (soil)	,,
Horn	Kā	Koh	,,
House	Ki	Kih	Thochu
Iron	Tejje	T'ich	Nankin
Salt	Metsā	Tsā	Tākpa
Sky	Ti	T'ien	Nankin
Tree	Si	Shi	Gyārung
Water	Dzü	Shui	Pekin
Cold	Si	Sidi	Gyāmi
Long	Chā	Ch'ang	Nankin
Eat	Chi	Ch'ih	Pekin
Kill	Sā (dead)	Sah	Shanghai

[1] From McCabe.

[2] The "Nowgong Nāgā" given here is Ao (Chongli division) as spoken in the village of Merangkong, on the Langbangkang range, called "Naogaon" by the Assamese. The similarity between Angami and Chongli Ao is considerably less than one might infer from this list.

Compare also :—

English.	Angāmi Nāgā.	Eastern Nepāl.	Types.
Mine	Ā	Ā	Chourāsya
Little	Kache	Kachi	Bāhingya
Not	Mo	Mo	Khāling
Father	Āpo	Āpo	Bāhingya
Fire	Mī	Mī	,,
Foot	Phi	Philu	Rodong
Hair	Tā	Tā	Serpā
Man	Mā	Mi	,,
Sun	Nā ki	Nā	Sunwār
Bitter	Kekwö	Khakwa	Rungchenbung
Laugh	Nü	Nhyü	Newār
Sit down	Bā	Bāk	Sunwār
Take	Lê	Le	Limbu
Tell	Pu	Puu	Nachhereng
Bone	Ru	(Tibetan) ruko	
Elephant	Tso	(Japanese) zo	
Eye	Mhi	(Japanese) me	

The Chinese, Nepalese, Tibetan, and Japanese words are mentioned by McCabe as having been taken from Hunter's "Comparative Dictionary of the Non-Aryan Languages of India."

The following is a comparative table of Angami Naga, Sema Naga, Chang Naga, and Burmese :—

English.	Angāmi Nāgā.	Sema Nāgā.	Chang Naga.	Burmese.
egg	(thevü-)dzü[1]	(awu-)khu	(au-)tei	u
salt	metsa	amti	chăm	hsa
fire	mi	ami	wàn	mi
water	dzü	azü	tei	ye
earth	kijö, kidzü	ayeghi	gau	mye
path	cha	ala	lăm	lan, lam
thou	no	nă, nŏ	nô	min
two	kenna	kini	nyi	hna
three	se	küthu	săm	yet
five	pengu	pongu	ngau	nga
twenty	mekwü	muku	sau-chie (= score, one)	huase
eat	tsü, tsi	chu	shau	sah
go	vo	gwo, gu	hau	thwa
go to the fields	chu	hu	ko	
this	hau, te	hi, ti	hau	thi
to-day	kinhi (day = zha)	ishi tsü-kinyheh = sun)	thāt (chanyu = sun)	kane
field	le	alu	siek	le(t)
dead	satate[2]	keti	haibu	thede
not	mo	moi	a . . . ki (=not . . is)	ma . . . bu
father	'po (apo=my father)	apo (i po = my father)	apo	aba, abe
sun	neki	tsü-kinyheh	chanyu	ne
speak	pu	pi	lau	piaw
bone	ru	ashogho[3]	luo	ayu

[1] dzü = water, the Angāmi word for egg = "fowl water." So in other Naga languages except Sema. Thus the Chang au-tei = "bird-water."
[2] The root is sata or sa. Te is merely the suffix of the past tense In the same word keti, the root is ti, and ke the adjectival prefix.
[3] R in Angami usually becomes gh in Sema.

The construction used in Burmese for expressing the date is also similar to the Angami construction, *e.g.*, " The third " (*date*) = *zha-se*-NHE (*zha* = day and *se* = three) in Angami : in Burmese it is *thone-yet*-NE (*thone* = day, *yet* = three).

Another similarity of construction is visible in the method of reporting speech, *e.g.*, " They are going " = Angāmi, *uko voya we* ; Burmese, *thudan thwade* ; Chang, *hauan hauta*. " It is said (*or* they say) that they are going " = *uko voya we* SHE and *thudan thwade* DE respectively. So in Chang with *tügh* :—*Hauan hauta-tügh*.

The Sema uses the word *pani* (< *pi ani* = is saying) in the same way :—

> *pa wuni* = he will go.

> $pa\ wunipani = \begin{cases} \text{he says} \\ \text{they say} \\ \text{it is said} \end{cases}$ that he will go.

In pronouncing Angami the method followed in McCabe and Grierson is as follows :—*à* = *a* in " pan," *â* or *å* is used to represent the broad *a* in " ball,"[1] *o* = *o* in " hot," *ö* = the German *ö* in schön, *ü* = the German *ü* in " brüder," *ê* represents the sound of *ey* in " they " or *ai* in " aim." Otherwise the vowels are given their continental qualities, long and short being distinguished by the usual signs. *Th* is pronounced as in " pot-house," not as in " think," and the *u*[2] in the word *un* = " thy " is not really pronounced at all, '*n* being a better rendering of the sound. The value of both vowels and consonants varies a good deal from one group of villages to another, and changes such as that from *kw* in Khonoma to *pf* in Kohima are frequent.

[1] As a matter of fact in Khonoma and Jotsoma at any rate the sound represented by *â* in McCabe's Grammar is nearer an English *o* sound than anything, and in the monograph generally, apart from this part dealing with language, I have used *o* or *ô* and not *â* in writing words containing this sound. I have also followed the current Naga Hills usage in writing *ü* for both the sounds here given as German *ö* and German *ü*, which do not perhaps quite represent the value of the sound we usually write as *ü*, which probably falls somewhere between the two.

[2] Sir G. Grierson, " Linguistic Survey of India," vol. III, part 2, p. 206, says that " the *n* . . . is very faintly sounded." *n* here is doubtless a misprint for *u*.

Prefixes and Suffixes.[1]—Angami expresses the various meanings which a root can assume partly by the aid of suffixes and infixes and partly by the aid of prefixes. These will be explained in their proper places, but the following prefixes require to be mentioned here. They have no special meaning of their own, and they are frequently dropped :—

1. The following prefixes are used in forming adjectives, adverbs, and present participles :—

ka or *ke*
me
pe
re. Thus :—

ke-zhā, large.	*ka-ti*, black.
ke-vi, good.	*ke-me-thi*, strong.
ke-re-ku, concave.	*pe-tē*, or *me-tē*, all.
ke-me-ku, ditto.	*ke-ɔor*, coming.
pe-sâ, me-sâ, or *re-sâ*, above.	*ke-chi*, doing.
pe-krâ, or *re-krâ*, below.	*ka-ngu*, seeing.

The adjective usually follows the noun it qualifies. When this is the case, and an indefinite article is also used, the prefix *ke* is not dropped. When, on the other hand, the adjective is a predicate, the prefix is elided. Thus :—

Themmā ke-zhā po.
    Man   big one, *i.e.*, a big man,
but—*Themmā hāu zhā*
    Man   this big, *i.e.*, this man is big.

2. In names of animals and objects the prefixes *the, te,* and *mi* are often dropped when the sentence is definite, and no misapprehension is likely to arise from the elision.

Thus, *te-füh*, a dog, but *ā füh*, my dog.

3. Nouns of agency are formed by suffixing *mā*, man, to the present participle. Thus, *bā*, to sit ; *ke-bā*, sitting ; *ke-bā-mā*, a sitting man, a sitter.

4. Other nouns are formed from verbs by prefixing *the* or *te*. Thus, *bā*, to sit ; *the-bā*, a chair.

5. The prefix *u* often replaces *te* or *the*, or, rather, in most cases both are used indifferently. Thus, *the-vü* or *u-vü*,

---

[1] From this point up to the specimen of Angami Naga, I have reproduced Grierson *literatim.*

fowl ; *the-vo* or *u-vo*, pig ; *si* or *u-si*, wood ; *te-fü* or *u-fü*, dog. *U* is always prefixed to nouns signifying parts of the body when used in an indefinite sense, and when a personal pronoun, or the word *mā*, an individual, is not employed. Thus, *u-phi*, the foot or feet ; *u-bi*, the hand or hands ; *u-tsa*, the head or heads. So :—

> *u-phi pe themmā-no* *chā-toyā-wē.*
> the-feet by men \walking-in-the-habit-are,
> the feet are used in walking.

> *u-tsa gi tepē pfayā-wē.*
> the-head on loads carried-are.

Like the Lhota *ō*, and the Sema, Rengma and Mikir *ā-*, this *u-* is almost certainly derived in such cases as the above from an old possessive pronoun meaning " his," which has in most instances lost its original signification.

Articles.—The numeral *po*, one, is used for an indefinite article. Thus *mā po*, a man.

For definite articles *hā-u*, this ; *lu*, that ; and the relative particle *u*, he who is, are used. Thus *te-khu hā-u* or *te-khu lu*, the tiger.

> *Nichu-mā andu kevor-u.*
> Young-male yesterday come-he-who-is, *i.e.*, the boy who is the one who came yesterday, the boy who came yesterday.

As in the above examples, the article invariably follows the noun which it qualifies. If there is an adjective, it follows the adjective. Thus, *te-füh, ka-ti po*, a black dog.

Nouns.—Nouns descriptive of parts of the body, or expressing relationship, must always be preceded by a possessive pronoun. Thus, *ā-phi*, my feet ; *po-phi*, his feet. *Phi* cannot be used by itself. So, *ā-po*, my father ; *un-po*, thy father. *Po*, father, cannot be used by itself.

Gender.—This is only apparent in the case of animate nouns. It is indicated in the case of nouns of relationship by the use of different words. Thus, *ā po*, my father ; *ā zo*, my mother. In the case of other nouns it is indicated by the following suffixes :—

> Masculine : *pfö, chü, dâ, dzü.*
> Feminine : *krü.*

Some nouns take one suffix and some another. The prefixes *the*, *te*, and *mi* are commonly dropped, as explained above, when these generic suffixes are added. Examples are :

Te-füh, a dog ; *füh-pfö*, a male dog ; *füh-krü*, a bitch.

Tsu, an elephant ; *tsu-chü*, a male elephant ; *tsu-krü*, a cow elephant.

(This last pair of suffixes is used for almost all wild animals.)

Mi-thu, a cow ; *thu-dâ*, a bull ; *thu-krü*, a cow.

(This pair is commonly used for domestic animals.)

The-vü, a fowl ; *vü-dzü*, a cock ; *vü-krü*, a hen.

(This pair is commonly used for birds.)

If a pronoun or adjective follows a feminine noun, it takes the suffix *pfü*, instead of *u*. Thus, *thu-krü lu-pfü*, that cow ; *thu-krü ke-ji ka-ti lu-pfü*, that good black cow.

Number.—Number is only indicated when it is not evident from the context. In such a case, the singular is indicated by suffixing *po*, one, and the plural by suffixing *ko*. This *ko* is the plural of the suffix *u* used as a definite article. It hence invariably has a definite signification. Thus, *mi-thu*, cow or cows generally ; *mi-thu po*, a or one cow ; *mi-thu-u*, the cow ; *mi-thu-ko*, the cows. So :—

Ā   un-ki   nu te-füh po ngu-lē

I   your-house in dog   a   saw, *i.e.*, I saw a dog in your house.

Te-füh-ko tēlē-chē

The-dog-s catch, *i.e.*, catch the dogs.

The particle *ko* follows the noun, and if there are adjectives it follows them. It also follows the generic suffix, if any. Thus :—

Vü-krü ka-chā hā-pfü-ko

Hens white these, *i.e.*, these white hens.

Note the irregular form *nânâ*, children, the plural of *nâ*, a child.

The pronouns form a dual number, which is used to form duals of substantives as follows :—

No   u-sāzāu   u-nā   mhūchē shâbāwē.

You your-brother you-two sick   are,   *i.e.*, you and your brother are sick.

Case.—Cases are formed by suffixes, added to the nominative, which remains unchanged. The accusative and genitive usually take no post-positions. The genitive precedes the noun on which it is dependent. The nominative sometimes takes *no* (corresponding to the Lhota *nā*) when it is the subject of a transitive verb.[1] Mr. Davis has only heard it used with interrogative pronouns. *No* is also occasionally used as a suffix of the genitive, generally with proper names. *Nā* serves the same purpose in Sema. We may also compare the Ao locative suffix *nung.* For the accusative verbs of asking require the suffix *ki.* The usual suffixes are :—

nu, in, to, or from.

lā, for.

pē, by (literally " taking in the hand and carrying," hence only used with inanimate nouns).

ki, to, used with proper names of persons only. Proper names of places take no suffix in the dative.

Examples of the various cases are the following :—

Nominative : *Themmā hā-u vor-wē.*

Man this came, this man came.

Sopo-no hā-u chi-lē-wē?

Who this did ?

Accusative : *Ā themmā hā-u ngu-lē.*

I man this saw, I saw this man.

Po-ki ketsochē.

Him ask.

Po-ki rakā chālēchē.

Him money ask-for, ask him for money.

Instrumental : *Nhā-si pē po vā pevülē-nitā-shē.*

Jungle-fruit by his belly to-fill-wished, he wished to fill his belly with jungle-fruit.

Dative : *Ā tisonhā lē nu tsu-yā-wē.*

I daily fields to go-habitually, I go to the fields every day.

Po Sāhā ki vo-te-wē.

He the-Sāhib to went, he went to the Sāhib.

---

[1] There is a similiar inflection of the agent nominative with *no* in Sema.

but   *Ā Kohirā*[1] *vo-te-wē.*
      I to-Kohima   went,   I went to Kohima.
      Ā   ā-sāzāu   lā   kwe   po   lē-to-wē.
      I   my-brother for   cloth   a   take-will,
      I want a cloth for my brother.

Ablative :   *Ā   thevā   lē   nu   vor-wē.*
      I   at-dusk   the-fields from   came, I re-
      turned at dusk from the fields.

Genitive :   *Themmā   hā-u   zā.*
      Man's   this name, this man's name.
      Lhurukrē-no   mā.
      Lhurukrē's men.
      Luvanu-no   ki.
      Luvano's house.
      No   kiu-no   rā   mā   gā?
      You   what-of village   man are?
      Ā   Kekia-no   renā   mā   po   wē.
      I   Kekia's   village man one am.

Locative :   *Lē   nu   thezu   chāperē-wē.*
      Fields in   rats   many-are, rats abound in
      the fields.

There are many other such post-positions ; *e.g.*, *mho*,
mho-ghī, on ; *ki*, *vākri*, across ; *lā-nu*, according to ; *dā-nu*,
between ; *ki*, by ; *ghī*, above ; *mho-dzū*, before ; *sā*,
behind ; *zē*, with ; *krā*, below ; *matsā-nu*, through ; *sā*,
except.

Adjectives.—When it is necessary clearly to distinguish
the gender of the noun with which it agrees, the addition of
the suffix *pfü* makes an adjective feminine. Thus, *the-nu*
ke-vi-pfü po, a good woman. Otherwise, adjectives undergo
no change. An adjective follows the noun it qualifies,
unless it is so intimately connected with the noun it qualifies
as to form one compound word with it. Thus, *themmā*
ke-vi po, a good man, but *kevi-mā po*, a good man *par excel-*
lence, *i.e.*, a warrior. So *lu-krö*, that month, *i.e.*, last month ;
hāu-krö, this month, *i.e.*, the present month.

---

[1] *Kewhira* would be a better rendering of the Angami word.

The particle of comparison is *ki*. Thus :—

Themmā hā-u lu ki vi-wē.

Man this that than good-is, this man is better than that.

Sibo hā-u petē-ko ki zhā.

Tree this all than large, this tree is the largest of all.

The numerals are given in the list of words. They follow the words they qualify. Thus :—

Te-füh ke-zhā sē.

Dogs large three, three large dogs.

Ordinals are formed by adding *u*, he who is, to the cardinals. Thus, *po*, one ; *po-u*, he who is one, first. We have also *ke-rā-u*, he who is in front, for " first," and *ke-nâ-u*, he who is behind, for " second."

Pronouns.—The following are the *Personal Pronouns*. They have a dual :—

Singular : *Ā*, I   *No*, thou   *Po*, he, she, it.
Ā, my   *Un*, thy   *Po*, his, her, its.

Dual : *A-vo*, thou and I. *U-nā, ne-nā*, you two.
Hā nā, they two, near.
He-nā, he and I. *Lu-nā*, they two, distant.

Plural : *He-ko* (I and you), *Neko*, you.
Hā-ko, u-ko, li-ko, lu-ko, they.
u-ko, we (I and they).
He-ko, he, our. *Ne-ko, nē,* your. *Hā-ko,* etc., their.

The genitive is in most cases the same as the nominative. The *n*[1] in *un*, thy, is very faintly sounded. These genitives always precede the nouns on which they depend. Thus, *ā nupfö*, my husband ; *un ki*, thy house.

The *Demonstrative Pronouns* are :—

Hā-u, feminine *hā-pfü*, this. Plural, *hā-ko*.

Lu, feminine *lu-pfü*, that. Plural, *lu-ko*.

There is no *Relative Pronoun*. The suffix *u*, he who is, feminine *pfü*, she who is, plural *ko*, is used instead. Thus :—

Themmā ke-vor-u.

Man come-he-who-is, the man who is come.

---

[1] This is as it stands in the " Linguistic Survey." This *n* must be a misprint for *u*.

The-nu   lu   ki   nu   ke-bā-pfü.
Woman that house in dwelling-she-who-is, the
woman who lives in that house.

The *Interrogative Pronouns* are :—

So-po, feminine *so-pfü,* who ?

Ki-u, feminine *ki-pfü,* which ? adjective.

Keji-po, kedi-po, so-po, what ?

The *Reflexive Pronoun* is formed by suffixing *thē* or *thâ,*
as *ā-thē vor-wē,* I came myself. *Ā-thē,* I myself. *Ā-thē ā-,*
my own ; thus, *ā-vē,* my property ; *ā-thē ā-vē,* my own
property.

Verbs.—There are five different verbs, with different
radical meanings, which are used to express the verb substantive. The most common is *bā,* be. The others are *to,*
root meaning " exist " ; *zhü,* root meaning " recline " ;
ni, root meaning " possess " ; *tā,* root meaning " stand."
Verbs do not change for gender, number, or person. Tenses
are formed by suffixes. As in other cognate languages,
there is little or no distinction between present and past
time. The main distinction is between time which is
future (indicated by the suffix *to*) and time which is non-
future (no special suffix). Every verbal form which contains
a direct statement usually ends with the syllable *-wē,* closely
corresponding to what is called the categorical *ā* in Mundā
languages. This syllable (which is sometimes dropped
when no ambiguity will ensue) serves to define the verbal
character of the word to which it is suffixed. It hence
converts adjectives and nouns into verbs. Thus, *mā po,*
a man, *mā-po-wē,* (I) am a man (of such and such a village) :
ke-vi, good ; *vi-wē,* is good. It is most often dropped in
the past and in the future. Two other suffixes which
should be noted are *shi* and *lē.* They do not appear to affect
the meaning of the verb in any way. They are, however,
generally (unless they accompany the *to* of the positive
future) used with a past tense, either singly or both together.
Some verbal roots can take either of these suffixes, while
some affect one and some the other. The root meaning of
shi is " to place," and that of *lē* either " to take " or " to go."
Instead of *wē* we often meet the suffix *m',* which is used in

exactly the same way, and is quite as common. Thus, *ā puwē* or *ā pum'*, I speak ; *ā pushiwē* or *ā pushim'*, I spoke ; *po so-du vortowē* or *vortom'*, he will come to-morrow. Subject to these remarks, the tenses of the Angami verb may be said to be formed as follows :—

The suffix of the present, of the present definite, and of the imperfect is merely the categorical *wē*. Thus, *ā pu-wē*, I speak, I am speaking, or I was speaking. So also in the past.

A present definite is also formed by *zhü*, as in *si tetsu-zhü-wē*, the tree is falling.

The suffix of the present habitual is *yā-wē*, as *ā tisonhā pherē-yā-wē*, I am in the habit of walking daily.

The suffixes of the past tenses generally are *wē*, *lē-wē*, *lē*, *shi-wē*, or *shi-lē-wē*, as—

Ā injösā po ngu-wē.
I last-year him saw, I saw him last year.

Ā un-ki ke-pu mhodzü po ngu-lē-wē.
I thee-to speaking before him saw, I had seen him when I spoke to you.

Ā mhā-chi-lē-wē.
I thing-ate, I have eaten.

Ā po-ki pu-shi-wē.
I him-to spoke, I spoke to him.

The suffix of the positive future is *to-wē* or *to*. Thus, *ā vor-to-wē* or *ā vor-to*, I shall come.

The suffix of the negative future is *lelho* or *lelho-wē*, as *ā vor-lelho-wē*, I shall not come.

The suffix of the future of doubt is *nhià* or *nhā*, added to the positive future, as *ā vor-to-nhià*, I may come.

The suffix of the imperative is *chē*, as *pu-chē* or *pu-shi-chē*, speak ; *vü-chē*, strike ; *totā-chē* or *totā-lē-chē*, go away. In the third person of the imperative, the suffix *bo* or *bu* is added to the subject, as *po-bo ki-nu vor-chē*, let him come into the house.

Similarly, *mi-thu-bu tizà nu lē-hē-chē.*
cows-permit garden in enter-not- (imperative suffix), don't let the cows into the garden.

Lhurukrē-bu pu-shi-chē, let Lhurukrē speak.

Ā-bu to-tā-chē, let me go.

This is properly a causative or permissive particle. It can be attached to any noun or pronoun, and when this is done the verb acquires a permissive or causative sense. Compare causal verbs below.

The negative imperative is formed by inserting *hē*, as *pu-hē-chē* or *pu-shi-hē-chē*, do not speak ; *zē-chē* or *zē-lē-chē*, sleep ; *zē-hē-chē* or *zē-lē-hē-chē*, do not sleep. When the suffixes *shi* and *lē* are used with the positive imperative, and when they are not used with the negative imperative, the suffix *chē* can be omitted ; *to-lē-chē, to-shi-lē-chē, to-lē*, or *to-shi-lē*, move on ; *po-ki pu-shi*, tell him ; *po-bu vor-hē*, do not let him come.

The suffix of the conditional is *râ*, as *po vor-râ*, if he should come.

The suffix of the infinitive of purpose is *lö* added to the positive future, as—

Ā   un-ki   pi-to-lö vor-wē.

I your-house to-see came, I came to see your house.

The suffix of the future infinitive is *ye* added to the infinitive of purpose. The whole is then conjugated as an independent verb, as—

Ā   tâ-to-lö-ye-wē.

I about-to-start-was, I was going to start.

The suffix of the adverbial present participle is *ki*, in, the prefix *ke* being also used as explained above. Thus :—

Ā dē ke-pu-ki themmā lu ā vü-wē.

I words speaking-in man that me struck, while I was speaking that man struck me.

The suffix of the past (or conjunctive) participle is *di*, with or without the prefix *ke*, as—

Po dē   pu-di   tâ-te.

He words having-spoken, went-away ; having spoken, he went away. *Ke-zā-wā-di*, having divided.

The idea of passivity is indicated by the suffix *te*, which, if it is not followed by *wē*, is pronounced *ta ;* thus, *po andu ngu-te*, he was seen yesterday. Sometimes *wāte* is used, as *ā vü-wāte*, I was beaten, also *wāho*, as *ā vü-wāho*, I was beaten. This *wā* is merely an intensive infix. See below.

The suffix *te* is also used with intransitive verbs, as in *themmā hāu vor-te-wē*, this man has come. *Ho* often merely emphasises a verb, as in *po vor-mo-ho*, he has not come.

As in other connected languages, Angami uses a large number of infixes which can be added to a verbal root in order to modify its meaning. The following are a few of these infixes. There are many others.

Infix.	Meaning.	Examples.
hu	entirely	*mhā-chi-hu-lelho-di*, things to eat *all* not being able.
lā	again	*ngu-lā-lēwē*, found again is.
mē	always	*to-mē-yā*, living always are.
ni	desire	*pevülē-ni-tā*, to-fill desire was.
pi	much	*chi-pi-tādi*, arisen greatly having.
prē	all	*kezēchi-prē-rā*, together-feasted all having.
pu	all, entirely	*peji-pu-ā*, lost entirely.
se	very	*ni-se-di*, glad very being.
tâ	entirely	*mhā ji-tâ-tā*, things wanting entirely were.
tē	entirely	*chi-tē-lē-di*, devoured entirely having.
wā	gives an intensive force	*tsü-wā-chē*, give out and out.
zo	gives emphasis[1]	*un vē zo-lē*, your goods assuredly-are.

The last mentioned, *zo*, is always used in the formula for oaths : *ā un vē regu mo-zo*, I your things steal not-most-assuredly, I assuredly did not steal your property.

Reciprocity is expressed by prefixing the syllable *ke* to the verbal root. Thus : *mengu*, desire, love ; *ā-vo kemengu-to-wē*, we two will love each other ; *vü*, beat ; *kevü*, mutual beating, to fight ; *ngu*, see ; *kengu*, to see each other, to meet ; *henā chā-nu kengu-wē*, we two met on the road ; *zā*, share ; *kezā*, to divide.

Potentiality is indicated by the suffix *lēto*, as in *ā tâ-lēto-wē*, I can go. The negative of this is indicated by the suffix *kalēji*,[2] as *ā tâ-kalēji-wē*, I cannot go. Here *kalē* means "physical power," and *ji* is the negative verb

---

[1] *Zo* also implies the continuance of an action in the immediate present, *e.g.*, *Po ki nu kerzowe* = "He is coming down from his house" (at this moment). The infix *ya* has a similar sense denoting continuance of action n the present.

[2] Or *kenniadzü*, *e.g.*, *a pule kenniadzü we* = "I cannot say." It is to be noted that with this suffix the infix *le* is always used, whereas when using the other suffix *kaleji* (*kale-dzü*) it is never used. Using the latter "I cannot say" = *a pu kaledzüwe*, never *a puLE kaledzüwe*.

substantive. Potentiality is also expressed by the words *vi*, good, and *shâ*, bad, used with the verbal root with *lē*. Thus, *ā thā Khonorā* [1] *vo-lē-vi mu shâ-gā*, I to-day Khonoma to-go well or bad is ? can I go to Khonomā to-day ? The same construction occurs in Āo with the words *zung*, good, and *māzung*, bad.

The idea of a frequentative verb is indicated by the suffix *tàzo*, as *ā tâ-tàzo-wē*, I go frequently. The same suffix signifies continued action, as in *ā chi-tàzo-wē*, I go on working.

A verb becomes causal by suffixing *bu* or *bo* to the object (compare the third Singular Imperative). Thus *po the-vo kwē-wē*, he tends or tended pigs, but *ā po-bu the-vo kwē-wē*, I caused him to tend pigs.

The negative particle is *mo*. The tense suffix *wē* may be omitted when it is used. It is suffixed to the verb, before *wē*, *lē*, or *te*, when they are employed. Thus, *ā pu-mo*, I did not speak ; *ā po ngu-mo-wē*, I did not see him ; *po betsā-wā-mo-te*, it was not broken. When both *lē* and *wē* are used, *mo* comes between them, as *ā si-lē-mo-wē*, I did not know. When both *te* and *wē* are employed, *mo* precedes both, as *po vor-mo-te-wē*, he did not come. Regarding the negative imperative, see above.

Angami possesses a negative verb substantive, *ji* or *ji-wē*, is not. Thus *rakā jirâ neko mhā-po-ri kri-lelho-nhā*, money not-being you anything buy-will-not-perhaps, if you have no money, you will probably not be able to buy anything.

The interrogative particles are *gā*, *ro* and *mà*. They are always placed at the end of a sentence. *Gā* and *ro* are used with interrogative pronouns, *mà* without. Thus :—

No   kitsā   vo-to-gā (or *vo-to-ro*) ?
You whither   will-go ?   where are you going ?
No   vor-to-mà ?
You will-come ?   are you coming ?

When *gā* and *ro* are used without an interrogative pronoun, they must be preceded by the words *mu-mo*, or not, thus :—

No   lē-nu   tsu-to-mu-mo-gā ?
You field-to   will-go-or-not ?   are you going to the field ?

---

[1] Better *Khwünora*.

Any word can be treated as a verbal root, and conjugated throughout. Thus, from *ke-vi*, good, we have *vi-wē*, it is good. From *ki-u*, which ? *ā ki-to-gā*, what shall I do ?

The word *pe* prefixed to an adjective converts it into an adverb. Thus, *vi*, good ; *pe-vi*, well. Adverbs cannot be treated as verbs. Thus *pevilēchē* is meaningless, and does not mean " do (it) well." In such cases another verbal root must be prefixed, as in *hāu chi-pe-vi-lē-chē*, this make (*chi*) well, do it well.

Order of Words.—The usual order is subject (with its adjuncts), direct object, indirect object, verb. Adverbs usually follow the words they qualify. When they qualify verbs, they usually, but not always, follow the root. Thus *pevi* is " well " and *chi-pevi-lēchē* means " do it well." The adverb *lā*, again, precedes the roots of intransitive verbs, and follows those of transitive ones. Thus, *lā-vor-chē*, come again ; *chi-lā-shichē*, do it again.

The following specimen of the Angami Naga language is also taken from Grierson :—

Jĕsu po ki-mā sā-tā, po nânâ kennā the-nu-mā
Jĕsu his wife died, his children two (were) girl

po the-pfo-mā po. Mā po u-nā-bu dzükhu-nu
a boy a. Man a these-two-let the-well-from

dzü u chi-mo-te. Vor po
water to-draw made-not. (So they) coming their

pu ki pu, " Henā-bu urā-mā dzükhu-nu
father to said, " Us-two-let our villagers the-well-from

dzü u chi-mo-te-lē, henā ki-to-gā ? "
water to-draw make-not, we what-shall-do ? "

Sirâ Jĕsu, " O, mhā-mo-wē. Mā nenā-bu dzükhu-nu
And Jĕsu, " O, it-is-nothing. People you-two well-from

dzü u-mō-tā-râ, ā dzükhu ke-sā po
water drawing-prevent-if, I well new a

kwē-shi-to-wē," i-di, dzükhu ke-sā po kwē-shē. Sesā
make-shall," saying, well new a made. Afterwards

po nânâ dzü u tsumu, derri dzü
his children water to-draw went, but the-water

krä-reniēbā. Po nânâ lā ke-vor-ki
dirty-was. His children back the-coming-at-time

po pu-wē, " kitoi-di nenā dzü ke-krā pfü
he said, "why you water dirty bringing

vorāgā ? " " Hē, ā-po, si-mo-lē.
have-come ? " " O, our-father, (we)-don't-understand.

Henā mhodzü mā-po vo pe-krā-wayā-lē."
Us-two before some-one going dirty-made (it)."

" Tidjü bā-hē ; mā po vo-mo. Ne-tidjü-râ ā
" Lies tell-don't ; man a went-not. You-lie-if I

nenā vü-to-wē." " Henā tidjü si-râ,
you-two shall-beat." "Us-two lying (you)-understand-if,

no kodu-â tsu, dzü u-di, vor henā
you one-morning going, water drawing, coming us-two

râ-chē," i-di, po pu-ki pu-lē. Po pu
rate," saying, their father-to said. Their father

kodu-â tsu dzü-u-shē. Dzü krā-niē-bā-râ,
one-morning going water-got. The-water dirty-being,

" Hē, ā nânâwē ketâ-wē. So mā dzü
" O, my children truth-spoke. What man the-water

perhuā-shi," i-di, po 'zhü po ngu chi-pfü-di,
dirtied-has," saying, his shield his spear taking,

tsu dzükhu lāzü-shē.[1] *Sirâ terhöwümiā tsu*
going the-well watched. And goddesses descending

dzü u-tā. Ketsē ke-zhā po dzü ki
the-water drew. Stone large a the-water near

zhü-shē.[1] *Terhöwümiā po mi pē-di*
was-lying. The-goddesses their head-ropes bringing

ketsē-gi pe-zhü-di, dzü-relutā-shē.[1] *Jĕsu*
the-stone-on (them)-placing, bathed. Jĕsu

---

[1] This is the *shē* of reported speech mentioned above. The relater does not commit himself to vouching for the accuracy of the story.

ngu-lē-di   po-ngu   pē-di mā-po   mi   kekā-lē
seeing-(this) his-spear taking one's head-rope   stole.

Kekā-pē-râ   po-bā   pē   bā-lē.   Sidi
Having-stolen-it his-seat making (it) sat.   Then

mā   kekri-mā
persons the-other

" *se-vór-mo-râ'   u-pípfu-mā'*
" don't-bring-if   our-parents

" *u-râ'tomú   dzü   sé-voké,*"
" us-will-scold water taking-go-let-us,"

i-di,   vo-tā.   Po   mi   ke-ji-pfü.
saying,   went-off.   She (her)-head-rope the-losing-one.

" *Hē   ā-kro-mā,   ā   mi   ji-te-lē,*"
" O   my-comrades,   I   (my)-head-rope have-lost,"

si-shē, derri po   ke-zē-ko   po   kwē-mo-di   vo-tā.
said, but her companions her awaiting-not had-gone.

Po   ke-zē-ko   vo-tā   meta,   Jĕsu   prâr,
Her companions had-gone as-soon-as, Jĕsu coming-forth

po tese-lē-shē. Po po-ki,   un   zā   so-po-ro ?   Un
her seized. He her-to, your name what-is ? Your

zā   pumorâ,   ā   un   mi   lāshi
name   (you)-tell-don't-if, I   your   head-rope   back

un-tsü-lelho-wē,"   *i-di,   lu-pfü,   " ā pu-shi-to-wē,*
you-give-will-not," saying, she,   " I shall-tell (you),

ā   zā   Vihuju-wē." *Sirâ Jĕsu,   "no   ā ki-mā*
my name Vihuju-is." And Jĕsu, "you my wife

chi-to-râ,   ā un   mi   lāshi   un-tsü-to-wē."
will-become-if, I your head-rope back to-you-give-shall."

" *Oh sirâ,   ā   un   kimā chi-to-wē,*" *i-di,   Jĕsu,*
" O then, I your wife will-be," saying, Jĕsu (said),

" *kwē,   ā-vo   u-ki   vo-to-kē.*"
" come, us-two house-to go-let."

Free Translation of the Foregoing.

How Jĕsu got a Goddess for his Wife.

Jĕsu's wife died, leaving him two children, a daughter and a son. Someone would not let these two draw water from the (village) well, so they came and said to their father, " Our villagers would not let us get water from the well. What shall we do ? " Then Jesu said, " O, never mind, I will make a new well for you," and accordingly made a new well. Afterwards his children went for water, but the water was all muddy, and when the children came back, their father said, " Why have you brought dirty water ? " They replied, " O father, we don't know. Somebody has been there before us and has dirtied the water." (Jesu said) " Don't tell lies, no one has been there. If you tell me lies, I will beat you." " (All right)," they said, " if you say we are lying, go one morning and get water, and then come back and rate us." So their father went one morning and got water. He found the water dirty and said, " O, my children spoke the truth. Who has dirtied the water ? " So taking shield and spear, he went and watched the water. And (as he watched) goddesses came down and drew water. There was a big stone at the edge of the well, and the goddesses put down their head-ropes (*i.e.* head bands used for carrying loads) on the stone and bathed. Jesu, on seeing this, stole away a head-rope, and after stealing it, sat upon it. Then the rest exclaiming,

> " If water (quick) we do not bring,
> Our parents will us rate,"

went away. And she who had lost her head-rope cried out, " O, comrades, wait for me, I can't find my head-rope." But her comrades had gone without waiting for her. When her companions had all gone, Jesu came forth and seized her, saying, " What is your name ? Unless you tell me your name, I won't give you back your head-rope." She (replied), " I will tell you, my name is Vihuju." Then Jesu said, " Be my wife, and I will give you back your head-rope."

(She replied) " O then, I will be your wife." Jesu (then said), "Come along, let us go home."[1]

The Angami numerals given here and the notes on tonal distinctions which follow are taken from McCabe's Grammar.

NUMERALS.

1. *po.*		27. *serr pemo thenā.*	
2. *kennā.*		28. *serr pemo thethā.*	
3. *sê.*		29. *serr pemo tekwü.*	
4. *dā.*		30. *serr.*	
5. *pangu.*		31. *serr o pokrō.*	
6. *suru.*		32. *serr o kennā,* etc., etc.	
7. *thenā.*		37. *lhidā pemo thenā,* etc., etc.	
8. *thethā.*		40. *lhidā.*	
9. *tekwü.*		47. *lhi pangu pemo thenā,* etc., etc.	
10. *kerr.*		50. *lhi pangu.*	
11. *kerr o pokrō.*		57. *lhi suru pemo thenā.*	
12. *kerr o kennā.*		60. *lhi suru.*	
13. *kerr o sê.*		67. *lhi thenā pemo thenā.*	
14. *kerr o dā.*		70. *lhi thenā.*	
15. *kerr o pangu.*		77. *lhi thethā pemo thenā.*	
16. *kerr o suru.*		80. *lhi thethā.*	
17. *mekwü pemo thenā.*[2]		87. *lhi tekwü pemo thenā.*	
18. *mekwü pemo thethā.*[2]		90. *lhi tekwü.*	
19. *mekwü pemo tekwü.*[2]		97. *krā pemo thenā.*	
20. *mekwü.*		100. *krā.*	
21. *mekwü pokrō.*		101. *krā di po* or *krā mu po.*	
22. *mekwü kennā,* etc., etc.		1000. *niê po.*	

NOTES ON THE NUMERALS.

Eleven = *Kerr o pokrö.*

The word *krö* means " added to," " increased," " more," *e.g.* " Give me one more " = *po ā rekröshichê.*

Seventeen = *Mekwü pemo thenā.*

Lit. The seven falling short of the twenty, *cf.* The money falls short of what I want = *Rakā ā kechāu pemowê.*

Thirty = *Serr*—most likely a contracted form of *sê kerr* = " three ten."

One hundred and one = *Krā mu po, kra di po.*

Mu and *di* are equivalent to " and." *Di* is really the particle used in forming the past conjunctive participle : *Vordi* = having come.

---

[1] See Appendix XIII, p. 458.

[2] The straightforward method, *e.g. kerr o thenā*, etc., is now supplanting

INTONATION.

" Like the Chinese and many of the so-called Lohitic
languages, which are still in a very primitive stage of the
agglutinating class, Angami Naga is peculiarly rich in
intonation. In illustration of this statement I append a
few examples showing the variety of meaning a simple word
may have. I have not attempted to mark tones, or emphasis ;
these can only be learnt by ear, and the beginner can always
avoid mistakes by using qualifying words to render his
meaning clear.

Chŏ	... =	{ Wild animal ; head. }	*Si* ...	... =	{ Cold ; to know ; wood. }
Chi	... =	{ To eat ; to do ; pain. }	*Kwe*	... =	{ Clothes ; voice ; meaning ; to await. }
Ki ...	... =	{ House ; place ; than ; season ; to. }	*Krŏ* ...	... =	{ To wash ; to buy. }
			Lê ...	... =	{ To take ; field ; warm. }
Ni ...	... =	{ Pleased ; loin-cloth. }			
			Khā	... =	{ To close ; steep. }
Mi ...	... =	{ Fire ; tail ; root. }	*Tekhu*	... =	{ Tiger ; fields ; grasshopper ; jew's harp. }
Zhā...	... =	{ Day ; pay ; large. }			

" Many Nāgās will tell you that there is a marked difference
in the intonation of these words, but for one Nāgā who
clearly marks these tonal distinctions, twenty fail to do so."[1]

KEZAMA AND MEMI.

The following notes on the Kezama and Memi languages
together with the specimen of the latter are also taken
verbatim from Sir George Grierson's " Linguistic Survey of
India," where, however, the notes on Kezama are given
somewhat tentatively.

[1] Similar distinctions of meaning according to tone are equally common
in Sema and Chang, but they are usually well marked in pronunciation.

"*Kezama.*

"Nouns have a prefix *e*, corresponding to the Sema and Rengma *ā*, which was originally the pronoun of the third person and means 'his,' but often has the force only of the definite article, or even has no meaning whatever, as in *e-nē me-chü*, a distant town. Corresponding to the Angāmi relative suffix *u*, we have *o*, as in *kachü-o*, he who was the younger. The Angāmi *mā*, person, is represented by *mi*.

"In nouns, the nominative singular takes the suffix *nyi* before transitive verbs, corresponding to the Lhōta *nā*. As in that language, the suffix can be omitted when no ambiguity will ensue. Thus, *kachü-o-nyi pu*, the younger said ; but *pu*, not *pu-nyi*, *gwo-lâ*, he went.

"The genitive, as in other cognate languages, takes no termination, and precedes the governing noun, as in *sü e-nē mi kelē kē*, that town's man one's house, the house of a man of that town.

"The dative takes the suffix *nhà*, as in *e-pfü-nhà*, to his father.

"The locative takes *chē*, as in *e-lâ-chē*, in the field, and *àzo* means 'with,' as in *krokromu-àzo*, with harlots.

"The sign of the plural is, as in Angāmi, *ko*.

"As regards pronouns, we have the following forms :—

"*Yē* or *iyē*, I ; *āwu-ko*, we. The word *vē* means 'property,' as in *ā-vē*, my property, but is also used to give the force of various cases to the personal pronouns, as in *ā-vē*, with me. *Ā*, by itself, is used as a prefix meaning 'my,' as in *ā-pfü*,[1] my father.

"*No*, 'thou' and 'you'; used as a prefix, *i* means 'thy,' as in *i-pfü*,[1] thy father ; *i-vē*, thy property, with thee ; *no i-vē* means 'thy son.'

"*Pu*, he ; *āwu-ko* means 'they' as well as 'we.' The prefix is *e* or *pu*, as in *e-pfü*,[1] his father ; *pu-vē*, his property. *Pu-ē*, apparently for *pu-vē*, is 'to him'; *pu-nhà*, to him. The nominative before transitive verbs is *pu-nyi*.

"*Sü*, that ; *hi*, this ; *tu-o*, who ? *di*, what ?

"As to verbs, we have *bā*, is, was. Adjectives take verbal terminations, as in *vē-ā*, it is good. . . .

[1] Or *-pvo*.

" The usual suffix of the past tense is *nā*, as in *psü-nā*, gave; *chü-nā*, as well as *chü*, did. Sometimes we find *lâ*, as in *gwo-lâ*, went ; *e-nyi-lâ*, was happy. Another suffix is *ā* or *wā*, as in *pu-ā*, said ; *gwo-ā*, has come ; *me-lho-wā*, has given food. Finally, there are several instances in which no suffix is used, as in the present. Thus, *pu*, said ; *gwo*, went ; *chü*, did.

" The suffix of the future is *dà*, as in *pu-dà*, will say; *e-nyi-dà*, will be happy.

" The suffix of the imperative seems to be *nē*, as in *psü-nē*, give.

" The usual suffix of the conjunctive participle is *ngi*, as in *ngu-ngi*, seeing. There is also *pfâ* in *ke-zē-pfâ*, dividing ; *me-lo-pfâ*, sending.

" *Kâ-ke-lâ* seems to be an infinitive of *kâ*, call.

" The causal suffix, corresponding to the Angāmi *bu*, is probably *lâ*, as in *pu-ē-lâ mā-pfu-lo*, cause him to wear.

" The following are examples of negatives: *psü-mo*, gave not; *pyē-mo-tà*, I am not worthy ; *e-nyi-mo*, was not happy ; *liü-mü-bā*, did not wish ; *mo-tà-mo-lio*, transgressed not ; *psü . . . mo*, gavest not. We have also *ho-tà*, was not ; *to-huē-hotà*, who cannot eat, the root *to* meaning ' eat.'

" Memi.

" *Prefixes and Suffixes.*—The otiose prefix *u* is very common. It corresponds to the prefix *u* of Angāmi, and to the *ā*, *ē* or *ō*, which we find in Mikir and in many of the Nāga languages, including Sema and Lhōta. As elsewhere, it is dropped when the noun to which it is prefixed is preceded by a possessive case. Thus *unnā*, son, but *ni-nā*, your son. It should be noted that, as in this instance, the first consonant of a noun is often doubled after the *u*. Thus *unnā* is equivalent to *u-nā ;* *ubbā*, a hand, for *u-bā*. This prefix, as in the other languages, originally meant ' his,' and still often does so. Thus *u-chi* means both ' house ' and ' his house.'

" In the case of nouns of relationship *a* is often used instead of *u*, *a* properly means ' my.' Thus *a-pū*,[1] my father, or,

[1] Or perhaps *-pvū*.

simply, 'father.' We have both *a-pū*[1] and *u-pū*[1] meaning 'father'; *a-pū*,[1] my father; *u-pū*,[1] his father; and (with the prefix dropped) *ni-pū*,[1] your father. A good example of the use of these prefixes and of the way in which they are dropped is in *ni-pū*[1] *chi-lē*, in your father's house. Here 'house' is *u-chi*. The prefix is dropped because the word is preceded by the genitive *ni-pū*. In *ni-pū*, the prefix *a* or *u* of *a-pū* or *u-pū* has been dropped for similar reasons.

"Just as adjectives in Angāmi Nāga take the prefix *ke*, so in Mao they take *ka* or *kā*. Thus *kāyi*, good ; *kasi*, bad ; *kakrā*, white.

"Note the use of the word *mai*, meaning 'person,' which is frequently employed like the Hindūstānī *wālā*. Thus *chi-lē-mai* (? the man in the house), a slave ; *utākata-mai*, a cultivator. It is the same as the Angāmi *mā*.

"Nouns.

"*Gender.*—Nouns of relationship, as usual, have special words to indicate gender. Thus :—

a-pū, father.	*a-pē*, mother.
pū-to-mai, man.	*ni-to-mai*, woman.
nā-pū-to-mai, son.	*unāmoni-to-mai*, daughter.

" In other cases *fodo*[2] usually means male, and *kru* (Angāmi *krü*), female. Thus *kuri fodo*, a horse ; *kuri kru*, a mare. Variations of this are :—

u-si silo, a dog.	*u-si sikru*, a bitch.
u-khro fodo, a male deer.	*u-khro tu-kru*, a female deer.

"*Number.*—The usual plural suffix is *inūi*, all, as in *apū-inūi*, fathers. Pronouns take *kru*, and connected with this appears to be *pū-tomai kāyi krohĩ*, good men, the plural of *pū-tomai kāyi*. In *unnā-hã-hi*, to his two sons, we have a rudimentary dual.

"*Case.*—As in Lhōta Nāga, the *Nominative* takes *nā* (corresponding to the *Kezhāmā nyi*) when it is the subject of a transitive verb. This *nā* is also occasionally used with

---

[1] Or perhaps *-pvū*.

[2] *Cf.* Sema (*a*)*du*, though this is used only for birds. The Sema female termination for all beings is (a)khu.

the verb substantive, and with intransitive verbs, but not as a rule. Thus always *yi-nā dāi*, I strike ; but *yi-nā soē*, I am ; *yi notē*, I shall be ; *ikru-nā tāwē*, we went ; *nilēkru tāwē*, you went. Other examples are :—

> *nonau-nā pē-ē*, the younger said.
> *u-pu-nā kojū-piē*, his father divided.
> *ni-thēhū* (not *thēhū-nā*) *khēwē,—ni-pū-na* (not *ni-pū*) *koto koso piwē*, your brother has returned,—your father has given eating and drinking (*i.e.*, a feast).

" This *nā* is, properly speaking, the suffix of the Instrumental case, so that sentences in which they are used are really passive constructions. *Nonau-nā pē-ē* is literally ' by the son it was said.' In the pronouns, *no* is sometimes used instead of *nā*.

" The *Accusative* takes no suffix, as in *u-nā kojū-piē*, he divided his wealth. Here *nā* means ' wealth ' and is not the nominative suffix.

" The suffix of the *Instrumental* is *nā*, as in *ubba-nā poē*, (we) hold (two spears) by means of our hands.

" The usual suffix of the *Dative* is *hĩ*, as in *apu-hĩ pēē*, (he) said to his father ; *unnā-hã-hĩ kojū-piē*, he divided to his two sons. Sometimes we find the instrumental suffix *nā* or *no* used for this case. Thus, *mai kali-nā*, to one man (there were two sons) ; *ma kali-no*, (he went) to a man.

"Motion towards is usually indicated by *lē-khē*, as in *ido lē-khē*, (sent him) to the field ; *u-chi lē-khē*, (as he came) to the house. Sometimes the locative suffix *lē* is used, as in *iniū kali-lē*, he went to (*literally*, in) a country.

" The suffix of the *Ablative* is *hĩ-ā*, as in *a-pū-hĩ-ā*, from the father. Note, however, *po-hino*, (take) from him ; *ubbalētino*, (draw water) from the well.

" The *Genitive* takes no suffix. It is simply prefixed to the noun signifying the thing possessed. Thus *a-pū chilā-mai-nā*, my father's servants. In the pronouns, *chu* is sometimes used as a genitive suffix.

" The sign of the Locative is *lē*, as in *u-chi-lē*, in the house ; *ido-lē*, in the field. ' On ' is *khē*, as in *ubbā-khē*, on his hand ; *upfiwā-khē*, on his feet. *Cha-hē lodē* is translated ' to enter in the house.'

" Adjectives.

" These usually, but not always, follow the nouns they qualify. They do not change for gender or number. When a case suffix is added to the noun, it comes after the adjective. The adjective prefix is *ka* (compare Angami and Mikir *ke*).

kuri kakrā, the white horse.
pūtomai kāyi kali, a good man, lit. man good one.
nitomai kāyi kali, a good woman.
pūtomai kāyi kali-hī̃, to a good man.
pūtomai kāyi krohī̃-hī̃, to good men.

" The following are examples of comparison :—
kāyi, good.
kāhē̃ kono ka-li-yi, better (*kāhē̃* means ' two ').
mainiū kono kaliyi, best.
ūsā pāji kāyi, very excellent coat.
atukru, high.
kāhē̃ kono kali atukru, (two than one high), higher.
mainiū kono kali atukru, (all than one high), highest.

" Pronouns.

" The *Personal* Pronouns are *yi*, I; *ni*, thou ; and *hana* or *po* (as in Angāmi), he, she, it.

" *First Person.*—The nominative is *yi* before intransitive verbs. Thus, *yi māē* or *yi-ū māutē*, I sinned. Before Transitive verbs, the form is *yi-nā*. This pronoun has a form *āi*, which is used as an oblique form. Thus, *āi dāi*, beats me, I am beaten. *Āi pikorosa*, to be received by me. *Āhā̃ kūā*, is translated ' with me.' The genitive is *a*, which is used as a prefix. Thus *a-pū*, my father ; *a-nā*, my wealth ; *annā*, my son. In the last example (as in *unnā* referred to under the head of prefixes) the initial *n* of *nā* is doubled after the prefix.

" The plural is *i-kru* (-*nā*). ' We Mao people ' is *im-mēmē*.
. . .

        ā-chu pēwā, my.
        yi, mine.
        ikro-chu, of us. . . .
        inilē-kru, our. . . .

" *Second Person.*—The nominative is *ni* or *nē* before intransitive verbs, as *ni-ū ãhã kūā chithiūchikro-bōē*, thou dwellest ever with me. Before transitive verbs we have *nē-nā*, as *nēnā koto koso piwē*, thou gavest a feast. Sometimes we find *nē-no* instead of *nē-nā*. In *ni pimoē*, thou didst not give, the suffix *nā* is not used, though a transitive verb follows.

" So we have in an interrogative sentence *nē ti thē-hino hrali-nā*, from whom did you buy that ? The oblique form of this pronoun, which is also used as a genitive prefix, is *ni*. Thus we have :—

> *ni-jū*, your name.
> *ni-pū*, your father.
> *ninnā* (with the n of na doubled), your son.
> *ni-nā*, your wealth.
> *ni-thēhū*, your brother.
> *ni-wā*, your service.
> *ni-chū*, your word.
> *ni-hĩ*, . . . to you.
> *ni-hĩā*, . . . before you.

" A genitive absolute is *nilo*, yours, in *a-nā inūi kabbūsa nilo pitē*, whatever is mine is thine. With this are connected most of the following forms :—

> *ni-et* (nom.), thou.
> *ni-chu*, thy.
> *ni-yē*, thine (? it is thine).
> *ailē-kru*, you, your.
> *nilē-kru-chu*, of you.

" The suffix *ū* added to these pronouns gives definiteness, as in *yi-ū moza thinobūdē*, whereas I die of hunger ; *ni-u ãhã kūā chithiūchikro-bōē*, you on the one hand dwell with me (while your brother, etc.).

" *Third Person.*—This is *hana* or *po*. The nominative is *hana* (-*nā*), as in *hana-nā annoē*, he asked. The accusative is *hana*, as in *hana matāa*, sent him. So we have for the genitive *hana thihū*, his sister ; *hana kēna*, his wife ; but the most usual word for ' his ' is the prefix *u*, as in *u-pū-nā u-nā*, his father (divided) his wealth. So (with doubled *n* as usual) *unnā*, his son. This *u* has in many cases become quite otiose. See the remarks on prefixes. *Hana-chu* is 'of him.'

"From the base *po*, we have *po-hino polo*, take from him ; *poē fulo*, bind him ; *po-hē kāhē̃*, from among those two ; *poilē-kru*, they ; *poilē-kru*, their ; *poilē-kru-chu*, of them.

"The following are examples of *Demonstrative* pronouns :—

"*This :—kuri-hē*, this horse ; *annā hana-hē*, this my son ; *kasha-hē*, this rupee.

"*Ha-dono, sa-dono*, for this reason ; *sa-chū*, (hearing) this word ; *sa-thēcha*, therefore.

"*That :—kasha ti*, those rupees ; *nē ti thē-hino hrali-nā*, from whom did you buy that ? *iniū lē ti*, in that country (note the position of the demonstrative after the case suffix).

"*Mai chi-nā*, that man (sent him) ; *sato ka-chi-thē*, at that time ; *mai cha-nā chowāsoā būli sē*, that man can live happily.

"*Interrogatives* are :—*nēthiyē*, who ? *thē-hino*, from whom (did you buy that) ? *adē*, what ? *ni-jū thētē*, what is your name ? *ada-soē*, what is (this) ? *ada-lē*, why ? *chiwē*, how many (years) are there ? *chia boē*, how many (sons) are there (in your father's house) ?

"The only instance of a *Reflexive* pronoun is *hana-nā alliā pēē*, he said to himself.

"VERBS.

"The verb substantive is *so*, be.

"The following forms have been noted :—

> *yi soē*, I am.
> *yi soē*, I was.
> *yi nolē*, I shall be.
> *yi solisē*, I may be.

ni-nā so, (fit) to be your son ; *ido-lē cho-ē* (alternate spelling for *so-ē*), he was in the field. We have also *nilo pitē*, is thine, and (a compound with *bū* or *bō*, to remain) *so-bū-lē*, let us remain.

"An example of the negative Verb Substantive is *mai-mo-ē*, (I) am not (fit).

" As in other cognate languages, the sense of time in the Finite Verb is very loosely felt. Once a tense base is formed, it does not seem to change for number or person. . . .

" In order to show how loosely the temporal suffixes are used, I here give (a) the future of the verb dā, strike, and (b) the present of the verb tā, go. It will be seen that, as given in the list of words, the conjugations are practically identical.

(a) I shall strike, etc.		(b) I go, etc.	
Sing.	Plur.	Sing.	Plur.
dā-lē	dā-lē.	tā-lē	tā-lē.
dā-lēwā	dā-lē.	tā-lēwā	tā-lē.
dā-lē	dā-lē.	tā-lēwā	tā-lē.

" The following is the way in which the various tenses are formed :—

Present.—The suffix is *ē* (Angāmi *wē*), sometimes written *i*. Thus, *bōē*, (he) lives ; *khoē*, (he) is pasturing ; *toē*, (they) eat ; *poē*, (we) hold (spears in our hands) ; *dāi*, (he) strikes ; after vowels, a euphonic *w* is sometimes inserted, as *dā-w-ē*, (I) am striking. Sometimes the suffix *dē* of the past is used, as in *bū-dē*, (he) remains (serving the God) ; *khai-dē*, (he) is kept (like a slave). So *thi-no bū-dē*, am about to die, literally, am in a condition to die.

" We also find the future form used, as in *tā-lē*, (I) go ; *ni-lē*, (he) is found.

Imperfect.—The only example is *dā-khē*, (I) was striking.

Past.—The usual suffix is *ē* (Angāmi *wē*)—the same as in the present ; thus following cognate languages. Examples are *pē-ē* or (with euphonic *w*) *pē-w-ē*, (he) said ; *pi-ē*, *pi-w-ē*, (he) gave (compare *kojū-piē*, (he) divided) ; *mohoē*, (he) wasted ; *mami-y-ē* (euphonic *y*), (he) became wretched ; *koazil-ē*, (he) went and joined ; *wēl-ē*, (he) came ; *mā-ē*, (I) have sinned ; *chol-ē*, (he) heard ; *annoē*, he asked ; *khē-w-ē*, (he) has returned ; *lobbo-ē*, he refused ; *za-w-ē*, (he) entreated ; *tā-w-ē*, (we) went ; *hral-ē*, (I) bought. The forms of the past of *tā*, go, are very instructive :

we have, *tā-w-ē*, (we, they) went; *tāwē-wā*, (you) went; *ti-tāwē*, (I) went; *tā-lēwā*, (and *tā-dē*), (he) went; *ti-tālēwā*, thou wentest. The verb *dā*, strike, inserts *bb*. Thus *dā-bb-ē*, (I) struck; *dā-bb-ēwe*, (thou) struckest; but *dāi*, (he, we, you, they) struck.

The syllable *dē* (Angāmi *te*) is also used to form the past, as in *tā-dē*, (he) went (to a far country); *dā-u-dē* (with inserted *u*), (I) have struck (his son). With the last compare *mā-u-tē* or *mā-ē*, (I) have sinned.

Other forms of the Past are *mono*, (two sons) were born; *matā-a*, he caused to go, sent; *maki*, he kissed.

Perfect.—The only true perfect which I have met is formed by compounding the verb with the auxiliary, as in *tā-so-e*, (I) have walked (a long way to-day).

Pluperfect.—This is the same as the Past.

Future.—The suffix is *lē*, as in *dā-lē*, (I) shall strike; *no-lē*, (I) shall be; *pē-lē*, (I) shall say; *so-bū-lē*, let (us) remain.

Present Subjunctive.—*Yi so-li-sē* is translated 'I may be,' and *yi-nā dā-sē*, I may strike.

Imperative.—The following forms occur :—*pi-yo*, *pi-yū*, give; *tho-piyū*, place; *pol-o*, take; *ful-o*, bind; *sithēpal-ō*, draw water; *dāo*, strike; *tāo*, go; *kot-o*, eat; *hebb-ū*, sit; *hēk-o*, come; *ālāch-o*, stand; *mos-o*, take (me for a servant). Other forms are *thiyē*, die; *tū*, run; *ponobā*, cause to wear.

Verbal Nouns, etc.—Suffix *ā*.—*ho-ā*, (rice) being dear (he became wretched); *bū-ā*, (a man) who lived (in that country); *ichū tā-ā*, arising (up going) (he went to his father); *pū-w-ā*, bringing (the best garment clothe him); *to-ā so-lā*, eating drinking (let us remain) (compare *koto koso* below); *thi-ā*, having died (is alive again); *kulē-ā*, calling (a servant); *sa-chol-ā*, hearing (this); *pi-ā*, giving (to harlots has wasted).

Suffix *li-ā*.—*ni-li-ā*, having found (him, they rejoiced); *thē-li-ū* (? *thi-li-ā*), when-dead (we hold two spears).

Suffix *li-ē.*—*dā-li-ē*, striking, having struck ; *ka-li-ē*, after (some days) remaining.

Suffix *o.*—*pō-tā-di-y-o*, having gone (he wasted his substance) ; *ichapē-li-y-o*, becoming sensible (he said to himself) ; *khol-o*, embracing (he kissed him).

Suffix *lē.*—*poi-lē*, carrying (his wealth to a far country).

Suffix *thē.*—*woi-thē*, at the time of coming ; *ho-ka-ti-thē*, when (all) had been wasted ; *tā-kochi-thē*, gone.

Other forms.—*tū-ko*, running (he kissed him) ; *kho-to*, (he sent him) to pasture (swine) ; *tā-no*, going ; *thi-no bū-dē*, I am about to die ; *ko-to*, food, rice ; *ko-to ko-so* (compare *to-ā so-lā* above) *pi-w-e*, gave food and drink.

Passive Voice.—The force of the passive is thus expressed :—*āi dāi*, beats me, *i.e.*, I am beaten.

Causal Verbs.—The following are probably causals : *mo-ho-ē*, he caused to waste, he wasted ; *ma-tā-a*, he caused (him) to go, he sent (him to the field) ; *mo-so*, cause to be, make.

Interrogative Sentences.—The interrogative particle is *nā*, corresponding to the Kachcha Nāga *mē*, and the Angāmi *gā*, *ro* or *mā*. Thus, *hral-i-nā*, (from whom) did you buy (that) ?

Negative Sentences.—The negative particle is *mo*, as in Angāmi. Examples are *pi-mo-ē*, (anyone) gave not ; *ni* (not *nē-nā*) *pi-mo-ē*, thou gavest not ; *pēthōki-mo*, (I) did not disobey ; *fa-pi-mo*, he is not released. Note that the negative *follows* the word qualified.

" SPECIMEN OF MEMI LANGUAGE.[1]

Im mēmē thēli-ā ēhū̃ kāhē̃ ubbānā poē.
We Mao-people when-dead spears two hands-by hold.
Ēhū̃ Orāmē Pēkujikhē fēlē. Fēlilā
Spears the-God Pēkujikhē is-for-piercing. If-able-to-pierce

---

[1] This is also taken direct from Sir George Grierson's " Linguistic Survey."

mai chanā Orāmē iniū lē chowāsoā būli sē.
man that God's country in happily to-live can.

Fēli • kokromainā Orāmē Pēkujikhē ukrūso
To-pierce who-cannot-man God Pēkujike serving

būdē, chilāmai soā khaidē, tinā fapimo.
remains, slave like is-kept, ever is-not-released.

Orāmai hana pi jisūē, kota maicha. Hana kēnā,
God's that head is-very-big, beard grows. His wife,

' *ochū mai nolo mai hai adasono mathiwē,*'
' aged man young man as-well-as why are-killed,'

annoē. ' Maina kososi miya to mima to. Mai
asked. ' Men chillies old eat unripe-also eat. Man

thēfrā yiā ochū mai nolo mai hai fūē,' *sata*
following I-also old man young man also catch,' saying

Orāmē hananā pē-ē.
God that said.

" FREE TRANSLATION OF THE FOREGOING.

When any one of us Mao people dies, two spears are put
into his hand. These are for piercing the God Pēkujikhē.
If the dead man can pierce him, he is allowed to live happily
in the God's country. If he cannot pierce him, he has to
become a servant to Pēkujikhē. He is kept like a slave,
and is never released.

" This God's head is very big, and he has a beard. His
wife once asked him why he killed young people as well as
old. He replied, ' Men cut chillies both unripe and ripe,
and after their example I catch both young men and old
men.' "

In order to show the close relation between the languages
of the tribes classed in this monograph as the Western
group (see Appendix III), a comparative list of words is given
on pp. 328 and 329. Of these words the Tengima are taken
from McCabe, the Memi, Kezami, Tseminyu Rengma, and
Lhota from Grierson, except for the words marked† which
are added by the writer. The Sema and Isenikotsenu

Rengma lists are also added by the writer.   Sir G. Grierson gives no vocabulary of the latter, and his vocabulary of the former is based on the Lazemi dialect, which is only spoken by a small group of villages in the Doyang Valley and understood with difficulty by the vast majority of Semas. It will be noticed how the two Rengma languages together link on Lhota to Angami and Sema.

NAGA ASSAMESE

The subject of language would hardly be complete without a few remarks on the " pigeon " Assamese, which forms the *lingua franca* of the Naga Hills, and through the medium of which most of the information necessary for this monograph has been collected.

The Assamese spoken in the Naga Hills is a bastard tongue which varies a good deal. " S " and " ch " are given the English quality as a rule, instead of being pronounced " h " and " s " respectively as in the Assam Valley, and a large number of Bengali, Hindustani, English, and even Naga words are in common use.   The first and second personal inflexions of the verbs are generally disregarded in favour of the third person, and Naga idioms and Naga constructions are commonly put literally into Assamese.   A good instance of this is in the Sema trick of saying in Assamese " I spoke *in his direction* " (তাহাৰ ফালে) to translate the Sema idiom " *pa vile pi* " = " I spoke to him," but such " dog " Assamese is in equally common use among the Angamis and other tribes of the district.   Such alterations also as that of *ŏkra* (= " crazy ") into *wŏkra* are very common, and the plural number is largely ignored.

Naga Assamese, though a somewhat clumsy vehicle of conversation, is very easy to pick up and with a little application can be spoken perfectly—provided the learner has no previous knowledge of real Assamese.   It is, moreover, an excellent vehicle for the expression of Naga turns of speech and thought, and therefore infinitely better as a medium for conversing to Nagas than Hindustani, or even English, would be, being capable, as it is, of representing almost the precise shade of meaning required.

1. English.	2. Memi.	3. Tengima.	4. Kezami.	5. Sema.	6. Rengma. (Tseminyu.)	7. Rengma. (Iseni-kotsenu.)	8. Lhota.
one	kali	po	kele	laki	me	küsu	ekhā
two	kāhē	kenna	kenhi	kini	kongu, ko-hung	kenyi	enni
three	kosa	sē	katsü	küthu	kingshan	kechü	etham
four	pādai	dā	pedi	bidhi	pezi	mezü	mezü
five	pongo	pangu	pangu	pongu	(shat†)pfü	munga	mingo
six	choro	suru	sarr	soghu, tsoghu	saro	togho	tirōk
seven	chānē	thenā	signi	tsini	(shat†)sanü	tāghü	ti-ing, tsecang
eight	chāchā	thethā	tichē	tache	tetsē	teza	tiza
nine	choko	tekwü	tepfü	toku	tekhē	teku	tōkü
ten	chiro	kerr	chiro	cheghi	serr	tegha	taro, tero
twenty	make	mekwü	mechi	muku	nki	mekweru	mekwi, mekwü
fifty	re pongo	lhi pangu	lha pangu	lho-pongu	hem-pfü	tenyi	ti-ingyā
hundred	kre	krā	kri	akeh	tsi	meza	nzo, nzü
I	yi	ā-	iye	niye	āle	hi	ā, ai
my	yi, āchu pēwā	ā-	iye	i-..	ā	i-..	ā
arm	ubba	bu	ba	aou	ubet	makha	okhe
leg	upfi	phi	phe	aphuku	pha	matsü	mpo, ocho†
nose	unghüng	'nhichā	nhukā	anhiki	nhikā	anyatsa	kenno
eye	unghē	'mhi	nhēchū	anyeti	āyehte	anyong	ōmyhek
mouth	ummē	me	keti	akichi	amaung	apang	ōpang
tooth	uhü	'hu	efü	ahu	ahe	akuna	ōhō
ear	nübbi	'nie	kenü	akini	nyeti†	ayesseh (of head), akenyeh (of face, body, etc.)	enno
hair	pisū	thā (human), mā (of animals)	etā	asa (of the head), amhi (of face, body, etc.)	peheh	ali	ōtsā
head	uppi	'tsu	kepsü	akütsü	peh	ali	kurr, kuri†
tongue	mali	mewü†	meli	amili	ingi, ayi†	amilli	nli, nni
belly	uppü	'vā	mevo	apvo	aghinda	apvu	opok
back	upfē	chē, nāku	kechē	akicheh	nse	akesü	mānkü, eche†

1. English.	2. Memi.	3. Tengima.	4. Kezami.	5. Sema.	6. Rengma. (Tsemīnyu.)	7. Rengma. (Iseni-kotsenu.)	8. Lhota.
brother	athēhū	'dzerāu (elder) / 'sazāu (younger)	jūkeri (elder) / itsikozü (younger)	amu (elder) / atūkuzu (younger)	ātsā (elder) / sangüzangü† (younger)	api (elder) / atsünoa, inyia (younger)	ota, ata† (elder) / ōnyü, ongo† (younger)
sister	athui (elder) / thihu, thehu (younger)	'üpfü†	epi	afu (elder) / achepfu (younger)	alegi	atsüghü	oyülōe, oilo†
woman	nĕtomai, nitomai	thenuma	nichümi	totimi	taninyu	nenza	elüā
child	nătomai	nichuma	kachümi	itimi	ints-anyu	anga¹	ōtsōe
boy	nătomai-puto	nichuma, krisā	numi	apumi	(pōniyu)	puza	nungori, (epüē† = *male*)
girl	nătomai-nito	thenunāma	elümi	ilimi	lenyu	alla	elüēroro
husband	achou†	'nupfō	'kāmi	akimi	ochoinyu†	mpoza	orapo†
wife	akō	'kima	'kāmi (*same as the word for husband*)	anipfü	ānu	mao-pvu	eng, kikamu†
house	uchi	ki	ekiē	aki	kā	azheng	oki
cow	uto	mithu	echō	amishi	metu	amesü	mangsü
dog	usi	tefüh	etsü	atsü	tēhi	afo	furho†
leech	eve†	revā	reghye†	aiveh	jombeh†	āwü	iva†
die	thiyō	sata	tsitā	ti, tive	silātā	süüta	tsa†
give	piyo	tsu	psüdo	tsü	pyi,† kishitā	psi	piā
good	kāyi	kevi	kevō	akevi, allo	gwā kemu	makhei	mhōnā, mhōm
bad	kāsi	keshā, vimo	kesü	alhokesah	mhodēkā, kerinyu†	makheh	m'mho
before	āja	mhodzü	ejhüpā	azu		athuwi	ōvangi
behind	āthōpo	sātsā	etsipā	athiu	siki	asang.	silamwē
sun	chengheng	tināki	tenyinhu	tsü-kinhyeh	iyēkā	aghani	eng
moon	ūkhro	krō	ekrü	akhi, akü	she	ashah	choro
stars	ovü	themü	eghe	ayeh	shenü	āōla	shantiwo
fire	ummi	mī	ene	ami	mā	ami	omi
water	uza	dzü	ejü	azü	dzü	atsü	otsü†

¹ *anga* is the same as the Sema word for "infant."

APPENDICES

APPENDIX I

BIBLIOGRAPHY

ALTHOUGH there are a number of books dealing directly or indirectly with the tribes inhabiting the Naga Hills, those that deal with the Angamis are not numerous, and are the reverse of exhaustive. The list given here contains the names of the books and articles dealing with the Angamis to which I have had access, together with the names of works dealing with other Naga tribes, which have been referred to in this monograph. The list is a very short one, and a few notes have been added with the object of indicating as far as possible the relative value of the authorities, which varies considerably.

1. "Travels and Adventures in the Province of Assam." Major John Butler. Smith, Elder & Co., 1855.

2. "Rough Notes on the Angāmi Nāgās," by Capt. John Butler, son of Major Butler. *Journal of the Asiatic Society*, Part I, No. IV, 1875.

Capt. Butler is by far the most valuable of the printed authorities on the Tengima Angamis, dealing as he does with the tribe at a period when they were in a warlike condition now already half forgotten. Capt. Butler's notes are not voluminous, but contain, as also do Major Butler's, a good deal of information as to the practice of war by the Angamis, which is no longer obtainable from the people themselves. Major Butler's "Sketch of Assam" (Smith, Elder, 1847) contains some information, probably second-hand, about Konyak tribes.

3. "Notes on the Wild Tribes inhabiting the so-called Naga-Hills." Colonel Woodthorpe. *Journal of the Anthropological Institute*, August to November, 1881.

Colonel Woodthorpe's notes contain some excellent drawings and the letterpress is valuable in so far as it is a *résumé* of Capt. Butler's "Rough Notes." Colonel Woodthorpe's dangerous distinction between the "Kilted" and "Non-kilted" tribes does not appear in Capt. Butler's notes.

4. "The Naga Tribes of Manipur." T. C. Hodson. Macmillan & Co., 1911.

This contains much information as to the Memi and Marami Nagas, the former of which, if not the latter, may be regarded as divisions of Angami to whom they are undoubtedly very closely allied. The Memis immediately on the Angami border are so closely connected with the Chakrima and Kezama Angamis as to make it possible to speak of these three tribes together as "Eastern Angamis," but for the Memi and the Marami in general Mr. Hodson is the authority, and I have not presumed in this monograph to trespass much upon his demesne.

5. I have had the use in writing this monograph of some unpublished notes on the Memis by Major Kennedy, formerly D.C. of the Naga Hills District, as well as some valuable notes by Colonel J. Shakespear, which are reproduced in the Appendix.

6. "Narrative of an Expedition into the Nāgā Territory of Assam." Lt. G. R. Grange. *Journal of the Asiatic Society*, 1839.

7. "Extracts from the Journal of an Expedition into the Naga Hills on the Assam Frontier." Lt. G. R. Grange. *Journal of the Asiatic Society*, 1840.

8. "Extract from a Report of a Journey into the Naga Hills in 1844." Browne Wood. *Journal of the Asiatic Society*, 1844.

These three contain occasional references to Angami customs, but are principally taken up with details of military or political importance and are likely to be of comparatively small value to the anthropologist.

9. "Fading Histories." S. E. Peal. *Journal of the Asiatic Society*, 1894.

10. "Human Sacrifices in Ancient Assam." E. A. Gait. *Journal of the Asiatic Society*, 1898 (p. 56).

These authorities contain some references to the Naga tribes in general, and the latter contains a valuable note from Mr. Davis relative to the Angamis which has been quoted in full in the text of this monograph (Part III).

11. "Census of Assam, 1891," Vol. I, pp. 237–251. A. W. Davis, Assam Secretariat, Shillong, 1892.

Mr. Davis in his notes here deals with the Nagas in general and not with any particular tribes, so that it must not be assumed, unless explicitly stated, that his remarks hold good of any Naga tribe in particular. Mr. Davis, however, had a very intimate acquaintance with the Naga Hills, and his observations carry considerable weight.

12. " Notes on the Naga Tribes in Communication with Assam." Owen. Carey & Co., Calcutta, 1884.

These notes have been referred to in one instance in this volume. They deal with the Konyak tribes, and not with any of the tribes to the south of Tamlu and the neighbouring Konyak villages.

13. " The Tribes of the Brahmaputra Valley." Lt.-Col. L. A. Waddell, I.M.S., *Journal of the Asiatic Society of Bengal,* Part III, 1900.

These accounts contain a great deal of anthropometrical data, and some excellent photographs, but the letterpress, in so far at any rate as it deals with Naga tribes, contains a number of inaccuracies and in some cases is misleading. It is, for instance, quite wrong to speak of Naga tribes as " endogamous." Not one of the nine tribes with which I am fairly well acquainted attaches the least importance to endogamy. Wherever two tribes march intermarriage is common, while tribal endogamy is really practised only where the force of geographical circumstances compels it.

14. " Ethnography of Nagas of Eastern Assam." W. H. Furness, *Journal of the Anthrop. Institute,* Vol. XXXII, 1902.

Account necessarily rather superficial but good in some points on Aos, Rengmas. and Konyaks (miscalled *Miri* in the article), in spite of some inaccuracies such as regarding the Chongli and Mongsen divisions of the Aos as exogamous units, while a bad mistake is made in confusing the people of Chima, a Konyak village, with the Sema tribe. This is probably due to Assame interpreters who speak of the Konyaks of Chima as " Sima."

15. " Naga and other Tribes of N.E. India." Miss G. M. Godden, *Journal of the Anthrop. Institute,* Vol. XXVI.

A *résumé* of information collected from other sources, most of them already mentioned in this bibliography.

16. " Outline Grammar of the Angāmi Nāgā Language." R. B. McCabe, I.C.S. Calcutta, 1887.

17. " Linguistic Survey of India," Vol. III, Part II. Sir George Grierson, Superintendent of Government Printing, India. Calcutta, 1903.

These two are the chief authorities for the Angami language. Both are of great value, and the latter, of course, deals with a number of other Naga languages as well as Angami. It contains a complete list of all former authorities on the Angami and other Naga tongues, but McCabe and Sir George Grierson have entirely superseded these as regards Angami. The map of the Naga tribes in the " Linguistic Survey " is not quite accurate.

18. "History of Upper Assam, Upper Burma, and the N.E. Frontier." Col. L. W. Shakespear. Macmillan, 1914.

Contains a chapter or two on the Naga tribes. Has some good illustrations. Letterpress, though giving a good idea of the frontier in general, is inaccurate when dealing with the habits, customs, and tribal divisions of the Nagas, and in cases a little misleading.

19. "Gazetteer of the Naga Hills and Manipur." Assam District Gazetteers. Also Supplement to Vol. IX of this Series. Assam Secretariat Press, Shillong.

20. "History of the Relations of the Government with the Hill Tribes of the North-East Frontier of Bengal." Alexander Mackenzie. Calcutta, 1884.

These last three are perhaps the most convenient works of reference dealing with the political history of the Angamis after they came in contact with the British Government, but which has not been treated of at all in this monograph.

APPENDIX I IS CONTINUED IN APPENDIX XIII ON P. 458.

APPENDIX II

NOTES ON THE MEMI

N.B.—These notes are drawn entirely from materials very kindly lent me by Colonel Shakespear, whose notes are, for the most part, reproduced verbatim. The marginal notes are mine.—J. H. H.

i. The following six gennas are proclaimed by the *Mohvu*[1] of Pusemi (Pudunamei) every month. They are observed by thirteen of the sixteen Memi villages. The *Mohvu* when proclaiming an ordinary genna mounts on a pinnacle of shale in Pusemi and shouts from there. His shout can be heard in Pusemi and is passed on to the other five villages at Mao, but the rest of the thirteen have to trust to luck, and often do not hear of a genna being proclaimed till some days later and observe it whenever they happen to hear. When the genna is over the *Mohvu* mounts a higher pinnacle and shouts from there. These two pinnacles are called *Tini-kashāba* and are said to be man and wife. War gennas are proclaimed from a stone in front of the *Mohvu's* house. The six monthly gennas are :—

1. *Pureishi.*—The *Mohvu* admonishes the people not to eat much rice, but no one pays any attention to him. No cultivation is done and the *Mohvu* remains chaste.

2. *Urumāni.*—*Mohvus* fast, taking only *zu* and ginger till the evening, and keep chaste. The rest of the community abstains from cultivation. This is said to keep off sickness.

3. *Tok-kaw.*—This is to improve matters generally; the prohibitions are the same as in Urumāni.

[1] *Mohvu* is the Memi equivalent of the Tengima *Kemovo.*

4. *Uramoni*.—For success in war and the chase. The whole community remains chaste, *Mohvus* fast, no cultivation.

5. *Umigaiyi*.—That no destruction may take place. *Mohvu* fasts and is chaste. Every householder spills out some water. No cultivation.

6. *Kehogāsi*.—*Mohvu* fasts and keeps chaste ; others idle. When an earthquake occurs there is a one-day genna called *Molugashu*. The *Mohvu* fasts and remains chaste ; the rest remain idle.

ii. *Personal Gennas*.—If a cow calves, or a cat kittens, the owner has to remain chaste for three days (formerly five) and in the first case abstain from eating beef. No one from another village may enter his house during these days. On the death of a cow or a cat, the owner abstains from cultivation for one day. For the birth of dogs and pigs and hatching of chickens only one day genna has to be observed and none for their deaths.

iii. *Wild Animals*.—The killer must fast for one day. For a tiger all sixteen Memi villages observe one day genna.

iv. *Klokawtimoni*.—During the moon of October, the *Mohvu* selects a day by the look of the moon, and declares that the next day will be genna ; no work of any sort can be done and the *Mohvu* remains chaste. This is especially for the moon.

v. *Uklokao-e*.—The twenty-ninth or thirtieth day of each moon is kept as a genna for the sun ; no work is done and the *Mohvu* remains chaste.

vi. The Memi of Mekrima (" Maikēl ") are said to observe four monthly gennas :—

1. *Utok-kawh*, to improve crops. *Mohvu* fasts in the morning and remains chaste, the rest of the villagers may do no work except bring water.

2. *Krehemani*.—For war and the chase. Whole village chaste and idle, only allowed to carry water.

3. *Uratawh*, to keep off illness. *Mohvu* fasts in morning and is chaste. Villagers idle.

4. *Poshimani*.—Same as *Uratawh*.

The other gennas named under Mao are observed, by order of the *Mohvu*.

vii. The following articles of diet are prohibited to all *Mohvus* and to stone pullers and others with high social status :—Fowls, eggs, flesh of wild animals, beans, and a small fish called *Kureu* ("Peru" in Manipuri).

Colonel Shakespear was told that it was impossible to say what awful thing would happen if a *Mohvu* were to fail to observe a genna strictly.

viii. *Death*.—On a death occurring, the village is genna for a day. The body is washed and dressed in fine clothes. The grave is dug by a son or a near relative. The grave is dug east and west. Males are placed facing east, females facing west. Cows and pigs are killed according to the wealth of the family. The dead are buried about 4 or 5 p.m. The grave is a simple pit, no coffin is employed, the body is carried out on a plank. With a man are buried two spears, a dao, a shield, an empty *zu* gourd, his pipe, and a bow ; with a woman, her iron walking-stick, a gourd, weaving apparatus, and her rain-shield. In the case of a child that was still being suckled some of its mother's milk, a little from each breast, is squeezed into two "chungas," and these are placed beside the head of the corpse in the grave. The grave is filled in by those who dug it ; the first part dug in the refilling is not thrown away, as is done in Maram. After the grave has been filled in, a small chicken is strangled and then hung by the neck from a small stake on the grave so that its feet just touch the ground, and some chaff is placed before it and set on fire. It is said that in this detail custom varies somewhat, but a fowl is killed in every case.

For five days after the death the house is genna, and at all meals a little of the food is placed in each of the corners at the back of the living room, and after the five days similar offerings are placed there once a month until the last month of the year (*Uklaw-kluh*). The person who cooks these offerings must do no other work and must remain chaste. The offerings are left there till the next ones are placed. On the last of the five days, if any flesh of the cattle killed remains it must be taken out of the house and given away. A new hearth is made and the house swept clean, but the new fire can be lit from the old one or any other. On the grave of the child that was buried while Colonel Shakespear was there he found his bracelets and Manton's " Sportsman's Register." No one would touch these.

ix. *Accidental Deaths.*—No different procedure except in case of death from drowning or by tiger, in which case a genna in all sixteen villages ; the corpse is buried in matting. No animals are killed, nor are offerings of food placed.

x. *Deaths in Childbirth.*—There is a day's genna for a woman who dies in childbirth, but no difference in the funeral rites.

Children dying within five days of birth are buried in an old pot wrapped in old clothes, inside the house, under the floor of the living room, without any ceremonies, because they have not been named.

xi. *Cats.*—Only the *Mohvu* and those who have acquired high social status (see para. xxiii) may keep *cats.* *Cats* used not to be killed, but nowadays people kill them, and no one is any the worse. But the oath on killing a cat is still held to be efficacious. Cats are buried with ceremony and people pretend to weep.

xii. *Tiger.*—If a tiger is shot the body will be brought into the village and buried. The killer is hailed as a fine fellow ; on his death a dog must be killed in order that its ghost may frighten away the ghost of the tiger, which will be waiting to trouble the ghost of his slayer on the road to Mārābu.[1]

xiii. *Belief as to the World beyond the Grave.*—Life in the other world is thought to be much like life here. Those who have acquired social status [2] by pulling stones, etc., and head-takers have an easier time, just as they have here. On the road to Mārābu waits Pekujikhe,[3] who challenges the ghost to single combat, the spirits of brave men accept the challenge, and then the earth heaves with the mighty

---

[1] This is a Sema custom also. The dog is buried with the dead man by most Semas, but in the Chophimi clan its flesh is eaten, following the Ao custom.

[2] *Vide* para. **xxiii.**   [3] Teṅgima — " Metsimo."

struggle and we call it an earthquake, but less brave spirits humbly pick the lice out of his head and are allowed to pass.

xiv. *Fire.*—The first fire which they brought from Mekrima was bad and burnt down their houses, so they fetched fresh fire from Liyai.[1] Clean fire is required to start the fires again, after a village has been burnt, for cooking the head of shikar, after bringing back a human head, for cooking during two days in Salani [2] when men eat apart, and for father and child when eating together (*vide* birth). No woman may make clean fire.

xv. *Birth Customs.*—1. (*a*) A pregnant woman must not eat the flesh of a cow or sow which was pregnant and died. (Memi Nagas do not eat goats.[3])

(*b*) If either parent dream of a spear or a cock, the child will be a boy ; but if the dream is of a woman's iron walking rod or a hen, the child will be a girl. Boys are generally preferred, and in order to get a son the parents must meditate on *Uräme*.[4] No attempt at abortion is ever made.

2. After the birth the father may not eat green vegetables for one day, and must not go out at night for six or seven days.

3. The ear-piercing is done by an old man, who gets a piece of wood for his trouble. Some day after the seventh the parents eat a fowl together and meditate on Uräme ; after this the child is given rice, gradually. The afterbirth is buried very carefully in a pot under the floor of the home, because should it be eaten by a dog or pig the child would die. On this day the mat on which the mother lay and her cooking pots are thrown outside the village. After a child has been named a garland of Kollaw grass is placed round its neck.

4. Twins are thought *very lucky*. No work is done on the day twins are born. The event is thought to presage

---

[1] Another village in the Manipur State.

[2] The Saleni genna among the Memi corresponds either with the Sekrengi or the Tsongi of the Tengima, perhaps combining features of both.

[3] Or rather, perhaps, do not allow their women to do so.

[4] This is clearly a plural form. *U-ra-me* is the equivalent of the Tengima word *te-rho-ma*, apparently, and probably therefore means deities in general.

good fortune for the *Mohvu*, it is therefore not surprising that twins always are helped first when any food is being distributed.

5. The body is buried under the spot on which the birth took place, if the child dies within five days of birth.

6. When the child is two years old, several fowls are killed and his friends are regaled. There is no special ceremony when he first goes to sleep in the young men's house.

xvi. *Birth Ceremonies.*—Only the father may be present, if he cannot be there an old woman takes his place. The mother herself cuts the navel cord with a bamboo knife, and buries the afterbirth in the room alongside of the birthplace. The delivery takes place on the floor to left of the central hearth, as you enter the living room, and the mother remains there for five days. When the mother has buried the afterbirth an old woman brings in stones to make a new cooking place, and if the child be a boy six stones, to make two new fireplaces, as for five days the father and mother must have their food cooked separately and eat separately ; and if the child be a boy a new cooking place must be made for the father also. As soon as the new fireplace has been made, water is warmed to give the child a bath, after which a cock or a hen, according to the sex of the infant, is killed by a boy, and cooked by the mother, who eats it all herself, except small portions given to *Urāme*. Then if the parents are wealthy a pig and several fowls may be killed and a feast given. On the day of the birth the father must do no work. For five days the mother must not leave the house, even for purposes of nature. On the fifth day the name is given. The father thinks of the name at the moment of birth, but should he subsequently dream of broken weapons, torn cloth, or killing animals, the name must be changed. A cock or a hen is killed and eaten by the mother, helped, if necessary, by an old woman. On the same day a bull is killed for *Urāme* and the flesh divided among the villagers.[1] Then the name is given as

---

[1] That is apparently only done for boys, and then only in certain circumstances. *Vide* last sentence of this paragraph.

follows. An elderly male relative holds a spear in one hand and a piece of burning fir-wood in the other, and somehow also takes the child. He first stands on the birth-place, then he crosses to the other side of the house and announces the name. The mother now throws away the pots she has been using and the special fireplace is removed and the mother rejoins her husband on the family couch.

On the sixth day the father and mother eat together, and then the mother takes the child just outside the village and then returns. On the seventh day the mother leaves the child in the house and goes and fetches water. Then she cooks rice and the flesh of some animal and places a little on the breast, mouth, and forehead of the child. The mother then takes her child, and with it a little dhan and a sickle to the house of another woman who has children living. The dhan and the sickle are left there and others brought in exchange. If after several girls have been born a son appears, the parents sometimes celebrate the event by killing a bull and feasting the villagers.

xvii. *Ear-piercing.*—This must be done within two months of birth. The parents must remain chaste for the remainder of the month in which the piercing is done, so most of them perform it on the last day of the two months. Some time later, within a year or two, the *Ale-we* genna is celebrated. The father and mother keep apart for five days and the mother and child eat together. During these days the mother does no work. When the child is two or three he gives a feast to his little friends—this is called *Muchāzue*. This terminates the ceremonies connected with birth and childhood.

xviii. *Ikhuichi* = boys' dormitory, *Iloichi* = girls' dormitory. Even if a boy has an unmarried sister he may sleep in his father's house, but from shame he does not. The girls mostly sleep in the *Iloichi*.

xix. *Marriage.*[1]—Price having been fixed by negotiation, the dreams of the young couple are noted; if those are

[1] Compare with the account of the Memi marriage ceremonies from Colonel Kennedy's note given in Part IV. The two accounts do not tally precisely.

favourable, both families prepare *zu*. An old woman goes from the bridegroom's house to that of the bride, taking with her two pots of *zu* and two hoes. She receives two pots of *zu* in exchange from the bride's house. On the day fixed for the marriage the bride is taken to the groom's house and they exchange leaf cups of *zu* which they have each made ; the cups are hung on opposite walls of the house. The bride gives her cup with her left and the groom with his right hand. That night the pair remain chaste. The next morning the girl's ear-rings are removed and she bathes and fasts, taking only *zu*. She stays in her new home, her husband going elsewhere ; he makes a new bamboo spoon and puts it in his house and goes back to the *Ikhuichi*. On the following day he returns to his house and makes a new hearth and brings a new pot and the pair eat together ; then the bride goes to her home, but returns in the evening with friends carrying food and drink, and the elders of the *sagei*[1] are called and drink, and then the younger members feast, and from then the young couple live together. After the marriage, in the month of *Sa-le-kluh* or *Chi-thu-ni-kluh*, June or December, *Salani* has to be performed. This is a two days' feast, during which the males of the *sagei* eat apart, using clean fire. The bride's parents send twenty or thirty loads of food and drink and all the males feast thereon. The people of the groom's *sagei* make a collection, which the groom gives to his father-in-law.

xx. *Mengu.*—On the death of his wife, the husband must give her parents a hoe ; but sometimes on her death-bed she tells him to give something else as well, in which case he must do so.

After marriage the young couple live with the husband's parents, but build a new house as soon as possible.

xxi. *Illegitimate Children.*—The parents are made to marry ; if they are of the same *sagei*, or of *sageis* which cannot intermarry, or if the father cannot be found, the girl is turned out of the village. She may return later, but must not

---

[1] *Sagei* = sept. *Cf.* Tengima *saiyeh*, which is no doubt the same word, though in this case *thino* would probably be used by a Tengima as equivalent *sagei*.

bring the child. It was declared that no case of irregular intercourse within prohibited degrees was known. Such intercourse would be punished by a tiger eating the culprits, but the village or *sagei* would not suffer.

xxii. *Memorials of Departed Heroes.*—Rich people have stone memorials called *Katetokhu* put up in their memory outside the village. A pig is killed in the house of the deceased and cooked there. The whole *sagei* fetch the stone and place it in position, and then return and feast in the deceased's house on pork and *zu*. Everything provided must be eaten and drunk that night, and all the *sagei* must remain chaste. If all is done properly the dead will be happy and comfortable.

xxiii. *Feasts of Merit.*—The aspirant for fame must perform the Yuhongba ceremony before he can do the greater one of pulling a stone. He must give notice of his intention to do so in the month of *Bellu-khuh*, corresponding to October. He renews all his cooking pots and changes the hearth-stones, and for one month from the date of giving notice he remains chaste. During this time he is busy getting *zu* brewed; when all is ready he kills a pig and calls the villagers. His friends bring presents and contributions of *zu*, which are very welcome, for it is up to the giver of the feast to provide *zu* for all the village for the whole of the month of *U-klaw-kluh*, and if it runs short he would fall into dire disgrace. On the first of *Chi-thu-ni-kluh* he again renews his cooking pots and changes the hearth-stones, and having eaten from the new utensils he may sleep with his wife. The next or any succeeding *Bellu-kluh* he may give notice that he will perform the stone-pulling. New pots and new hearth-stones are procured and the stone-puller must keep chaste for the next ten months. In the month of *Chi-thu-ni-kluh* he gives a feast called *U-tuzur*, killing a big cow or two small ones and feeding the whole village and providing *zu* for the *sagei*. During the next month the village collects wood for *zu* making, and the puller has to provide them with *zu*. In the next month *zu* in quantities is made and stored. The stone has to be chosen during this month. Having selected the stone, he puts some *zu* and " Kollaw " leaves under it and goes home to dream ; if he does not dream at all it is bad. When the stone has been approved of, the pulling is arranged. The puller wears a special dress with a head-dress, white cloth gaiters, and special cloths ; the others all dress in their finest. Two old men dressed as the puller, except that they do not wear the special cloth *Zawshishu*, go to the stone, and one of them places some ginger and *zu* in a leaf by the stone and then lets a white chicken go that the stone may move as easily as the chicken runs away. The young men chase it and kill it. The *Mohvu* now walks round the stone with a spear in his hand and then gives the first pull. (The stone has been put on the sledge before the ceremony.) Then two chaste young men who have followed the *Mohvu* holding *Chhip-pe* wands and " Kollaw " leaves and some cocks' feathers take up their position in front of the stone and throw the *Chhip-pe* wands in the direction in which it is intended to go. They mount on to the stone and shout to it to go quickly, after which they rejoin the *Mohvu* and give a pull at the ropes. They get on to the stone a second time, and then the hauling begins, and if possible the stone must be got to the site on that day, but certainly by the next. This done, all go and drink. The *Mohvu* and the old men of each *sagei* go into the puller's house with him and an old man who has pulled a stone sits outside. *Zu* is distributed in leaves ; those inside the house except the *Mohvu* drink theirs ; the old sentry also does not drink his ; the rest of the people assemble outside, and when they have drunk their portions all shout " Ho ! " The old sentry goes into the house and he and the *Mohvu* drink. Then all go home ; the *Mohvu* and the old sentry must remain chaste that night. The next day but one more *zu* is made, and five days later a pig is killed, and the day after a cow and buffalo, and two days later whatever meat has not been eaten by the puller and his household is divided among everyone with *zu*. The village is cleared of strangers. The unmarried girls and all males are called and come with their *zu* cups, get them filled, take them home, and return and stand or sit in rows and are given drink in leaves ; this goes on for four or five days, but the cups are not brought on the later days. The puller receives small cash presents from his friends, to whom he gives a special drink. New *zu* is then prepared, and when it is ready everyone is again treated. Again *zu* is prepared, and when it is ready the villagers go and hoe the puller's field and erect the stone which all this time has been waiting on the sledge. This ends the show. The puller is not allowed to eat fowls, eggs, and certain vegetables. At every feast a Yuhongba gets two shares, a Lunchingba four, and one who has pulled two stones ten shares.

xxiv. *Calendar.*—Year begins in December which is

> *Chi-thu-ni-kluh.*
> *Chaw-zu-lappa.*
> *Thok-klulawpa.*
> *Klaw-nu.*
> *Kāna.*
> *Pu-zur-kluh.*
> *Sa-le-kluh.*
> *Raw-le-kluh.*
> *Un-ru-kluh.*
> *Moyalapukluh.*
> *Bellukluh.*
> *U-klaw-kluh.*

xxv. This month *U-klaw* is the genna of that name. The first day is *Mi-kuru-kraw;* on this day offerings are made for those who have died by fire ; on the second day, *Se-zur-kraw*, offerings are made for those who have been murdered ; on the third day, *I-kraw-ji*, offerings are made for all other deceased during the preceding year. On each evening the offerings are thrown away. The three days are very strictly *penna*.

xxvi. *Rain making and stopping.*—The *Mohvu* of every village calls for rain or fine weather and a one day's genna is proclaimed.

xxvii. *Sickness.*—Some dhan and a fowl are taken to the Maiba, who from looking at the dhan tells in which direction the fowl should be released and an egg thrown away If this does not bring about a cure, a rich man will kill a bull inside the house ; a little of the flesh from the lips, its four feet, and liver are wrapped in a plantain leaf and put in the thatch. The sick man eats a little of the flesh, and the rest is distributed round the village, each house getting a piece. If anyone were to steal the meat the patient would die. The household is *kenna* for the day.

xxviii. About the fifteenth day of the month *Chaw-zu-lappa, i.e.* January, the *Mohvu* of Mekrima has to go alone very early in the morning, before anyone is about, and build two small houses for Ura[1] and his son. In the house he places two plantain leaves and on these *zu* and ginger. He prays that all may be well with the villages. He must return to his house without speaking to anyone. This day is called *Rapekosha*. The *Mohvu* fasts and he and the whole village remain chaste, and the next seven days are *penna*. About the twelfth day of the next month the *Mohvu* again goes as before and builds one house for the servant of the god and places offerings ; this day is called *Ukruchi* and is followed by five days' genna as above. If everything is properly carried out the whole sixteen villages benefit. Should they suffer in any way they attribute it to the *Mohvu's* neglect and get angry with him and demand that he should take the necessary steps to appease Urāme.

xxix. *The Durbar at " Maikel "* (Mekrima).—This is the version given to Colonel Shakespear by the *Mohvu* of Mekrima.

Ura a god produced Jilimasa,[2] who lived in Mekrima. A cloud came from the south and had connection with Jilimasa, who gave birth to a god. On the occasion of the intercourse, a tiger was the result. Three more times the cloud came and three beings, called Asapu, Tuthoh, and Kepi, were produced. When the progeny grew up they demanded to see their father, and Jilimasa told them they must not be afraid of him when they saw him. Then she put *zu*, rice, and flesh on the plate and called on their father to

---

[1] *U-ra* here probably = *the* god, *i.e.* the particular spirit associated with Mekrima ("Maikhel") village, *cf.* para. xxix.

[2] Jilimasa is apparently an equivalent in some respects of Ukepenopfü. Compare the stories in Part V.

appear, and when he did so the first born, the god, ran under
his arm, Asapu and Tuthoh caught him by the knees, but
Kepi after one look fled to his mother. What the tiger did
was not related. Then the father carried off the god.
Then the tiger said he would become a man, and the others
said "Very well; whoever touches one of the three stones
near Mekrima shall become a man." So they ran and the
tiger got there first, but the others said it must be run again,
and they shot the stone with an arrow and so they became
men and the tiger ran into the jungle. Kepi stayed there
and was the ancestor of the Haus,[1] Tuthoh went to the valley
and from him the Meithei, and Asapu went westward and
from him the Mayang. After two months Tuthoh returned,
and after six Asapu arrived, and in the seventh month
Jilimasa gave Asapu a white cock, Tuthoh a sareng fish,
and Kepi a mithan. They were going to eat those in turn.
First the fowl was cooked and all were going to eat, when
the bird stood up in the dish, and they said "How are we
to eat this?" Then Asapu took a dao and applied magic
and the bird lay down again and was eaten. Then the
sareng was cooked and it behaved in the same way, and
Tuthoh repeated Asapu's performance and the fish was
eaten, and then the mithan was cooked and they ate as
much as they could and put the remainder in a pot, and
Kepi saying "Don't touch" went away, but the other two
put their hands into the pot and they stuck there, and
when Kepi returned they were unable to pull them out,
but he was merciful, and taking a white cock he offered to
east and west and besought *Urāme* to release them, and
when they got free they admitted that Kepi was their
superior. They put up a stone and separated and each
went to his own place, and it was agreed that the one which
looked back should pay tribute, and poor Kepi turned round
to look, and so they said "You must pay" and went away,
leaving this written on a stone and giving him a letter on

---

[1] *Hau* = Hillmen, a Manipuri term apparently used in contempt
Meithei = Manipuri; *Mayang* = men of the plains of Assam. *N.B.* The
Changs use *Haung* as a contemptuous term for plainsmen whom they
distinguish from *mǎtmei* (= "real man") which they use for all Naga
tribes.

leather which the rats ate, so poor Kepi never learnt to write.

xxx. The Mao version is a little different.

The children came to Mekrima from Keshur[1] and held the Durbar. The story of the feast is the same. When the three brothers returned they found their mother sick. The spirit son saw her first. She had fever, the tiger then came and selected the parts of her he would eat first ; then the three men came and took care of her, which pleased her, but she died and they buried her and cooked their dinner on her grave so that the tiger might not find it, therefore they may eat on graves. The names of the men are given by Hodson. Then the three men parted and each marked out his road with white sticks and many followed Alapa and Tuto. Memo wanted to go, but their father said he was to stay and eat his rice, so Mao has always stolen Mekrima rice.

[1] Kezakenoma. Compare the stories in Part V.

APPENDIX III

In dealing with the Naga tribes as a whole I should be inclined to divide them into four rough divisions :—(1) The Southern Nagas, consisting of Kacha Naga and Kabui tribes and the majority of the tribes of the Manipur State described by Mr. Hodson in his monograph and not specifically mentioned here. (2) The Western Nagas, consisting of the Angamis (including the Memi and Maram sub-tribes in the Manipur State), the Semas, and perhaps the Rengmas and the Lhotas. (3) The Central Nagas, viz., the Tangkhuls, Aos, Sangtams, Yachumi, and perhaps Changs and the Phom villages. (4) The Eastern Nagas—the Konyak tribes of Tamlu and the area north-east of the Dikhu extending along the borders of the Sibsagar and Lakhimpur districts to the Patkai range and apparently southwards along that range to the east of the Phom and Chang countries. Of the tribes east of the Changs, Yachumi and Sangtams, however, so little is known that nothing can be definitely asserted. But there is a tribe extending from the river Ti-ho (see Tuzu in maps), a tributary of the Chindwin up to the Patkoi range, some villages of which call themselves *Kalyo-Kengyu*, —*i.e.*, the men who live in stone houses, since they all use slate for roofing their houses. This is the tribe otherwise known as Bosorr or (to the Sema) as Tukhemmi and to the Chang as Aoshed. On the Burma side they are called Para. I place this tribe in the Central Naga group. It is in this unknown country that the western tribes locate the villages of Amazons, ogresses, cannibals, and tiger-men of which their legends tell. In any case, the division into four groups is at best a rough one, and of course the Manipuris themselves, despite their Hinduism, are probably of Naga stock.

(1) *Southern Group.*

KACHA NAGA (called *Mezama* by Angamis).

The only tribes of the southern group which are located inside the Naga Hills administrative district are the divisions of the Kacha Nagas, the Zemi, Lyengmai, and Maruong-mai. These tribes are situated to the south of the Angamis and have been very much influenced by them, the Zemi having been long virtually subject to the Angami village of Khonoma. The Angami dress is worn, though the kilt is merely put round the body and not fastened between the legs, and in some villages the exogamous clans have the same names as those in Khonoma. Some of the more northern villages along the Barak river have terraced fields—in some others jhuming prevails. The languages are quite distinct from the Angami, and each of the three divisions has its own. These Kacha Naga tribes seem to be closely allied to the Kabui tribe in Manipur, and some of the Kacha Nagas are situated as far south as the North Cachar Hills. The dancing and singing of the Kacha Nagas and Kabuis are of a very much more advanced development than is found among the Western Nagas, and the "morung" is an important feature of the village.

The Maruong-mai are said to practise teknonymy.

A grammar and vocabulary of Empeo (the name given to the Kacha Nagas in Haflong and probably equivalent to Maruong), together with a short account of the tribe and its manners, customs, and beliefs, was compiled by Mr. Soppitt ("Short Account of the Kacha Naga (Empeo) Tribe, with Outline Grammar," C. A. Soppitt, Assam Secretariat Press, Shillong, 1885). Sir George Grierson ("Linguistic Survey," Vol. III, Part II) classes the Kacha Naga language in the Naga-Bodo group.

(2) *Western Group.*

I have included with the western group the Memi and Maram Nagas and the Lhota tribe. Both these have been otherwise classed by Sir George Grierson on the score of language. As regards the Memi and Maram sub-tribes, however, he says that he might equally well have classed them with the Western Nagas. So that I think I need not further apologise for having done so myself. As regards the Lhotas, I have grouped them with the Angamis, Semas, and Rengmas on other than linguistic grounds,[1] as there seem to be several points of varying importance in which the practices of the Angamis, Semas, Rengmas, and Lhotas generally agree in differing from that of the Central Nagas and Konyak tribes. Seven points may be mentioned :—

(1) *The Use of Tattoo.*—Tattooing is not practised by any of the Western Nagas, though it is practised by all the central as well as the Konyak tribes.

(2) *Disposal of the Dead.*—All the Western Nagas bury their dead. The Central Nagas and the Konyak tribes expose their dead on " machans," the latter treating the head separately. The Changs, however, practise burial not infrequently, while the Yachumi are said to bury their dead beneath the deceased's bed, throwing out any bones they may find there in digging the grave. This is quite contrary to any practice of the Western Nagas. The Tangkhuls bury their dead, but they continue to erect over the grave a model of the " machan " as used for the body by the Aos.

(3) *Disposal of Heads taken in War.*—Heads taken in war are buried or hung up outside the village, usually in some particular tree, by the Western Nagas, whereas the Central Nagas hang them up in their houses.

(4) *Knowledge of the Legend of the Dispersion from the Kezakenoma Stone.*—The legend has been given in Part I of this monograph. It is known to all the Western tribes,

---

[1] At the same time a comparison of Lhota with Inseni-Kotsenu Rengma (not given by Grierson) shows much similarity.

and so far as I can learn it is not known to the Central tribes. It is certainly not known to the Aos. In several other cases I have found that legends known to Angamis, Semas, and Lhotas alike are not known to the Aos and Changs, who do, however, know one another's stories.

(5) *Method of Sowing.*—The Western tribes when jhuming sprinkle the seed paddy carefully and cover it with earth (using a hoe) after sowing. The seed is spaced to facilitate subsequent weeding. The Aos and other Central tribes merely throw down their seed broadcast on the ground and leave it to take its chance, and to come up very thin in places, in others so close that weeding is very difficult. The Tangkhuls, however, have adopted terraced cultivation.

(6) *Stone-pulling.*—The practice is common to all the Western Nagas except the Semas, who believe that they used to practise it formerly (*vide infra*). It is not practised by the Central tribes, except the Tangkhul.

(7) *War Drums.*—All the Central tribes make large wooden war drums of the trunk of a tree hollowed and carved to represent a mithan or other animal. These drums are, at any rate by the Aos, regarded with a good deal of veneration and play an important part in village ceremonies. They are not made by the Western tribes, except in one or two Sema villages bordering on the Sangtams and occupied by men of the Chophimi clan, which is almost certainly of Ao or Sangtam origin itself.

An eighth point of contrast might possibly be found in the method of taking oaths (see under Aos).

It is no doubt possible that these points of resemblance and difference are adventitious. In any case, all Naga tribes seem to have had, in part at any rate, a common origin ; but for the purpose of dealing with a number of tribes like those inhabiting the Naga Hills some sort of grouping is desirable, and perhaps that sketched here will serve as well as any other. The Lhotas have undoubtedly been affected by Ao influences, an explanation of which is offered in the note on the Lhotas.

ANGAMI (called *Tsungümi* by Semas, *Tsüngung* by
Lhotas, *Monr* by Aos).

The Angamis fall roughly into five groups, the Chākrōma,
Tengima, Chăkrĭma (or Chĕkrăma), Kezami, and Memi.
The first two, and as far as possible the second two, have
been dealt with in this monograph. The Memi have also
been touched on, as one village at any rate falls into the
Naga Hills District, but a fuller account of them has
already been given by Mr. Hodson in his " Naga Tribes of
Manipur."

SEMA (SIMI) (called *Sema* by Angamis, *Chümm* by
Lhotas, *Moiyarr* by Mongsen Aos, *Simrr* by
Chongli Aos, *Sümrr* by Sangtams, *Samli* by Changs).

Of the non-Angami tribes of the Western group, the
Sema, or as they call themselves Simi, seem to be most
nearly related to the Angamis. The language shows a
very close approximation, particularly to Kezami.

The Semas are situated north-east of the Angamis and
stretch from the upper Dayang valley, where they border
on the Rengma and Lhota tribes, northward into the Ao
country and eastward across the Tizu to the Tita valley,
where they border on the Yachumi and Sangtam tribes.
The Semas of Lazemi and the neighbouring villages in the
Tizu valley differ considerably in dialect, in customs, and
in dress from the bulk of the Sema tribe grouped round the
headwaters of the Kileki and Dikhu rivers, and on both
sides of the Tizu. The Semas of Lazemi and the upper
Dayang valley seem more closely connected with the
Angamis and Rengmas and perhaps contain an admixture
of both these tribes. It is primarily the Semas east of the
Dayang valley of whom I am speaking here.

In general appearance the Sema is decidedly inferior to
the Angami. The men rarely have fine features and the
women are usually ugly. In stature and physique, however,
many of the chieftains of the higher villages, particularly
those across the frontier, can compare well with almost any
Angami. The Sema is generally regarded, and probably

with justice, as one of the most warlike of the Naga tribes, but otherwise in some respects the Sema character has been maligned, *e.g.* by Mr. Davis in the Census Report of 1891. No doubt the usual Sema oath, taken by biting a tiger's tooth and thus rendering a false swearer particularly susceptible of falling prey to a tiger, was very lightly and irresponsibly taken. But as tigers, probably once a continual source of fear when settling new villages in heavily forested country, had become almost extinct in the Sema country, this was perhaps only what one might expect to find. If the general average be taken, the morality of the Sema, judged by European standards, is probably no lower than that of any other Naga tribe, while Semas on whom reliance or responsibility is placed seem to rise to the occasion as well as most Nagas. In his domestic life the Sema man is an excellent husband and father, while the women have a far higher standard of chastity than other tribes and are very good mothers of large families.

The dress of the Sema is much more scanty than that of the Angami. Apart from cloths, the prevailing pattern of which is black with a border of three parallel red stripes along each side, the principal garment of the men is a narrow flap, about ten to twelve inches long by three to four broad, of black cloth embroidered with a few lines of red, and some times with a few cowries. This flap is the end of a strip of cloth which is rolled to form a girdle tied round the waist, and fastened so that the flap hangs down in front, though it conceals little of the wearer's nakedness. This garment is nowadays giving way to a " lengta " like that of the Aos and Lhotas, while in the villages in communication with the Yachumi and Sangtam tribes a form known as *lapuchoh* is worn, which consists of a sort of a bag which contains the private parts and is pulled up under the girdle and hangs down in a flap in front, embroidered with crimson dog's hair and a circle of cowries. The Sema women wear a short petticoat, over which a broad girdle of loosely strung beads is worn, coming down below the hips and suggesting that this was originally the sole garment. In ceremonial dress the Sema wears a cowrie apron about fifteen inches square, a red sash across his chest with a long fringe of scarlet goat's hair, a tail of basket work and human hair either hanging straight down (*asaphu*) or sticking out behind (*avi-ke-saphu*—mithan-horn-*saphu*), and a circlet of bear's hair round his head carrying two or three hornbill feathers worn as a sign of head-taking. Handsome gauntlets of cowries with a fringe of scarlet hair are worn at all times by warriors, and white conch-shell beads and boars' tusks are very popular as necklaces. The women wear heavy armlets above the elbow of some metal resembling pewter, and both men and women brass bracelets, but the men rarely, if ever, more than one on each wrist. The weapons of the Sema are like those of the Angami, except that the dao always has a long handle and the spear has a smaller head. The shield is rounded at one end and sometimes covered with mithan or bearskin. In war the rounded end is carried downwards, but for ceremonies upwards and garnished with a red and white hair plume. Some of the Semas in communication with the Yachumi and Sangtams use the crossbow. Like the Rengmas, Lhotas, and Central Naga tribes, the Sema cuts his hair in a straight line round the head, shaving below the line.

Except for the fact that he does not practise the wet cultivation of rice, the agricultural and domestic life of the Sema is very similar to that of the Angami. In the matter of manufacture, however, he is far more primitive, and while the blacksmith's art seems to be quite a new acquisition in the Sema country, the art of weaving is only known to a few villages. It is practised by the Dayang valley villages and by one or two of the villages between the Kileki and the Dayang. In the other Sema villages cloths are not woven, and it is sometimes said to be genna to weave. This latter assertion possibly arises either from an unwillingness to admit ignorance of the art, or from an attempt to explain its absence, for though some clans do not weave at all and say it is genna for them, there are also large sections which cannot weave among the clans for whom weaving is undoubtedly not genna.

In internal organisation the Sema offer a most striking contrast to the other tribes of the western group in the existence of hereditary chiefs. The chieftainship goes down from father to son, the elder sons becoming chiefs in their own villages during the father's lifetime, provided the sons are able to found separate villages, and one of the younger sons probably succeeding in his father's village. Where, however, the elder sons are not able to found villages of their own, the eldest son succeeds his father and his brothers become sort of satellites. In some cases, of course, the chief is succeeded by his brother, on whose death, however, the office reverts to the elder line. The chief is in the first instance the sole owner of land in his own village, but when the village is unable to throw out colonies the land becomes divided and subdivided among brothers, though the younger brothers who have not married by the time their father dies do not necessarily get a share. The chief's subjects cultivate land belonging to the chief and owe him labour on the land which he reserves for his own cultivation. The right to free labour, like the land, is apt to get split up where the chief's sons cannot separate. The subject cannot leave his village without the chief's consent, as he owes him various services ; but in return for service from the subjects, the chief looks after them, providing them with wives and often feeding them, or at any rate lending them food in times of scarcity. On the whole, the subject receives from his chief quite as many benefits as he gives, and the system works well. It is usually the unsatisfactory and the bad characters who try to run away or who quarrel with their chief. The subject can acquire land of his own by purchase, and often does so. In some villages, such as Seromi and Satami, the organisation is much more democratic, while the chief system hardly exists at all in the Lazemi group of villages. It may be worth notice that the Semas use the same word (*müghemi*) for " orphan," " subject," and " pauper."

Unlike most Naga tribes, the Semas show no trace of any dual organisation. They call their fathers *apo* and their mothers *azo*, which suggests that they are a branch of the division which is represented by the *Kepezoma* among the Angamis. There are a score or more of principal clans originally strictly, and still to some extent, exogamous, the name of the clans being explained as patronymics in some cases and as nicknames in others.

The Semas practise polygyny, a chief or a rich man sometimes having as many as five or seven wives, who generally seem to dwell in excellent harmony together. Premarital chastity is the rule rather than the exception among Sema women, the girls being very carefully looked after by their parents. They are rarely, if ever, married against their will, but marriage prices run high, particularly for chiefs' daughters, for whom the equivalent of as much as Rs.300/- is not infrequently given.

The religious beliefs of the Semas are broadly similar to those of the Angamis, and both public and private gennas roughly correspond, though those of the Semas are fewer and simpler. The gennas of social status are marked among the Semas by the erection of Y-shaped posts carved with mithan heads, to which the beasts are tied for slaughtering. The Sema dances are less stately than those of the Angamis, but more intricate with more movements and very much more attractive to watch. Angami and Sema singing is very similar.

As a special monograph on the Sema tribe is ready for publication, and will probably be published by the Assam Administration, no further particulars of the tribe are given here, though its position among the Naga tribes is a very important one.

RENGMA (INZONN) (called *Mezama* by Angamis, *Mozhumi* by Semas, *Moiyuï* by Lhotas, *Monr* by Aos).

The Rengmas are a small tribe of which the main body is situated to the immediate north of the Angami country. There are, however, other sections, part of the tribe having migrated across the Dayang to the Mikir Hills about a century ago, owing to the hostile pressure of the surrounding tribes, and part, a naked section, being located to the east of the Angami country and the Tizu river in Sohemi, Melomi, and Lapvomi and (in part) Temimi, which is a mixed village of Naked Rengma and Sangtam. Some Rengmas claim to be an offshoot of the Semas,[1] but the prevailing belief is that they came to their present habitations from Sopvoma in the Memi country by way of Kezakenoma. Sohemi claim to be a colony from the Western Rengmas and to have originated in a hunting party which got benighted on the bank of the Tizu. Melomi and Lapvomi are colonies from Sohemi. It is easy to reconcile these versions if we suppose that the Rengmas occupied a much larger area than they do now, and stretching eastward from their present habitat. The inroads of Angamis and Semas would account for the separation of the Naked from the other Rengmas just as the "Tukomi" Sangtams and "Lophemi" Sangtams have been pushed apart by the Semas more recently. This explanation also accounts for Rengmas who had been pushed west by Semas saying that they had come from the Sema country. Genuine Aos who have been pushed back north by the Lhotas are sometimes said by the other Aos to be of Lhota stock "because they have come from the Lhota country." That it is the true explanation is shown by Sema villages west of the Tizu being called in old maps *Mezhamabagwe*, which is Angami for "formerly Rengma."

In appearance the Rengma is of poorer physique than most of his neighbours. His dress is noticeable for a very handsome cloth of broad black and white bands with three or four narrow red stripes down each side of the cloth. The women whose husbands have done the necessary gennas wear a dark blue or black cloth ornamented with cowries arranged in circles or trefoils. The wearing of cowries by women is noticeable, as among Nagas generally cowries are worn by men only, though the Sema women wear a string of cowries round the waist. The cloth worn by the Dayang valley Semas closely resembles that of the Rengmas. Ceremonial dress as worn by the Rengmas resembles that of the Semas except in the case of the Angami shield (used also by the Dayang valley Semas), the Lhota "lengta," and

---

[1] Many must have been driven out of land now occupied by Semas, a process which generally seems to cause legends of this sort, and there is no doubt some admixture of Sema blood, particularly in the Inseni-Kotsenu division of the tribe.

a sash approximating to the Angami pattern. Cane leggings
are worn as by the Angamis, and the Rengmas who migrated
into the Mikir Hills still retain the black *pissôh*, or cane
rings, worn by the Angamis below the knee. The Rengma
cuts his hair like the Sema, but generally shaving the head
a good deal higher—that is when he does cut his hair, for
he frequently allows it to grow untrimmed and unkempt.
The Naked Rengmas are really naked, wearing no " lengta "
at all, and, in the case of Sohemi, are remarkably expert
swimmers and divers.

The Rengma village generally resembles an Angami
village, but the house is built with porch resembling an apse
in shape. Morungs are built and used, being of more
importance than among the Angamis and Semas. The
polity of the village resembles that of a Lhota village.
" Jhuming " is the only form of cultivation in the Western
Rengmas, but the Naked Rengmas have excellent terraces.
Themokedima is noted for its blacksmiths.

The Rengmas are divided into two clearly distinguished
linguistic groups talking different languages. The southern
villages are known with reference to their language as
Tseminyu, and the northern as *Inseni-Kotsenu*. In Tesifima
village one clan speaks the latter and one the former. The
Tseminyu are divided into *Ketenenyu*, calling their fathers
aphu and their mothers *avyo*, and *Azonyu* using the terms
apyu and *apfsü* respectively. The *Inseni-Kotsenu* appear
to use *apa* and *azha* throughout. Among the Tseminyu, the
Azonyu are divided into exogamous clans, as are the Inseni-
Kotsenu Rengmas, but the Ketenenyu, although divided
into a considerable number of patronymic septs, form a
group still exogamous, at any rate in the large village of
Themokedima, the different septs never intermarrying, but
taking wives from the Azonyu or elsewhere.

In religion the Rengmas resemble the Angamis and Semas,
and their gennas roughly correspond. As among the
Angamis, there is a female " first reaper," and stone-pulling
is practised.

The Rengma is ordinarily monogamous, but sometimes
takes a second wife and builds a separate house for her.

The Rengma folklore and traditions approximate closely to those of the Semas and Angamis, with whom they claim a common origin. They know the legend of the Kezakenoma stone, and add to the legend given me at Kezakenoma by saying that the stone was defiled as Atalanta defiled the temple of Zeus, in order to expel the god.

Sir George Grierson's "Linguistic Survey of India" contains a note on the Rengma language and a short vocabulary, but of the Tseminyu dialect only. A list of words of both dialects has been given in Part VI.

LHOTA (KYONG) (called *Chizima* by Angamis, *Choimi* by Semas, *Tsindrr* by Aos).

The Lhotas who call themselves *Kyong* are located to the north-east of the Angami and Rengma country, having the Semas to the east of them and the Aos to the north-east. They are divided into two divisions, *Liye*, comprising the villages to the north of the Dayang river, and *Ndreng*, those located to the south of it. This division into *Liye* and *Ndreng* is dependent purely on locality, and the variation of customs between the two is very small, and no more than the presence between them of a river impassable for at least four months in the year would account for. According to existing traditions, the Lhotas moved north from the country now occupied by the Angamis, some of them crossing the Dayang near Changsang at the edge of the plains where the Bagti stream joins it, and others going north through or round the Rengma country. The villages of Pangti and Okotso mention in their gennas the name of a site called Haimung near Keromichomi in the Sema country, where their villages were located till a large number of persons were carried off by a tiger. They came to Haimung from the direction of the Themoketsa Hill (the Lhota name for it has the same meaning as the Angami name, "the place of the killing of the fowl"), having come originally from the direction of Manipur. Some fragments of stone, apparently meteoric, are still shown in Pangti as having been broken off the stone on which the paddy put to dry became miraculously doubled

and caused the quarrel separating the Angami, Sema,
Rengma, and Lhota tribes—the stone, that is, located by
the Angamis at Kezakenoma. The Lhotas believe that
they left half of their tribe to the east and that each half
regards the other as deserters from the tribe.

During the whole of this northward movement the Lhotas
seem to have been in conflict with the Aos, who occupied
the greater part of the country now occupied by the Lhotas.
At any rate, at least all the country north of the present
bridle path from Wokha to the plains was formerly occupied
by the Aos, and the conflict between them and the invading
Lhotas was so persistent that the Aos are still commonly
spoken of by the Lhotas as " Uri," " the Enemy." Whole
villages of Aos were expelled, and only a few months ago a
man of Pangti village, digging down to make a fresh foundation for his house, dug up an earthen pot full of Ao ornaments.
It was reckoned in the village that these must be at least
five generations old, and buried when the Lhotas turned
the Aos out of the village site at Pangti. It is possible
that the Lhota method of building has been affected by the
occupation of Ao villages, perhaps taken over as they stood,
for like the Ao the Lhota builds in streets, though he erects
stones to commemorate his gennas in rows down the middle
of the street. Further, while the Ao builds his house with a
raised bamboo floor, using earth, like the Kuki, only for the
hearth, the Lhota, while sometimes building on the ground
with a " machan " outside at the back only, more often
than not builds with a raised floor of bamboo which he
covers with earth all over, a process which makes the house
as dirty and verminous as if it were built on the ground,
and rather suggests that he found the Ao floor draughty or
for some other reason objectionable, and saved himself the
trouble of building a new house by just earthing it over,
and having once started the practice, adhered to it. However this may be, it is likely enough that there is an admixture
of Ao blood in the Lhotas, for it is common for an invading
tribe to incorporate into itself small bodies of the invaded.
The Changs incorporated what were once the Ao villages of
Noksan, Longla, and Litam in this way, while the Semas

across the Tizu mix and intermarry freely with the Sangtam
and Yachumi tribes, at whose expense they are migrating
eastward and seem to have already absorbed large numbers
of Tukomi Sangtams into their tribe.

Sir George Grierson has drawn attention to the resemblance of the Ao and Lhota languages, and it may be taken
as certain that there has been some infusion of Ao blood
in the Lhota tribe as now constituted, since the Aos, as
has been pointed out above, once occupied much of what
is now Lhota country, but in character the two tribes are
in many ways a contrast. While the Lhota tends to be
quiet, dour, thrifty, and on the whole perhaps inclined
to be introvert, the Ao is more extrovert, communicative,
and a ready and very voluble speaker. The Lhota is more
definitely dolichocephalic than the Ao, and like the Angami
has a tradition of having left the half of his tribe somewhere
to the east. In the Lhota case, however, this half can
probably be identified with the Southern Sangtam tribe
(see Mills, *The Lhota Nagas*, p. 4), whereas the Angami
speak of their lost half apparently as the Karen (Karenoma),
the Karen on their part, according to Smeaton (*The Loyal
Karens of Burma*), making a reciprocal claim. All that
one can say for certain is that the bulk of the forefathers
of the Naga tribes entered their present habitat piecemeal
from the east, or south-east.

In dress the Lhota resembles the Sema and Rengma.
He wears a " lengta," however, and not a mere flap like the
Sema, the " lengta " being white or blue with three red
horizontal stripes. His cloths are very carefully graded
according to the position of the wearer. Plain dark blue
or plain white cloths called *Sinimukshi* (="white and
black ") cloths with alternate blue and white stripes, *Sitamm*,
and dark blue cloths with a broad blue band, *Shipang*, may
be worn by anybody ; *Shipang* being also worn by women
as a petticoat. After a man's first social genna, called
Wozhetaksu, the cloth *Pangdrop* (black with red stripes with
a narrow white[1] band down the middle) is worn ; on the
next genna, *Shishang*, the stripes are widened, while some

---

[1] In the Ndreng villages it is a broad blue band.

of the Ndreng Lhotas, who wear *Pangchang* (black with three red stripes down each side) instead of *Pangdrop*, add red embroidered patches to *Pangchang* and call it *Sinyiku*. After *Shishang* the genna called *Eta* is performed and the cloth *Etasü* is worn ; this cloth is *Pangdrop* with still wider stripes. After *Eta* the genna *Sirutso* is performed, and this is followed by the dragging and erection of one stone, *Etu*. After the erection of this stone *Etusü* is worn. After this the genna *Esham*, the erection of two stones (*esham* = pair), is performed and *Eshamsü* is worn. *Etusü* and *Eshamsü* are classed together as *Lungpensü*. This cloth is dark blue with five stripes, about 1½ to 2 inches broad, of lighter blue, and also with narrow marginal stripes on each side, three in the case of *Etusü* and four in the case of *Eshamsü*. The man who has put a spear into the body of an enemy, even if a dead one, may wear the cloth *Chamtessü*, which is of the same pattern as *Pangdrop*, only with a blue band instead of a white one. A warrior who has taken a head may wear *Rokissü*, of the same pattern as *Pangdrop* but with figures and patterns in black gum laid on to the white band. The cloths mentioned are those in use among the more Northern Lhotas. The others vary somewhat to the south, but the *Lungpensü* cloths are universal in the Lhota country, one or two villages only using yellow stripes instead of blue.

In ceremonial dress the Northern Lhotas resemble the Semas, but use the small leather shield of the Aos, Changs, and other central tribes. The Southern Lhotas use a leather shield resembling the Angami shield in shape and wear sashes similar to the Angami sash.

Occasional specimens of an obsolete form of dao called *yanthang* are to be seen among the Lhotas, but they are preserved as relics, not used. They belong to that type in which the hilt is pointed so that it can be stuck into the ground, as in the cases of Khasia and Garo daos. A dao with this type of hilt is also used by the Kabuis, while an illustration of a dao identical with this Kabui type is given by Major Butler as a Bhutanese dao (" Sketch of Assam," p. 190). Possibly the type is of Tibetan origin. It is the top dao of those figured in the illustration mentioned.

In domestic life, agriculture, and occupation the Lhotas resemble the Semas and Rengmas. The morung, however, is more important than among the Semas and the Angamis, and there are often several in a village. The Lhotas swim and dive very well (using a stone carried in the waist-belt) and at fish "poisonings" will bring up a live mahseer weighing 10 or 12 lb., more or less intoxicated but still full of kick, which they have caught in 30 feet of water in their hands and mouths. They bite into the fish behind the head and bring it up held in that way to prevent its wriggling out of their grasp. They will do this sometimes in muddy water merely, without using any "poison." The Lhotas also make dug-out boats which they use on the Dayang. No other tribe in the Naga Hills District makes boats of this sort, though the Aos and Konyaks of Tamlu make bamboo rafts.

In internal organisation the Lhota is very similar to the Angami. The polity of the Lhota village, like that of the Angami village, is democratic, and the exogamous system of the Lhotas corresponds very closely to that of the Angamis. There is a division of the tribe into two bodies, one of which call their mothers *Ayo* and the other *Apvu*. The former are again divided into two groups, *Muripvi* and *Ngulipvi*, as in the case of the subdivision of the Angami Kepepoma into Thevoma and Sachema. The latter remain in one group, *Chammipvi*. The Lhota name for father, however, is constant, all three using *apo*. The real names of the three groups are *Mipongsandri* [1] and *Izumontsürre*, calling their mothers *ayo*, and *Tompyaktzerre*, calling their mothers *apvu*. Each of these groups is divided into a number of clans (*Chibu*), which in the northern villages are still exogamous, but which in some villages have become subdivided to a considerable extent. The names of these clans are in each case the names of the founders of the clan, who were originally brothers, the Mipongsandri clans being descended from four brothers the sons of one man, and similarly with the others. The name of the eldest brother is sometimes

---

[1] I am not sure of the correctness of the term "*Mipongsandri*" for this phratry.

used to indicate the group, and hence the terms Muripvi, Ngulipvi, and Chammipvi. The groups are divided thus :—

Group.		Principal Clans.
Mipongsandri	.	*Muri, Uthiu, Yamthang, Izong.*
Izumontsürre	.	*Nguli, Shitri, Humtsoi, Kithang, Mozoi, Thungwe.*
Tompyaktzerre	.	*Chammi, Kikong, Pathong, Tsoboi.*

The Lhota is ordinarily polygynous to the extent of having two wives. Three are sometimes married. A rich man almost always takes a second wife when he does an important genna, if he does not happen to have two at the time, and sometimes takes a third if he has. The girls are married young, and bride-prices are often high, varying from Rs.20/- to Rs.150/-. This price is paid in instalments which sometimes extend over ten years or so and constitute some guarantee of the wife's good behaviour, as if she gives trouble the instalments are apt to cease. Divorce is common, the reason being the youth of the brides. Whereas among the Semas and the Angami girls are always consulted before they are married, the Lhotas marry their daughters off without consulting them, and when they grow a little older they develop inclinations of their own. In most if not all villages it is the practice for a man to allow a brother or near relation on the father's side to enjoy his wife when he is absent from home for any length of time, but when this is done specific permission is given, and unless given, any interference with a man's wife during his absence would entail a claim to compensation. Any sexual relation between members of the same exogamous clan is strictly genna.

In his religious ideas the Lhota differs little from his neighbours. " Apotia " or accidental deaths, corresponding to Angami *Sesho*, entail the throwing away entirely of all the dead man's property, and his house must be vacated and left to fall to pieces, its occupant going to live in a rough shelter in the jungle near the village for thirty days. His eschatology has been noticed in speaking of that of the Angamis. He believes in a village of the dead inside Wokha

Hill on the road to which he must struggle with the spirit
Echlivanthano, to whom he gives a bead (tied to the dead
man's wrist), in return for which Echlivanthano gives him a
drink of water. The village gennas are regulated by an
official known as *Puti*, whose functions correspond to those
of the Sema *Awou*. The Lhotas used to take oaths by, and
still venerate, a huge boulder on the ridge of the Changkikung
range close to Lakuti village. This boulder is called *Diulung*
and is believed to fight with a similar boulder, on the same
ridge but much further to the north, called *Changchanglung*.
Changchanglung is in the Ao country near Waromung
village. Diulung used to fight with other stones also, and
fought with a great boulder at Lungithang called *Tarrlung*,
which it succeeded in overthrowing, so that the latter fell
into the middle of the Dayang river, where it now is. When
the floods rise above Tarrlung's head the surrounding fields
suffer great damage. These beliefs as to the fighting stones,
Diulung, etc., may be compared to the Khasi stones of
U Kyllang and U Symper mentioned by Colonel Gurdon
in his book on the Khasis (p. 170). Generally speaking,
the folklore of the Lhotas is intimately, sometimes verbally,
related to that of the Angamis and Semas, and has far more
in common with it than with that of the Aos. There is a
story current in some Lhota villages of a cave (other than
the cave of the dead) in Wokha Hill painted with pictures
of every sort of man and animal and with a mysterious
writing. There is, however, only one man living who claims
to have seen it, and he has forgotten the way back though
he has often tried to find it. He is a man of Niroyo village.
Probably the story is a myth.

The Lhotas accepted British rule fairly readily ; they
had a legend that the swallows had foretold the coming of
a white race which would unite all Nagas under one rule,
and warned the Lhotas not to fight against this race.

The Lhotas are a particularly musical tribe and pick up
bugle calls and English tunes very readily. They play the
former on long wooden trumpets ; the latter are, of course,
only learnt by occasional individuals whom I have known
to play them on the tin whistle or the concertina, learnt

purely by ear. The best song in the Lhota country is said
to be that composed on the death of Mr. Noel Williamson
in the Abor country. He had been for several years
Subdivisional Officer of Mokokchung in the Naga Hills.
The song was composed by the Lhota coolies who went
as carriers on the Abor expedition that exacted punishment
for his death, and the first two stanzas run as follows, repetitions and meaningless sounds interpolated in singing
being omitted :—

Chopa tyindro okaro Williamson, Williamson, youngest of the sons of the Sahibs,[1]

Ndi 'rina tchhücho la ? What enemy killed you ?

Kipangri na tchhücho. He died at the hands of men of Kipang.[2]

Yantsuosen elammdo wocho alo ? Did you go for gain of money ?

Nyingthang elammdo wocho la ? Or did you go for the sake of honour ?

Mongsanguri elammdo wocho sana? Or did you go to kill an enemy ?

Chopa tyindroi panina The great ones for some of our young men

Nchingtsungo wothan erhema tsata This very day are coming to take to go with them.

Pongla yingsang kumoina tchhü-chola ? On what mountain did he die ?

Zakto echa ! Show us quickly !

Kipang tyindro pani chenini, Two brothers, men of Kipang

Ndotsosi etsuo Williamson tsen-sochola ? Why did you kill Williamson Sahib ?

For the Lhota language the best authorities are the Rev.
W. E. Witter—"Outline Grammar of the Lhota Naga
Language," Calcutta, 1888—and Sir George Grierson's
"Linguistic Survey." Neither, however, contains any
specimen of the language. It has been mentioned that Sir
George Grierson has classed Lhota with the central Naga
languages. He bases his classification on the position of
the negative, but notices that Angami shows a trace of the
negatives preceding the verbal root in *m'bawe* (= is not).
He might also have instanced a similar trace in Sema,
where the ordinary word for "don't know" is *mta* (< *mo iti
ani*). The Sema and Lhota vocabularies show a number of
similarities, *e.g.* :—Sema *apu* (= boy), Lhota *epue* (male),

[1] The youngest of many sons is believed to be the best of them all.

[2] Kipang—the village which was responsible for Mr. Williamson's murder.

Sema *illi* or *ali*, Lhota *elue* (= girl), likewise the suffixes -*khu* (Sema) and -*kho* (Lhota) to denote the female of animals, and such words as *iva* (Lhota) and *aïveh* (Sema) = leech, for which the Angami again is *reva*. The Aos call it *pangchu* or *pangchi*.

A monograph on the Lhota tribe is at present being written by Mr. J. P. Mills, now Assistant Commissioner at Mokokchung.

(3) *Central Group*.

The difference between the Western and Central groups has already been dwelt on. One characteristic which holds good of all the tribes here classed as " Central," except the Chang and Phom, is the use of the termination -*rr* or -*rü* or -*re* to denote the men of a given village or tribe, turning a place name into a collective noun.[1]

Ao (AORR) (called *Cholimi* by Semas, *Uri*or *Chongli* by Lhotas, *Aorr* by Sangtams, *Ao* by Changs, *Païmi* by Konyaks).

The Aos claim to have come from six stones called Lung-trok (*lung* = stone, *trok* = six) on the hill of Chong-liemdi east of the Dikhu, and more or less opposite Longsa village.[2] There is a legend that the Aos, Changs, and Semas were all one, but there was so little room at Lungtrok that they split up, the Changs going one way, the Semas another, and the Aos coming west across the Dikhu. This legend, however, does not agree with the Chang and Sema accounts of their own origin, the Sema in particular disclaiming any

[1] See Assam Census of 1891, p. 175. Mr. Clark denies that it means " man," and says it is the present tense of an old verb " to be." For every example given by Mr. Clark, however, there is an exact parallel in the use of the Sema termination -*mi*, which is identical with the Angami -*ma*. Whatever the precise original meaning of the terminations -*ma*, -*mi*, and -*rr*, they have clearly the same force in use, and there is no reason why the words for " man " and for " being " should not be in some cases virtually equivalent.

[2] Mrs. Clark (" Ao Naga Grammar ") gives a legend of the Chongli to the effect that they and some Ahoms came into the Ao country together, the Aos settling at Chongliemdi and the Ahoms at Longmisa (or *Tsimer menden* == Plainsmen's site); the Mongsen Aos being also settled near Chongliemdi when the Chongli were at Chongliemdi itself.

connection with the Ao, whom he scorns, and derives his origin from Japvo mountain to the south. The Aos at one time inhabited the country now occupied by the Lhotas, or at any rate all of it as far south as Chingaki at the least, and the Sema country as far south as Emilomi and the Kileki river, and some Aos who are said to be of Lhota origin by their brother Aos seem to have been Aos who came north-east again when driven out of their villages by the Lhotas.

The people of Yacham and Yiong, and also of Tangsa, all just east of the Dikhu, which is the Ao border, seem to be very closely connected with the Aos, though speaking somewhat different dialects.

The Ao is apt to be a fluent talker and very voluble, not least in disputation, and an excellent carrier. The women are good-looking, but the men, except in Nankam village, are perhaps of poorer physique than their neighbours. In dress and weapons the Ao has borrowed much from his neighbours. The present Ao " lengta " is believed by the Lhotas to have been copied from theirs, while the ceremonial " lengta " is called *Moiya langtam* = " Sema apron." The men are not tattooed, but the women are tattooed on the chin, neck, bosom, arms, and legs. The patterns of the arms and legs are different for Mongsen and Chongli women, but the four vertical marks on the chin running down into an $\times$ pattern zigzag of two lines ending between the breasts is the same for both. The tattooing is done with an adze-shaped implement set with cane thorns like the bristles of a tooth-brush, only much longer. The end of this implement is ham-mered into the body with a hammerlike root and the process is excessively painful. Girls being tattooed have to be held down by several men, and the process occasionally cripples a girl for life, and sometimes causes her death. The women wear brass rings on their heads (rather like the Eastern Angami, but threefold instead of single) and great squares or circles of crystal in the lobes of their ears.[1] In ceremonial dress they cover themselves with bells. The Chongli women tie their

[1] A precisely similar ornament is worn by the Tangkhul women in the Somra tract, who say that they get them from the plains of Burma.

hair with black plaits of human hair, the Mongsen women with white cotton.

The Ao house is built on a machan, all except the front room, which serves the purpose of a porch and a pigsty. The fireplace is made on a square covered with earth as in a Kuki house. The village is built in streets with the eaves of the houses touching one another, so that a fire runs from one end of the village to the other. It is usually situated on the top of a ridge rather than on a spur like the Angami village. There is an excellent description of an Ao village, taken from a Survey report by Colonel Woodthorpe, in the Assam Census of 1891 (p. 242). The Ao's house is cleaner than the houses of the Western Nagas, but his feeding habits are filthy, as the Ao never washes any of his utensils ; he will offer you drink in a cup caked with the dirt of years, and cooks and brews in like vessels, offering in this respect a great contrast to his Sema and Lhota neighbours. His person, too, is usually dirtier even than the rather grimy Sema, and as he smokes incessantly and never cleans his pipe, he always stinks of tobacco fouling and nicotine. The women smoke too, using both wooden and iron or brass pipes.

The Ao community is controlled nominally by a council of elders (*tātăr*), who deal with disputes in the community and usually exact a fee for the dealing of justice, or injustice, for they are by no means always fair. The *tātăr* also, on payment of a fee, allow members of the community to put on boar-tusk necklaces, cowrie gauntlets, warriors' cloths, and other insignia of war and head-hunting which have not been earned in any way at all except by the payment of three or four rupees.

The Aos are divided into two groups, distinguished by the language used. These two groups, Chongli and Mongsen, exist side by side in many Ao villages, speaking dialects so distinct that they might almost be called different languages. Not unnaturally in the majority of Ao villages one dialect or the other has got the upper hand and become the ordinary language of the village, but there are villages in which there are, here and there, both Mongsen Aos ignorant of the

Chongli and Chongli Aos ignorant of the Mongsen dialect, and it is common for Chongli and Mongsen Aos conversing together to speak each his own language. The word for " father " varies little, being *oba* in Chongli and *aba* in Mongsen, but the word for " mother " is *ocha* in Chongli and *ave* (or *avü*) in Mongsen, except in the Yimchen clan (Mongsen Airr) of Nankam, where the word for mother is *ala*. Chongli and Mongsen are alike divided into three exogamous clans (*kidong*), Pongen, Langkam, and Chami, who take precedence in that order, and may not intermarry even with the corresponding *kidong* of the opposite linguistic division.[1] Although the exogamous nature of these units still persists, many sub-clans have come into existence. Both the clans and sub-clans are, generally speaking, patronymic. They observe a number of food tabus, some of which are mentioned in the Appendix on Totemism. There seems to be no conscious totemism underlying these food tabus.

In religious observances the Aos are noticeably more prolific than their neighbours. At the Tsingemung genna the young men and girls have a tug of war. The men have to pull uphill, but there is little real pulling. The women sing while pulling. The war-drum is looked upon almost as a village god. When it is burnt a new one is carved out of a whole tree and pigs and chickens are sacrificed to it. The priest harangues it and calls upon it, among other things, to protect the village from venereal diseases, after which it is dragged to the village.[2] *Amung* (abstention from work, Angami *penna*) is found, and so are other gennas of various sorts. Contributions are levied yearly for the performance of sacrifices and for the entertainment of distinguished guests. This levy has recently been divided by order of Government into two parts, in order that the Christian Aos, of whom there is an increasing number (it

---

[1] Mrs. Clark mentions a tradition to the effect that there was a time when the Chongli and Mongsen did not intermarry at all. I once asked an old Ao of position whether he knew of a time when the Chongli and Mongsen did not intermarry. He said he had never heard of such a tradition, but that as they spoke different languages it was possible ; until comparatively recently Ao-Sangtam marriages were rare.

[2] Compare the pulling of a village door by Angamis.

pays the Ao financially to turn Christian), may not be called on to bow the knee in the house of Rimmon. The levy for the entertainment of distinguished guests is called *Aksü*. The guest is given a definite part of the animal slain and the rest is eaten by the elders. There is a special branch of *Aksü* known as *Sibainga Aksü*, levied in the clan for the entertainment of related clans in other villages, in order to keep up the memory of the relationship ; at times of distress certain nominal services are expected from a clan in one village by its relation in another—*e.g.*, when a village is burnt related clans send a small present, a couple of daos and some rice, or something of that sort, to the village in trouble,[1] while if a man dies away from home it is the duty of the nearest clan related to the one to which he belongs to bring home his corpse. There is nothing religious in the *Sibainga Aksü*.

Egg-breaking is practised by the Aos for the taking of omens, the omen being determined by the fall of the pieces of the shell, as among the Khasis (Colonel Gurdon, " The Khasis," p. 106), though with less elaboration. No board is used ; any flat stone will do.

The Ao method of taking oaths contrasts with that followed by all the western group of Nagas. Both parties must take the oath (by biting a bit of the disputed land, sacrificing a chicken, etc.) and an account is kept for thirty days, and whichever suffers a misfortune (from his own illness or death to the loss of a chicken or a pig, or even the most trivial mishap conceivable) within that time loses the oath. A form of ordeal is also practised, both parties beheading a chicken. The party which fails to make a clean job of it in one stroke loses.

The Aos are notorious for the unchastity of their women. Divorce cases are never-ending. From a tender age girls are free to do as they like before marriage, and are thus with difficulty prevented from doing so afterwards. The unmarried girls sleep in small houses, built for the purpose, in twos and threes, and the unmarried men sleep with them,

---

[1] When such a present is given by one village to another it is called *ubocha* (" father calling ").

only the quite young boys remaining in the "morung." The Ao house has no outer room, as the Sema and the Angami houses have, that is convenient to sleep in, and it is regarded as improper for any except very small children to sleep in the same room as their parents. The result is that quite young children sleep in the "morung" or in the girls' houses. The Christian villages have resorted to a girls' dormitory with an aged dame in charge, but it may be doubted whether they are very much more chaste than their heathen sisters.

When dead, the Ao is smoked in his own porch and buried on a platform with his ornaments, utensils, and weapons, or with wooden imitations of them.

The Ao legends and folklore approximate more closely to those of the Sangtams and Changs than to those of the Lhotas and Semas. They do not seem to know the story of the Kezekenoma Stone, but many of their stories, unknown to the Western Nagas, are identical with those of the Changs.

The chief authorities for the Ao language are Sir George Grierson ("Linguistic Survey of India," vol. iii, part ii, pp. 269 et seq.) and Mrs. E. W. Clark ("Ao Naga Grammar. with Illustrative Phrases and Vocabulary," Shillong, 1893). The latter deals with the Chongli dialect only. The dialect spoken by Changki and some of the neighbouring villages differs much from the ordinary Mongsen dialect, of which it seems to be a branch.

SANGTAM (PIRR,—ISACHANURE) (called *Lophomi* or *Tukomi* by Semas, *Sangtamrr* by Aos, *Sangtam* by Changs).

This tribe appears at one time to have stretched right down the east border of the Aos and Semas from the Chang country to that of the Tangkhuls and Naked Rengmas, but has become separated into two divisions by an eastward movement of the Semas and a westward movement of the Yachumi. The tribe is now divided into two or three distinct groups, the northern separated by Sema and Yachumi villages from the rest. The northern group known to the Aos as " Sangtamrr " from their principal village, seem to call themselves *Pirr*, while the central group are said by Mr. Davis (Grierson, " Linguistic Survey," vol. iii, part. ii, p. 290) to call themselves *Isachanure*, though *Tsingare* was the form given me by Yezatsimi. The two groups, northern and central, are called by the Semas *Lophomi* and *Tukomi* respectively, and these two words have been used in this book to distinguish these two groups of this tribe. The third group I have called South Sangtam. It includes the villages of Primi, Photsimi, Phozami, and probably Thachumi and Thomami, all of which adjoin the Naked Rengmas. Temimi is partly South Sangtam, partly Naked Rengma. Karami, Niemi, and other villages to the east belong to the Kalyo-Kengyu tribe and not to the South Sangtams.

Little is known about the tribe generally. The Lophomi group seems to resemble the Aos most nearly, though finer in physique and greatly superior in war and hunting. The Tukomi group, which used to extend quite as far west as the Tizu valley, has mixed a good deal with eastward-going Semas, who quickly gain the ascendancy in most Sangtam villages which they enter.

As in the case of the Aos, the women are tattooed in the calf and arm, but the men not at all. In many villages the women are also tattooed on the forehead and chin.

The language is classed by Sir George Grierson as Central. Mr. Davis mentions that it resembles Lhota in sound.

Like all the central Naga tribes except the Aos, the Sangtam use the crossbow, which is not employed by any of the western tribes, except by such villages of the Semas and Naked Rengmas as have borrowed it from their Tukomi neighbours. In their dress the northern Sangtams resemble the Changs, while the southern dress more like the Yachumi.

The course of Sangtam migration is said to have been from Yatsimi to Yezatsimi (both " Tukomi ") ; thence to Katarimi (now Sema), thence to Kungizzu (a vacant site in what is now Sema territory), and thence to Tsantomghi, where the village of Sangtam was founded whence all the " Lophomi " villages derive their origin. The Pirr villagers themselves, however, merely told me that they came from Chongliemdi, still in Sangtam territory but on the line of the above sketched migration.

YACHUMI (YACHONGR). (called *Yachumi* by Semas, *Yamsongrr* by Aos, *Yamchongrr* by Sangtams, *Yamsung* by Changs).

This tribe, calling itself *Yachongr* and called *Yachumi* by the Semas, is situated at the head of the Tita Valley and borders on the Changs, the Sangtams (on two sides), and the Semas (on the west).

Little is known about the Yachumi. The termination in -rr suggests a fairly close connection with the Aos, as in the case of Sangtams. The Yachumi are less warlike than the Semas, who dominate the nearer villages and take tribute from them. The Changs, however, claim close kinship with the Yachumi.

The Yachumi use a shoulder-headed hoe not unlike that of the Khasis (see Colonel Gurdon's monograph, p. 12). The Yachumi name for it is *thou*, the blade alone being called *yünchi*. The Yachumi are said to bury their dead beneath the deceased's bed, throwing out the bones of any of his ancestors that are encountered in the process. The Kiungrr clan of the Yachumi is believed to correspond to the Awomi clan of Semas.

The Yachumi do not appear to tattoo.

CHANG (called *Mochumi* by Semas, *Mochungrr* by Aos, *Machongrr* by Sangtams, *Mojung* by Konyaks of Tamlu).

This tribe, sometimes spoken of as " Mozung," is situated across the Dikhu to the east of the Ao country. Its principal village is Tuensang (or " Mozungjami "), and from this village all or most of other Chang villages are derived. The tribe is very warlike, being second to none, not excepting the Semas. They are of fine physique, tall but lean. They wear a small " lengta " like the Sema *lapuchoh*, and that worn by Sangtams and Yachumis, worked in red dog's hair and with a circle of cowries. The Chang belt is very noticeable, being a band four to six inches broad, sometimes worked with circles, more often completely covered with cowries. The red dog's hair, like the red goat's hair on the dao-handle and sash, is explained as representing the fire which they apply to the enemy's village ; the cowrie circles represent the moon ; and the trefoil and quatrefoil groups of three or four cowries each, with which they also embroider "lengtas" and belts, represent the stars, as raids are undertaken by night by the light of the moon and the stars. The dao-sling is more of the nature of a sheath than is the usual Naga wooden sling, as it is made of a flat piece of wood eight inches long with edge and guards to keep the dao in. The dao has a long blade and a long handle and is drawn from the back over the right shoulder. The Changs are very skilful in the use of the crossbow and use poisoned arrows for hunting, but not for war, except in the case of a village which is hard pressed by an attacking party and has poisoned arrows handy. The use of poisoned arrows in war is regarded as unfair, and a war party does not take poisoned arrows with it when going on an expedition. Warfare among the Changs contains a number of such conventions.

The poison on the arrow is covered with a leaf, and a man wounded with a poisoned arrow can save his life by cutting out the head before the poison under the leaf has got wetted by the blood, as it takes some time for the poison to get wet and it does not act until it does so. A man so wounded will eat raw gourds (because they are " cold ") and the dung of dogs and chickens (" because they are the nastiest things known "). If any inconvenience is experienced from eating the flesh of an animal killed by a poisoned arrow, a little of the poison itself is eaten as medicine. The poison is made from the sap of a tree.[1]

The houses are built on the ground as far as the hearth and the remainder on a machan, so that the inner room is half on the ground and half raised. The village is built in streets if possible.

The Changs have an æsthetic sense more highly developed than their neighbours. They practise a sort of " poker-work," burning patterns on bamboo or wood, which i very

[1] See Appendix XIII p. 459.

handsome. The main theme of the pattern almost always takes the form or a variation of the form of the pattern tattooed on the chest of a warrior. Men who have taken heads are tattooed with this pattern, which resembles two or four conventional leaves springing from a common stem. The women have a diamond-shaped patch tattooed on their foreheads and either vertical or horizontal lines (the custom varies in different clans) on their chin. They also have two rays tattooed from each corner of the mouth. This tattoo is put on before

PATTERN TATTOOED ON THE CHEST OF A CHANG WARRIOR.

puberty is reached. After tattooing, the girl's hair is allowed to grow and she is married about two years later. From the time she is tattooed she has to observe the food tabus observed by women. Before tattooing she can eat all that men eat. The poker-work ornamentation is used for drinking-horns, pipes, dao-slings, and any other wood-work. The Changs are also good at cane-work, though their cane helmets and gauntlets are imported from the " Aoshed "[1] tribe to the east of them. This tribe also makes the axe-shaped dao used by the Naked Rengmas and other tribes, which used to be used by the Changs at one time.

The Chang polity resembles the Sema somewhat in the existence of chiefs in each village, though they are not so powerful as the Sema chiefs, since they have not the same monopoly of land. They also resemble the Semas in having no clear dual division, for though the tattoo on the chin is vertical in some clans and horizontal in others, the names for " father " (apo) and " mother " (anya) are constant, and the clans seem to derive their origin from a single, not a dual stock. The Changs seem to be divided into the following clans :—Chongpo (subdivided into Shangdi, Hangwang,

[1] See below, under " Kalyo-Kengyu."

Hagiyung, Ungpong, Maava), Ung, Lumao, Kangcho, and Kudamji. These clans are exogamous. Unmarried girls are not expected to be chaste.[1] They sleep in the outer room of the house, into which the young men force their way at night, the girls defending themselves with sticks and firebrands. Intrigues of this sort are, however, usually followed by marriage with the lover. Strangers are never admitted in this way.

The Changs have a superstitious awe of tigers and pythons. One of the subdivisions of the Chongpo clan (Chongpo Hagiyung) is regarded as being intimately connected with tigers, and its members are lycanthropists like the Semas, while it is genna for all true Changs to touch tiger or python, though the former is killed when accidentally encountered and the latter under certain circumstances. When a tiger is killed the man who killed it is genna for thirty days and may not leave the " morung " during that time. Pythons are killed under the following circumstances. In times of famine someone, probably one of the most severely affected by the famine, will volunteer to kill a python, and everyone in the village will subscribe rice and salt, chillies, etc., and send this man out to kill a python. When the man finds a python he will say to the python, " I am going to cut you here," " I am going to cut you here," threatening it with his dao in different parts of his body, but not in the real place, as if he did this the python would turn the edge of his dao like a stone. He then says to the python, " When I have cut you, give me all your wealth " ; saying this he cuts him through the neck. He then throws away the dao and spear which he was carrying, and the clothes he was wearing, and returning to the village remains thirty days in the morung. During these thirty days he cannot cook rice in earthen pots, but must use bamboos only for cooking. Persons bringing him food must not put it into his hand, but place it down and go away. When this thirty days'

---

[1] Pairs of lovers sometimes sleep together in the jungle, but while they have connection a bough of a tree must be pulled down for the girl to recline on, so that the leaves prevent the face of the man from looking at, or being seen by, the earth. Afterwards the bough is released and allowed to swing up again.

genna is over, a pig is killed and the war-drum is beaten
by the young men at dawn, and, when the men go to the
fields, also at midday and finally at sunset. The village
burier is sent for. He takes a chicken and lays upon its
head all the misfortunes liable to come to the clan from
the killing of the python. He then cuts off the chicken's
head and tears out its liver, spitting the latter in three pieces
on a bamboo skewer. Everyone in the clan spits on the
chicken, the males on the liver, and the females on the body.
Children too small to spit have some spittle taken from their
mouth on their parent's finger and put on to the chicken.
The people as they spit say that their misfortunes shall fall
on the chicken's head. The body and head are then impaled
on a panji outside the village. The liver is stuck on to an
arrow and tied up near the body, so that the arrow may
drive off the avenging spirit that is angry at the python's
destruction.

In their folklore and legends the Changs show great
resemblance to the Aos, but the account of their origin is
different. They believe that they came up north from the
Tizu Valley and that they are connected with the Yachumi.
They give the following account of the separation of the
Naga tribes :—

In the beginning a rubber tree (*Chong*) was felled by the
founder of the Chongpo clan. The top branches were taken
by the Semas, Yachumis, Sangtams, Aos, Aoshed and
Konyak tribes. It is the tops of trees that sing, and these
tribes carried off the tops singing, and left only the trunk
and roots for the Changs, and these make no sound. Therefore it is that the Chang songs are poor compared to the
singing of other tribes. When the rest of the tree was
divided the ancestor of the Ung clan said, "I am going home"
(*ungla*). Hence the name of that clan. One share was
spoken of as loot (*mawü*) and hence the Lumao clan. The
ancestor of the Kangcho clan said he had lifted up (*kang*)
his share. The Kudamji went to look for water, but the
others had taken it all and there was none left, and so they
are always poor. They get their name because when they
went to war they came up last and only got the *kudam* (the

last and inferior share) of the enemy's head. They are like the "huluk," ape. It, too, was too late to get any water, and now never drinks from streams at all, but catches it in the hands from rain or off leaves.

Some of the Changs bury their dead (inside the house), some expose them on platforms. In either case some six months to a year later the head is wrenched off or dug up and cleaned, and taken to the heir's house and put under the bed while a feast takes place, after which it is returned to its grave or put back under the platform, as the case may be. In the latter case the exposed body is buried after the joints have been counted to make sure that none are missing. A fire is built under the machan to show by the smoke which way the wind is so that the smell may be avoided.

The Chang language is grouped by Sir George Grierson, who gives a vocabulary, in the eastern sub-group with the Konyak tribes. I am very doubtful whether I ought not to have grouped the Chang tribe likewise myself. In grouping with the central Nagas I have relied on its folklore, which connects it with the Aos, on its own claims to connection with the Yachumi, and on a superficial resemblance to the Sangtams in appearance and in dress. The Konyak tribes to the north of the Phom country are naked. The Changs believe that about three generations ago all their customs and dress underwent a radical change, and that platform burial was then introduced because someone remarked that it was not possible to breathe under the earth. It was at this time also that the practice of tattooing was adopted from the Phom and Konyak tribes to the north and east of the Changs.

PHOM.

This tribe consists of four villages only, Hukpang, Pongching, Ourangkong, and Mongnyu, and seems closely allied to the Changs. The tattoo pattern of the men is the same, but while the Changs cut their hair like Lhotas, Semas, Aos, Sangtams, and Yachumi, the Phom sometimes have a lock hanging down behind, suggesting some of the Konyak tribes which border on them. The tattoo of the women is different from that of the Chang, as the Phom tattoo them on the legs and not on the face. The Phom women also wear different beads from the Chang women, though the men dress exactly the same. Mirinokpo or " Assiringia " village in the Ao country, which Sir George Grierson mentions, is a colony from Ourangkong in the Phom country. The Phom expose their dead on platforms, keeping the head in the house for a month.

KALYO-KENGYU.

This is a name [1] for the tribe living to the east of the Changs, Yachungs, and Sangtams which is used for the tribe generally by some of the villages of that tribe situated east of the Changs, whence the tribe extends southwards as far as the Somra tract, including, among other villages, Makware, burnt in 1911, Niemi, and Karami. The tribe is called *Aoshed* by the Changs, *Tukhemmi*, apparently, by the Semas, and *Para* on the Burma side. This tribe is noted for its ironwork, its daos and spear-heads being particularly fine, also for red cane helmets and leggings, and for blue cloths with red squares of dog's hair embroidery. Its country is so far unexplored.

(4) *Eastern Group*.

KONYAK TRIBES (called *Taprongumi* or *Minyumo-Nagami* by Semas, *Mirirr* by Aos, *Chagk* by Changs).

I have used the word " Kŏnyăk " for the tribes to the north-east of the Aos and Changs, the group spoken of by Mr. Peal as " lying between the Dikhu and the Disang rivers and north of the Patkai " range, and " all reputed to be descendants of one village called Changnyu : a sort of tribe-mother to whom many of them salaam, and annually

[1] *Kalyo-Kengyu* = " Dwelling in stone (*i.e.* slate-roofed) houses," slate being used instead of thatch for roofing, as it is the best, if not the only, material available locally.

send small presents, which, however, are not tribute." It is possible, however, that I should have done better to include the Changs with the Konyak tribes. The names *Kŏnyăk* and *Hāhā* are applied by the people of Tamlu to themselves and to the very closely related tribes to the east of them, whose clothes, nakedness, method of hair-dressing and tattooing present great similarities. The names both apparently refer to method of hair-dressing. These tribes are known usually by their Assamese names as Tablungias, Banparas, Mutonias, Namsangias, etc. Until quite recently they were all naked tribes, and even now only those quite near the edge of the plains wear an apron. This dress is, however, spreading further into the hills and the expression " Naked Nagas " for these tribes has ceased to serve. Tamlu adopted a short blue apron within the memory of officers now serving on the Assam Commission, and Wanching (Tablung), Wakching (Jaktoong), and the neighbouring villages, are now in the process of adopting it. Very tight belts are characteristic of the men of these people. They are made of cane or of the bark of the " Agar " [1] tree and reduce the waist of the wearer to a very small compass indeed. [2] The hair is allowed to grow in a long tail, which in some villages is wound up into a knot at the back of the head about a wooden or bone support which passes through the hair horizontally. In this, and particularly in the physical appearance of the women, some of these people remind one in a way of the Kuki tribes, and there would seem to be an undoubted touch of Shan blood in the villages round Tanhai and Pungkhung (Borgaon) above Choraideo in Sibsagar. This is the place where the Shans are believed to have emerged into the plains of Assam from Burma, and later on an Ahom king of Sibsagar took refuge in Tanhai when dethroned, and married Watlong, the daughter of the chief. Later he was restored to his kingdom, and went down to

[1] *Aquilaria agallocha.*
[2] They seem to abide by Mr. Neil Munro's way of thinking, when he exhorts young men to " keep down the waist o' ye," since

> " Endurance and elegance, youth, dash and daring
> Depend on the belt ye can put round your wame."

Choraideo with his Naga bride, preceded by dancing and
singing. As part of her bride-price he built a tank, a paved
road, and a stone bridge, the remains of which may still be
seen at Tanhai, where the footprints of the king and of his
horse are also shown. The word used for tank in Tanhai
is a Shan word, and other Shan words are in use in the
language. The Konyak men artificially blacken their
teeth. All along the edge of the plains they are confirmed
opium eaters.

The houses of the Konyak tribes in the Naga Hills District
are built partly on the ground and partly with a raised floor.
The " morungs " are large and have great posts carved with
the figures of men, tigers, snakes, monkeys, etc. The upright
poles project through the roof and are thatched over with
straw, which is tied in to the post at intervals, giving an
effect decidedly suggestive of the pinnacles of Sibsagar
and other Assamese temples.

The Konyaks of Wanching and Wakching are great
makers of daos, for which they have a large market.

The Konyak tribes immediately east of the Ao country
are divided into two groups, *Thendu* and *Thenkoh*. The
Thendu tattoo their faces while the Thenkoh do not. The
tattoo on the women of the two divisions is different also,
and there is said to be a further division of the tribe generally
into three classes,[1] the chief or Ang in all villages being of
an exclusive class which takes precedence of the other two
and always provides chiefs.[2] The men are tattooed on
taking a head, but in the villages recently annexed where
heads are no longer available the young men have taken to

---

[1] *Cf.* the division of the Aos into Chongli and Mongsen with different
tattoo patterns crossed by a triple division into three clans of which the
Pongen probably corresponds to the Ang clan though it has not the same
pre-eminent position in the tribe. It does, however, take precedence of
the other two and is considered in some way superior.

[2] These chiefs must be of Ang blood by *both* parents. An Ang (at any
rate if he is chief of his village and not merely of the Ang clan) marries
as his principal wife the daughter of the Ang of another village, and only
a son of such a union can succeed to the chieftainship, though an Ang
usually has many subsidiary wives taken from other clans, and children
by them.

assuming the tattoo after the pretended killing of wooden figures.

The dead are buried on platforms like those of the Aos, after being smoked, but the head is wrenched off later on and put in an earthen pot which is thatched with palm leaf and put under the machan, the heads of the dead being ultimately collected in one place.

The married women are in some villages quite naked. In others they wear a very narrow horizontal strip of cloth, which though sometimes only about four inches wide contrives to be perfectly decent. The unmarried girls are naked, but wear a cloth when they leave the house, at any rate when there are strangers about.

There is in several superficial details a likeness to Angami Nagas, otherwise so extremely different, which must be more than fortuitous, and suggests that at some time the tribes were in contact one with another, or in common touch with some other people from whom they borrowed the same habits. Although none of the tribes in between wear them, both the Angami and Konyak tribes wear the cane knee-rings, though the Konyaks dye theirs red. Both tribes, and none of those intervening, make a bugle of the buffalo horn. Again, both the Konyak tribes and the Angamis weave precisely the same variety of palm-leaf rain-cloak worn by none of the tribes in between. Rain-hats too, though not of quite the same pattern, are very similar, and again are not used in the same way by the intervening tribes. In one Konyak village I found a woman making twine and cloth of fibre exactly like that used by the Angamis, and called *gakeh*. This is not used by Semas, Lhotas, or Aos, though the Yachumi are said to make cloth from nettle fibre (Angami *wüve*). Finally, the Angami method of hair-dressing, leaving a lock behind and tying it into a knot and wearing a fringe in front, also suggests the Konyak method.

"Notes on the Naga Tribes in Communication with Assam," by John Owen (Calcutta, 1884, W. H. Carey & Co.), deals with Konyak tribes. Sir George Grierson gives a survey of the language spoken by them in his " Linguistic Survey of India " (Vol. III, Pt. II, p. 329). Mr. S. E.

Peal's " Eastern Nagas of the Tirap and Namtsik " (*Journal of the Asiatic Society of Bengal*, No. 1 of 1896, p. 9) deals with related tribes, as also does the same author's " Visit to the Tribes inhabiting the Hills south of Sibsagar " (J.A.S.B. Pt. I, No. 1, 1872), and the account of " the Nagas " in Major Butler's " Sketch of Assam " (Smith, Elder, 1847).

AUTHOR'S NOTE TO APPENDIX III, SECOND EDITION

Since the above was written much work on the Konyak Nagas has been done by Dr., now Professor, Christoph von Fürer-Haimendorf—see his article on " The Morung System of the Konyak Nagas, Assam " in the *Journal of the Royal Anthropological Institute,* vol. LXVIII, 1938, and his " The Naked Nagas ", London, 1939.

A small volume on the Nagas of the Tirap and Namtsik valleys has been published by Sri Parul Dutta of the North East Frontier Agency under the title of " The Tangsas " (Shillong, 1959).

Names used by some of the Naga Tribes

(The name the tribe uses for

Names of the tribes in common use in English.	Angami.	Sema.	Rengma.	Lhota.	Ao
Angami	*Tengima*	Tsungimi	Tsugenyu	Tsüngung	Monrr
Sema	Sema	*Simi*	Semu	Chümm	Moiyarr (Mongsen) Simrr (Chongli)
Rengma	Mezama	Mozhumi	*Nzonyu*	Moiyuï	Monrr
Lhota	Chizimi	Choemi	Tsugwenyu	*Kyontsü*	Tsindrr
Ao	—	Cholimi	Nankanyu (< name of village Nan-kam)	Uri (= "the enemy") Chongli	*Aorr*
Sangtam (northern) „ (others)	— —	Lophomi Tukomi	—	—	Sangtamrr
Yachumi	—	Yachumi	—	—	Yamsongrr
Chang	—	Mochumi	—	—	Mochungrr Mozungrr
Konyäk	—	Taprongumi Minyumo-nagami	—		Mirirr
Kacha Naga ...	Mezama (pronounced slightly differ-ently from the word for Rengma)	—	Mezhenu	—	—
Foreigner (of the plains)	Teprima	Koiami	Asanyu	Osomm	Tsimarr

N.B.—The Angami word for the Rengmas, Mezhama or Mezama, is also used for all the Aos for the Rengmas and any one else to the south of them. In a similar way the Semas use the indefinitely. The names Konyäk and Haha are used in Tamlu and Wakching for their own

for one another and for foreigners.

itself is printed in italics.)

Sangtam.	Yachumi.	Chang.	Konyak.	Kacha Naga.	Foreigners.
—	—	—	—	—	{Dawansa (Kachari) {Gnamei (Manipuri)
Sümrr	Shimrü	Samli	—	—	—
—	—	—	—	—	—
Taünrr	—	Tsinrü	—	—	{ Lhota Naga Miklai (both used by the Assamese. Miklai < the village Mekula)
Aorr	—	Ao	Païni	—	Hathiguria (Assamese)
{Pirr {Isachanure	—	Sangtam	—	—	—
Yamchongrr	Yimchurr	Yamsung	—	—	—
Machongrr	Machungre	Chang	(?) Mojung	—	—
Tablungre	—	Chagk	Konyǎk or Hǎhǎ	—	" Lengta Naga," Tablengia, Bordubia, Namsangia, etc.
—	—	—	—	Zemi Lyengmai Maruongmai	—
Litsürr	—	Chanap Haung (= West plainsman). Chang Haung (= East plainsman, i.e. Burmese)	—	—	—

other tribes north and north-east of them collectively, just as the Ao word, Monrr, is used by the expression *Tushomi* for the tribes to the north and east of them—Sangtam, Yachumi, Chang, etc. and similar tribes and refer primarily to the method of hair-dressing.

APPENDIX IV

TOTEMISM

I HAVE said nothing about Totemism in the text of this monograph, as I have not been able to discover any trace of it, or of anything approaching it, among the patronymic and omnivorous clans of the Angamis. There are, however, one or two traces of ideas which may be totemistic among other tribes, and as the close connection of the Naga tribes is indisputable, it is possible that these ideas are, or have been, also present among the Angamis, particularly as the various clans of one tribe often point to clans of other tribes with which they believe themselves related. The belief in such a relationship usually seems to be based on pure tradition, such as that connecting the Lankamrr clan of the Aos with the Shitri clan of the Lhotas. Other reasons, such as similar food restrictions, are said to exist. If they do exist, it is possible that they indicate an organisation in exogamous clans dating back to a time before the present division into tribes speaking different languages. On the other hand, three of the clans of Lazemi of the Semas claim connection with some of the clans of the Angami village of Kohima, but the connection seems to be based on an admixture of blood, which may be the real reason of all such alleged relationships between clans of different tribes.

Among non-totemistic tribes one might expect to find traces of totemism, if any existed, in stories of their origin, and in their tabus on foods, and here and there we find, not only a story of descent from some animal or plant, but also a corresponding tabu. These, however, are very rare.

Among the Lhotas we have the Tsoboi clan of the Tompyak-
tserre phratry, which traces its descent to a woman who was
weaving, when a hornbill (*Dichoceros bicornis*) flew over
and dropped a tail feather into the partially woven cloth.
She put the feather into her waist-belt (or wove it into the
cloth) and became pregnant as a result. Some members
of the Tsoboi clan and the allied clans of Chammi and
Kikong abstain from the flesh of the great hornbill, but the
tabu is neither universal in the clans nor very strict, nor
is it prohibited to kill the hornbill. There is a corresponding
clan among the Aos ; the Wozakumrr kindred of the Pongen
clan have a similar story of their origin and tabu the flesh
of the hornbill. In the story of the Wozakumrr, the feather
was put into a basket and then turned into a stone. This
was thrown out and turned into a bamboo. This turned
into a man, who refused to have anything to do with anyone
but the woman who had picked up the feather, and the
Wozakumrr are descended from this pair. The other
clans used to deride their descendants as the children of
a bird, and they denied this and resented the imputation
so much that it led to fighting. In the fight a man of the
Wozakumrr was killed down by the river and his head taken
and his body cut up into bits. Then the hornbills came in
numbers and washed the bits of flesh with water from the
river. The Wozakumrr fled, but seeing what happened,
saw that it was true that they were of hornbill descent and
admitted the justice of the imputation, to which, however,
they still strongly object.

These stories of a hornbill ancestor are particularly
interesting in view of the great veneration with which the
hornbill is regarded by all Nagas of whatever tribe and
whatever clan ; its flesh is not eaten by any of the Sema
tribe, but it is to be noticed that among the Aos to tell
a man that he belongs to the family of the bird is a piece
of very serious abuse. The words, " You are of the Wozakumrr, don't come near me " (*i.e.*, because I am of the
genuine Pongen clan, or of some other clan descended from
human parents in the orthodox way), is a saying that has
led to fines of many pigs, whether actually addressed to

one of the Wozakumrr or to someone quite unconnected with them. Again, while most Semas tabu the flesh of the great hornbill (*Dichoceros bicornis*) but do not mind killing it, it is genna for all true Semas so much as to touch the *awutsa*,[1] which the Ayemi clan sometimes assert vaguely to be in some way related to them,[2] though their descent is definitely derived from a human progenitor, and they go further than the Tsoboi and Wozakumrr in that, as a rule, they refrain from killing it. It is, however, the great hornbill which the Semas, like all other Nagas, regard as the emblem of bravery, its tail feathers being the insignia of the successful warrior. The selection of the hornbill by Nagas is easy to understand. It is the largest bird in the country, of magnificent appearance, and makes a great impression soaring slowly overhead with very loudly whirring wings, audible at a distance and height at which the bird itself is barely visible.

Another case which appears to be totemistic at first sight is to be found in a claim of the Zümomi clan of the Semas to be descended from a certain red plantain, from eating which some of them abstain. This explanation, however, is open to grave suspicion. I have been told at least six explanations of the name Zümomi, all quite different, all equally far-fetched, and all from Zümomi men themselves. Besides the plantain story, there is one which ascribes their origin to a spring in some red earth in the Sema country, another which explains the word as meaning those who drink from large plantain leaf cups (because the clan were originally few in number and therefore had plenty of liquor—which does not follow at all), and there are other similar stories. The real meaning of the name, however, is said by all the other Sema clans to be " men of no blood "—*Azhü* = blood, *mo* = no, *mi* = men. The ancestor of the Zümomi was the bastard son of a girl called Putheli and the whole genealogy is known. The various explanations

---

[1] *Aceros Nepalensis.*
[2] The explanation of its tabu which is usually given, however, is that anyone eating its flesh is liable to choke with . dry, coughing sound, like that emitted by the bird.

of the word given by the Zümomi themselves are, as their
very variety and discrepancies show, merely attempts to
evade the slur of bastard origin. Putheli was the daughter
of Kaghamo, ancestor of the Chesholimi and Chishilimi clans,
and it is almost certain that she really was the ancestress of
the Zümomis and an historic character ; the clan is one
that has sprung to pre-eminence among the Semas comparatively recently and in a few generations. They were
originally a small group which left the village of Awohomi
to found Nunomi, and all the present Zümomi villages are
colonies from Nunomi, most of them having been founded
within the memory of man. It is conceivable that the
story of the ancestry of the Tsoboi and Wozakumrr may
have really originated in an accident, such as that which
happened to Putheli, in which case the hornbill might
have been chosen to take the responsibility owing to the
veneration in which it was already held.

There are two other instances of quasi-totemistic ideas
among the Semas which are worth mentioning. One
is the tabu of a species of edible fungus by the Asimi, or some
of the Asimi clan, on the ground that it grows in large
quantities at that place where the ancestors of the clan
emerged from the earth, the soil being particularly rich at
that place, a story which does not quite fit in with the
usual account of descent from the man Nikhoga, the ancestor
of all the Semas. The other is a connection which is believed
to exist between the Wotsami clan and the huluk ape. The
flesh of the huluk is tabued to the Wotsami because some
of the clan turned into huluks after their death. This clan
is generally looked down on by the other Semas ; it is
small and poor and scattered. It is sometimes said to
correspond with the Shitri clan of the Lhotas, but without
any apparent reason and in the face of apparent probabilities.

It might, of course, be argued that the totemistic and
quasi-totemistic ideas which I have mentioned are survivals
of what was once a complete totemistic organisation, in
which case it would be possible to give the names of several
of the Naga clans a totemistic origin. *Thevoma*, for instance,
the name of one of the largest of the Angami clans, might

be translated " Pigmen," and *Awomi*, the name of a Sema clan, the same. The condition, however, of the Naga languages makes any such translation wholly unreliable. It is, moreover, totally at variance with the tradition of the clans themselves and with their own explanations of their names, which are in most cases patronymic, though these are sometimes explained as nicknames. It is likewise always possible that even if the names of clans proved to be the names of plants or animals they might have been acquired in some such way as, for instance, the village of Setikima and Khonoma get their names. Setikima means " the men of the pipal tree," the name being taken from a huge pipal tree on the crest of the cliff selected by the village for its site, while the name of Khonoma, properly Kwünoma, is taken from the name of a species of tree felled in large numbers when the site was cleared.[1] As these villages contain men of several clans, a totemistic explanation of the name is hardly possible. It is possible, however, that some totemistic idea may underlie the nicknames by which Naga clans sometimes explain their clan names, and a few instances are given from the Sema tribe for what they are worth. Similar instances have already been given in the notes on the Chang tribe in Appendix III.

The Semas have a story to the effect that one Nikhoga was the first man. He had six sons, but could only find a wife for the eldest, and as the others kept intriguing with the eldest son's wife, he determined that the other five must separate and make families for themselves. Accordingly he made a feast, cooked rice, and killed a pig, a dog, and a goat. The second son (the eldest, *Asimi*, stayed with his father) chose the dog's head, and so his family are named *Chunimi*, " Eaters of everything," like the dog. The third chose the pig's head, and his descendants are called *Awomi* (*awo* = pig). The fourth called out and made a

---

[1] Men of such a village migrating to another village might form a clan in the new village which would be known as *Setiki-nu-ma* or *kwüno-nu-ma*, as the case might be. Instances of such nomenclature are to be found in Angami villages (*v.* App. X), and if the original village were forgotten owing to migration an ætiological explanation of the name of the clan would naturally arise.

noise when carrying firewood to cook the feast, whence the clan of *Ayemi* (*yeye* = chatter). The fifth, who was the first to start eating rice, founded the *Achumi* (*ana* = rice, *chu* = eat). The sixth stood looking on silently and not joining the others, so his descendants are called *Yeputhomi* (*aye* = clan, *putho* = silence, depth, though the ordinary meaning of *putho* is " night.") [1] These explanations of clan names are clearly not of the sort one would care to put much faith in. The names of many of the clans are patronymic. Chesho and Chishi, the sons of one Kaghamo, founded the *Chesholimi* and *Chishilimi* clans, the *Kinimi* are descended from Kinishe, the *Khakulimi* from Khaku. The names of other clans are explained in similar ways, the name of one of them, *Wotsami,* being given because the founder, when trying to snatch some rice from a pig, got bitten by it in the hand (*awo*=" pig," *aou*="arm," *tsa* means " bite "). It is interesting to compare these explanations with some of those given by the Changs, to which they are very similar. The Wotsami, who are looked down on by the other Sema clans and who are in some way associated with the " huluk " ape, may be compared to the Kudamji clan of Changs, which are also looked down on and also regarded as being like " huluks." The fact that the Aos despise the only one of their clans which claims descent from a bird has also been noticed.

Tabus of flesh among the Semas and Aos have been mentioned. To quote one or two instances, the Awomi clan, and its branch the Kinimi, of the Semas tabu the flesh of both dogs and goats. Here it should be noticed the Awomi while tabuing dog and goat meat, explain their name as meaning " Pigmen." Among the Aos the Chongli division eat all flesh except in the case of the Pongen clan, which abstain, or used to abstain, from dogs, though recently they have taken to eating them, owing, as they say, to the medicinal qualities of the meat (a connection between the Pongen clan of the Aos and the Awomi of the Sema is sometimes propounded owing to a common tabu of dog's

[1] Another version makes the Ayemi and Yeputhomi descend from one father named Kaka.

flesh). The Mongsen Aos all abstain from frogs and from pig's intestines, while the Yimchin and Achonchangrr abstain from beef, dog's flesh, and the remains of tiger or leopard kills. These abstentions from certain foods do not seem to me in any sense totemistic, but of a nature similar to the food tabus observed by Angami women or by Angami men who have done the Zatse genna. In all Naga tribes the women are subjected to a much stricter series of food tabus than the men. The cases of abstention from the hornbill, and perhaps from the " huluk " monkey in the case of the Wotsami, fall, of course, into a different category, but as regards the abstention from various other meats, I think myself that the origin is originally due to a fear that some bad quality of the thing eaten will enter into the eater, or to a belief that such food has proved dangerous to the eaters in some particular case. In this connection Mr. Hodson (" Naga Tribes of Manipur," p. 199*a*) writes " that there are tabus affecting social units both among the Meitheis and the Nagas, is a fact upon which I cannot insist too often or too strongly. In so far as Colonel Shakespear has found evidence of the origin of these tabus among the Meitheis, it is clear that the objects tabued are believed to have been proved dangerous to some individual member of the social unit." One is reminded of the reason given by some Semas for reaping by hand only, because one man once slashed his stomach and killed himself when reaping with a dao.

Not is it by any means impossible that the tabus affecting the hornbill and the " huluk " among the Semas, and the python among the Changs, have not had a very similar origin. How easily such a notion may spring up can be gathered from a single instance which came under my notice of a tabu on an Angami. I was going up from Zubza to Kohima with Srisalhu, of Khonoma, when we met a large snake in the road. I started to beat it, but Srisalhu would not join in. When I had killed it he said that it was *kenna* for him to kill snakes. The reason was that his home in Khonoma, or rather his father's home, had been inhabited by a snake. When Srisalhu removed to a new site the snake appeared in the new house.[1] It still lives in Srisalhu's house and is frequently seen, having survived two rebuildings. This fact impressed Srisalhu, who talked it over with the other men of his kindred, who considered that a man who had a snake like that in his home ought not to kill snakes at all. Accordingly it is now regarded as *kenna* for Srisalhu and his household to kill snakes. If Srisalhu's descendants are prolific this *kenna* will doubtless in time affect a whole kindred.

In conclusion, I cannot do better than quote Mr. Hodson again : " What these facts seem to prove is the existence in this area not so much of totemism, as of a mental attitude, a *Weltanschauung*, which in other parts of the world have permitted totemism to flourish and prosper."

For a survey of totemism in Assam seen in its relation to totemism in India generally, see J. V. Ferreira's " Totemism in India ", Bombay, 1965.

[1] It might easily be transferred from one building to another in a " dhuli " of paddy or in part of the thatch.

APPENDIX V

OF THE FAMILY

As will be seen from the foregoing pages, there is very little trace or indication among the Nagas of anything but a patriarchal constitution of society. There are, however, one or two points which should be noticed, in that it is possible that they may be taken to be survivals of a different organisation of the family.

The supreme deity of the Angamis, Ukepenopfü, has a female termination, and though sometimes regarded as having male attributes, she appears in at least one legend as a woman. This might perhaps suggest that the matriarchate at one time existed among the Naga tribes, as it is undoubtedly remarkable that a people with such patriarchal instincts should have a female as their supreme deity. On the other hand, it may be pure chance, as there are other Angami deities with the same female termination, Telepfü for instance, as well as " ropfü," while the Sema supreme deity, Timilhou (= " creator of man "), seems to have purely male attributes. It is, however, interesting to notice that a Naga *in extremis* almost always calls "mother, mother ! " though she may have been dead for fifty years.

I have pointed out that descent and relationship on the female side are hardly recognised at all by the Angamis, nor are they, so far as I know, by any other Naga tribe. I have found, however, one instance to the contrary among the Angamis, an instance which is particularly noticeable in view of prevailing customs and beliefs. In Kohima Village the Cherama and Rösuma clans do not intermarry, the reason given being that the founder of Cherama married the sister of Rösu, the founder of the

Rosuma clan. This reason is striking, as in all other cases of similar prohibitions of marriage between two clans or kindreds the reason given is that the clans are descended from two brothers. There is a certain mild prejudice among Angamis against marrying first cousins on the mother's side, though it is permitted by the rules of exogamy, and is nowhere regarded as *kenna*. As to this prejudice extending beyond one generation—it is a thing which I do not think any Angami would dream of propounding except in the instance given above, or in some similar case if such exists. Possibly the theory which ascribes the prohibition to a marriage between the founder of Cherama and Rōsu's sister has been invented to explain a prohibition the reason of which has been forgotten. The explanation that the founder of the Cherama clan of Kohima and Rōsu were brothers was barred by all the village traditions, which draw an explicit distinction between the Cherama and the six Pferonuma clans. Perhaps a prohibition which applied to one generation only has been accidentally perpetuated, or it is a survival of a matrilineal system. However that may be, the prohibition remains and the reason given by the Angamis is relationship on the female side.[1]

As for the position of women in the family, the head-taking genna as observed in Kohima which has already been described suggests a position of some authority for aunts on the paternal side. Women, however, are generally somewhat prominent in head-taking, sisters owing a lock of hair to their victorious brother and unmarried girls refusing husbands who had not taken a head.

S. E. Peal's ingenious theory of exogamy and premarital licence has been mentioned in Part III. In view of that and other theories of exogamy a Sema legend of the origin of exogamous clans is interesting. Nikhoga, the first man, had six sons, but was only able to find a wife for the eldest. Consequently the other five were always intriguing with their brother's wife until Nikhoga drove them forth to found separate families and ultimately exogamous clans. This story might perhaps support Peal's theory, or it might

[1] *See* Appendix XIII, p. 460.

suggest some period of polyandry in the past. It has been suggested that the promiscuous relations between the sexes before marriage are the result of ignorance as to the cause and method of procreation. This theory has to be reconciled with the practice of abortion and infanticide by unmarried girls. Where the cause of pregnancy was not known, it is difficult to see how shame can have attached to it in the case of the unmarried as distinct from the married, and unless the institution of marriage was subsequent to the acquisition of knowledge on this point, one would have expected pregnancy in unmarried girls to have been an accepted state of things. At present, when an unmarried girl does become pregnant it is usual for the man responsible to marry the girl. Chang girls seem to make a practice of admitting their lovers only on the promise to marry them later on. Moreover, as has been noticed, in most Naga tribes at any rate, probably in all, any sexual relations between two persons of the same exogamous group are regarded as criminal.

Possibly the resemblance between the Angami word for " husband " ('*nupfü*) and the Sema word for " wife " (*anipfü*) is worth notice. The Angami word appears to have a feminine termination. The Sema word for husband is *akimi* (" house man "), which seems the same word as the Angami '*kima* = " wife." In Kezami the word for both " husband " *and* " wife " is *akami*.

APPENDIX VI

THE rain-making gennas of the Angamis have been noticed, but there is rather a marked difference in the rain-making practices of some of the other tribes, which are worth alluding to.

The Semas take the head of a " huluk " ape and put it in the water at a salt-lick. They also drive a stake into the ground in the same place, saying as they do so, " *Tsüna tsüna li*," " *Ttsüna tsüna li* " (Rain, rain, fall !) and when they have finished and are going away they sing " *Tsüga thoile, yegathubo*," which is the song sung by children playing in the rain. When enough rain has fallen and they want it to stop they remove the head and pull out the stake, otherwise the rain would fall continuously.

The Lhotas also place a huluk's head in water, any stream or pool will do, and take it out when they wish the rain to stop.

Captain Porter, of the 17th Infantry, told me that when the Lhotas wanted rain they caught a land crab and tied him by the leg in a nullah, putting an egg beside him. The crab's business was to call the rain spirit, and the egg was put there for the crab to give to the spirit. If this resulted in rain the crab was let go again, but if no rain came the unfortunate crab was hung on to a tree and left to die, as being an incapable and useless intermediary. This is not practised by the northern villages.

The Lhotas also turn out in numbers and beat the earth with sticks when they want rain, calling to it to come and soak the earth well, and when going away singing (like the

Semas) "*O, dapotsisi, dapotsisi,*"[1] which is again the song sung
by children when dancing in the wet, and is almost untrans-
latable ; it represents the fall of the rain wetting their heads
and trickling down their bodies, and might be rendered
" Rain, rain, soak me."

The Changs have an ingenious method of making the
Earth ask the Sky for rain. A stake is buried horizontally
in the ground and earth broken up fine and heaped in over it.
Over all a bamboo mat is put to keep it down. A cane
thong is passed through the mat and under the stake and
up through the mat again. This thong is sawn backward
and forwards, just as the thong used on the fire-stick is
sawn, and makes a dull, groaning sound. When the Earth
calls thus the Sky hears it and sends rain in three days at
the outside.

N.B.—The use of the " huluk " ape by the Semas and Lhotas is probably
due to the Nagas' belief (which I fancy is more or less correct) that the
" huluk " never comes down to the ground to drink, but collects rain-
water, etc., from the leaves of trees. Possibly the idea is that the sky,
seeing the " huluk " reduced to drinking from pools on the ground, and
(in the case of the Semas) brackish water at that, will send rain. I have
not, however, been able to extract any explanation from the Semas or
Lhotas themselves, except that " it is the custom to do thus when rain
is needed."

[1] The Ndreng Lhotas sing "*Etsüsüsü, etsüsüsü* " referring to the coldness
or coolness of the rain. The words are " baby-talk " and not properly
formed words

APPENDIX VII

OF CELTS, AND STONES IN GENERAL

THE Angami belief that stone celts are thunderbolts
has already been mentioned. This belief is also held by
Lhotas, Semas, Changs, Aos, and other Naga tribes, and
by many of their neighbours. The Angami belief is that
the stone celt was first given to men by Ukepenopfü as an
instrument, but that the men, not knowing its proper use,
chipped and spoilt it, whereon it returned to heaven of itself.
Now it falls in lightning, but the place where it falls cannot
be found unless a man mark the exact hour and moment
of the flash and the place where the stone strikes the earth.
He should then cover up the spot with a basket or some
similar thing and look under it on the expiration of seven
years precisely to the moment of the flash, when he will
find that the stone has come up out of the earth and is lying
under the basket. Some say the time is seven months,
not years. In any case, the exact hour must be struck or
nothing will be found. The possession of a celt is regarded
by the Angamis as a sure means to prosperity and health.
It brings increase of cattle and fruitful crops. The more
perfect the celt is the more it is prized, though the Lhotas
are said to prefer them imperfect.[1]

The Semas, Lhotas, and other tribes say that the valuable
part of the celt returns to heaven in the flash, leaving
only a stone worthless as an instrument. The Aos do not
seem to prize celts at all. The Lhotas regard them with
some awe, and oaths are taken on them. The Sema regards
the possession of a celt as bringing fruitfulness to the owner's
Naga beans and other subsidiary crops of minor importance.

---

[1] As far as my personal experience of Lhotas goes the Lhota objects to
picking up a celt or even touching it at all.

These celts are called by the Angamis *methie*,[1] by the Semas *Pogopu-* or *Thogopu-moghü* (= toad's axe), by the Lhotas *Potsophu* (gods' axe), by the Aos *Kutakr-pu* or *Kutakr-vu* (= gods' axe), by the Changs *Mughka wo* (= spirits' hoe).

I have never seen shoulder-headed celts or closely corresponding iron implements as described by Mr. Peal in 1896 ("The Kol-Mon-Anam in the Eastern Naga Hills"—*Journal of the Asiatic Society*, August, 1896), although the Yachumi use a shoulder-headed hoe not at all unlike that used by the Khasis (*see* Colonel Gurdon's "The Khasis," p. 12). Of the celts, however, which I have seen, the largest is decidedly like the iron hoe still used by the Aos. Moreover, it was found quite recently in the Chebi river, which runs below Pangti, which used to be occupied by Aos till driven out by Lhotas. It is slightly worn at the shoulders. It might be compared also to the narrow iron hoe of the Lhotas or to the Angami hoe, which is on a much larger scale, but while the latter tribes lash their hoes to a crooked stick, the Aos more often insert the end of theirs into a hole in a straight stick.

The celts which I have seen in the Naga Hills are of two types, of which one is predominant, the other being very uncommon. The dominant type is roughly triangular with its widest part at the edge. The polished blade, like that of a Naga dao, is flat on one face and curved down to the edge on the other face. The smallest I have seen was about three-quarters of an inch in its widest part,[2]

[1] I have not been able to find out the meaning of *methie*, but perhaps it may be compared with the Yachumi word *thou*, meaning a shoulder-headed hoe. The Angamis also speak of celts as *terhoma guli* (= spirits' bullets) and regard them as being shot from some *terhoma misi* (spirits' gun). I cannot help wondering if whether the Sema name for celts is not a corruption of or euphemism for *teghami-moghü*, which would mean "spirits' axe." Indeed Vikhepu, one of the most intelligent Semas I ever knew, agreed with me that it was likely, but I have since found that the Sema associates the toad with the spirit Litsapa, who controls the rainfall, and this would perhaps be enough to associate the toad with the "thunderbolt." With *methie* and *moghü* we may compare the Khasi *mo-khiw* and the Burmese *mo-gyo*. *See* Gurdon, "The Khasis" (1914), p. 12 sq.

[2] Though no iron hoes as small as this are now in use, a minute iron hoe, less than an inch broad in the widest part, was found by me on the site of a long extinct Sangtam village near the present village of Mokokchung in the Ao country.

while the largest,[1] which I have mentioned as found in the Chebi river, measures 2½ inches across the blade. The other type is much longer in proportion to its breadth and perhaps resembles a Naga adze more than a hoe, though not unlike the narrow Lhota and Sema hoes. I have only seen one of this type about 3½ inches long and 1¼ inches in the widest part. These three celts and others from the Naga Hills are at present in the Pitt-Rivers Museum at Oxford. It is perhaps possible that the triangular celts were fitted into a hole in a wooden handle, while the wedge-shaped celts were bound to crooked sticks ; that is, if the two varieties of celts do not represent different races at one time occupying these hills.

The belief that celts are thunderbolts is said to be common among people who have recently emerged from the stone age, and (I quote Mr. Peal here) " it is well known that the earlier forms of iron implements and weapons are based on that of their stone prototypes." It might be added that they are also sometimes based on their wooden prototypes, for the cross-handled, iron-bladed, horseshoe-shaped hoe, used by some of the Lhotas and many of the Aos and Konyaks, is obviously based on the hoe which the Semas call *àkuwoh* or *achakha* and still use regularly, and which is made of a piece of pliant wood or bamboo bent into the form of a horseshoe with the ends prolonged to cross one another.[2]

[1] I have since seen one considerably larger. Both are in the Pitt Rivers Museum at Oxford with other celts collected in the Naga Hills.

[2] There is a method of slaughtering animals which is used in ceremonies by some Naga tribes, which may possibly be in part a survival from times when iron weapons were unknown. The animal is tied up and a cut made in the skin with a dao behind the animal's shoulder, and a pointed wooden stick inserted and driven home by hand. In the case of mithan killed in this manner by Semas the animal is also formally struck two or three times with a stick. It is easy to realise that it would take a long time to kill a mithan by beating it to death or with a stone axe, though the latter might be capable of making a cut for the insertion of a pointed stick. The Angami method of killing fowls with a stick at the ceremony of dragging the village door and with a bamboo at the Terho-rogi genna has been also noted in Part IV, as also the killing of pigs with sticks, though the latter is as much the usual method among the Angamis as the use of a pointed stick is with the Aos, both tribes using these methods respectively on ordinary occasions as well as ceremonially. These methods ensure that no blood is lost and that may be the reason why they are employed. Aos

Among the Angamis, as among all other Naga tribes, stones in general are particularly liable to become objects of superstitious awe. Many Angami clans, though not all perhaps, keep a genna stone called *Kepuchi*, usually near one of the village gates. This stone is prominent in head-taking gennas and should any earth fall on to it by any means, genna must be observed ; otherwise it does not seem to have any special significance, but may perhaps have originally been regarded as the abode of the deity of the village or locality. In Lhota morungs, too, round stones, not very large, are often to be seen, and are kept in the morung and seem to be regarded as the habitation of a spirit, but the ideas are very vague on this point. Oaths used to be taken on them.

Angami monoliths of two kinds have already been mentioned, the stones dragged and set up on the completion of the Ketseshe genna, and stones set up in memory of parents by the son who inherits the house. This latter custom only exists in some villages, whereas the pulling of stones, after the acquisition of high social standing by genna, is practised, not only by all Angamis, but by the Lhotas and Rengmas also, and possibly used to be practised by Semas. It is conceivable that the memorial stones were erected as a dwelling for the spirit of the dead, but I do not think that monoliths are usually regarded as the abode of spirits. A case came to my notice of a stone being dragged for a monolith which was regarded as possessed and was abandoned. In January, 1913, Zavire of Phulama went out with almost all Phulama village to pull in a stone. This stone was very big and could not be moved by the men who had gone to pull it. When the news reached the village a man named Pusann went out and helped to pull the stone, although he had a quarrel with Zavire. The instant Pusann started to pull, the stone moved as though it had lost its weight, but Pusann fell under the sledge and was nearly killed. His thigh was broken ; and the stone was abandoned. It was held to be *kenna* to bring in that or any other stone when killing a mithan ceremonially spear it after tapping it on the fore-head with a pointed stone. The Lhotas used, I believe, to kill mithan for ceremonial purposes by beating them to death long after it was usual to spear them for purposes other than ceremonial.

on that day. About five days later a small stone was pulled in.

Stones of noticeable appearance or peculiar shape or large size readily become the objects of awe. At Phesama there is a stone named "Nyielo," which may be seen white and shining in the bed of the stream. The raising of this stone is believed to be followed by fierce storms of wind and hail such as are related to have occurred on the occasion when the stone was first noticed. Phesama were fishing in the stream and rolled the stone to the bank. A storm got up immediately, so they rolled it back, when the wind and storm were miraculously stilled. Another case in which a stone was held responsible for storms came to my notice in Jotsoma. The late continuance of the March winds, in 1913, which were seriously interfering with terraced cultivation, was put down to the taking back to the village of a curiously-shaped stone by one of the Jotsoma clans. It was asserted that the winds would not stop until this stone was put back in the place from which it had been taken, and I was asked by the Tekronoma clan to compel the Tsyama clan to put it back.[1]

Special stones are regarded as the abode of spirits all over the Naga Hills. The Kezakenoma stone and the dream stone of Viyakiricha at Khonoma have been mentioned. So has the Lhota stone "Diulung" at Lakuti. At Nankam, in the Ao country, there is a pair of stones male and female, to which offerings are made, and at Longkai, a Konyak village, there is another. But these are only one or two among hundreds. At Lumami, in the Sema country, for instance, there is a stone at the side of the Government path to which everyone who goes by offers a present of a pebble or a bit of stone picked up from the path, making a pile of small stones which periodically slips down, to be picked up by other passers-by and presented again. There are one or two particularly interesting stones in the Sema country. At Natsimi (Cherema) there is a stone which has, at the time of writing, a new and widely increasing cult, particularly amongst the neighbouring Rengma villages. When I saw it, it was about 18 inches long, of an oily appearance and black in colour, quite unlike any local rock which

---

[1] *See* Appendix XIII, p. 460.

I have seen. It was roughly wedge-shaped, about 4 inches broad at the base and 4 or 5 inches in height. It proved to retain a surreptitious finger-print, but to leave no oil or grease on the finger. In 1912, when I saw it, it was said to have been in existence for six years and to have grown during that time from a hand's length to three times as long. It is said to change colour and to be quite white at times. It was found in a jhum field and transferred to a sheltered corner at the side of a cliff, where only one or two can come near it at a time. On genna days the neighbouring villages come and offer it pice. Many pice are always to be seen round about it, but I suspect the lion's share goes eventually to the "interpreter" of the stone, who holds converse with it in his dreams and asks it questions about the future. Omens as to trading ventures are taken on the stone itself by seeing whether a pice placed on the stone slips off or stays on, this depending partly, at any rate, on whether the "interpreter" places the pice near the apex of the wedge or towards the base where the slope is steeper. The stone takes human form at night, and it is in this form that he first appeared to his votary and told him to remove the stone from the field, and it is in this form that the latter meets him in his dreams. The approaches to the stone are marked with the remnants of numberlesss offerings of eggs, fowls, and pigs, and fowls released at the spot are reputed to stay-there of their own accord. I am myself inclined to regard the "interpreter" of the stone, who was also its discoverer, as an unrecognised genius.[1]

Black stones said to be similar in composition to that at Natsimi, but smaller and usually rounded, are kept by all tribes as charms, particularly for crops. They are said to "sweat" freely[2] and to breed, getting offspring like themselves, but smaller. They are called *thego* by Angamis, who keep them in the dhan dulis in their houses. It is genna to show them at all among Angamis. The Semas abstain from vegetables after touching them. Most tribes keep them in a pot or some such place covered with paddy, as they store their grain outside the village. Similar charm-stones are kept for success in warfare and in hunting.

[1] *See* Appendix XIII, p. 460.
[2] If the thumb is rubbed across one of these stones it leaves a wet mark.

The former are said to have white spiral lines on them and the latter to resemble a deer's foot and are cloven. The crop charms are feasted with bits of meat once a year. The others when their aid is required. The only charm-stone I have seen[1] had scratches on it said to be a test of its genuineness and the result of its fighting with mice in the owner's house. I was told that if I broke it I should find it white inside.

In Lazemi there is a pair of stones, male and female, which cohabit and breed, and whose safe-keeping and propitiation are looked on as very necessary to the prosperity of the village. No one knows where they are, except the priest and two of the old men of the village who unearth

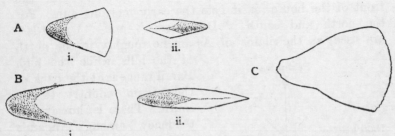

A. Sketch to show shape of triangular celt, i. surface, ii. side view.
B.   ,,   ,,   wedge-shaped celt.
The dotted part represents the surface left unpolished.
C. Outline of large celt found in the Chebi River.

them every now and then—about once in three years. The stones are said to come to the surface of their own accord at the proper date ; after they have been feasted with due ceremony they are again buried in private by the priest and his companions. I have met the idea that stone can produce offspring in other places in the hills and boulders or stones rounded by the action of water, etc. seem sometimes to be regarded as in a different category altogether from rocks and broken bits of rock, or the rough stones of which the soil is full. Mr. Hodson in his " Naga Tribes of Manipur," gives a number of Naga beliefs as to particular stones.

[1] I have seen a number of others since.

APPENDIX VIII

Points of the Compass.—The Angamis naturally take the rising and the setting of the sun to distinguish east and west, though the latter is also called " the side behind the house " because an easterly aspect is preferred for the front of the house, as it gets the early morning sun. For the north and south " Downwards " and " Upwards " are used, as the plains of Assam lie roughly to the north of the hills, while the high Barail range is at the back of the Angami country to the south. There is, however, a tendency among Angamis who have been to school to use " Upwards " for the north and " Downwards " for the south, because maps are printed with the north at the top and the missionaries at Kohima have inverted the Angami terms to suit their convenience in teaching. The south is given by McCabe as *Chakritsa* (*i.e.*, " Chakrima side ") but this can only apply to certain villages.

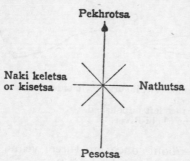

Pekhrotsa

Naki keletsa or kisetsa

Nathutsa

Pesotsa

POINTS OF THE COMPASS.

The Sun and Moon.—The moon and sun are regarded by the Angamis as male and female,[1] man and wife, respectively. The sun, being a woman, is afraid to go out at

---

[1] The Khasis also make the moon male and the sun female, and explain the spots on the moon as the result of ashes flung at his face. (Col. Gurdon, " The Khasis," Second Edition, p. 172). A similar story is reported from Mexico, though it is a hare that is flung at the moon instead of ashes or dung.

night and therefore moves out during the daytime, her husband coming out at night. (The Semas and Lhotas believe that the functions of the sun and moon were originally the opposite of what they are now, so that the sun shone at night and the moon by day. The latter, however, was so hot that the earth and everything on it was scorched and every form of life made almost impossible. At last a man took some cow-dung and threw it at the moon's face, ordering it to shine at night only, in the cool, and the sun to shine by day. This change took place and the cow-dung is still to be seen on the moon's face). See also Part V, *supra*, " Legends."

Eclipses are explained as follows. The earth is very big and the sun was therefore unable to heat the whole of it. So he had to borrow heat, and from time to time repays the loan. When he is wholly or partially eclipsed he is at that time making a repayment of his borrowed heat. Eclipses of the moon are explained in a similar way. Some Naga tribes explain eclipses as the eating of the sun or moon by a tiger or a spirit, but in the case of the Lhotas at any rate the idea seems borrowed from the Assamese, the Lhota expression merely being that the orb " dies."

Calendar.—The Angami year is divided into twelve months as follows :—

Thennyê, roughly corresponding to October.			
Zipe	,,	,,	November.
Redê	,,	,,	December.
Doshü	,,	,,	January.
Keno	,,	,,	February.
Kezi	,,	,,	March.
Kerāu	,,	,,	April.
Ketsu	,,	,,	May.
Chachü	,,	,,	June.
Chādi	,,	,,	July.
Chirê	,,	,,	August.
Rêyê	,,	,,	September.

Normally the months consist of thirty days each, and an intercalary month is inserted vaguely every three or four

years, the year of insertion being spoken of as *krü kerr-o-se
titsi*, " the thirteen month year," though the extra month
has no name of its own.[1]

The Stars, themü, are often regarded by the Angamis as
men who have been translated to the heavens after death.
No distinction is drawn between stars and planets except
in the matter of size. Names are given to some of the more
conspicuous stars and constellations.

The *Milky Way* is called *Pfiüdzücha* (Pfiü's water channel),
which is the name of the Barak river dividing the Kacha
Naga country. Why the name of the constellation should
have been given to the river, or whether the name of the
river was given to the constellation, is not known. When
Pfiüdzücha is visible fine weather is expected. It is most
visible at the beginning of the cold weather, when it lies from
north to south like the Barak river.

The *Morning Star* is called *Tizhepfü*, and was a girl of
that name who during life was a great coquette and made
all the lads in the village think she was in love with them.
When they found out how they had been deceived, they
swore that they would never look upon her face again ;
but she said that she would turn into a big star when she died
so that every one would look at her. Women who are fickle
or loose are still compared to Tizhepfü. (*? Tizhepfü* <
tise-pfü, " morning bringer.")

The *Evening Star*, appearing in the south-west just
after sunset, is known as *Kerügu-Vaphi*," the "Thief
Watcher."

The three stars of the *Belt of Orion* are known as *Thepeko*,
or *Rhupeko* (? = the Carriers). They were three men who
were carrying a post for a house and were attacked by their
enemies and killed. The smaller stars dependent from
the belt and forming Orion's sword are the enemies who
ambushed and killed the three post-carriers. (The Lhotas
say that the three stars of the belt are three men looking for
a mithan).

The *Hyades* are known as *Themü-tikru*, " the Rain-shield
stars," and were a woman's rain-shield. She suddenly missed

---

[1] The Changs have an intercalary month of which it is tabu to mention.
[1] *See* Appendix XIII, p. 460.

it from her shoulders and looked round to find it had been snatched away from her and set in the sky as a constellation.

Zuthekroko, the " Rat diggers," are pointed out as the *Pleiades*. They were seven men who were digging out rats in the jungle when they were suddenly set upon and killed by their enemies. Hence, perhaps, the unluckiness of the number seven among the Angamis. (The Semas describe them as a number of young girls who were killed when making *modhu* and spinning cotton in a rich man's house).[1] (The *Zuthekroko* were once pointed out to me as the seven stars of the Plough, but the latter are really known as the *Themü-pisu*.)

Themü-rüü, " the Star-Girls," probably = the Gemini. I have been unable to identify them with absolute certainty, as different stars are pointed out by different persons. They are two stars close together which were two girls who were killed by raiders when spinning in front of the house, or, according to another version, two girls who were killed, when catching snails and fish in the rice terraces, by a tiger, which is the "big red star" (probably Aldebaran) seen "just behind them".

Comets are known as *Zudio-Khupu*, " Zudio's pipe." A man named Zudio, who was dying, said that seven days after his death he would smoke his pipe, and everyone should see the smoke of it in the sky, and, further, that after seven generations had passed he would show himself again. A comet appeared after his death and is seen at rare and long intervals and is known as Zudio's Pipe or Zudio's smoke, *Zudio-Mikhu*. (The Semas believe that great warriors become comets after their death.)

---

[1] The Angami, as in some other Assamese tribes, sees seven. The Sema sees six and (like the Greeks) says that there used to be seven.

APPENDIX IX

DETAILS OF THE *LI-SÜ* (OR *LĔSÜ*) CEREMONY FOR THE ACQUISITION OF STATUS IN KOHIMA VILLAGE

The details of the *lisü* ceremony here set down are taken almost verbatim from an article of mine in the *Journal of the Royal Anthropological Institute* in 1922 (see No. 24 in Appendix I).

The carved stone monoliths at Dimapur seem to represent the final efflorescence in Assam of a forgotten civilization of which survivals appear sporadically from the eastern Himalayas through South-East Asia and Indonesia down into the Pacific, and which seems to have spread from Indonesia to Madagascar and even to West Africa.[1] It seems to have reached Assam partly at any rate from the south-east, and is represented there by the monolithic stone jars of the North Cachar Hills, which are clearly related, and that pretty closely, to the stone jar necropolises of Vietnam, Celebes, and Sumatra, and also no doubt to the monoliths at Dimapur and the later group at Jamuguri.[2]

The monoliths of North Cachar contained the ashes of the dead, and are probably represented further west by the familiar stone cists and monoliths of the Khasia Hills, where the Khasi and Synteng migrating westwards had to do their best with a hard gneiss instead of a tractable sandstone. The stone cists, in some villages carved according to sex, which house the skulls of deceased Konyak Nagas, doubtless represent a degenerate form of the same cult, as also do the standing stones and wooden posts of other Naga tribes. In all Naga tribes the fertility of the crops and the prosperity of the village are closely associated with the dead, whose life-substance is conceived of as forming a continuous cycle of reproduction, passing from

[1] See "West Africa and Indonesia: a Problem in Distribution" in *Journ. Royal Anthropological Institute*, LXXVI (1946).

[2] See "Carved Monoliths at Jamaguri in Assam" in *J.R.A.I.*, vol. LIII (1923).

men to cereals sown, and thence back through grain eaten, or through the flesh of animals that have eaten it, to man again. It is this theory that forms the philosophic basis of headhunting,[1] and while one form of social status is acquired by the taking of heads and bringing additional life-substance to the community in that way, another is acquired by the distribution of acquired wealth and an attempt thus made by a successful man to inform his family, clan, or fellow-villagers with his superfluity of that life-substance which is the secret of his success.

The highest rank is generally associated with the erection of a pair of standing stones. The *lisü* ("post-placing"?) *genna* is the next one before the pulling of a stone, at any rate in the Kohima group of villages, though not practised in the Khonoma group. The details here recorded were taken down from the joint account of two old men of Kohima village, Lhosele of the Puchatsuma clan, and Saniyu of the Dapfetsuma clan, who were selected for me as the two men in the village most expert in this ceremony. For this *genna* is not, as most *gennas* are, dictated by the official priest (*pitsü*), but is observed according to the direction of any old man who is well known to be expert in the details that have to be observed. I have myself witnessed what I could of the ceremony, but it would obviously be difficult to be present throughout.

First of all a preliminary ceremony, called *Zhuhetsü*, is performed in the month *Thenia-krü*, beginning on the sixteenth day of it. The first day of this observance is called *kizhe*. Rice and liquor are fastened to the centre post of the house, as in all Angami *gennas*, for the spirits, and the performer of the ceremony observes *penna* (i.e. he must not go to the fields to work). He kills four cows, or about that number, and feasts his personal friends on this meat and on liquor got ready beforehand. Three new pots must be used, one for male and one for female friends, and that third for the performer and his *thugiyu*. Three new hearths are also made, two in the outer room, the other in the inner room, but away from the household hearth. The male guests cook at one of the hearths in the front room, the female guests at the other. At the

[1] See "The Significance of Head-hunting in Assam" in *J.R.A.I.*, vol. LVIII (1928).

third new hearth the performer and his *thugiyu* are to cook.
Only the performer's own household, himself excluded,
are allowed to use the regular hearth on this occasion.

The *thugiyu* referred to is a boy called in for such a
genna; the chaste son of any neighbour will do.

For three days the performer and his *thugiyu* remain
kenna (tabu), and cook and eat together thus. A new
gourd, a new ladle, and a new funnel are used by the
performer's wife, who may put *zu* (rice liquor) down near
at hand in the new gourd, when the two may pick it up
and drink. On the evening of the third day the *thugiyu*
goes home, taking with him a leaf of *zu* and cooked meat
wrapped in a leaf.

The next day the performer must remain in his house,
but on the fifth day he may go out as usual. This day is
called *zhangu*.[1] He may not, however, enter anyone
else's house on this day. On the sixth day (*zhakre*)[1] he
has to remain in his own house again. On the seventh
day he goes to cut fuel for the ceremony proper, and on
that day he kills pigs or cattle, according to the number
of his personal friends. This day is called *si-du* ("wood-
cut"). Forty pieces of meat and several gourds of *zu* are
on this day taken to the place where the fuel is cut, and
there consumed by the performer and his *thugiyu* and two
of the performer's most intimate friends. This completes
the preliminary *genna* in the month *Thenia-krü*, and the
persons concerned are again free to do as they please for
the present.

The following month, *Zhepeo-krü* ("rice-ripening-month"),
is then allowed to elapse, and is followed by the month,
Redeo-krü ("reaping-month"), in which the rice for the *zu*
to be used at the ceremony has to be pounded. On the
fifth day of this month is the *Kevakethe genna*, marking the
beginning of the harvest, and the whole village keeps *penna*.
On the sixth day the village goes to the fields, and on the
seventh (*ngisie*) the *pitsü* warns the village that the ninth
day will be *thuzhoh*, when the rice (for *zu*) is to be watered
by all about to perform the *Lisü genna*. On this (seventh)
day the two intimates of the performer above mentioned

---

[1] The word *zha-ngu* apparently = "fifth day"; *zha* = day; *pengu* = 5.
But *zha-kre*, if it = "sixth day", must be from some obsolete form,
as the current word for 6 is *soru*.

(they are called-*nasa*) bring each a wee basket of rice to the performer's house, which he takes and sets aside, no use at all being made of it; but after this, all the performer's friends are at liberty to bring their contributions, a little basketful each, to the performer, who puts it all in an empty rice-bin of woven bamboo in his house.

On the ninth day, called *thuzhoh*, the friends of intending performers go into the jungle and get plantain leaves for making cups, etc., a load each, and to split wood to fence in the porch where the cattle are to be killed in front of the performer's house. On this day, too, the whole village gets ready their food and *zu* for the *genna*, the actual performer having started to do so from *ngisie*, as he must complete his much more elaborate preparations by the end of *thuzhoh*.

On the tenth day of the month the rice brought by the two *nasa* is cooked and eaten by the performer, a small portion of the rice being kept over uncooked. This is taken on that day or the next, together with two halves of plantain leaf, of which the ends have not in the usual way been torn off, and a new basket, a little one; the rice is wetted in the basket and put upon the leaves. This wetted rice is then spoken of as having dried, and two little grasses, of the kind called *tsaka* and *pipfe*, are taken and shaken over the rice, when it is said that the fowls have been driven away. (The husband says to his wife, "Fowls are eating the paddy!" The woman shakes *tsaka* and *pipfe* twice over the rice on the leaves, and says, "I have driven them away.") Then the husband goes out and says, "Rain has fallen on the Sema side" (i.e. to the north-east). Then the woman picks up the rice, wraps it up, and puts it in the little basket and places it at the foot of the centre post of the house in the back partition of the room in which the hearth is.

This is followed by the pounding of the rice for the brewing of liquor (*zu*) for the feast itself. As this calls for much outside help, it cannot be completed on one day if there be any considerable number of performers in the village. Accordingly, some pound on the eleventh, others on the twelfth and the rest on the thirteenth. If, however, performers are few enough, the pounding is finished on the eleventh. This pounding of the rice is done by the young

men of the clan, who drag up paddy-pounding tables
outside the performer's house and there pound out the
performer's rice, wearing full gala dress. In the evening
they come back to the performer's house and drink *zu*
with him, and receive ten pieces of flesh each, each piece
to be the size of a handful. The women of the clan also
put on gala dress and sift the rice pounded by the men.

On the fifteenth day of the month the *bohu* is made;
that is the new fence about the performer's veranda, inside
which the cattle are to be killed. On the sixteenth, the
whole village observes *kizhe* (as at the *Zhuhetsü*). On the
seventeenth day the performer is to kill the cattle for the
feast.

On the eve of the seventeenth is the part of the ceremony
called *sangi*. A new basket is set in the house, and in it a
woman's brass bracelet, a pair of girl's earshells, and a
fragment of a woman's cloth (new), with a bit of scarlet
hair tied up in it. This bit of cloth, with the hair, is called
theko-pfe, "sheep-cloth",[1] because blue cloths ornamented
with red sheep's wool (cf. the present Rengma woman's
cloth) are said to have formerly been worn, and a cornelian
bead. To these women's ornaments the following male
things are added: a bit of elephant's hide a few inches long,
as a shield; a very short spear a few feet long; a "dao";
a *chapri* (sporran of cotton ropes) in miniature; a little
bit of cloth, woven on purpose, as a man's cloth; a miniature
man's stool of wood; a bit of shell, to represent a neck
conch; and a bit of human hair, formerly given by some
sweetheart of the man's, but now taken from four or five
old women.[2] These men's things are carefully kept separated from the women's things already in the basket.
The next morning the performer, with his cloth wrapped
over his head, takes the basket with its contents, and puts
it in the veranda and comes in again. His wife asks,
"*Ki a ga?*" ("What happened?"), and her husband

---

[1] This is noticeable as the Angami have no sheep, nor are there any
in their country, except such as have been imported recently by Europeans,
and these survive with difficulty. No other Naga tribe that I know has
a real word for "sheep". The Semas and Changs call them "foreigners'
goats". The Semas, Rengmas, Sangtams and other tribes using red
wool for embroidering cloths use that of dogs. Goat's hair is often dyed
scarlet, but is too stiff for embroidery.

[2] Perhaps to avoid giving grounds for jealousy to his wife.

answers, *"Po niredi lilewe"* ("He took it willingly"). Both husband and wife lie down again, each on their own bed. Some one else in the house then says, "Get up! The cock has crowed". The wife asks her husband what dreams he had, and he replies that his dreams were good, and asks the same question of his wife, who answers in the same terms.

Then all the cattle to be killed are driven into the *bohu*, where they are killed, the *thugiyu* first touching each with a little spear.

The bodies are laid out with the heads to the east, and the performer, with his cloth over his head, takes a corner of his cloth and touches with it the near hind leg of each slain beast after saying, "I never told anyone to kill all these cattle! I must be given more in their place." Then his wife takes *zu* from the vat and fills a leaf in her husband's hand, and he touches it to his lips without drinking, and puts it down by the vat.

After this, the two *nasa* cut up the first beast killed. The others are cut up either by other men outside the *bohu*, or by the *nasa* inside. Of the first animal's liver, nine minute fragments are cut and sewn by five and by four on a little sliver of cane, and put by the king-post (*kizhe*) of the house. This concludes the part of the ceremony called *tsüseoe*. The men and women now cook separately in the house.

The next episode is called *therhüza*. Still on the seventeenth day (called *voyezhu*) an old woman and a virgin, wearing complete sets of bracelets and armlets and new clothes, take rice from the performer's house and wet it and put it on the pounding-table and pound with a special song. The old woman sings:—

Sie	*thudeh*	*zhuhi*	
pestle	strike	(?)	
zhatsü	*tsulilo*		*kralilo*
pound	victuals-must-be-saved		drink-must-be-saved
kechukehie-zhu	*thutole*		
first-in-rank	make		

i.e. "Strike down the pestle and pound! Meat and drink must be accumulated that he may reach the highest rank of all."

The meaning of *zhuhi* is no longer known. The song is perhaps a sort of spell to ensure the performer's duly passing on from the observance of the *Lisü genna* to the still more expensive final ceremony in the series by which social status is acquired by successive steps. The pestle is either a big heavy wooden pole, used standing on the pounding table itself, and driven down with both hands into a socket cut or burnt in the table, or a heavy crooked stick like an inverted V, with one side longer than the other, which is manipulated from the ground by the side of the table.

On the same day two bits of meat are sent to two old men of each clan invited, with the news that the performer will do *lisü*, and to ask for help.

Meanwhile the performer and his wife sit apart behind a mat put up so as to partition off a corner of the house, and no one may approach them but the *lowüü*. The *lowüü* is the functionary who presides over and directs private as opposed to public, religious, or quasi-religious ceremonies, being summoned by individuals, much as a physician or a priest or both might be called in by one of ourselves as well as carrying out the duties of the undertaker.[1] The *lowüü* feeds the performer and his wife with meat from a specially reserved leg of beef taken from one of the beasts slaughtered and hung up within reach. He also sleeps with them on the same mat.

At this stage in the proceedings the *lowuu* ties together with two strands of red cane, a wee iron hoe and a scrap of meat; he makes a number of such bundles, and gives one each to every man in the village who has done the *Lisü genna*, while to men who have only done the preceding *genna* of *zhatsü* similar bundles omitting the hoe are given.

This completes the episode called *therhüza*. But meanwhile the *lowüü*'s official assistant, who must for this purpose be an old man past work in the fields, has been

---

[1] I have used the term *lowüü*, as that is the term in use in Kohima village, where this ceremony is performed. Hitherto the term *Zhevo*, which is the term used in the Khonoma group of villages, has been used. I have also stated, I think, that the *Pitsü* in the Kohima group performs the offices performed by the *zhevo* in Khonoma, as well as those of Kemovo. This is not absolutely correct, though he performs some of them, as the *lowüü* is the person who really corresponds to the *zhevo*. The *lowüü* also corresponds precisely to the Sema *laχü*.

getting ready the marks on the emblematic posts which are to be carried round the village. The cutting out of the posts, carved as they are with a *mithun* head in high relief, has been completed beforehand, but the zigzag lines on the forked posts and the crosses on the straight one must be done by the *lowüü*'s assistant, and they must be cut from below upwards.[1]

On the eighteenth day, in the morning, the performer and his wife are to wash ceremonially. Taking a spear and a reaping-hook respectively and two bits of soap-vine each, they go to the washing pool followed by the *lowüü*. Two new gourds are cut, one for each of them. Each of the pair draws water in the gourd, pours some into the left hand, rubs in a little soap, and touches it twice to his head. The *lowüü* does not wash. Then all three return to the house, where each of them wraps in a leaf a few grains of cooked rice, and tucks it under his (or her) waist-belt. Then *kizhe* is observed, the wild vegetables known as *zhuhe, tserowü, chede, chephoh, zomhu, kube, rothu, chakra, bocha, phekwe* and *tehu* being added to the usual offering of rice and *zu*, and the whole being put by the *lowüü* high up on the centre post outside instead of on the inside central post as usually.

Next, an absolutely black bull is killed inside the *bohu*, by the *lowüu*, who ties two leaves to the dead beast's off fore-leg. This is followed by the incident called *mhopeva*. The woman fills a leaf in her husband's hand from the vat, and he touches it to his lips and throws it away. (N.B., *pe* = "throw away".) The bull is then cut up, and *kerrle* follows, which consists in the cooking of the liver and other titbits in separate pots for men and women, and the eating of them by the guests.

The next episode is called *katsidze*. A shelf is made across a corner of the inner room by putting first a piece of branch of the tree called *pre*, inside that a bit of *chephoh*, and, across the two, sticks of *zomhu*, and overall plantain leaves. All those in the house wrap up rice, and put it under their belts, and thirty tightly rolled plantain[2] leaves are tied

[1] Many of the Sema forked posts have precisely similar zigzag marking.

[2] The plantain leaf is used for all sorts of utensils, particularly for cups, plates, and for wrapping up the cold rice taken to the fields, whence its name, *te-kwe-ni* = "rice-cover-leaf".

to the *pre* branch. The head of the black bull is put on the shelf together with the off hind-leg, the foot of which must point towards the front door. Then the *pitsü* and some very old woman come and eat in the house. The *pitsü* is given thirty-one pieces of cooked meat, and the old woman twenty-nine, and both drink *zu*, and are given thirty pieces of uncooked meat each. Then the *pitsü* gives one bit of cooked meat to the old woman, so that they have an equal number. The *pitsü* then gets up and puts a corner of his cloth over the old woman "as though he was going to have connection with her", and then sits down again. Again, thirty scraps of meat are cooked as *kemevo-mocha*.[1] The *lowüü* takes these and puts them on a leaf, and holds them over a small new bamboo basket, the basket being first held upside down. "Is it from this side it is eaten?" he asks. "It is not!" is the answer of the assembled guests. He then turns the basket right way up, and asks again, and is this time answered "It is!" so he doubles the leaf which holds the scraps and puts it into the basket, and eventually the old woman takes it away with all the rest of her shares of meat put into the same basket.

Next the *lowüü* sets out a miniature stool about 3 inches long and says to the *pitsü*, "There is your stool." The *pitsü* replies, "It is not fitted for me to sit upon", to which the *lowüü* answers, "It is the stool of our remote ancestors." To this the *pitsü* says, "Very well", and lets the corner of his cloth fall on to it.

Then in the front room the black bull's off fore-leg, with the leaves tied to it, is set down, and first the performer, then his wife, then all the inmates of his house touch it in turn with their cloths, and withdraw into the inner room, where they remain with their backs to the door through which they have just passed. Only the *pitsü*, the old woman who came with him, and four young boys, remain. The *pitsü* and the four youngsters then give the "spirits' call" (*terhoma-whi*) three times, calling softly "*Oö-whe-whi*". Then the *pitsü*, taking his spear, peers out of the front door, saying, "*La terhuma kia ?*" ("Perhaps

[1] The *Kemovo* (or *kemevo*) is the hereditary priest, representing the original founder of the village. His functions in the Kohima group are performed by the *pitsü*, and anyone who has performed the full series of social *gennas* is called *Kemevo*.

an enemy ?").[1] Then the *lowüü* pours *zu* into a leaf cup
in the *pitsü*'s hand, and the *pitsü* goes out, followed by the
four boys, each likewise with leaf cups filled by the *lowüü*.
Then the old woman, with two gourds of *zu* for herself and
two more for the *pitsü*, and in her basket three bits of rib
for the *pitsü*, and two more bits for herself, follows them
out. As, however, the basket is too heavy for her to
carry, it is lifted on to her back and then taken off again,
and the *pitsü*'s share is taken for him separately by a
young man. Now that they have gone out the household
may look round again.

After this, thirty-two scraps of meat are cut by the
lowüü, and a little wormwood is burnt, and the meat is
put in a pot and placed on the fire and taken off again with
the statement that it is cooked. Then the performer
takes a little gourd, to which he ties thirty of these pieces,
leaving two in the pot. He takes his spear and goes out,
carrying the gourd on his back, followed by the *lowüü*,
but leaving his wife in the house. The performer goes to
where the emblematic posts are, and blesses them in the
following words:—

> *Perin*[2]*-u-li,   perin-u-cha   ria   sievoghe!*
> Post of fertility, path of fertility willingly rise up!

The posts are now "pulled" to the performer's house.
Actually the Y-shaped post is carried by a warrior, who
holds it in a horizontal position, the foot of the post forwards,
by walking between the arms and supporting one of them
in each hand. To the foot of the post long ropes of creepers
are attached, and these are pulled on by a horde of small
boys. The straight post is carried in a vertical position

---

[1] So, at least, it was explained to me. One is tempted to wonder
whether there has not been a confusion between *terhoma*, "spirit", and
terhüma, "enemy", particularly as neither the old men who gave me the
formula, nor the exceptionally intelligent interpreter who helped me,
himself one of the leading men in Kohima village, could give any explanation at all of any part of the ritual other than "thus the *genna* must
be performed".

[2] The word *perin* is apparently obsolete, like *zhuhi*, and the old men
either did not know its meaning for certain—they thought it might mean
"mithun", i.e. gayal, the present Angami word for which is *gwi*—or
they forebore to translate from motives of delicacy. I have here avoided
the difficulty by using an abstract noun which gives the sense, though
the meaning of the Angami word is more likely to be concrete, abstracts
being foreign to their language.

by another warrior,[1] who holds it in front of him with both hands and walks just in front of the forked post between the creeper ropes, which are attached to it. All the young men, the warriors, and the veterans of the performer and the assisting clans precede the pulling boys; the whole company is decked out in full ceremonial dress from the youngest boy to the oldest man, the warriors and young men carrying fully ornamented shields and spears, or, if they have them, guns which they fire off at intervals. Preparations are made for this display for months beforehand, articles of dress, etc., being borrowed from all the villages of the tribe within reach. The whole spectacle is most impressive.

After reaching the performer's house, the performer is left standing there while the procession moves off to the village. Until the posts reach his house again, there the performer must stand. Meanwhile the procession perambulates the village, visiting all the open spaces in it. These open spaces are reserved areas of flat ground, among the houses crowded at different levels on to the top of the hill, and serve for playgrounds and for all sorts of public purposes. Each has its name, being known as such and such a "pool". When the procession reaches one of these "pools", it first circumambulates it with loud cries, firing of muskets, and brandishing of weapons. The warriors line up at one side, and the small boys drop their ropes, and run and jump across the open space. Then they return, pick up their ropes and the posts, move to one side, leaving room for the men to form up in lines, dance *en masse* across and around the "pool", and draw aside to allow individuals to display their athletic prowess by leaping into the air to considerable heights with amazing agility, followed by a furious stampede of the whole crowd across the "pool". Eventually the procession moves on to repeat the performance at the next "pool". All this to the accompaniment of the most barbaric shouts and cries and the incessant firing of guns.

When the procession gets back to the performer's house, he puts the gourd, which he took with him when he sent

---

[1] In 1920, when no suitable warrior was available for the purpose, a young man carried the forked post under explicit orders of old warriors, who said that no evil should befall him for it.

to bless the posts, into the back room, hanging it upon a post there. He never touches it again. Then he comes out and looks at his posts; then goes inside again, takes new rice (cooked), wraps it up and tucks it under his belt; then comes out again and watches the *lowüū* take the ropes off the posts. He then goes back into the house, where he and all his household change the rice under their belts. He then goes out, selects a site for the erection of the posts, and, having pointed it out to the *lowüū*, returns inside. The *lowüū* digs holes for the posts, sets them up, ties a bit of creeper round them, and sticks in a wee leaf of *zu*, as at *kizhe*. A little of the blood of the black bull is put by the *lowüū* on each post. The performer then blesses the posts in these terms:—

"Zhatsü	*ha*	*nengule*	*kechukehie-zhu*
Pounding	this	taking-pleasure-in	first-in-rank
tsülilo	*kralilo*		*perin-u-li*
food-to-be-saved	drink-to-be-saved		post of fertility
perin-u-cha	*ria*	*lhurnlo!"* [1]	
path of fertility	willingly	become-heavy-with-life!	

Then a hole is made in the wall beside the front door and two pipes inserted, one for the Kimhoma clans, the other for the Sakuma clans of Kohima.[2] Inside these pipes, salt and *zomhu*[3] are placed as the shares of the Kimhoma and Sakuma clans respectively. *Zu* is then poured into the pipes from the inside of the house, so as to run through the wall and fall outside, washing out on its way the salt and the *zomhu*. The *zu* is poured into the Kimhoma pipe before the Sakuma pipe.

[1] *Lhurnlo* is apparently another obsolete word only used in this connection.

[2] Kohima village is, for ceremonial purposes, divided into two groups called *Kimhoma*, composed of the Dapfetsuma, Puchatsuma and Rosuma clans, and *Sakuma*, comprising the other four clans, Chetonoma, Horotsuma, Hrapvoma and Cherama. For other purposes they are usually regarded as being divided into *Pferonuma*, a phratry comprising the six clans first mentioned, and *Cherama*, which the Pferonuma speak of as "alien", *solhima*, with particular reference to an occasion, connected with the origin of the rain-making rite, on which the Cherama clan refused to co-operate with the other clans of the village. There are yet again other legends giving various and divers origins for the different clans. *Vide* pp. 238, 256–58, *supra*.

[3] *Zomhu* has already been mentioned in two other connections in this ceremony. It is a vegetable, valued for its acid taste.

Next the *lowüü* takes a basket called *köpe* on his back, putting into it a dog pup, to which he gives a miniature shield and spear, and ashes ("in the name of the clouds"), and cotton seeds ("in the name of hail"). With this basket he climbs up on to the roof of the performer's house, whence he throws out the ashes, saying that they are clouds, and then throws out the cotton seeds saying that they are hail, and finally throws down the puppy with its spear and shield. Whoever can get hold of the puppy carries it off and keeps it, but as there may be a hundred or so young men scrambling for it, it sometimes happens that the unfortunate animal is killed in the scrimmage.[1]

Next a bull-calf, also with a "spear" and a "cloth" (the spear is a rough miniature and the cloth a mere fragment of white cloth), is led out on a rope of creeper, and this calf, too, is scrambled for by the young men with much violence and more or less killed in the process, after which it is completely killed by stabbing it with a piece of wood, and its liver is torn out and given to the performer, and the carcass is torn in pieces by the young men. This calf must not be killed or cut up with iron in any way at all. The *lowüü* buries the liver inside the performer's house, and at the same time buries two *pre* sticks with the thicker ends towards the front of the house, or the east, and the smaller ends the other way, just as a house is built with its smaller end westwards.[2]

---

[1] The form of sacrifice in which the victim is hurled down from the top of the porch has one or two parallels worth mention. The unadministered Konyak tribes of the north-east Naga-Hills are reported to offer a human sacrifice in which the victim is cut down so that his blood falls from above on to the ladder (a notched pole) by which the house of the sacrificer is entered, these Konyak houses being built on a platform and not, like the Angami houses, on the ground. The ceremony at which the sacrifice takes place is, like the *Lisü* genna, one performed by prosperous families, for the benefit of the community at the time of the harvest home. An older and more striking parallel is to be found reported by Samuel Purchas, who, on the authority apparently of various ancient authors, describes the temple of Hierapolis in Asia Minor as having a great porch "almost an hundred fadome high" facing north, and in front of it two enormous phallic emblems ("*priapi*") "about the height of three hundred fadome". The victims (animals) to be sacrificed were cast down from the top of the porch. Children also were let down by ropes in sacks. *Purchas his Pilgrimage*, Bk. 1, ch. 15. No doubt the fall of the victim aided the fall of fertilizing rain.

[2] By preference the Angami orientates his house so that the front faces east, and catches the morning sun, but this preference is by no means rigorously adhered to. The front of the house is both higher and broader than the back end.

Then the *lowüü* makes fire in the corner partitioned off by a mat, and he and the performer and the performer's wife drink *zu*, after which the guests outside may also drink, and the ceremony is over.

But a month later the *lowüü* comes again, and pulls up the posts and puts them down in the *bohu*, in which they had been erected before, but against the side of the house where they remain. And until the First Sower[1] has sown the rice the following spring, the performer may not eat outside his own village, nor visit another village at all.

How far we may infer, from the details of this Angami ceremony, the rites that must have attended the erection of the huge megaliths at Dimapur, we can only guess. Elephants are depicted in the carving on many of the stones; no doubt they helped in the tremendous effort that must have been needed to haul the huge blocks through the forest from the Diphu gorge, but they may also have contributed their lives to the holocaust of sacrifice in a ceremony of which the *Lisü genna* can be at most a microcosm. Fights between tigers and elephants, also depicted on the carved megaliths, probably formed part of the spectacle, as they did at the festivals of the Ahom kings. And we shall perhaps not go far astray if we take the puppy-dog, with its spear and shield, and the bull-calf, whose liver is buried not eaten, and who is also vested by a spear and a cloth with sinister attributes of humanity to be the unfortunate latter-day representatives of more terrible offerings of human life.

[1] *Vide* p. 189, *supra.*

APPENDIX X

ANGAMI (TENGIMA) CLANS

Shown under the villages in which they are found.

Names of clans in Tengima Angami villages.

N.B.—S. after the name of a clan denotes that it belongs to the Satsūma *Kelhu*. The other Pezoma clans are all of the Thevoma *Kelhu*. The Pepfüma clans are all of one *Kelhu*, the Thekronoma (or Cherama).

A.—*Khonoma Group.*

KIGWEMA

Pezoma.	*Pepfüma.*
Kavema	Makuma
Kipoma (half)	Kipoma (half)
Merelitsuma	

KHONOMA

Thevoma	Merhema
	Semoma

JOTSOMA

Toloma	Thekronoma
Tseyama	
Kroma	

MOZEMA

Pfepetsuma
Vihotsuma
Nisonuma

THEKREJENOMA

Pezoma.	*Pepfüma.*
Kotsuma	
Petsuma	

SACHEMA

Nayatsuma S.	Vima-rhekrüno
Rhatsatsuma S.	

KIRUFEMA

Hozhama	Thekronoma

B.—Kohima Group.

KOHIMA

Pezoma.	*Pepfüma.*
	Puchatsuma
	Rosuma
	Dapfetsuma
	Chetonoma
	Horotsuma
	Hrepvoma
	Cherama

N.B.—Most of the Kohima clans contain Pezoma families who came from other villages.

MEREMA

Kiditsuma	Horotsuma
Seyatsuma	
Kesinoma	
Chakuma	

CHESWEMA

Kroma	Kewhinuma

N.B.—The Kewhinuma (= " From-Kohima men ') are composed of colonists of the Horotsuma, Chetonoma, Hrepvoma and Cherama clans of Kohima, and use the names of these clans.

KERUMA

Thevoma	Makwuma
	Kugwema

Rekroma

Pezoma.	Pepfüma.
Thevoma	Methoditsuma
Thevo-kretsuma	Cherama

Dehoma

Thevoma	Mekwuma

Chedema

Thevoma	Thapvünoma
Kilozuma (half)	Sakuma
	Kilozuma (half).

Nerhema

Chadi-zaproma	Solhima
Kratsetsuma	(? or Üsuma)
Chizisetsu-relhotsuma	

N.B.—The Chadi-zaproma contains some Pezoma who came from other villages and attached themselves to that clan.

Chichama

Rüpiechuma	Riema
Sügotsuma	
Methama	
Tephri-Methama	

N.B.—The Rüpiechuma, Sügotsuma, and Methama clans all contain Pepfüma families who came from other villages, while conversely the Riema contains several Pezoma families of similar origin. The Tephri-Methama (*i.e.*, "Foreign-methama ") are the descendants of a man said to have been a "Mān," *i.e.*, Burmese who came from the plains to Chichama and was adopted into the Methama clan. His descendants now number some twenty houses, and are reckoned as Pezoma. This Burman had three companions who were adopted into the Rüpiechuma, Sügotsuma, and Riema clans respectively, but two of them were killed by their adoptive clansmen and one died of diarrhœa. *Tephri* means " Foreign " as opposed to " Naga," not merely as opposed to " Angami." The four Burmese who came to Chichama probably wandered up from the plains of Assam at the time of the Burmese invasion.

TOFIMA

Pezoma.   *Pepfûma.*

Sohenoma
Chazuma
Pékroma
Sema

N.B.—The Sema clan is really Sema and not Angami, but, of course, the blood is now mixed.

C.—*Viswema (Dzuno-Kehena) Group.*

VISWEMA

Pezoma.   *Pepfûma.*

Rotsoma
Zirema
Krihezuma
Pavoma

KIDIMA

Téëma
Sima
Thama (? S.)
Mekroma (half)   Mekroma (half)

N.B.—The Sima clan is here, too, probably of Sema origin, the Semas having at one time probably been located in the present Kezami country.

KHUZAMA

Rotsuma
Zirema

JAKHAMA

Zema
Viyema
Nekima

MIMA

Thama S.
Tsoprama S.
Resoma S.

KEZOMA

Mekroma
Kehoma

PUCHAMA

Pezoma.   *Pepfüma.*

Kranoma
Nisema
Puniatsuma

PHESAMA

Merama   Mekuma
Sikama
Viyema

The small Tengima villages of Sachenobama, Choloma (Khonoma group), Sihama, Tichuma, and Nachama (Kohima group), and the half Sema village of Garifema have been omitted from this list. Sachenobama is composed of a dozen or so odd families from the various villages of the Khonoma group. Choloma, when I visited it, consisted of three houses only. Nachama is composed of various families of the different Chichama clans.

Where one clan is half Pezoma and half Pepfüma the reason usually is to be found in adoption or migration. It seems to have been frequent, if not usual, for persons migrating to another village to be adopted into clans of the opposite *Kelhu* to which they belonged. The reason is no doubt that they married as a matter of course into the opposite *Kelhu,* and were then adopted into the clans of their wives, having no clansmen of their own in the village, as in the case of Nihu's ancestor given in the pedigrees in Part III.

APPENDIX XI

ANTHROPOMETRICAL

1. MEASUREMENTS TAKEN BY PROFESSOR DIXON.
2. MEASUREMENTS TAKEN BY THE WRITER.

I

Tribe.	Sub-tribe.	Village.	Stature.	Reach.	Head.		Face.		Nose.		Remarks.
					Length.	Breadth.	Length.	Breadth.	Length.	Breadth.	
Angami ...	Tengima	Khonoma	1690	1790	182	145	135	140	62	41	
,,	,,	,,	1695	1751	182	142	124	140	55	35	
,,	,,	Keruma	1720	—*	190	148	130	149	62	35	*Partly crippled and unable to take reach.
,,	,,	,,	1623	1760	189	140	114	138	52	45	
,,	Chakrima	Zogazumi	1505	1660	170	149	110	142	52	42	
,,	,,	,,	1702	1760	183	152	120	149	57	42	
,,	,,	—	1575	1660	182	132	122	140	60	44	
,,	,,	—	1600	1640	186	133	110	132	50	42	
,,	,,	—	1610	1630	194	148	105	133	50	39	
,,	,,	—	1675	1720	189	141	113	134	55	40	
Sema	—	—	1650	1705	182	146	120	139	54	38	
,,	—	—	1665	1675	184	142	—	136	51	40	

I am indebted for these figures to the kindness of Professor Dixon, of Harvard, who took them at Kohima, Christmas, 1912, from coolies about to start on the Mishmi expedition of that year. Other figures may be found in Col. Waddell's article on "Tribes of the Brahmaputra Valley," *Journal of the Asiatic Soc. of Bengal* for 1900. The measurements that follow have all been taken by myself.

II ANGAMI

Name.	Sub-tribe.	Tribal Division.	Clan.	Kindred.	Village.	Approximate age.	Cephalic length.	Cephalic breadth.	Nasal length.	Nasal breadth.	Remarks.
Pozü	Chakrima	Pezoma	Kakretsoma	Yakatsuma	Cheswezuma	40	190	142	50	40	The Chakrima villages appear to be almost entirely Pezoma.
Théyésé	,,	,,	Kesonuma	Kesoma	,,	20	180	143	43	41	
Soleri	,,	,,	Nikatsoma	Ekwonuma	,,	35	191	144	44	40	
Etsowe	,,	,,	Kesonuma	Nkama	,,	25	190	145	45	40	
Velopra	,,	,,	Kamotsuma	Miyanatsoma	,,	35	181	152	42	36	
Tsorri	,,	,,	Nikatsoma	Rosanuma	,,	30	192	143	50	33	
Lhusa	,,	,,	Techetsomi	Chetalapunomi	Guozetoma	50	197	142	44	38	
Sole	,,	,,	Veyetsomi	Chedonumi	,,	35	185	155	44	35	
Tsorré	,,	,,	Mekritsetsumi	Hesenomi	Losama	40	190	141	53	42	
Pulhezu	,,	,,	,,	,,	,,	30	195	139	40	40	
Hipezü	,,	,,	Toganumi	Checheimi	,,	50	183	146	50	36	
Dalhuli	,,	,,	,,	Gazomi	,,	30	185	140	50	35	
Mesamm	,,	,,	Wezami	Higwenimi	,,	25	188	145	49	40	
Chetsü	,,	,,	Chedotzomi	Yezomi	,,	35	192	144	50	38	
Yekahe	,,	,,	Ekami	Zuimi	,,	25	187	149	40	37	
Tsitoghu	,,	,,	,,	Kwehimi	,,	25	190	149	43	37	
Kevise	,,	,,	Kezonumi	Kuluthomi	,,	50	193	145	45	36	
Pfütsomi	,,	,,	Hosimi	Pokoimi	,,	25	195	143	43	37	
Puzemo	,,	,,	Kesomi	Kizomi	,,	35	190	149	45	39	
Sodzüzhe	,,	,,	Lohemi	Zhohelemi	Kroma	50	192	146	49	35	
Zusarru	,,	,,	Tengyinumi	Niedzudemi	,,	40	190	149	47	36	
					Average	—	189	145	45	38	

ANGAMI—*continued.*

Name.	Sub-tribe.	Tribal Division.	Clan.	Kindred.	Village.	Approximate Age.	Cephalic Length.	Cephalic Breadth.	Nasal Length.	Nasal Breadth.	Remarks.
Tahemo ...	Kezama	Pezoma	Senomi	Mekrisunomi	Kezabama	45	195	147	44	34	
Tuveniu ...	„	„	Lekomi	Mewotsami	„	20	197	142	40	37	
Hetsolo ...	„	„	„	Tselhinumi	„	30	200	139	45	39	
Zogé ...	„	„	Chekhami	Enesunami	„	30	185	148	47	35	
Ediloh ...	„	„	Senomi	Mengelhi-Terrekho	„	55	195	152	47	42	
Tsüloni ...	„	„	Lekomi	„	„	40	184	142	52	34	
Zimolo ...	„	„	Chekhami	Tselhinumi	„	20	195	137	44	36	
Pfimi ...	„	„	Lohemi	Kehonumi	„	40	180	137	43	38	
Distolo ...	„	„	Semoma	Mekrisonumi	„	25	180	142	50	34	
Mollo ...	„	„	Venumi	Dilhinumi	„	35	197	140	50	40	
Chesü ...	„	„	„	Dalhemi	Mesolozumi	30	190	137	52	37	
Metsapi ...	„	„	Thelentsomi	Yasenomi	„	45	190	135	41	37	
			„		Average	—	191	141	46	37	
Srisalhu ...	Tengima	Pepfüma	Semoma	Chalitsuma	Khonoma	45	184	144	47	31	
Vitse ...	„	„	Merhema	Pelhenoma	„	25	193	150	45	34	
Lhutzuzhu ...	„	„	Thekronoma	Hozunuma	Jotsoma	20	190	145	51	35	
Kruvizo ...	„	„	Merhema	Viselenoma	Khonoma	36	201	149	50	40	
Dapusa ...	„	„	Semoma	Chalitsuma	„	50	184	142	42	34	
Viketo ...	„	„	Merhema	Sokrelenoma	„	25	187	143	48	36	
Lokrele ...	„	„	„	Savinoma	„	40	183	140	51	40	
Hovizo ...	„	„	Thekronoma	Nopeinoma	Jotsoma	50	190	138	51	40	
Hwesilhu ...	„	„	„	Kutsotsuma	Kirufema	30	199	152	49	41	
Vizirr ...	„	„	„	Lhuamenoma	„	30	188	146	54	40	

ANGAMI—*continued.*

Name	Sub-tribe	Tribal Division	Clan	Kindred	Village	Approximate Age	Cephalic Length	Cephalic Breadth	Nasal Length	Nasal Breadth	Remarks
Lhusele ...	Tengima	Pepfüma	Hreproma	Keletsuma	Kohima	45	185	145	52	41	
Vichathe...	"	"	Cherama	Zevichenoma	"	30	188	145	51	37	
Chavipre...	"	"	Chetonoma	Kotsoma	"	30	187	141	45	38	
Ketsuvi ...	"	"	"	Kemienoma	"	40	185	150	46	37	
Kranhele...	"	"	Dapfetsuma	Kerekonoma	"	35	174	149	49	39	
Hriehale ...	"	"	Rosuma	Pienunoma	"	35	185	154	53	40	
Lhopovi ...	"	Pezoma	Makroma	Yangotsoma	Kezoma	35	186	153	41	38	
Sokrele ...	"	"	Thevoma	Chatsuma	Khonoma	45	200	151	52	41	
Kruzeto ...	"	"	"	"	Puchama	25	190	146	46	37	
Nisozhü ...	"	"	Kranoma	Seletsuma	Phesama	45	179	144	52	40	
Sitsole ...	"	"	Merhema	Zasenoma	Kigwema	40	187	142	50	41	
Kepu ...	"	"	Kipoma	Zevichenoma	Dehoma	60	188	157	52	41	Nose aquiline.
Kriechale ...	"	"	Thevoma	Seratsuma	Viswema	55	189	151	59	35	
Vise ...	"	"	Rotsoma	Thenoselenuma	Kohima	36	181	157	50	36	
Salezu ...	"	"	Puchatsuma	Rutsanuma		55	177	159	52	44	
					Average	—	192	148	49	38	
Terrhü ...	Memi	Pepfüma	Thedoma	Mechonuma	Razama	25	183	144	40	37	

General average of Tengima, Chakrima and Kezama Angamis — 191   145   47   37

SEMA.

Name.	Clan.	Village.	Approximate Age.	Cephalic Length.	Cephalic Breadth.	Nasal Length.	Nasal Breadth.	Remarks.
Nizilhu ...	Chesholimi	Lukobomi	33	182	147	45	41	
Inakhu ...	Chishilimi	Sichimi	45	185	150	48	43	C.
Satakha ...	"	"	50	185	148	53	42	C.
Vukashe ...	"	"	50	190	147	48	46	
Wokiye ...	"	"	40	195	151	49	37	
Kunazhe ...	Chophimi	"	35	192	152	43	38	
Khokeshe...	Chishilimi	"	35	182	150	50	37	
Heshepu ...	"	"	30	188	151	48	37	
Hukiye ...	"	Phuyetomi	40	182	149	45	35	
Hozokhu ...	Yepothomi	"	25	185	155	54	38	
Nasaka ...	Achumi	Lumitsami	25	196	143	52	41	
Kiyetha ...	Chophimi	"	18	182	139	45	34	
Koyazu ...	Kinimi	"	40	190	155	48	34	
Nivalho ...	"	"	45	178	152	53	41	
Wulhoshe ...	Awomi	"	50	183	145	51	41	
Punuku ...	Kinimi	"	30	194	141	45	40	
Khukiye ...	"	"	25	190	147	51	39	
Wulhoshe...	"	"	30	181	142	45	35	
Khukiye ...	Chophimi	"	45	185	149	51	38	
Khukeshe...	"	"	30	190	151	46	38	C.
Meghilhoh	Shohemi	"	40	185	142	43	37	
Kulhoshe...	Chishilimi	"	25	185	153	43	35	
Khaishe ...	Awomi	"	40	181	150	49	44	

Remarks. C. against a man's name indicates that he is a chief or the son or brother of a chief.

There is no dual division, all Semas using the same terms for father (*apo*) and mother (*aza*).

The Chophimi clan is of Ao or Sangtam extraction.

SEMA—*continued.*

Name.	Clan.	Village.	Approximate Age.	Cephalic Length.	Cephalic Breadth.	Nasal Length.	Nasal Breadth.	Remarks.
Hethena ...	Kinimi	Lumitsami	30	197	144	49	36	
Inato ...	,,	,,	40	191	148	52	40	C.
Mithihe ...	Yepothomi	Vekohomi	30	190	145	45	36	
Zelelho ...	Achumi	Ghukia	35	175	147	49	34	
Kavilho ...	Chesholimi	Phusumi	55	178	146	53	35	
Wokuheh...	Zümomi	Lizimi	40	184	143	51	32	
Sulhoshe ...	Asimi	Phusumi	30	186	135	40	34	
Shoghopu...	,,	L'tami	40	195	148	47	34	
Vikhepu ...	Ayemi	Serromi	25	183	160	50	35	C.
Kupvuhe ...	Chishilimi	Lokobomi	45	190	147	46	35	C.
Lohazu ...	Ayemi	Tichipami	40	178	144	45	39	C.
Lhozeshe ...	Morrumi	Sotomi	35	192	145	43	42	The Mcrrumi clan are ultimately of non-Sema extraction. Sotomi is a transfrontier village of mixed Semas and Sangtams, though this particular man is of a family long absorbed by Semas and came from a genuine Sema village.
Hezekhu ...	Zümomi	Sheyepu	20	180	150	46	35	
Yethazü ...	Chophimi	,,	35	179	142	43	42	
Thaishe ...	Achumi	Lumami	40	181	145	42	42	C.
Vikiye ...	Kinimi	,,	40	184	142	52	38	C.
Inazïe ...	Awomi	Phuyetomi	25	183	152	50	38	C.
Average				*186*	*147*	*48*	*38*	

RENGMA.

Name.	Linguistic Group.	Tribal Division.	Clan.	Village.	Approximate Age.	Cephalic Length.	Cephalic Breadth.	Nasal Length.	Nasal Breadth.	Remarks.
Nrilo...	Tseminyu	Ketenenyu	Hoseninenyu	Themokedima	35	193	146	45	37	The Rengmas are divided into two linguistic groups speaking different languages, known as *Tseminyu* and *Insenikotsenu*. The former is divided into *Ketenenyu*, calling their fathers *aphu* and their mothers *anyo*, and *Azonyu*, using the terms *appu* and *apfü*. The *Inseni-kotsenu* all use *apa* and *azhao*. The *Ketenenyu* division, although divided up into a number of clans, still forms an exogamous group. Deeply pitted between eyes.
Kezütha	„	„	„	„	55	193	143	53	39	
Nyinno	„	„	Kumtsanenyu	„	25	185	146	41	38	
Wasang	„	„	„	„	30	191	141	44	37	
Rhiga	„	„	„	„	30	182	146	51	33	
Mashato	„	„	Kepyeninenyu	„	30	185	146	36	35	
Nosang	„	„	Mitsangnenyu	„	30	185	139	47	38	
Tesimvyu	„	„	Tesempvinenyu	„	30	190	146	44	40	
Lhosanyu	„	„	Kacheninyu	„	25	193	145	47	39	
Gwasang	„	Azonyu	Zumahonenyu	„	45	184	148	47	38	
Kehga	„	„	Sompvenyu	„	50	175	129	40	36	
Küthongpong	„	„	„	„	20	189	140	42	34	
Zanga	„	„	„	„	33	182	142	41	36	
Hilo ...	„	„	Stibinyu	„	25	195	139	45	37	
Kikü	„	„	Kizonyu	„	50	191	145	45	36	
Dzomü	„	„	Sevinyu	„	30	188	150	45	34	
Gwalo	„	„	Tepwinyu	„	35	195	140	45	34	
Stimtivi	„	„	Rasenyu	„	20	185	137	46	38	
Zalepu	Insenikotsenu	—	Maghatha	Insuma	50	199	148	47	37	
				Average		188	143	45	37	

LHOTA.

Name.	Division.	Phratry.	Clan.	Village.	Approximate Age.	Cephalic Length.	Cephalic Breadth.	Nasal Length.	Nasal Breadth.	Remarks.
Asao	Liyé	Mipongsandri	Uthiu	Pangti	23	180	141	40	35	The division into Liyé and Ndreng is one of locality merely, the Lhotas west of the Dayang river being called Liyé and those east of it Ndreng. The three phratries of Mipongsandri, Izumontsürre, and Tompyaktzerre correspond to the Angami divisions of Sachema, Thevoma, and Cherama, and, like them, fall into two groups, one consisting of Mipongsandri and Izumontsürre, who call their mothers *ayo*, and the other of Tompyaktzerre, calling their mothers *aphu*. The term *Mipongsandri* is probably incorrect, but I have retained it here for want of a better.
Chamimo	"	Izumontsürre	Nguli	"	40	185	148	43	37	
Etsizao	"	"	Shitri	Okotso	35	186	147	43	39	
Rishamo	"	Tompyaktzerre	Tseboi	Pangti	40	186	147	41	37	
Tsengyimo	"	"	Kikong	Aré	35	192	145	45	41	
Lichamthang	"	"	"	"	45	182	150	46	39	
Yibonthang	"	"	"	"	25	190	145	45	40	
Lasheto	"	"	"	"	25	190	150	43	37	
Koppé	"	"	"	"	40	185	140	44	37	
Yanko	Ndreng	Mipongsandri	Yamthang	Changsü	30	184	140	40	37	
Izanthang	"	"	"	"	45	181	150	44	40	
Kithango	"	"	Uthiu	"	45	194	151	51	39	
Pyobemo	"	"	Izong	Koio	25	183	145	38	37	
Yankoso	"	"	"	"	30	181	142	37	38	
Konchamo	"	"	Izong	"	25	191	148	37	38	
Santhamo	"	"	Mori	"	40	182	145	34	34	
Langtsimo	"	Izumontsürre	Izong	Chingaki	45	182	146	45	38	
Thonlothang	"	"	Nguli	"	35	182	142	37	36	
Tamcho	"	"	"	"	40	178	133	43	38	
Chinyero	"	"	"	Koio	20	182	142	34	34	

LHOTA—*continued.*

Name.	Division.	Phratry.	Clan.	Village.	Approximate Age.	Cephalic Length.	Cephalic Breadth.	Nasal Length.	Nasal Breadth.	Remarks.
Sülamo ...	Ndreng	Izumontsüre	Nguli	Koio	30	193	145	45	35	
Thengbamo	,,	,,	Thangwé	Changsü	55	205	156	51	42	"Pathong" is generally re-
Risso ...	,,	,,	Hmtsoi	,,	30	190	153	44	36	garded as the same class as
Zanasha ...	,,	Tompyaktzerre	Pathong	Koio	30	179	153	44	37	"Kikong." In any case they
Rakho ...	,,	,,	,,	,,	35	178	157	47	38	are so closely connected that
Chendramung	,,	,,	Kikong	,,	25	182	143	40	38	intermarriage is not allowed.
Ngwoshio ...	,,	,,	,,	,,	25	185	143	39	37	
Lamanthang	,,	,,	,,	,,	50	183	148	45	45	
Yanchamo ...	,,	,,	,,	,,	40	190	150	40	37	
Konyamthang	,,	,,	,,	,,	25	190	147	40	36	
Nlio	,,	,,	,,	,,	25	186	152	35	37	
Wochibemo	,,	,,	,,	,,	30	180	145	40	34	
Kamtemo ...	,,	,,	,,	,,	55	191	154	42	40	
Yanaro ...	,,	,,	,,	,,	45	192	157	48	39	
Limomo ...	,,	,,	,,	,,	45	172	141	42	32	
Shombemo...	,,	,,	,,	Chingaki	35	186	141	43	37	
Minthango ...	,,	,,	,,	,,	35	193	155	42	41	
				Average		*186*	*147*	*42*	*37*	

AO.

Name.	Tribal Division.	Clan.	Village.	Approximate Age.	Cephalic Length.	Cephalic Breadth.	Nasal Length.	Nasal Breadth.	Remarks.
Kamsangliba ...	Chongli	Lankamr	Ungma	30	179	156	48	37	
Noksangba ...	"	"	Mokokchung	37	182	147	49	40	
Marilabzak ...	"	"	Longsa	40	185	145	50	40	
Innamiran ...	"	"	Mokokchung	55	185	155	49	40	
Wolpa ...	"	"	Akhoia	18	176	147	44	35	
Limalamba...	"	"	Ungma	35	188	147	44	42	
Merangchiba	"	"	Nankam	40	185	153	50	40	
Matsanshinok	"	"	Khensa	50	180	152	46	37	
Ripayangba	"	"	Changki	25	187	147	38	37	
Yimpilamba	"	"	Khensa	50	183	143	38	35	
Methangmayang...	Mongsen	"	Mongchen	50	183	149	48	31	Probably of Chongli extraction.
Lengtinoktan ...	Chongli	Pongen	Akhoia	22	180	146	45	35	
Imtipogyin...	"	"	Longchang	30	187	151	43	35	
Mirisinga ...	"	"	Nankam	45	176	148	42	36	
Chongpongsangba	"	"	Chuchu	30	176	143	43	40	
Labzangtsiba ...	"	"	"	40	184	149	51	39	
Imsitakba ...	"	Imsong	Longchang	35	175	146	46	38	*Imsong* seems to be a sub-division of Pongen.
Imtisashi ...	"	"	"	20	181	151	41	36	
Longrikapa ...	"	"	Waromung	40	185	141	45	38	

AO—continued.

Name.	Tribal Division.	Clan.	Village.	Approximate Age.	Cephalic Length.	Cephalic Breadth.	Nasal Length.	Nasal Breadth.	Remarks.
Lanukamzak ...	Chongli	Chongli airr	Waromung	23	194	147·	45	35	AI is of the same clan as Pongen. Sangsutang aī is a branch of Mongsen aī.
Karinungba ...	Mongsen	Mongsen airr	"	23	175	151	40	40	
Chongponglamba ...	"	Sangsutang airr	Longchang	35	175	145	39	40	
Reppatangba ...	Chongli	Chamirr	Ungma	40	195	148	46	36	
Marichongsi ...	"	"	Chuchu	40	181	155	42	42	
Karinangtang ...	"	"	Khensa	35	184	154	49	36	
Zillusangba ...	Mongsen	"	Nenkam	35	193	156	46	36	
Takasusang ...	"	"	Changki	40	185	154	47	41	
Moyaleptan ...	"	"	Nankam	41	177	157	51	35	
Akhaba ...	"	"	Mokokchung	30	192	157	50	42	
Marimayang ...	"	"	Waromung	40	175	151	48	40	
Makanleptan ...	"	"	Khensa	50	180	152	46	40	
Pangchongkapa ...	"	"	Imchenkimong	30	182	144	43	37	
Karikamba... ...	"	Uchi	Longchang	18	185	147	40	31	Uchi is of the same clan as Chami.
Youngchihang ...	"	Mongsen ungrr	"	35	184	142	40	34	Mongsen ungrr merely means " Chief of Mongsen," and may belong to any of the three exogamous clans of which the chief family has become a subdivision.
			Average		183	149	45	37	

CHANG.

Name.	Clan.	Kindred.	Village.	Approximate Age.	Cephalic Length.	Cephalic Breadth.	Nasal Length.	Nasal Breadth.	Remarks
Taakam ...	Hawang	Hawang	Litimm	40	195	141	44	31	
Ngaku-lakpo	,,	,,	Longtang	30	198	145	40	39	
Yangba ...	,,	,,	Yangpi	35	186	141	43	30	
Ngaku ...	,,	Chongpu	Yangemdi	35	182	147	45	36	
Saiyo ...	Ung	Ungpang	Nakcho	50	194	144	48	35	Very deep pit between the eyes.
Mongba ...	,,	Kawanchi	Longtang	30	198	145	40	39	
Peëlong ...	,,	Chongwangchi	Hakchang	40	190	140	49	32	
Thungpang...	,,	,,	Yangemdi	30	185	145	45	43	
Chingma ...	,,	Longshu	Hakchang	45	193	141	50	37	
Chaolu ...	Hung	Naktung	,,	40	185	144	46	35	
Chualen ...	Kangsho	Yauloshi	Longtang	25	182	140	40	40	
Yemlong ...	,,	,,	Yangpi	40	190	141	51	35	
Chaulih ...	Hagiung	Asseri	,,	40	171	140	50	34	
			Average		*188*	*143*	*45*	*36*	

PHOM.

Name.	Clan.	Kindred.	Village.	Approximate Age.	Cephalic Length.	Cephalic Breadth.	Nasal Length.	Nasal Breadth.	Remarks
Kaolam	Nameithang	Nameithang	Hukpang	20	176	142	45	33	

KONYAK.

Name.	Tribal division.	Clan.	Village.	Approximate Age.	Cephalic Length.	Cephalic Breadth.	Nasal Length.	Nasal Breadth.	Remarks.
Matna	Thenkoh	Kongnok	Tamlung	45	196	149	43	41	Cheek bones unusually prominent.
Lipwong	"	Augwanhu	Wanching	40	191	145	51	37	
Lam'ong	"	Pimlonghu	Kongan	45	185	150	41	36	
Chingham	"	Hentokhu	"	45	192	149	35	41	
Thaopong	"	Yanlam	Tanhai	35	191	149	50	40	
Acham	"	Angnophang	Wakching	18	183	146	43	40	
Lauching	"	Laktuhu	Kongan	55	175	145	43	35	
Ganpai	"	Yanlam	Tanhai	30	193	137	45	42	
Chingohen	"	Yingshanghu	Kongan	20	188	147	40	39	
Thapyong	"	Paiknok	Wanching	25	185	148	42	39	
Allong	"	Matpisün	Punkhung	25	187	140	45	34	
Matlong	"	Kongnok	Tamlung	45	198	148	38	42	
Thongban	"	Yinshauhu	Kongan	45	185	150	41	36	
Onyé	"	Shishohu	"	40	195	147	42	36	
Shohpong	"	Manching	"	25	183	142	40	37	
Panglao	Thendu	Wongnantim	Wangla	35	185	151	46	41	
Hakwang	"	Wonghu	Hungfoi	40	191	147	55	43	
Hatnung	"	Wongnanyum	Lonkai	30	190	155	49	36	
Maktah	"	Wongchimpong	Auting	30	197	144	44	36	
Photai	"	Wongnanyum	Lonkai	30	193	145	43	43	
Yongnyai	"	Wongnanyum	"	40	186	146	44	45	
Chingau	"	Wonghu	Hungfoi	30	188	150	46	36	
Average				—	189	147	44	39	

The cephalic and nasal indices respectively, worked out to the nearest unit from the averages for each tribe, give the following results :—

Angami ...	...	Cephalic index	76	Nasal index			79
Sema ...	...	,,	,,	79	,,	,,	80
Rengma ...	...	,,	,,	79	,,	,,	82
Lhota ...	...	,,	,,	79	,,	,,	88
Ao ...	...	,,	,,	81	,,	,,	80
Chang ...	...	,,	,,	79	,,	,,	80
Konyak ...	...	,,	,,	77	,,	,,	89

What is noticeable about these figures is the comparative height of the nasal indices of the Lhota and Konyak figures, and the low figure for the Angami cephalic index and the high cephalic index of the Aos. For the sake of comparison I have worked out the cephalic index from the figures given by Colonel Waddell as the average of each tribe in his paper on the tribes of the Brahmaputra valley.[1] The Lhota nasal index as resulting from my figures is perhaps fortuitous or erroneous. In any case, Colonel Waddell's figures show a nasal index for the Lhotas of 79, with a cephalic index of 77. The figures for the Konyaks measured by me with their possible infusion of Shan blood may be compared with the cephalic and nasal indices respectively, according to Colonel Waddell's figures, of the Fakials (a Shan tribe), c. i. 78—n. i. 82, the Kukis, c. i. 76— n. i. 91, and the Tsak-ma of the Chittagong Hill Tracts, c. i. 80—n. i. 91. The low figure of the Angami cephalic index is caused by the low cephalic index of the Kezami Angamis, which is 74 against 77 each for the Tengima and Chakrima. It is also quite possible that the Lhotas and Semas would show figures approximating more nearly to the Angami standard if measurements were taken over the whole tribe, but my measurements were taken from the more northerly villages where there is almost certainly an admixture of Ao blood, particularly in the case of the Lhotas. The Rengmas measured by me were unfortunately all from the village of Themokedima, where there seems to have been a good deal of miscegenation when the Military Police outpost was at Wokha. The cephalic and nasal indices of the Ao are particularly interesting in view of the legend recorded by Mrs. Clark of a mixed settlement of Aos and Ahoms (c. i. 82—n. i. 82), but may also be compared with the indices of the Miris (c. i. 81—n. i. 84) and of some of the sub-Himalayan Mongoloid tribes recorded by Colonel Waddell, such as the Kiranti (c. i. 82—n. i. 86) and the Tibetans (c. i. 81— n. l. 82). With regard to the Aos it must be remembered that miscegenation has in any case gone a good deal further than in any other Naga tribe treated of in this monograph. Gurkhali sepoys might be responsible for a certain approximation to the standard of sub-Himalyan tribes in one or two villages in the case of individuals, but there has been an undoubted admixture of Assamese blood from the plains in a large number of Ao villages. At one time, probably that of the Burmese invasion of Assam, Assamese families fled to the hills in some numbers and in many cases settled there and adopted Naga customs and dress. They are now

---

[1] *Journal of the Asiatic Society*, 1900.

indistinguishable from the ordinary Ao except by their being liable to be abused as being of Assamese blood by some irritated neighbour. This admixture of plains blood might explain a tendency towards an Ahom head. Whatever explanation is sought for, one must bear in mind the peculiarly broad views entertained by the Aos on pre-marital chastity and post-marital fidelity.

APPENDIX XII

GLOSSARY

A

Ăgār ... ... A valuable wood from which oil is extracted for the manufacture of perfume. *Aquilaria agallocha.*

Ăhū dhān ... ... Paddy grown in jhum fields as opposed to paddy grown in irrigated land.

Ăpŏtia ... ... (<Assamese *āpădīya*[1] = " accidental " or " causing misfortune " ; Bengali *āpăd* = a calamity) applied to death by certain particular misadventures, *e.g.*, death in childbirth, killing by a tiger, loss in the jungle, drowning, killing by the fall of a tree or by a fall from a tree, death by snake-bite. These are not all regarded as " Apotia " deaths by all tribes, but the first three seem to be invariably so regarde d.

C

Chābĭlĭ ... ... A form of currency formerly used in the Ao country and consisting of a narrow strip of iron from 6 to 8 inches long with a triangular projection at the end. It represents a conventionalised *dao* of an obsolete type. *Chabili* ?<*chabi* = a key, pronounced *Săbĭlĭ.*

Chŭnga ... ... A section of bamboo used as a drinking vessel or for carrying water. In the latter case a length of 3 or 4 feet is used, the joints being pierced to admit the water down to the bottom.

D

Dao ... ... A sort of bill of varying shape used both for wood-cutting and as a weapon by the tribes of N.E. India and Burmah. Sometimes spelt *dah.*

---

[1] The Assamese word is *āpad*, অাপদ meaning a calamity.—P. R. GURDON.

Deo-mǎni ... ... (*lit.* " god-bead "). A variety of bead made from a reddish - brown stone flecked with black. The stone seems to be found in Nepal and beads made from it are very highly prized by Nagas. Possibly dug from ancient graves.

The Bengal Asiatic Society's Journal, volume xvi, p. 713, contains a notice by H. Piddington of the " Deo-Monnees or Sacred Beads of Assam."

Dhān ... ... The unhusked grain of the rice plant, commonly called " paddy."

dhōti ... ... Loin-cloth. A strip of broad muslin cloth wrapped round the waist, drawn between the legs and tucked in in front. It forms the ordinary nether garment of Assam and Bengal.

dhūli ... ... See *dūli*.

dūli ... ... A large basket averaging about 5 feet in height and 2½ feet in diameter with a pointed cover. Used for storing grain by the Angamis.

dǔrbār ... ... A gathering of persons for conference ; an official reception.

dzu ... ... See *zu*.

G

Gaonbura ... ... (*lit.* = village elder). The head man of a village or of a " khel " holding his appointment from Government.

genna ... ... See note preceding Part I, and also Part IV under heading " Genna."

genna-bura ... ... (*lit.* = genna elder). A Naga-Assamese term used more or less indiscriminately for the four religious officials of the Angami village (see Part IV), and for the corresponding functionaries in other Naga tribes.

J

Jǎppa ... ... A four-footed carrying basket with a pointed lid narrower at the bottom than the middle. It is made of two thicknesses of split bamboo or cane, with a lining of bamboo leaves in between to keep out the wet. Generally from 3 to 3½ feet in height and 18 to 20 inches in diameter.

jhūm ... ... Land cultivated by " jhuming."

jhūming ... ... A form of extensive cultivation in which an area is cleared of jungle (which is burnt, the ashes being dug into the ground), and sown for two successive years. At the end of this period weeds come up too thickly for convenient cultivation, and the fertility of the soil is to some extent diminished. The land is then allowed to remain uncultivated for from five to fifteen years, at the end of which time there is a fresh deposit of leaf mould and the growth of tall vegetation has killed off the small weeds that interfere with cultivation. In jhuming only one crop is sown in the year, rice in the first year being followed by millet in the second where this cereal is cultivated.

K

Kăcheri	... ...	or " cutcherry," the magistrate's court.
kăchu	... ...	The arum, *Colocasia antiquorum*, grown largely as food by the more northern and eastern Naga tribes.
kălăs ...	...	Narrow-necked earthenware jar for storing liquid ; two to three feet in height.
kang ...	...	A basket wide at the top and pointed at the bottom used for carrying.
khang	... ...	See *kang.*
khalsi	... ...	See *kalas.*
khĕl ...	...	The word for an exogamous group among the Ahoms. Hence applied to the Angami *thino,* and as the different *thino* in an Angami village usually live in separate quarters, the word has consequently been applied to a subdivision of a Naga village regardless of exogamy, to which, as in the case of the Semas for instance, it has frequently no reference at all.
kodali	... ...	See *pharua.*

L

Lao ...	... ...	Gourd used for carrying and storing liquor.
lengta	... ...	A narrow strip of cloth tied round the waist, passing between the legs from behind and up to the waist again in front, whence it falls down again in a square flap.

M

Machăn	... ...	A raised platform made of bamboos split and interwoven, of simple bamboos, or of wood.
mĕnitessa	... ...	A cereal used in the concoction of fermented liquor— the great millet (? *sorghum vulgare*).
mĭthăn	... ...	The domesticated variety of *Bos frontalis,* one of the species of Indian bison.
mŏdhū...	... ...	Fermented liquor brewed from rice, of which there are three or four varieties known to Nagas, viz.:— *pita modhu,* made from uncooked rice and fermented after the addition of water, a very mild drink ; *kachāri modhu* and *rohi,* made from rice boiled and subsequently fermented; and *sākā modhu,* made by infusion, boiling water being poured through previously steeped and fermented rice, like the first a mild concoction.
mŏrung (or *deka chăng*)		The house in which the bachelors of the clan sleep. Also used as a centre for clan ceremonies and a sort of men's club generally.

P

Paddy...	... ...	Rice growing or in the husk.
pănikhĕts	... ...	(*lit.* " water-fields "). Irrigated and flooded terraces for growing wet rice.

pānjis... ... ... Spikes of hardened bamboo used to impede the passage of an enemy, impale wild animals in pits, etc. They vary from eight inches to four feet in length, and when well seasoned by exposure to the weather are sharp enough to pierce the sole of a boot.

pharua ... ... An implement used for hoeing and digging and made like a spade with the blade at right angles to the handle. The term is also applied to Naga hoes.

pice ... ... A small coin roughly equivalent to a farthing.

S

Sărkăr... ... ... The British Government.

serow ... ... *Nemorhhoedus rubida,* a species of antelope allied to the goat and living on jungle-clad precipices. The variety alluded to in this monograph is the Burmese or red serow. The Assamese call it *deochaguli* (= " god-goat "), probably owing to its extraordinary elusiveness.

shikāri ... ... A tracker, hunter of game.

Z

zū ... ... Fermented liquor. See Part II. (*Zu* is an Angami word.)

APPENDIX XIII

AUTHOR'S SUPPLEMENTARY NOTES TO SECOND EDITION

P. 47

[1] Sir J. Frazer ("Golden Bough", viii, p. 100) referring to Dr. Burton Brown says that such memorials are intended to deceive the spirits as to the place where the real grave is, but I think myself that they represent a change in funeral customs from exposure of the corpse, as, e.g. by Konyaks, to interment.

P. 73.

[1] Subject of course to the possession of a right in the water to be taken, there is apparently a right to dig a water-channel across unirrigated land in someone else's ownership, but a polite and formal request *must* be made from such an owner. The old men of Kohima village in my time had never heard of any case in which leave asked in this way had been refused, and they were of the opinion that it could not be refused, and said that the same custom applied to a right of way asked for across unirrigated land. A case in point came into my court in 1922 in which a man wished to cut an irrigation channel across the wood-plantation of a personal enemy. To avoid having to ask him for a favour, he offered, through a go-between, to exchange an unirrigated field for the right to cut the channel without other obligation. His enemy refused the offer but invited the offerer to come and see him about it in person. Instead of doing that, however, he went to court and complained that his right of making a water-channel was being obstructed. With the occurrence and approval of all the headmen and interpreters present it was decided that the channel for the water should be cut, but that the litigant was guilty of a serious breach of village custom in that he tried to offer land as though he had no right to cut the channel, and had complained of obstruction when he had not himself complied with the customary and necessary preliminaries to cutting it. He was fined Rs 30. The case is worth recording as a typical illustration of Angami psychology in regard to customary rights, and of behaviour and manners.

P. 74.

[1] If a terraced field be sold when the time for transplanting has come, it is customary to transfer the rice seedlings needed for transplantation with the field.

P. 83.

[1] Dr. N. L. Bor tells me that in Phekrokejima lemon grass (*cymbopogon sp.*) is used. The leaves are rubbed and squeezed into a small ball; the perfume is puffed into the hive of the common house-bee, which becomes unconscious enough to allow the removal of its honey.

P. 84.

[1] The Dalleburra tribe of Australians in Queensland use the same method of discovering hornets' nests. See *Journ. Ryl. Anthrop. Inst.*, LVII (Dec. 1927), p. 410.

P. 87.

[1] A larger type of the same snare with a bamboo string about 7 ft. long is used for snaring leopard-cats, etc.

P. 100.

[2] As a remedy for a cough the gall of a crow is used, no doubt from some association between the hoarse cry of a crow and the sound of a cough.

P. 103.

[1] And I have seen a man of the Kezami village Tekhubama having thrown his spear high in the air and caught it like a drum-major's staff, hold it level parallel to the ground in one hand and jump over it from side to side while holding it in that position.

P. 135.

[2] Provided always that in the case of ancestral (as distinct from personally acquired) property the persons who would ordinarily inherit in default of such verbal directions are present and assenting when the verbal bequest is made. If they refuse to agree to its alienation ancestral land *must* be left to them, and they are also entitled to so much of its produce as may be contained in the grain basket nearest to the entrance of the house.

P. 140.

[1] Property bought by the husband and wife after their marriage goes to the survivor, and then to the children, males, I think, inheriting before females. When direct descendants of both sexes fail it goes to the heirs of whichever one of the original pair survived the other.

P. 144.

[1] The principle involved is identical with that of the Anglo-Saxons whereby an accused man could prove his innocence by producing twelve compurgators willing to swear to it, a system out of which the jury system seems to have arisen.

[2] As in the case of warriors on the warpath. See p. 151.

P. 145

[1] Or, alternatively, that the evil consequences of the oath may visit the twig instead of the swearer and be thrown away with it. (*Cf.* Cordington, " The Melanesians ", p. 186).

[2] We may compare this biting with that of Malcolm Kenmore, King of Scotland, who confirms a grant of land with the words " for the more sooth I bite the white wax [of the seal] with my tooth before Margaret, my Wife, and Mall, my Nurse ", these two being witnesses to the deed.

P. 167

[1] The real basis of head-hunting among all the Naga tribes is the belief that the head is the seat *par excellence* of the life-essence which informs human beings as well as (in a lesser degree no doubt) many other animals. This life-essence is brought back to the village in the head which is placed upon the sacred stone (*kipuchie*) of the village from which apparently the life-essence diffuses itself to the villagers, their crops and their stock. This explains the necessity for taking heads to replenish the life of the village when the population has been weakened by disease or scarcity. It explains also the great importance which attaches to head-taking as a young man's preliminary to marriage. If he has not " touched meat ", as the expression is, he is not nearly so likely to beget a child, for there is no surplus life hanging about him. Similarly, it explains why a woman's head with long hair is so much prized, as life-essence lodges in the hair of the head. It also explains the custom of cutting short the hair of unmarried girls as it makes them less likely to give birth to illegitimate babies. (*See* my " The Significance of Head-hunting in Assam " in the *Journal of the Royal Anthropological Institute*, vol. LVIII, Dec. 1928).

P. 179.

[1] The reaping hook itself in this case is a protection because it is made of iron, and iron is a deterrent of evil spirits. Thus in Phesama in 1921 when a man who had been adopted from the Niyema into the Makuma clan wished to change back again, iron was buried at the gateways of both the clans (different clans commonly occupy separately fenced wards in a village) to prevent any possible evil consequences, e.g. sickness or death, that might follow such a change. So too in Kohima village in 1922 bits of iron (hoes) and chickens were put outside the village by each clan on its own approach road to prevent epidemics. It should be noted in this connexion that whereas iron can be put out on anyone's land in the case of a *bona fide* illness, iron put out to deter the evil consequences of a sin, i.e. of some tabooed action, most emphatically cannot be left on the land of anyone other than the culprit himself.

P. 189.

[2] The penalty for starting to harvest crops before the Lidepfü is expulsion from the village for seven years. A man was so expelled from Keruma in 1921, and neither objected nor appealed. But in a case in Kohima in the same year the culprit was turned out for five days only, but the whole village observed them as *penna*, which must have made him extremely unpopular.

P. 190.

[2] I am inclined to think, however, that the real reason was a feeling that it was wrong or dangerous to make fun of the dead monkey.

P. 191.

[1] It is the বহ মদাব of the Assamese, *Erythrina fulgens*. Cf. p. 229 *infra*. It is perhaps significant that this tree is preferred by the Garo for the pyre on which the dead are burned. See Playfair, *The Garos*, p. 109.

P. 204.

[2] The ancient Slavs seem to have agreed with the Lhota for the Bulgars sacrificed dogs (in vain) when investing Constantinople in the IXth century. (Howorth, "The Bulgarians" in *Journ. Anthrop. Inst.*, XI, iii, 1882). The medicinal use of dog flesh has been more common. Hippocrate recommends a diet of puppy-flesh for consumptives; "dog-oil" is still used, externally, in the north of England for rheumatic ailments, and a prescription for making it was given by Nicholas Culpeper in his *Pharmacopoeia Londoniensis* of 1659 (*The Lancet*, Nov. 12th and 26th, 1921).

P. 213.

[1] I was told at Kigwema, which had one of the finest doors in the Angami country, that the tree from which their door was to be made was chosen by finding one the girth of which was three times the breadth of the doorway. It was cut in the rough, in a single piece of course, at the spot where the tree was felled—in this case about five miles from the village—and finished off at the village. A chicken was released where the tree was felled, and when it was dragged to the village a bull was killed. The remainder of the huge tree was entirely wasted, as it cannot be used for anything else. It would have made a number of paddy-pounding tables (see page 53 *supra*), but must not be used for them as women would have to mount on them to pound, and this would be equivalent to their mounting on to the village door, and that of course is taboo (*kenna*).

P. 214.

[2] For other instances of this method, see Hose and McDougall, "Pagan Tribes of Borneo", II, 152 (Kayan), Skeat, "Malay Magic", p. 334 (Malay), and Cole, "Wild Tribes of Davao District, Mindanao", p. 100, and "The Tinguian", p. 264 (Philippines).

P. 227.

[2] Spears thus put on a grave or cenotaph may be retrieved when the superstructure rots and falls, but must not be touched by deceased's own kin or clansmen, and are therefore usually taken by deceased's sister's husband or some other relative who belongs to another clan.

P. 238.

[3] In Theniazuma there is a grave on which water is poured to cause rain, and from which grass is pulled up to stop rain. In either case this proceeding is accompanied by a day's *penna*.

P. 240.

[3] For close parallels in remote parts of the world, see Frazer, "The Golden Bough", viii, pp. 236, 244.

P. 242.

[1] The Angami share the common belief about the possibility of causing a person harm by operating on some part of his person, e.g. hair- or nail-trimmings, at a distance. I had a complaint from a man of the Chetonuma clan in Kohima against a fellow-clansman, who, he said, after kindly cutting his hair for him took away the cuttings, worked magic on them, and so caused him to go mad.

P. 274.

[2] This story may be compared with that of *Jogeshwar's Marriage* given by Bompas in "Folk-lore of the Santal Parganas" (LV, p. 273), and Matsno's account of his transparent ceiling recalls Colin Dubh's castle "with the highest ceiling in the world".

P. 314.

[1] I have given this story as it is given in " The Linguistic Survey of India ", vol. III, part ii, by Sir George Grierson, but Sir Charles Pawsey has pointed out to me that there is no Angami word *mi* meaning "head-rope", and that the only known meaning nowadays is "tail". Grierson's informant clearly thought that goddesses do not have tails (an attribute of devils, perhaps ?) and placed his own interpretation on the word *mi*, an obsolete word of which he did not know the real significance. The similarity of this story to the widespread legend of the swan-maidens is obvious, and it is worth pointing out that there is a Sema word *mhi* = "feather", and I should myself venture to translate *mi* in this context as "plumage" rather than "headrope".

P. 336.

[1] In Appendix VI to the late J. P. Mills' " The Ao Nagas " (London, 1926) I have given a fairly comprehensive bibliography of books and articles relating to the Naga tribes from 1792 to 1925. I add here, therefore, only a few which deal with the Angami specifically or with some important aspect of their culture insufficiently covered in this volume :

21. Jenkins, Major F., " A Sketch of our Relations with the Angami Nagas " (Calcutta ? *circa* 1854 ?).

I have never seen this work.

22. Brown, Dr R., "Report on the Exploration of the Angami Naga Country made in connection with the Survey of the Naga Hills and Manipur Boundary, 1873-74" (Calcutta? 1874).

I have never seen this. Dr. Brown was Political Agent in Manipur.

23. Prain, D., "The Angami Nagas" in *Révue Coloniale Internationale*, V, vi, 472-494 (Reprinted and revised, Sept. 1890).

I have never seen this. I think Prain was in the I.M.S.

24. Hutton, J. H., "Carved Monoliths at Dimapur and an Angami Naga Ceremony", and "Meaning and Method of the Erection of Monoliths by the Naga Tribes", both in the *Journal of the Royal Anthropological Institute*, vol. LII, 1922.

25. Hutton, J. H., "Angami Naga Dye Processes" and "Sacrifice by Hurling from the Roof" in *Man*, vol. XXIII, 1923.

26. Hutton, J. H., "The use of Stone in the Naga Hills" in the *Journal of the R.A.I.*, vol. LVI (1926).

27. Hutton, J. H., "The Significance of Head-hunting in Assam", in the *J.R.A.I.*, LVIII (1928).

28. Mills, J. P., "The Angami Nagas" in *The Assam Review*, vol. I, no. 6 (Calcutta, 1928).

29. Wood, Rev. W. H. S., "British Relations with the Angami Nagas" in *The Assam Review*, vols. II and III, 1929/30.

This account is derived primarily from Mackenzie (no. 20 above), from the District Records of Cachar, and, for the account of the siege of Kohima in 1879, from a MS. belonging to Canon Williamson of Cheltenham (at one time vicar of Bredwardine) who had received it from his relative Capt. Williamson of Garo Hills fame, who had obtained it himself from the Mrs. Cawley who had recorded it during the siege. I myself placed the copy which I had from Canon Williamson in the Kohima Record Room some time before 1929.

30. Fürer-Haimendorf, C. von, and Mills, J. P., "The Sacred Founder's Kin among the Eastern Angami Nagas", in *Anthropos*, Band XXXI, 1936.

31. Reid, Sir Robert, "History of the Frontier Areas bordering on Assam from 1883-1941", Shillong, 1942.

This volume is a continuation of no. 20 above, by Mackenzie, and brings the political history of the Naga Hills down to the time of the second great war.

P. 378.

[1] Arrow-poison, obtained from tribes to the east, is believed to be made from the sap of a tree. In fact it is aconite, the tree belief perhaps reflecting some contact in the far past with the *upas* tree of Malaya.

P. 399.

[1] I am indebted to Mr. E. T. D. Lambert for the information following :

Apparently both clans claim to have been the first to build on the Kohima site. Chera's wife was named Meseü; Rosü may have been her brother, but seems in any case to have been a dependant of Chera who, at his death, was given some land called Kruzihe, where the scratching of a fowl led to the discovery of an unknown spring. There Meseü made a terraced field. Once when she was drawing water there Rosü slapped her buttocks in a familiar way. She took offence saying "I am the cock, not you", and smacked on the ground the bamboo stick which she was carrying. The bamboo split into slivers, and Meseü laid a curse on the intermarriage of Chera's and Rosü's families who would split up like the bamboo if they did not observe her interdict. Chera's family then moved down to the new water supply, and since then the two clans do not intermarry.

P. 407.

[1] It had probably been brought to the village by the Tsyama clan as a fertility charm, being roughly phallic in shape. When I visited Jotsoma next I found it erected by the wall of the Tsyama ward. Thekronoma's complaint was probably due to the fear that its presence there would promote the prosperity of a bitterly rival clan.

P. 408.

[1] This stone was broken by a Baptist preacher in 1923. It proved to be an imposter, being only a piece of shale which had been treated with oil or fat to look like a genuine baetyl or charmstone. See "The Sema Nagas", p. 254.

P. 412.

[1] This intercalary month is inserted when it becomes obvious that the Terhengi genna, which falls on the 16th day of the moon Redê, and should coincide with the end of the rice harvest, is falling too early in the year, but the matter seems to be decided further to the east, for Kohima take the dates for their gennas from Jakhama (one of the origin stories of Kohima derives from the little tarn at Jakhama where their footprints were still "till recently" to be seen) and Jakhama from Mao. The tiresome deviation of the lunar from the solar year can also be checked to some extent by careful observations of the solstices, which are made, at any rate in Kohima village, by such persons as happen to be interested. The Revd. J. E. Tanquist told me that a man named Sitsalie of the Dapfutsuma clan did this in Kohima, having been taught to do so by his father, by noting the position at which the sun rose day by day in regard to the mountain peaks on the eastern horizon, but the furthest point, north or south, which the sun reaches cannot be determined with precision because on that particular day the sky is always overcast. The summer solstice is taken as the approximate time for the transplantation of the rice seedlings to the irrigated terraces (pp. 74, 198 supra).

INDEX

INDEX

ABLUTIONS, of head-taker, 239
Abor Expedition, 369
Abortion, 171, 172 ; practice of—precludes ignorance of laws of procreation, 400 ; not practised (Memi), 341
Adoption, 117 et seq. ; effect on marriage cu tom, ·120 ; inheritance in case of, 136, 137
Adultery, punishment of, 150, 168, 225, (Lhotas) 367
Adze (Kethi), 66
Affinities, 16
After-birth, disposal of (Memi), 341, 342
Agriculture, 72 et seq.
Ahom, kings enlist Nagas and have dealings with Manipur, 13 ; king seeks refuge in Tanhai, 384
Ahoms, dual organisation of, 110, n. 2
Aksu, Ao levy for entertaining guests, 374
Alders, pollarding of, 76 ; use of, in birth ceremonies, 216
Amazons. See under Legends
Amung, Ao equivalent of Penna, 373
Angami, Eastern, definition of term, 15 ; physical type of, 20 ; style of hairdressing, 22 ; cloths used by, 25 ; bead necklace worn by, 23 ; leggings worn by men of, 31 ; use of " pissoh " by, 24 ; unmarried men's cloth, 26 ; spears used by, 34 ; dao, 36 ; women's cloths, 26 ; dress, 26, 27 ; ornaments worn by, 28 ; house ornamentation among, 55 ; memorials of dead, 47 ; look-out places, 47 ; method of keeping mithan, 80 ; Kemovo among, 187 ; First Reaper among, 189 ; gennas among, 197, 200 ; Sekrengi among, 205 ; marriage rites of, 222, 223 ; provision for widows, 168 ; prostitution among, 173

Angami, origin of term, 14
Angamis, 16, 27 ; classification of, in Census of India, 8 ; habitat, 5, 14, 15 ; included in Western Nagas, 351 ; division into groups, 15, 355 ; origin of, 110 ; Butler's story of Origin, 20 ; ancestors of, 112 ; affinity to Khoirao Nagas and Kacha Nagas, 16 ; dual organisation, 110 ; allied to Memi, 7, 8, 294 ; probably of same stock as Lhotas, Rengmas, and Semas, 10, 17, 18 ; points of resemblance between, and Konyak tribes, 386 ; appearance and physical characteristics of, 20, 21 ; mentality and intelligence, 37 ; character, 38 et seq. ; relations with Manipur, 13 ; enlisted by Ahom kings, 13 ; defeat Semas, attacked by Lhotas, 7 ; state of, prior to arrival of British—feuds in villages, 12 ; methods of warfare, 12, 13 ; admit authority of priests of Mao and Maikel, 7
Animal as embodied spirit, 180
Animals killed by birds or beasts tabu to First Sower and Reaper, 189 ; restriction on moving, during genna, 198 ; legend of friendly, 271 ; domestic, origin of, 202 ; birth of, entails " kenna," 214 ; birth and death of, entail " kenna " (Memi), 338
Animals, wild, hunted at Sekrengi, 205 ; killing of, entails fast (Memi), 338
Animatism, 179
Anthropometrical measurements, vary little, 10 ; tables, 423 et seq.
Anvil (Rekri-chi), 63
Aos, descriptive note on, 370–375 ; origin of, and affinities, 370,

SUPPLEMENTARY INDEX